Brief Contents

The Vocabulary of
Critical Thinking

The Vocabulary of Critical Thinking

Phil Washburn
New York University

New York Oxford
OXFORD UNIVERSITY PRESS
2010

Oxford University Press, Inc., publishes works that further Oxford University's
objective of excellence in research, scholarship, and education.

Oxford   New York
Auckland   Cape Town   Dar es Salaam   Hong Kong   Karachi
Kuala Lumpur   Madrid   Melbourne   Mexico City   Nairobi
New Delhi   Shanghai   Taipei   Toronto

With offices in
Argentina   Austria   Brazil   Chile   Czech Republic   France   Greece
Guatemala   Hungary   Italy   Japan   Poland   Portugal   Singapore
South Korea   Switzerland   Thailand   Turkey   Ukraine   Vietnam

Published by Oxford University Press, Inc.
198 Madison Avenue, New York, New York 10016
http://www.oup.com

Library of Congress Cataloging-in-Publication Data

Washburn, Phil.
The vocabulary of critical thinking/by Phil Washburn.
   p. cm.
Includes bibliographical references and index.
ISBN 978-0-19-532480-8 (pbk. : alk. paper)
1. Critical thinking.   2. Reasoning.   I. Title
BC177.W37 2009
160–dc22   2008035088

Printing number: 9 8 7 6 5 4 3 2 1

Printed in the United States of America
on acid-free paper

Contents

This book is dedicated to the next generation:
Mary, Sara, Mark, Michael, Mara, and Charlotte

Preface

This book offers a novel way to help students improve their thinking. I believe it is also an effective way. The book is based on several assumptions.

One is that when people talk about thinking, they are talking about many different things. Mathematicians have their views about thinking and problem-solving; psychologists have theirs; management consultants have theirs, and so on. I have assembled a range of books on thinking and ways to improve one's thinking in the bibliography ("For Further Study") to illustrate the great variety of viewpoints.

Even within the relatively restricted domain of "critical thinking," practitioners advocate different methods of instruction. Some emphasize teaching traditional logic. Others believe students should follow steps of problem solving. Others explain experiments in psychology and the cognitive bases of thinking. Many say good class discussions are the best way to improve students' thinking.

I believe all these different ways of teaching thinking have merits. Thinking is multifaceted, and each approach highlights part of the whole phenomenon. But which approach is best? I did not want to adopt one of these conceptions of thinking, because to do so would minimize or exclude the others. That created a conundrum, which leads to another assumption.

A second assumption is that, in spite of the differences among disciplines and methods of teaching, some very basic mental operations are common to all of them. Before one can succeed in science, or history, or the arts, one must understand certain crucial relationships. Teachers and other educated people can recognize these basic operations in students' work and in other writing. Examples are comparing things, making generalizations, explaining causes, assessing sources, and others. All the disciplines use these basic operations, but they elaborate them and apply them in different ways. They assign different priorities to different skills. For example, assessing sources is very important in history and journalism, whereas recognizing vagueness, irony, and connotations of words is more important in literature. Thus when people in different disciplines talk about "thinking," they often emphasize different things, even as they recognize basic skills.

I have tried to step back, as it were, and find the common, fundamental operations or skills that students should master before they proceed into the specialized disciplines. I believe there is such a set, and I've organized the chapters in this book around those fundamentals. Thus the book is primarily for people beginning their college careers. But it could be useful to others as well. I have learned that going back to fundamentals from time to time is helpful, so more advanced students could also benefit from reminding themselves of the complexities in these basic operations.

I suspect that professors of logic and psychology and math might say that they also teach the fundamentals. That is probably true, but I believe they teach only selected fundamentals. For example, courses in logic emphasize the analysis of arguments, and arguments are fundamental to thinking. (Each chapter after the first two includes examples of arguments for analysis.) But there is more to good thinking than analyzing arguments. And students must understand certain concepts before they can analyze arguments. Courses on problem solving in math teach techniques of solving problems. That is fundamental, but it's only part of thinking effectively. I have tried to broaden the scope of this text to include a wider range of the basic operations than some conventional approaches to critical thinking include. One way to do that is to try to uncover even more basic processes than stating an argument, for example. This book gives students the preparation they need before they study logic and problem-solving.

I have also assumed, in the third place, that a good way to *begin* practicing the fundamental skills is to learn words to name them. I am guided in this by the other disciplines. In physics, for example, one of the first things students learn is a specialized vocabulary—*acceleration*, *momentum*, *kinetic*, and so on. In art history, students learn the particular way art historians use the word *perspective*, as well as technical words such as *chiaroscuro* and *negative space*. Learning the terms is essential. It allows students to see things and notice things they would not—probably could not—otherwise see. After they have learned the vocabulary, they can go on to investigate problems and questions that arise within that specialized discipline.

If there is a set of operations common to all the different disciplines, we might call the study of those operations "basic thinking," or "effective thinking," or "critical thinking." The words in this book constitute the vocabulary of "critical thinking." I believe that learning this vocabulary is the best way to begin improving one's proficiency with the basic skills. It is not the whole of critical thinking, but it is an introduction that all students can appreciate.

It is even more productive than learning the vocabulary of the other disciplines, because many of the words in this book refer to actions, or products of one's actions. The words are about comparing, generalizing, explaining, inferring, judging sources, evaluating, referring, assuming, and creating. As students gain a more precise and layered understanding of these words, they also gain a better understanding of the operations. When they examine other writers' uses of the words, e.g., *inference*, they are seeing how to perform the operation. When they themselves apply the words in different contexts, they are actually practicing the activity, e.g., inferring. By learning the words, they are improving their thinking skills. Other vocabulary books teach students unfamiliar words, which enable them to understand what a writer says. They may teach students certain concepts, so the students can recognize a phenomenon when they encounter it, e.g., momentum. But as students learn the words in this book, they are learning how to perform basic operations, such as comparing and generalizing. They are learning and improving skills. They also acquire names for the skills, so they can reflect on their own practice.

Mastering the words in this book will not make a person an excellent thinker. That takes years. But informed practice is essential. I believe the approach in this book is the best way to begin that practice.

Acknowledgments

I would like to thank the following people for their thoughtful comments on an earlier version of this book. The flaws that remain are due to my inability to adopt all their suggestions. John Bird, Winthrop University; Mary Bozik, University of Northern Iowa; Benedict Hughes, Northwood University; Keith Krasemann, College of DuPage; Ann Lewald, Tennessee Technological University; David Louzecky, University of Wisconsin-Sheboygan; Catherine E. McCartney, Bemidji State University; and Genevieve Migely, California State Polytechnic University in Pomona.

I am also grateful to my wife and partner, Marianne. She has taught me dimensions of thinking that I would never have known without her.

The Vocabulary of Critical Thinking

Introduction

What Is Critical Thinking?

Different people answer that question in different ways. Perhaps the first thing to say is that it is not being critical of people. Words often have more than one meaning, and when people talk about "critical thinking," they mean the kind of thinking that enables a person to make a good decision. It is thinking about whether or not something you heard is true, or thinking about the best way to get your work done on time. Having a critical attitude means looking for some basis on which to judge something. For example, watching a movie critically means looking for strong points and weak points, features that make it excellent and features that make it average or boring. Critical thinking includes finding flaws and problems ("criticizing"), but that is only part of the activity. It is also praising and valuing. It means thinking about all the aspects of a statement, a person's action, a film, a government policy, or anything else, so that you can understand it and make the best judgment of it—positive, negative, or neutral.

Why Should Anyone Study Critical Thinking?

You can already think, of course. You can probably think pretty well, if you are reading this book. But everyone can improve. I try to improve my thinking continuously, even though I've written books about it. I know I can get better. Thinking is like swimming, or playing tennis. You can raise the level of your game.

To understand how to improve, we have to have a clearer idea of what critical thinking is. As I said, it is trying to make good decisions, but I have a theory about how people do that. To me, critical thinking is seeing relationships among things. Many different kinds of relationships. It is seeing how two things are similar or different. It is seeing the causes of something that happened, or the effects of something. It's looking at a large group of things, such as cars in a parking lot, and seeing something they all have in common. (That's called *generalizing*.) We can see all sorts of relationships, and we can get better at finding them and understanding them. Sometimes we make mistakes. For example, a person might think that forgetting to wear his "lucky socks" caused his team to lose the game. But that would be a mistake. Superstitious thinking is one kind of mistake, and there are others.

The chapters of this book are about the different kinds of relationships we can see. Some relationships have one chapter; some are so important that more than one chapter is devoted to them. For example, thinking clearly about causes and effects is so important than three chapters are devoted to that relationship.

If you practice seeing and thinking about these relationships, your thinking in every other area of life will benefit. That is because they are so basic. For example, imagine that a bank offers you a job. You have to make a decision, and you need information. What would it be like to work for the bank? Here's where critical thinking comes in. One important relationship is between your belief about something and the source of the belief, that is, where it came from, or what the belief is based on. Suppose your parents tell you one thing about working in a bank, your friends tell you something else, the bank has its story, and a web site online gives you a completely different description. What do you believe? Which source should you trust? Critical thinking will help you decide. You can learn more about the relation between your beliefs and where the beliefs came from. You can get better at making good decisions if you improve your understanding of sources.

The other relationships are just as basic. All the subjects people study in college use these relationships. If you take a course in biology, for example, you will learn about experiments and theories. Experiments are scientists' ways of trying to determine causes and effects. A theory is a type of generalization. So if you have already studied the relation between cause and effect, and generalizations, you will be better prepared for more specialized courses. In studying history, sources are extremely important. If you have already learned to think carefully about sources—even if it's to decide whether to take a job or not—you will have a head start in mastering the specialized thinking required in a history course.

What Does This Book Try to Do?

This book tries to give you the basic tools that will help you improve your critical thinking. The basic tools are words. Since we think about several different kinds of relationships, we use different types of words to talk about the relationships. For example, if you must make a decision about the job in the bank, you have to think about which source of information you should trust. Several words will help you: *reliable*, *first-hand*, *expert*, *credentials*, *objective*, and *confirm*, among others. If you learn exactly what these words mean, and apply them to your situation, you will make a better decision. After doing that you will be much better at seeing the relationship between any belief—yours or other people's—and the source of the belief.

The same applies to other basic relationships. Being creative is a kind of critical thinking. It enables you to make better judgments and decisions. A creative idea or a creative solution is one that uses a new relationship, a combination of things that no one thought of before. For example, someone thought of combining tape with note paper and invented Post-it® notes. You can think creatively now, but you can also improve. I believe the first step in improving is learning words to describe what creative people do. What exactly is *brainstorming*, or *fantasy*? You have some idea of what these words mean, but you can deepen your understanding of them, find out about variations and types, and see how people apply them in specific situations. By expanding your understanding of the *word*, you are also increasing your *ability* to do the things the word names. Absorbing these words and making them a part of your everyday thinking will sharpen your skills in all the areas of critical thinking.

Here's another example. Comparing is probably the most basic kind of thinking we do, and you can do it easily. But there are different kinds of comparing. Moreover, that mental operation can be broken down into simpler parts. In Chapter 1 you will study words like *analogy*, *metaphor*, and *model*. All name different ways of comparing things. If you have a name for something, it's much easier to do it. Think about cooking. If you want to improve your cooking, you will make progress much faster if you learn the words *simmer*, *broil*, *bake*, *sauté*, *fry*, *stew*, and others. Learning the word is the first step to learning to do the action. The same applies to the action of comparing. Learning exactly what *metaphor* means doesn't automatically make you a better thinker, but it's a good step in that direction.

Isn't Learning Words Too Simple? Shouldn't the Book Be About Rules and Complicated Things?

Critical thinking can be as complicated as you want to make it. Scientists on the front lines of research are engaged in critical thinking. So are doctors, lawyers, and business executives. But their thinking is made up of simple parts, put together in complex combinations. That happens in other areas. Your genes carry a blueprint that specifies the color of your hair, your height, the pattern of your fingerprints, the tone of your voice, the shape of your face, and every biological trait you have. But genes are made of just four chemicals (symbolized as A, C, G, and T). It's the combinations and patterns, maybe hundreds of letters long, that produce the infinite variety of traits people have.

Critical thinking is also made up of a few simple parts. I believe the relationships I mentioned are the parts, and understanding the relationships is the best way to improve your thinking. The nine basic elements are: comparing, generalizing, reasoning, judging sources, finding causes and effects, making value judgments, referring, assuming, and creating. You will learn what these words mean in detail, and others related to them. Understanding and practicing these basic operations will make it easier for you to combine them and apply them in new, complicated situations later.

Your goal is to be able to *do* something better—find causes, judge sources, etc.—not to know a fact or memorize an answer. But the best way to raise your game and improve your performance is to take one step at a time, and build on earlier steps. If you follow the steps in this book, I believe that at the end you will be a much better thinker.

Step 1.

The best first step, in my opinion, is to learn the definitions of these key words. That by itself will help you a great deal, because you will gain a deeper understanding of what you read and hear. Teachers and journalists use these key words all the time. You already have some understanding of words like *plausible* and *controlled experiment* and *justify*. But meanings are complicated and slippery; they depend on context. You can get a richer, more exact understanding, and then you will have a much better grasp of what other people say and write.

The words in this book are the most essential words for understanding academic writing, in all the different disciplines, from anthropology to zoology. Those subjects have their own technical vocabulary, like *ritual* and *photosynthesis*. And the students in the classes think about different things, like pre-industrial societies or plant cells. But the kinds of thinking they do are similar in each subject. The words in this book are about the basic thinking.

Step 2.

The second step is to look at examples of people using the words. "The mayor *justified* her action by reminding us of the budget gap." A definition will give you an idea, but seeing real-world examples of the words shows you small differences in the ways people use the words. Or sometimes big differences. Examples show you different ways the words can be applied. Think again of learning to cook. A child knows the basic meaning of *knife*, but that's only the beginning. By watching experienced cooks at work, he can learn all sorts of ways of using a knife that he probably never imagined. If he looks closely, he will see that two operations with a knife that seemed the same are actually slightly different. He enriches his understanding of what a knife is and what he can do with it.

Step 3.

Steps 1 and 2 are like what you do if you study a book on general vocabulary. Those books list the definitions of 1,000 words or so, with an example or two to illustrate how the word is used. If you learn the words you will understand more of what you read. You can also express yourself in your own writing more effectively. But that's all. The vocabulary book isn't concerned with what the words are *about*.

This book is different. The whole purpose is to understand what the words are about—that is, basic processes of critical thinking. Studying the words is simply the best way to begin practicing critical thinking. But then you can go on to Step 3. In Step 3 you look at examples of people using the processes—justifying a decision, for example—without labeling it with the word *justify*. You have to recognize the process itself when you see it. It's like taking tennis lessons. Your coach tells you what "a two-handed backhand" is. Then he demonstrates it a few times. Maybe he points to some other players and says, "You see their two-handed backhands?" Now you know what the word means. Then you might watch a game on TV and suddenly say to your friend "Wow, did you see that two-handed backhand?" The announcer didn't tell you what the player did. You can recognize it yourself.

This is a more advanced level of understanding. You have not only learned the word; you have learned the concept, the idea the word conveys. And you can use the concept to see things and understand things you probably wouldn't have understood before. For example, if I don't know what a two-handed backhand is, I just see two people batting a tennis ball back and forth. If I don't know what *simmer* or *stew* or *fry* mean, then when I see a person cooking, all I see is a person and a stove. But if you have learned what those words mean, you see far more than I do. It all makes sense to you. You know why he uses the pan he does, and sets the heat at a certain level. But to me it's all just puttering. The same is true for *classifying*, *experimenting*, *confirming*, *inferring*, *valuing*, and all the other words in the book. The goal is to understand what those words are about—the mental operations, the critical thinking itself—not just the words. Learning the words is only the first step.

Step 4.

Finally, you want to do the things yourself that the words describe. You want to compare, judge sources, think creatively, and do all the other things that make up critical thinking. If you learn to recognize a two-handed backhand, you can enjoy and understand the tennis matches you watch at a much higher level than someone who never heard of a two-handed backhand. But, of course, the main reason to learn the word is to get out on the court and use it yourself. If you study the word *analogy*, you will have a better understanding of what others mean when they use the word. You will also recognize analogies when you see them, even if no one calls them analogies. But the greatest benefit of studying the word and examples is that it makes it easier for you to make your own analogies. It empowers you to think for yourself. Your thinking becomes more skillful and effective, whatever you are thinking about.

If you learn about tennis, or cooking, you might enjoy watching others without ever participating. That can be fun. But thinking is different. You are already in the game. You think every day. You are not only in the game: You can't quit. Tennis balls are flying at you right now. And people are keeping score. That's a metaphorical way of saying information is flying at you, opportunities are flying at you, demands on your time, people's expectations, and changes in the workplace are flying at you. And other people notice how well you deal with these challenges. Your success depends on your ability to understand information, see how it fits together, and solve problems. Your thinking skills are vitally important.

To help you complete Step 4, each chapter includes a section at the end on writing. One way to practice using the thinking operations is to write about something. You can apply the particular words and the operations they name to new situations. You can use the ideas yourself, and in that way improve your skills. For example, the first chapter is about comparing. At the end, the exercise asks you to write a paragraph or two comparing two people. You can do that now, of course. But after studying words about comparing, and seeing how others do it, you should be able to raise the level of your game and write a better paragraph. (You will understand what makes your comparison better.) Other chapters ask you to write something using the other thinking operations. By the end of the book, you will have a lot of practice in actually using the basic elements of critical thinking. That's how you improve. And, in my opinion, nothing you can learn will help you more than improving your skill in thinking.

Comparing

1. to compare
2. to contrast
3. to distinguish
4. analogy
5. metaphor
6. model

By studying these words and learning how writers use them, you can improve your thinking. You already understand many of these words to some degree, but you can learn more ways they are used, and you can make your understanding more precise. Many of the words in this book name an action, like "comparing." When you practice using the word you are also practicing the action, and with practice you get better at it. Chapter 1 is about comparing, because it is probably the most basic kind of thinking.

Comparing is so basic that all animals do it. All animals can sense their environments in one or more ways. Dogs smell, bats hear echoes from flying insects, snakes sense heat. Even amoebas can move toward food and away from acid. So in some way they can detect similarities and differences between things. They may not consciously think about them, but they respond to them. (A bat can hear the difference between a flying moth and a falling leaf.) We can perceive similarities and differences in our environments as well, and unlike amoebas, we can consciously focus on particular similarities and differences.

You compare things automatically, so how can you improve this basic kind of thinking? It isn't just a matter of noticing things that others may not have noticed, although observing details is very useful. But beyond that, you can understand different ways of comparing, and the simpler parts that make up the process. When you improve your understanding of the process, you will gain insights into other people's thinking, because everyone compares things all

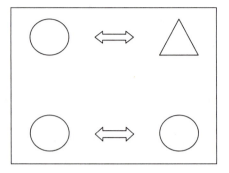

Figure 1.1
It's easy to see a difference between the top two figures and a similarity between the bottom two. But can you see any similarities between the top two, or differences between the bottom two?

the time without realizing it. You will also be able to compare things yourself deliberately, methodically, and creatively, and you will get better results.

I said in the Introduction that there are many different types of thinking, but one thread that runs through many of them is seeing some sort of relationship between things. Cause and effect is one kind of relationship; being a member of a group (for example, left-handed people) is another kind of relationship (between the individual and the group). When two things are similar or different, that's a third kind of relationship. And there are others. Thinking means recognizing different kinds of relationships.

Part 1. Definitions

1. to compare.   to find similarities or differences between things. "You should compare Bill Gates and Carly Fiorini to see how they are similar and what makes them successful."

comparison (noun). what you get when you have compared two things, usually a description of one or more similarities or differences between them. "Alice's comparison of Hamlet and Othello made me see how lonely they both are."

Comment

Many of the key words in effective thinking come in two forms: *verbs* and *nouns*. Verbs are words that indicate actions. Nouns are words that name objects or things. "To eat" is a verb; "meal" is a noun. "To run" is a verb; "race" is a noun. The word *compare* is a verb. Comparing is something you do. The noun is *comparison*. If you have compared two things, then you have made a comparison, which is a thing or a result. "Thinking" (verb) is an activity, and if you have been thinking you have produced "thoughts" (noun). This is simply a convenient way of talking about words, and I'll usually give both forms of the key words. Later you will learn about other forms as well.

Example

1a. I've been inundated [flooded] with requests to **compare** Reagan with other recent presidents, especially Bill Clinton.…Regarding their differences, I have found that, like most politicians of our time, Clinton is a work in progress. He didn't come to office with a set core of beliefs. Reagan, on the other hand, moved into the White House having said essentially the same thing for two and a half decades.…

They do have things in common. Both are tireless campaigners. Both genuinely love people. And Clinton, like Reagan, feeds off a live audience. Put both men in front of a joint session of Congress or at the podium of their respective conventions, and watch how they electrify the room.

Michael K. Deaver, *A Different Drummer: My Thirty Years with Ronald Reagan*, HarperCollins Publishers, 2001, pp. 121–122

Comment

In comparing Reagan and Clinton, Deaver points to differences as well as similarities. Comparing means finding both. Contrasting means looking only at differences.

2. to contrast. to point out differences between two things. "The principle contrasted Mrs. Cooper's relaxed style in the classroom with Mr. Peters' more formal style."

contrast (noun). a difference between two things. "The contrast between the two movies was striking, even though they were directed by the same person."

Contrasting is a narrower activity than comparing, because you are only considering differences.

Example

2a. Uncama's journey to the underworld, motivated by anger, is splendidly **contrasted** with the Ashanti tale of Kwasi Benefo's journey to Asamando, the Ashanti world of departed souls. Here is the story of a hero whose quest is motivated out of love, suffering, and a great compassion.

Clyde W. Ford, *The Hero with an African Face*, Bantam, 2000, p. 21

Question: What difference does the writer see between Uncama's journey and Benefo's journey?

3. to distinguish. to point out differences between two things that might otherwise be confused or lumped together; to differentiate. "We should distinguish between food that tastes good and food that is good for you."

distinction (noun). the difference that sets two things apart. "The teacher drew a distinction between warm-blooded animals such as birds and cold-blooded animals such as fish."

The word can also mean the difference that makes one thing outstanding, or better than another. "The Senator served his country with great distinction."

Example

3a. When is a spanking more than a spanking? When does parental discipline cross the line from an occasional spank to keep an unruly child in order to a beating?

The great parenting debate is now a great federal government debate here [in London]. As a new children's bill makes its way through Parliament, ministers and officials are debating whether all forms of corporal punishment—even by parents—should be banned. The government has taken state interference in personal behavior to a new level; it now seems to distrust parents so much that it thinks they can't **distinguish** between disciplining their kids and assaulting them.

Brendan O'Neill, Britain Debates: To Spank or Not to Spank, *Christian Science Monitor*, 4/19/04

Comment

To distinguish is not exactly the same as to contrast. People often use *distinguish* to talk about seeing a difference between two things that is not easy to see, or marking a difference that is important to keep in mind. In Example 3a, the writer is saying that the government seems to believe that parents can't see the important difference between discipline and child abuse.

4. analogy. a similarity between two things; a comparison of two things with an emphasis on several similarities, usually for the purpose of explaining the less familiar by its resemblance to the more familiar. "Dr. Reynolds explained viral infection using the analogy of an army invading a country. He said the virus invades the body."

Example

4a. I particularly enjoy watching the gliders soaring through the heavens. The only way those graceful yellow crafts can fly is to be tethered to a powered plane that takes them up to where they can catch a wind current. Then they disengage and sail free and alone until returning to land.

While watching that beautiful spectacle one day, I recognized an **analogy** between flying and child rearing as a single parent. There is a time when your children need to be towed by the "mother plane." If that assistance were not available, or if it were not accepted, the "glider" would never get off the ground. But, there comes an appropriate moment for a young pilot to disengage and soar free and alone in the blue heavens.

Dr. James Dobson, Teach Honesty by Example, Universal Press Syndicate, *The Grand Rapids Press*, 8/7/05

Comment

An analogy is a complex comparison. In this example, Dobson suggests that parents and kids are like tow-planes and gliders in several ways. Thinking about the similarities helps us understand the challenging process of bringing up children.

5. metaphor. an indirect comparison of two things. The speaker takes a term that usually applies to one thing, for example *shark*, and applies it to a second thing, such as a banker, suggesting that the second thing is like the first thing: "Mr. Jones at the First National Bank is a shark, a loan shark." Metaphors can be positive, too. "After his date with Mary, Jim floated home on a cloud."

Example

5a. What artists, poets and novelists all have in common is their skill at forming **metaphors**, linking seemingly unrelated concepts in their brain, as when Macbeth said "Out, out brief candle," talking about life. But why call it a candle? Is it because life is like a long white thing? Obviously not. Metaphors are not to be taken literally (except by schizophrenics, which is another story altogether). But in some ways life is like a candle: It's ephemeral, it can be snuffed out, it illumines only very briefly. Our brains make all the right links, and Shakespeare, of course, was a master at doing this.

V. S. Ramachandran, *A Brief Tour of Human Consciousness: From Impostor Poodles to Purple Numbers,* New York: Pi Press, 2004, p. 71

(*Ephemeral* means lasting only a short time. "Her fame was ephemeral; after six months no one remembered her.")

Comment

Ramachandran puts his finger on an important point about metaphors: They are comparisons, but the writer lets us—the readers—find the specific similarities. When Shakespeare indirectly compares life to a candle, he has thought of ways that they are similar. But he doesn't tell us what they are. It is *our* brains that must grasp the links. That's one reason metaphors are so much fun and make such an impact.

Metaphors and analogies are both comparisons of things. The difference is that metaphors are normally shorter and simpler than analogies. Shakespeare's metaphor—"Out, out brief candle"—is just a hint, a suggestion. Dobson explains his analogy of children and gliders more fully. He helps us see several ways that children are like gliders.

6. model. a smaller, simpler version of something, such as an architect's model of a building, used for the purpose of understanding the larger, more complicated thing. "In one room of the museum was a model of the solar system, about ten feet across, with all the planets moving around the sun, and even the moon orbiting the earth."

A model can also be a perfect example of a thing, worthy of imitation, as in "a role model." "June took her own mother as the model of what a mother should be." "PS 38 was a model elementary school."

Example

> 6a. When ancestral Polynesians spread into the Pacific around 3,200 years ago, they encountered islands differing greatly in their environments. Within a few millennia that single ancestral Polynesian society had spawned on those diverse islands a range of diverse daughter societies, from hunter-gatherer tribes to proto-empires. That radiation can serve as a **model** for the longer, larger-scale, and less understood radiation of societies on different continents since the end of the last Ice Age, to become variously hunter-gatherer tribes and empires.
>
> Jared Diamond, *Guns, Germs, and Steel: The Fates of Human Societies,* W. W. Norton, 1999, p. 28

Comment

Diamond is comparing two processes: the Polynesian expansion throughout the Pacific, and humanity's expansion over the globe. We don't fully understand the second expansion. But Diamond says that the Polynesian expansion was shorter, smaller, and is better understood than the expansion of the human race out of Africa to other continents. So it can serve as a model of the larger expansion.

One difference between models and analogies is that models can be completely artificial constructions, although they don't have to be. In other words, if you wanted to create a model of a baseball team, you could draw a large diamond on a piece of paper and put nine *X*s on it, or nine pennies, or anything to represent the nine players. That would be a smaller, simpler version of a real baseball team, even though it's an artificial construction. An analogy is usually a comparison of two natural things, like children and gliders, or learning and growing a garden, or a society and the human body.

Test Yourself

Match each word with its definition.

1. to compare
2. to contrast
3. to distinguish

4. analogy
5. metaphor
6. model

a. to point out differences between two things
b. an indirect comparison of two things; saying one thing is another thing
c. to find similarities or differences, or both, between things
d. a smaller, simpler version of something, which helps us understand the larger thing
e. to point out a difference between two things that may not be noticed, or that is important to keep in mind
f. a similarity between two things, usually one familiar and one not, that helps us understand the less familiar thing

Part 2. Understanding the Meaning

These six words are not completely new to you, but I hope you now have a fuller, more detailed understanding of them. You can deepen your understanding even more by looking at real-world examples. As you talk with people and read things, you will encounter these words, and learning these details should help you see aspects of people's comparisons that you didn't notice before. It should also help you make more complicated comparisons yourself. You know that there are different types of comparisons. Now you can use the words *metaphor* and *analogy* to distinguish between simple, indirect comparisons and longer, complicated comparisons. You can see the difference between comparing and contrasting. Having words to name things, such as analogies, makes it much easier to recognize them and think about them.

Comparing is one type of thinking. As you practice using the words, your mastery of this particular thinking skill will grow.

1. to compare.

1b. The French work twenty-eight per cent fewer hours per person than Americans, and the Germans put in twenty-five per cent fewer hours. **Compared** with Europeans, a higher percentage of American adults work, they work more hours per week, and they work more weeks per year.

One obvious result of this is that America is richer than Europe. In terms of productivity—that is, how much a worker produces in an hour—there's little difference between the U.S., France, and Germany. But since more people work in America, and since they work so many more hours, Americans create more wealth. In effect, Americans trade their productivity for more money, while Europeans trade it for more leisure.

James Surowiecki, The Financial Page: No Work and No Play, *The New Yorker*, 11/28/05

Comment

If you want to use words carefully—and doing so is an important part of thinking clearly—then you will use the words *compare* and *contrast* differently. Comparing is broader. It is finding similarities or differences or both, while contrasting is only finding differences. Example 1b is a comparison, not a contrast, because the writer mentions one way in which Europeans and Americans are similar. Did you notice it?

> 1c. Testing holds appeal for parents and politicians eager to **compare** preschoolers with each other or with benchmarks. And it is valuable in identifying children with learning disabilities, or in evaluating a program.
>
> Sue Shellenbarger, Falling "Behind" at Age 3; The Hazards of Pushing for Accountability in Pre-K, *Wall Street Journal*, 8/18/05

Comment

This example is a reminder that people compare things for a purpose. Comparing is fun, but usually you compare things (restaurants, teachers, prices) in order to find out some useful information. Comparing children might help teachers discover the ones who need help.

Figure 1.2
These identical twins are similar in many ways. Can you see any differences? *Source:* © *Kenneth Sponsler/Shutterstock Images LLC*

1d. For 14 years, scientists from the Scripps Institution of Oceanography in La Jolla, California, used a camera on a sled to study a stretch of seafloor 2½ miles down. They **compared** the numbers of sea cucumbers and other marine life present each season with available air pressure, temperature, and other climate data and found a striking correlation. Within a year or two of a major climatic event from either El Niño or La Niña, life in the deep was drastically altered. The numbers of individuals of each species radically went up or down.

Megan Mansell Williams, Surface Weather Affects Life at Bottom of the Sea, *Discover*, January, 2005, p. 49

Comment

Example 1d is interesting because it shows that scientists can not only compare two objects, such as a fish and a squid, but can compare relationships between things. The scientists in La Jolla first counted the numbers of sea creatures one year and measured the temperature and other climate features that same year. They recorded the relationship between the sea creatures and the weather. Then they compared that *relationship* in one year with the same relationship (between sea creatures and the weather) in another year and discovered that when the weather changed, the numbers of sea creatures changed. Weather events in the atmosphere affected animals deep down in the ocean.

Comment

You will find that people do not always use the six words in this chapter in exactly the same ways. Different people mean slightly different things when they say "compare," or "distinguish," and so on. This is true for all the words in this book. It's simply in the nature of language. Few words have a precise, exact definition that everyone can agree on. For example, how many people make "a crowd"? When is a person "ill"? Is your employer "demanding"? When is an employer guilty of "sexual harassment"? Sometimes the differences are small, but they can lead to misunderstandings. So it helps to be aware of them.

Compare means to find similarities or differences between two things. But people sometimes say that you can't compare two things. Everyone has heard the expression "They are like apples and oranges," or "It's a case of apples and oranges." Consider the following example.

1e. Re "2,000 Dead, in Context," by VH (Op-Ed, Oct. 27):

To **compare** the sacrifices of World War II with those of the war in Iraq is truly **comparing** apples and oranges.

In 1941 the United States was attacked by Japan. Shortly thereafter, Germany declared war on the United States.

Iraq neither attacked our country nor declared war against it. Many Americans who supported the war at first, including members of the Senate, apparently did so based on statements made by the

Figure 1.3
Like everything, apples and oranges are similar in some ways and different in others. *Source: Tamara Kulikova/ Shutterstock Images LLC*

administration. Many of those statements have subsequently proved to be incorrect or misleading....

HW, Letters: Don't Liken Iraq to World War II, *New York Times*, 10/28/05

Comment

When people say, "You can't compare apples and oranges," what they mean is that two things are very different, and it's difficult to find any similarities. Or they mean the differences are more important than the similarities. But actually you can find similarities and differences between *any* two things. For example, whales are similar to pencils. How? Surely they are so different that they can't be compared. But think of similarities: Both are made of atoms, both reflect light, both are organic, i.e., made of material that is or was alive, both are longer than they are wide, both are smooth on the outside, and so on. Of course, you could find many differences as well. But if someone says one thing is similar to another, you can never say that he or she is wrong.

Since any two things can be similar and different at the same time, people get confused and get into arguments. If you say whales are similar to pencils, someone else might disagree and say they are completely different. "That's like comparing apples and oranges." And that person would be right. You are both right. Things can be similar *and* different at the same time. In Example 1e, VH wants to emphasize the similarities between WWII and the war in Iraq, whereas HW wants to emphasize the differences. Remember that people compare things for a purpose. VH wants to persuade people that the war in Iraq might be worth the sacrifice, since WWII was worth the sacrifice, and the two wars are similar. HW thinks VH's comparison doesn't serve the purpose VH thinks it does.

The way to avoid this problem is to explain exactly *how* two things are similar or different. "Apples are similar to oranges in their sweet taste, but different in their color." Often you will read or hear people explain the similarity or difference they have in mind by saying "in this respect" or "in respect of" something. Someone could say "Humans and chimpanzees share over 90 percent of their DNA. They are similar in this respect."

2. to contrast.

2b. Indeed, Mr. Horie's internet company, Livedoor, is easy to **contrast** with the venerable economic model that Japan Post represents. The post office champions snail mail; Mr. Horie's customers use email. The post office built brick-and-mortar branches to help consolidate the Japanese islands; Livedoor and others are using the internet to decentralise decisions. And whereas the post office's huge state-run bank promotes financial isolationism and conservatism, Livedoor has got help from one of the big foreign investment banks that are changing Japan.

Japan's Election: Out with the Old Guard? *The Economist*, 8/27/05

2c. They were once neighbors, but as the rush of commuters waned on a mild April morning at the Ruggles Street MBTA [subway] station, Darnell Delaney and Terrell W. Hodge battled. Only Delaney survived....

"This is a case of self-defense," Delaney's lawyer, Larry R. Tipton, told Suffolk Superior Court Judge John P. Connor Jr. at the arraignment. "Mr. Delaney was attacked by Mr. Hodge."...

Suffolk Assistant District Attorney John P. Pappas said Tipton's account **contrasted** sharply with what nearly a dozen witnesses including MBTA workers, commuters, and passersby said they saw that morning. All described Delaney as the aggressor, he said.

John Ellement, Stabbing Suspect Is Arraigned, *Boston Globe*, 6/12/04

Question: What things are being contrasted here? What difference does the writer point out between them?

3. to distinguish.

3b. In the early 1940's, the American government instituted a series of denaturalization proceedings against foreign-born German-Americans who supported Nazi doctrines or were active in the German-American Bund, a pro-Nazi group. The Supreme Court held that these [government] actions were unconstitutional, explaining that an individual cannot be denaturalized for making "sinister-sounding" statements. The court sharply **distinguished** between radical dissent, which is protected by the First Amendment, and "exhortations calling for present violent action which creates a clear and present danger," which is not.

Geoffrey R. Stone, What You Can't Say Will Hurt You, *New York Times*, 8/15/05

Comment

The Supreme Court distinguished between radical criticism of the government (which it said was legal) and calls for violent action (which was not). Why does the writer say "distinguished" instead of "contrasted"? To distinguish is to contrast, but the word *distinguish* includes the idea that keeping the different things apart is important, or the idea that some people don't see the contrast and it needs to be emphasized. In this case, some people didn't see that radical criticism of the government or society (by American Nazis) is different from calls for violence.

3c. In a survey published earlier this year, seven of 10 parents said they would never let their children play with toy guns. Yet the average seventh grader spends at least four hours a week playing video games, and about half of those games have violent themes, like Nuclear Strike. Clearly, parents **make a distinction** between violence on a screen and that acted out with plastic M-16s. Should they?

Karen Wright, Guns, Lies, and Video, *Discover*, April, 2003

Comment

The writer in Example 3c says parents distinguish between violence on a screen and acting out violence with toy guns, but she also raises a question about the distinction. Maybe they should not distinguish the two things. Are the similarities more important than the differences? What do you think?

4. analogy.

4b. Most battlefield accounts out of Iraq have come from journalists, but a number of combatants are writing memoirs. That adds a new voice to the 24/7 information coming out of the war.

"I like to use a football **analogy**," says John Crawford, whose *The Last True Story I'll Ever Tell: An Accidental Soldier's Account of the War in Iraq* is now on sale. "A sports reporter can write in depth and give you a good idea of the game, but you really don't get it until you play it."

Carol Memmott, Soldiers Bring Iraq Battle to Books; Outlook Differs from Journalists, *USA Today*, 8/11/05

4c. Students are forced to take too many tests under No Child Left Behind and lawmakers should allow schools to use other ways to determine whether kids are learning what they should in each grade, according to a group of principals from across the United States.

The law, which President Bush signed in 2002, requires students to take math and reading tests in grades three through eight and in one year of high school. That's in addition to state-mandated tests and exams 12th-graders in many states must pass to graduate.

The principals said they support testing—but only to a point.

"One of my teachers likes to use an **analogy**: If the farmer spends all the time weighing the pig, you never have the time to feed the pig," said Jeff Miller, a high school principal in Spokane Valley, Wash.

"The pig never grows. You keep placing him on a scale. So we give all these tests, we weigh the pig a hundred different times."

Raju Chebium, Schools Need New Way to Measure Progress, Principals Say, *Gannett News Service*, 8/12/05

Comment

When you make an analogy, you are comparing two things, and you are saying that the similarities are important because they help us understand one of the things better. But sometimes people will disagree, and they will say you have made "a false analogy." (It's like saying, "You are comparing apples and oranges.") In other words, the two things aren't really similar, or you are ignoring important differences. As you study people's comparisons and analogies, you will see that some are better than others. Your practice with these words will improve your ability to make good analogies and avoid poor analogies (i.e., false analogies).

> 4d. For example, proponents of war with Iraq argue that peace demonstrations amount to mob action and liken it to Mussolini's fascists ("Democracy is not about the mob in the street," letter, March 14). Calling on our government—as millions around the world did—to consider alternatives to war was a far cry from fascist mobs demanding authoritarian rule and military adventurism. The analogy is simultaneously insulting and silly.
>
> Another common **analogy** is with the failure of the world to stop Hitler in the 1930s ("This time, America is doing something," column, March 14). Whatever one thinks of Saddam Hussein, the world showed considerable more resolve when he invaded Kuwait. There was an international coalition and it responded forcefully to that aggression. Is there any doubt that if Iraq were to launch an invasion of another country that countries that now shy away from a pre-emptive war would respond differently? This isn't the 1930s and seeking an alternative to war is not appeasement.
>
> FD, Letters, **False Analogies** Allow Sloppy Thinking to Thrive, *The Times Union* (Albany, NY), 3/23/03

analogous (adjective). the quality of being similar

Comment

An adjective is another type of word, besides nouns and verbs. An adjective is a word that describes a characteristic of something. In the phrases "a funny guy," "an expensive car," "a long trip," the words *funny*, *expensive*, and *long* are all adjectives because they describe the characteristics or qualities the things have. The words *guy*, *car*, and *trip* are all nouns. The word *adjective* comes from Latin words that mean "to add something." So an adjective "adds" qualities to objects.

4e. For commercial radio to work, it has to deliver a definable audience to advertisers willing to buy time. Conservative talk radio has been successful as an advertising vehicle targeting men ages 35–54.

What's the **analogous** demographic [population group] that liberal radio can deliver? Is it more female than male? Is it at the upper end of the 35–54 demographic? The lower end?

While these seem insignificant questions to the folks who just want to hear radio that doesn't parrot Rush Limbaugh, demographics drive radio.

Tim Cuprisin, Talk Radio Targets New Group: Liberals, *Milwaukee Journal Sentinel*, 3/29/04

5. metaphor.

5b. A powerful way to join ideas together is to make a **metaphor**. You can create this "wonderful harmony" simply by recognizing similarities between unrelated phenomena. Indeed, this is how our thinking grows: We understand the unfamiliar by comparing it to what we know. For example, the first automobiles were called "horseless carriages."

Roger von Oech, *Expect the Unexpected (Or You Won't Find It)*, The Free Press, 2001, p. 62

5c. It is a great matter to observe propriety in these several modes of expression—compound words, strange (or rare) words, and so forth. But the greatest thing by far is to have a command of **metaphor**. This alone cannot be imparted by another; it is the mark of genius,—for to make good metaphors implies an eye for resemblances.

Aristotle, Poetics, ch 22, sec 9, in Walter Jackson Bate, ed., *Criticism: The Major Texts*, Harcourt, Brace and World, 1952, p. 34

metaphorical. (adjective) the characteristic of something that is used as a metaphor, e.g., "When the coach said we need a snorting bull on our team he was using the words metaphorically."

5d. Part of what makes Jehovah such a fascinating participant in stories of the Old Testament is His kinglike jealousy and pride, and His great appetite for praise and sacrifices. But we have moved beyond this God (haven't we?)....If pressed, many people insist that the anthropomorphic [human-like] language used to describe God is **metaphorical**, not literal.

Daniel C. Dennett, *Breaking the Spell: Religion as a Natural Phenomenon*, Viking, 2006, pp. 265–266

6. model.

6b. We use **models** or analogues as stand-ins for the real things, sorting out problems with the **models** instead. There are, for example,

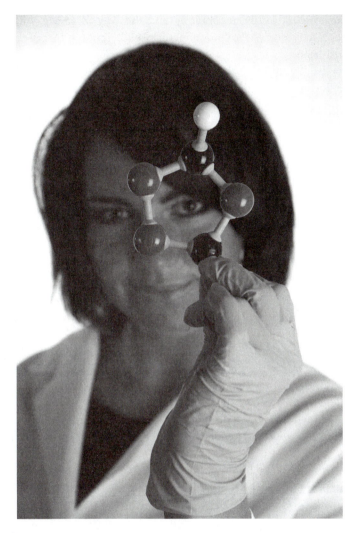

Figure 1.4
This woman is holding a model of a molecule made up of six atoms. Models can be simple, like this one, or very complex and abstract. *Source: © Jose Gil/Shutterstock Images LLC*

blueprints, mockups for aircraft, architect's **models** for buildings to be, casts of organs for student physicians, simulation games.

D. N. Perkins, *The Mind's Best Work*, Harvard University Press, 1981, p. 191

6c. Oil paintings often depict things. Things which in reality are buy-able. To have a thing painted and put on a canvas is not unlike buying it and putting it in your house. If you buy a painting you buy also the look of the thing it represents.

This analogy between *possessing* and the way of seeing which is incorporated in oil painting, is a factor usually ignored by art experts and historians....

It is usually said that the oil painting in its frame is like an imaginary window open on to the world. This is roughly the tradition's own image of itself—even allowing for all the stylistic changes (Mannerist, Baroque, Neo-Classic, Realist, etc.) which took place during four centuries. We are arguing that if one studies the culture of the European oil painting as a whole, and if one leaves aside its own claims for itself, its **model** is not so much a framed window open on to the world as a safe let into the wall, a safe in which the visible has been deposited.

John Berger, *Ways of Seeing*, British Broadcasting Corporation and Penguin Books, 1972, pp. 83, 109

Comment

Models are important. We often understand new, strange things—new ways of doing something, new people or behaviors, new concepts—by comparing them with things we already understand. We incorporate them into a model that we already have. Sometimes our models can mislead us. For example, early Europeans in Africa had a model of what a farm was like, and tried to fit the African activities into their model. They gave the natives tools, such as hoes, and expected them to farm the same way Europeans did. But the Africans didn't know how to use the tools and broke them. Africans had been growing food for centuries, but their practices didn't fit into the European model of farming.

Berger, the author of Example 6c, is a Marxist. He says historians have a model of making and buying oil paintings, and they use it to understand the history of art. Historians believe that a painting on the wall is like a window we look through. Art is about enjoying beauty. But Berger says this model is blinding us to the reality. A better way to understand what's actually happening with art is the model of a safe in the wall where a person stores the precious things he or she has bought. Buying a painting is a substitute for buying and owning the things the painting represents, according to Berger. Art is about wealth and property. A different model leads to a better understanding, in Berger's opinion.

Comment

Constructing models is an important way of comparing things, and understanding this word will help you improve your thinking. But you should remember that the word has another meaning that is probably more common: A "model" is also an ideal, a perfect example, or something worth imitating. For example, a person can be a role model, or "a model parent." These two meanings of *model* are related but not the same.

Part 3. Applying the Words

In Part 1 you studied the definitions of six essential words. I hope you learned more exact and more complex meanings of the words than you knew before. Consciously studying the definitions will help you improve your thinking. You use words in your thinking just as a tennis player uses strokes and movements in her play. If she stops playing and consciously focuses her mind on a serve, for example, and maybe goes through it in slow motion a few times, she will become a better tennis player. The same applies to your use of these words.

In Part 2 you studied other people's uses of the words. You saw different kinds of situations where the words apply, and different aspects of their meanings. Words can be more complicated than they seem at first.

In Part 3 you can practice applying the six words in various situations. You now have a richer, more detailed understanding of these vital concepts. By doing the exercises in Part 3 you will become more comfortable with your new understanding, and you will become more skillful in making comparisons of all kinds. After all, the goal is not just to know the definitions, but to improve your ability to think effectively. These exercises help you do that.

Exercise 1:   Choose the Right Word

For each sentence, choose the best word (or an appropriate form of the word) to fill in the blank. The appropriate form may be a verb (to compare), a noun (comparison), or an adjective (analogous). Verbs may be past tense (compared), future tense (will compare), or present tense (compares, is comparing). The exercise will help you master the meaning of the key words, and selecting the right form will help you choose the best words in your own writing.

1. to compare
2. to contrast
3. to distinguish
4. analogy
5. metaphor
6. model

a. Dr. Kovacs wanted to explain the feeling of weightlessness, so he used an _____ with going down in a fast elevator.
b. Although it was hard to see any differences between the two identical twins, their mother _____ them by the ways they looked at her.
c. The poet _____ the cold, dry, dead winter with the warm, wet, growing spring.
d. The kids built a _____ of a fort using doctors' tongue depressors.
e. Shakespeare is known for his _____, as when he says "All the world's a stage, and all the men and women merely players."
f. The essay _____ the American Revolution and the French Revolution, and seeing the similarities and differences helped us understand both revolutions much better.

Exercise 2: Apply the Words

Each of the following passages is an example of comparing, contrasting, and so on. Read each one and then answer the questions that follow.

1. As the Beagle sailed down the South American coast, Darwin noticed that the animals he saw in one place were replaced farther along by others that were similar but not quite identical. They belonged to the same genus, or family group, but were of different species, or particular types. Sometimes, instead, they belonged to the same species but differed in some slight way, such as having tails of different length. As Darwin wrote later in his *Autobiography*: "It was evident that such facts as these could only be explained on the supposition that species gradually became modified, and the subject haunted me."

Harry Henderson, Lisa Yount, *The Scientific Revolution*, Lucent Books, 1996, p. 67

What things did Darwin compare? Did he see only similarities, only differences, or both similarities and differences?

2. Males and females respond to pain differently, even as children. In most places, boys are expected to show a stiff upper lip when they get hurt, while girls wailing is, well, girlie. In part, this difference is learnt—or, at least, reinforced by learning. But partly, it is innate. It is hard, for instance, to blame upbringing for the finding that boy and girl babies show different responses to pain six hours after birth, or that male rats are more long-suffering than females. It is also life-long. Ed Keogh of the University of Bath, in England, and his colleagues have found that women report feeling pain in more bodily areas than men, and also feel it more often over the course of their lives.

Pain Perception: Sex and Drugs, *The Economist*, 7/23/05

In contrasting males and females, what difference or differences does this writer describe?

3. Many doctors and patients fail to understand the difference between physical dependence and addiction.

An addict uses a drug to get high, becomes tolerant and needs ever-increasing amounts to maintain that high. Patients taking narcotics for pain don't get high; they get relief from their pain, and when larger doses are needed, it is usually because their pain has become more intense, as often happens in patients with advanced cancer or degenerative diseases.

Physical dependence occurs in almost everyone who takes a narcotic for two weeks or more. The body becomes adapted to the presence of narcotics (that is, becomes physically dependent on them). A patient cannot go off them abruptly without suffering serious withdrawal. I asked Dr. Schneider how to go off narcotics safely. She suggested cutting back 10 milligrams every three days (the exact amount would depend on the dose a patient is on). If at any point in the weaning process my pain became more intense, I was to go back to the last dose, wait a week, then try to resume the weaning.

Jane Brody, Let's Get Serious About Relieving Chronic Pain, *New York Times*, 1/10/06

How does Brody distinguish between physical dependence and addiction? In what way are the two conditions also similar?

4. The pretext for this popular violence was found in the fact that from time to time armed bands of monarchist Tutsis who had fled into exile would stage raids on Rwanda. These guerrillas were the first to be called "cockroaches," and they used the word themselves to describe their stealth and their belief that they were uncrushable.

Philip Gourevitch, *We Wish to Inform You That Tomorrow We Will Be Killed with Our Families*, Picador, 1998, p. 64

The Hutus in Rwanda who called the Tutsi guerrillas "cockroaches" wanted to insult them (even though the Tutsis turned the metaphor around and used it as a badge of pride). Was this a good metaphor? Why would the word "cockroach" be an insult? What negative images or ideas does it call up in people's minds? (You can be more specific than saying "they're nasty," "they're yucky," or "they're gross.")

5. But however systematic our values may be, we have to live with the fact that at bottom, in our value postulates, we are not responding to some cosmic imperative, but rather inventing values for ourselves as we go along.

It seems to me that we are in the position of a company of players who have by chance found their way into a great theater. Outside, the city streets are dark and lifeless, but in the theater the lights are on, the air is warm, and the walls are wonderfully decorated. However, no scripts are found, so the players begin to improvise—a little psychological drama, a little poetry, whatever comes to mind. Some even set themselves to explain the stage machinery. The players do not forget that they are just amusing themselves, and that they will have to return to the darkness outside the theater, but while on the stage they do their best to give a good performance. I suppose that this is a rather melancholy view of human life, but melancholy is one of the distinctive creations of our species, and not without its own consolations.

Steven Weinberg, *Facing Up: Science and Its Cultural Adversaries*, Harvard University Press, 2001, p. 47–48

Weinberg is using an analogy to explain something. What two things is he comparing?

6. But meaning is not derived from knowledge. To try to manufacture it in this way, that is, out of the provable knowledge of what

can be made, would resemble Baron Munchhausen's absurd attempt to pull himself up out of the bog by his own hair. I believe that the absurdity of this story mirrors very accurately the basic situation of man. No one can pull himself up out of the bog of uncertainty, of not being able to live, by his own exertions; nor can we pull ourselves up, as Descartes still thought we could, by a *cogito ergo sum* [I think, therefore I am], by a series of intellectual deductions. Meaning that is self-made is in the last analysis no meaning. Meaning, that is, the ground on which our existence as a totality can stand and live, cannot be made but only received.

Joseph Cardinal Ratzinger, *Introduction to Christianity*, translated by J. R. Foster, Ignatius Press, 2004, p. 73

Like Weinberg, Ratzinger (who later became Pope Benedict XVI) is also using an analogy. What two things is he comparing?

7. Performing imaginary experiments on a computer is becoming ever more useful as the power of modern computers continues to increase. By the early 1990s it was possible on a computer to follow the fate of large numbers of atoms undergoing extremely fast reactions much more easily and in much more detail than by means of laboratory experiments.

Philip R. Watson, in David Calhoun, ed., *1994 Yearbook of Science and the Future*, Encyclopedia Britannica, Inc., 1993, p. 307

What kind of model are scientists using here? What are they trying to understand with the model?

Exercise 3:   Apply the Ideas in Writing

Think of two people you know and write a paragraph or two comparing them. You should describe at least two similarities and two differences. You could compare two teachers you have had, or two friends, or relatives, or even people on TV. One way to organize your ideas is to explain the similarities first and then explain the differences. Or you can explain one similarity and one difference, and then explain another similarity and another difference.

Improving Your Writing 1: Paragraphs

A *paragraph* is a set of sentences that convey one main idea. The sentences are all related to a single topic, and they develop that topic, in the sense that they present details about the topic. In Example 1a, the first paragraph is about differences between Clinton and Reagan, and the second paragraph is about similarities between them. A *topic* can be anything—your friend, democracy, volcanoes, the battle of Concord—and the *main idea* is what you say *about* that topic: Your friend is generous; democracy is difficult to maintain; volcanoes are unpredictable; the battle of Concord is often misunderstood. You can explain that main idea by adding details, facts, examples, and other things you know about it. But everything in the paragraph should be related to the main idea.

A good paragraph has a *topic sentence*, which states the main idea. Usually it's the first sentence. The topic sentence is relatively broad, since it covers all the more specific information in the paragraph. In Example 1a, the topic sentence of the second paragraph is "They do have things in common." The remainder of the paragraph explains that main idea.

CHAPTER 2 ⚑

Generalizing

7. to generalize

8. sample

9. stereotype

10. to classify

11. criterion

Comparing, the topic of the previous chapter, may be the simplest, most basic kind of thinking we do, but almost as fundamental is thinking about groups. When we compare two things—say, two dogs—and see that they are similar, we might go on to compare a third dog with the first two, and then a fourth, and so on. We see a canary and notice that it is different and doesn't belong with the dogs. Soon we have a whole group of things that are similar and that belong together. If we then say, "Dogs have wet noses," we have said something about the whole group, not just one or two dogs. A statement about a group of things is called a *generalization*, and it's a very important kind of statement. It's not the same as saying "Snoopy has a wet nose," because that sentence is about a particular dog, Snoopy. "Most of my friends like jazz" is different from "Sheila likes jazz."

We can think about specific, particular objects, or we can think about groups of things. Groups are also called *classes*. If you look at a taxi cab parked on the street you can notice its color, the dent in the front fender, the rubber bumper, the inspection sticker in the windshield, and all sorts of other specific features. You can compare two particular taxi cabs. Or you can think about taxis in general. Someone might ask, "Are all taxis yellow?" or "Do all taxis have a partition between the front and back seats?" If you have some experience with taxis, you can answer those questions with generalizations. "Yes, in this city they're all yellow," or "No, I've seen some that don't have a partition." These statements are not about a specific cab, but about the whole class of cabs.

We talk about groups all the time. "Most students in my school want to go to college." "Beef costs more than chicken." "Whales breathe oxygen just like us." Generalizations are essential in every area of life because we can't treat each particular thing as if it were unique and not part of a group. For example, we know that eggs are good to eat (in general), so when we get up in the morning and prepare breakfast, we don't have to wonder if this particular egg will be poisonous. When the Number 10 bus comes, we get on and expect it to go where all Number 10 buses go. We don't ask the driver if she is going to Canada or Mexico. In other words, we treat things as types. If we know what type of thing this little round object is—it's an egg—then we know a lot about it and we know what to do with it. We know a lot of generalizations about eggs and we apply them to this particular object.

But sometimes eggs are rotten. It doesn't happen often, if you buy your groceries at a regular supermarket, but it can happen. So the generalization "eggs are good to eat" is usually true but not always true. We can make mistakes with our generalizations. In fact, it's easy to go wrong in making generalizations. We might say *all* eggs are good to eat when actually only *most* of them are. Or we can be completely off track. A person might think about her friends in college, and she might decide that "most people in my college are athletic," when in fact a majority of the students at that school aren't interested in sports. She just happens to know a lot who are.

It is so easy to make mistakes with generalizations—especially about humans—that some people go to the extreme of saying that all generalizations are bad and we should never generalize. That is an overreaction. In fact, we must generalize continuously in order to function at all. If we didn't treat the hamburgers on our plates, or the elevators we ride in, or the sales clerks we buy from, as types, we would be paralyzed and couldn't act at all. On the other hand, we can all be more careful with our generalizations. In this chapter you will deepen your understanding of several key words involved in thinking about groups and making generalizations. Thinking about groups is more complicated than comparing two things, and it involves several relationships. Learning the precise and complex meanings of the important terms will help you avoid making mistakes, it will help you see other people's mistakes, and it will help you think broadly and systematically about groups of things.

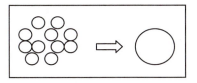

Figure 2.1
Generalizing means finding some feature that many particular items have in common. Here, all the items on the left have the round shape in common.

Part 1. Definitions

7. to generalize. to say something about a group of things, based on what you know about a few of those things. "I've been to Starbucks cafes in several cities and the coffee was always good but expensive. As a rule, Starbucks has a good product at a premium price." This person is generalizing about Starbucks cafes as a group. "In every sample we tested the new drug killed the bacteria. We conclude that the new drug will be effective against these bacteria in most cases." This person is generalizing about applications of the new drug to a type of bacteria.

generalization (noun). a statement about a group of objects, people, events, times, or other things, as opposed to a statement about a particular, individual thing. The sentence "Apples are red" is a generalization, but "This apple in my hand is red" is a particular statement.

Example

7a. One can make this **generalization** about men: they are ungrateful, fickle, liars, and deceivers, they shun danger and are greedy for profit.

Niccolo Machiavelli, *The Prince*, trans. George Bull, Penguin, 1999 [originally written 1514], p. 54

8. sample (noun). the particular members of a group that a person actually observes, and that form the basis of his or her generalization. "To find out what the students at State University think, I took a sample of opinions in my economics class. Eighteen people approved of the President's policy, and seven disapproved. That suggests that most people in this school support the President's policy."

(Here the speaker asks students in her economics class what they think. The students are her sample. Then she generalizes about the whole group of students at the university, although she hasn't actually asked all the students in the university what they think.)

A doctor takes a sample of blood or urine and tests it, and, on the basis of what's in the sample, makes a generalization about what's in your body as a whole.

to sample (verb). to try something, usually something to eat or drink. "I sampled the diner's cheesecake; it's first-rate." This person is saying that he or she actually tasted a small part of the cheesecake at the diner (one piece), and on that basis is generalizing about all of the cheesecake at that diner.

Example

8a. But let's say you go to each casino in the Chicago area and stop every 10th customer to go through the turnstiles, at different times of day and different days of the week, and get a representative **sample** of who goes to casinos. Then what kind of profile emerges of the typical casino customer?

That's an oversimplification of sampling methods, but Harrah's has been commissioning surveys by independent polling groups for years, and the surveys always have shown the typical casino customer to be slightly older, slightly better-educated and slightly more affluent than the average American adult.

John Gorchowski, Who Goes to Casinos? You Might Be Surprised, *Chicago Sun-Times*, 6/18/04

9. stereotype. a generalization about a group that is based on a very small number of examples, and that usually attributes some negative characteristic to the group. "Protestants have no conscience." "Catholics are just mindless sheep." "Jews are greedy." "Muslims are all fanatics."

Example

9a. Cabdrivers can no longer be **stereotyped.** One time the popular conception was of the balding, pot-bellied, cigar-chomping, middle-aged man, who'd drive like a bat out of hell and yelled at all the other drivers.... There are as many different types of cabdrivers, with as many different dispositions, as there are among the entire human race.

Studs Terkel, *Working*, Avon, 1972, p. 270

10. to classify. This word has two different meanings: 1. to divide a large group of things into subgroups, so that each member of the large group can be sorted into one of the subgroups; "The animals in the exhibit are classified as vertebrates and invertebrates." "Amy classified her porcelain collection into American, British, and Chinese pieces."

2. to put something into a group of similar things, i.e., into a certain class of things. "A lobster is classified as an invertebrate." "For tax purposes, Smith was classified as 'low income.'"

These two meanings are related but different, and they represent two different thinking operations. One way to consider the difference between the first meaning and the second meaning is to look at the object that is classified. In the first meaning, a group of things is classified; it is divided into parts. In the second meaning, an individual is classified; it is put into its appropriate group.

classification (noun). a. an arrangement of a group of items into sub-parts; b. the act of identifying one particular thing as belonging to a certain group.

Example

10a. A former member of the state's Sex Offender Registry Board is questioning the way it **classifies** its targets. The seven-member board ranks convicted sex offenders on a scale of 1 to 3, with level 3 considered the most likely to reoffend....

The board has **classified** sex offenders dating back to 1981. As of June, there were 2,496 level 1 sex offenders in Massachusetts, 4,936 level 2 offenders, and 1,191 level 3 offenders, he said.

Megan Woolhouse, Former Official Criticizes Offender Registry, *Boston Globe*, 7/16/06

11. criterion. some quality or mark that guides people in classifying things; the test by which people decide that something belongs in a certain category. "The criterion for being a mammal is giving birth to live young instead of laying eggs."

The plural of *criterion* is *criteria*. You can have more than one criterion for classifying something; you can have several criteria. "To be a senior here, you must be enrolled in the school, *and* you must be in your fourth year."

Example

11a. The experimental test is especially important, as the ultimate **criterion** for distinguishing scientific knowledge from philosophical speculation.

H. J. Muller, What Science Is, in George Levine and Owen Thomas, eds., *The Scientist vs. the Humanist*, W. W. Norton and Co., 1963, pp. 12–13.

Test Yourself
Match each word with its definition.

7. to generalize
8. sample
9. stereotype
10. to classify
11. criterion

a. taking a large group and dividing it into smaller groups
b. a statement about a group that is based on very limited experience with members of that group
c. noticing or deciding that a statement about all or part of a group of things is true
d. the part of a group that you have experienced, and that leads you to believe something about the whole group
e. the test, or standard, by which you decide that an object belongs in a particular class

Part 2. Understanding the Meaning

7. to generalize.

7b. I am shocked by the ignorance of the recent outcry against vegan diets in the media [i.e., diets that avoid all animal products—including eggs, milk, fish, etc.], most recently Nina Planck's article about the dangers and irresponsibility of vegan diets during pregnancy and infancy....

Generalizing from a handful of ignorant vegans to the entire vegan population does a disservice to those of us who have spent years educating ourselves on human nutritional needs and how to meet them on a plant-based diet.

Nicole Speer, Letters: Vegans and Their Children, *New York Times*, 5/23/07

7c. Frederick Schauer, who teaches a course on the first amendment at the Kennedy School of Government at Harvard [says]...society has become so obsessed with avoiding any stereotypes that it ignores reality.... A fair number of **generalizations**, he insists, turn out to be accurate....

Amid new concerns about identifying terrorists and old worries about the police using race and ethnicity as grounds for suspicion, Mr. Schauer says one of his goals is to fine-tune "profiling" and rescue it from being pejorative. "I defend the morality of decisions by categories and by **generalizations**," he writes.

Felicia R. Lee, Discriminating? Yes. Discriminatory? No, *New York Times*, 12/13/03

(*Pejorative* means "carrying a negative judgment, or conveying a sense that something is bad; disparaging." "The word *fat* is a pejorative word; you should say he is *portly*.")

Figure 2.2
What generalization can you make about the people you see in this photograph? *Source:* ©
J. McPhail/Shutterstock Images LLC

Comment

There are two basic types of generalizations: universal and limited. A universal generalization is about *all* of the members of some group, whereas a limited generalization is about *some* of the members of the group. For example, the sentence "Every box of cereal comes with a prize inside" is a universal generalization because it is about all the boxes. "In our survey, most people preferred coffee to tea" is a limited generalization because it is only about most of the people, not all.

You can express universal and limited generalizations in various ways. To state a universal generalization you could say, "None of the contestants quit the race," or "Without exception the people we met were friendly." You are making statements about the entire group of contestants and the entire group of people you met. Here are some limited generalizations: "Some dogs learn faster than others," "Many flowers have no fragrance at all," and "Quite a few cities sent representatives."

> 7d. To appreciate the Marxian conception of history it is necessary to remember that its author belonged to an age which recognized no limitations to the range of knowledge available to a single mind. Historical **generalizations** of the most far-reaching and universal kind were not merely admired but expected. In this regard Marx was a true Victorian, for faith in general theories was by no means confined to Central Europe, though German writers were among its foremost exponents. Taine, Tocqueville, and Gobineau in France, Mill and Spencer in England, were as productive of sweeping hypotheses as any German.
>
> George Lichtheim, *Marxism: An Historical and Critical Study*, Praeger, 1965, p. 141

Question: Lichtheim says Marx made universal generalizations. Lichtheim himself makes a generalization, indirectly. What is it? (Hint: He gives examples to illustrate it.)

8. sample.

> 8b. Television these days is loaded with sex, sex, sex—double the number of sex scenes aired seven years ago, says a study out yesterday....
>
> There were nearly 3,800 scenes with sexual content spotted in more than 1,100 shows researches studied, up from about 1,900 such scenes in 1998, the first year of the Kaiser Family Foundation survey....
>
> The study examined a **sample** of a week's worth of programming on ABC, CBS, NBC, Fox, WB, PBS, Lifetime, TNT, USA Network and HBO. Sexual content, as defined in the study, could be anything from discussions about sex to scenes involving everything from kissing to intercourse.
>
> Sex Scenes on TV Are on the Rise (from the Associated Press), *AM New York*, 11/10/05

> 8c. A large-scale government-financed study has concluded that when it comes to math, students in regular public schools do as well as or significantly better than comparable students in private schools....

Figure 2.3
If the grapes in the sample (in the woman's hand) taste good, can she know that the other grapes taste good?

> Taylor Smith, Jr., vice president for executive support at the Association of Christian Schools, which represents 5,400 predominantly conservative Christian schools in the United States, said that many of the group's members did not participate in the national assessment, which he thought could make it a skewed **sample**.
>
> Diana Jean Schemo, Public-School Pupils Do as Well in Math as Those in Private Schools, Study Says, *New York Times*, 1/28/06

Comment

A "skewed sample" is a small part of a group that is not like the group as a whole. It is weighted so that it leans in some direction. For example, if you wanted to find out about public high schools, but all the schools in your sample had more than 2,000 students, your sample would be skewed, because many public high schools have far fewer students. So your sample is not similar to the group as a whole. Or suppose you wanted to survey your community to find out about political opinions, and you gathered a sample of people by putting an ad in the newspaper that said, "We will pay $5 for your participation." Your sample would be skewed because you would attract those people who are willing to take out time to earn $5. Many people would be too busy to participate for $5. Another word for skewed is *biased*.

(*Skewed* literally means "at an angle, slanted." A doorframe can be skewed if it doesn't stand up straight.) The opposite of a skewed sample is a representative sample.

> 8d. Ethnographers have been rightly criticized for writing "The Hopi do (or believe) thus and so" without stating whether this generalization is based upon ten observations or a hundred or upon the statement of one informant or of ten informants representing a good range of the status positions in that society. No scientist can evade the problems of **sampling**, of the representativeness of his materials for the universe he has chosen to study.
>
> A. L. Kroeber and Clyde Kluckhohn, General Features of Culture, in William R. Taber, ed., *Man in Contemporary Society*, Columbia University Press, 1962, p. 54

> 8e. The Ms. Magazine Campus Project on Sexual Assault, directed by Mary P. Koss at Kent State and funded by the National Center for the Prevention and Control of Rape, reached more than seven thousand students at a nationally representative **sample** of thirty-five schools, to find out how often, under what circumstances, and with what aftereffects a wide range of sexual assaults, including date rape, took place.
>
> Ellen Sweet, Date Rape: The Story of an Epidemic and Those Who Deny It, in Alfred Rosa and Paul Eschholz, eds., *Controversies: Contemporary Arguments for College Writers*, Macmillan Publishing co., 1991, p. 424

Comment

This writer says her sample is "representative." That's another way of saying it's not skewed (or biased). The sample of colleges is just like the whole group of all the American colleges. It includes large, small, Eastern, Western, state, private colleges, and so on.

Question: Suppose you want a representative sample of the people who live in your town or neighborhood. If you went to the local McDonald's or Burger King or other fast-food restaurant and interviewed every person you could in one day, would you have a representative sample or a skewed sample?

> 8f. A cup of cooked pasta, the recommended serving, has around 200 calories. But when New York University researchers **sampled** pasta dishes served at local fast-food outlets and family restaurants in 2002, the serving sizes averaged almost *five* cups.
>
> Peter Jaret, The New Carb Rules, *Fitness*, July, 2004, p. 151

Comment

Notice that this writer is using *sample* as a verb. If you sample (verb) pasta dishes, you end up with a sample (noun).

9. stereotype.

9b. Half of all the students attending college today are 25 and over. "The Joe College **stereotype**—the eighteen- to twenty-two-year-old full-time student in residence on a campus—accounts for only 20 percent of the fifteen million students," says Harold Hodgkinson, the director of the Center for Demographic Policy at the Institute for Educational Leadership in Washington.

Sam Roberts, *Who We Are Now*, Times Books, 2004, p. 194

9c. Even the **stereotype** generalizations about scientists are misleading without some sort of detail—e.g., the generalization that scientists as a group stand on the Left. This is only partly true. A very high proportion of engineers are almost as conservative as doctors.

C. P. Snow, The Two Cultures, in George Levine and Owen Thomas, eds., *The Scientist vs. the Humanist*, W. W. Norton and Co., 1963, pp. 12–13

Comment

Stereotypes are inaccurate, misleading generalizations. Some people decide, therefore, that all generalizations are bad. But that's a hasty decision and it would prevent you from thinking effectively. Some generalizations are bad and some aren't. Good generalizations are essential. We couldn't live without them. For example, "Crossing the street without looking both ways sometimes leads to accidents" is a sound generalization, and is very useful. Bad generalizations are those that people make without enough experience to back them up. They are based on a sample that is too small, or that is skewed. Bad generalizations are stereotypes. If I meet one rude French person, and on that basis decide that most French people are rude, then I am making a generalization without enough evidence to support it. But if I take a thorough survey of many French people, I might be able to make a sound generalization about the group as a whole, e.g., "Many French people expect tourists to make an effort to speak French."

10. to classify

Comment

The word *classify* has two different meanings because when we classify things we go through two different steps, but we use the same word to talk about both steps. You can see this if you think of an example. The most famous classification ever made was Carl Linnaeus' classification of living things into animals and plants, phyla, orders, classes, genera, and so on. Linnaeus did two distinct things. First, he surveyed all living things and decided what subgroups they should be divided into. He decided that being rooted to the ground is an important difference from being able to move freely, and on that basis (and others) he divided living things into the subgroups of plants and animals. Among animals, he decided that having a backbone is an important characteristic, so he divided them into vertebrates (backbone) and invertebrates (no backbone). And then, within the two classes of vertebrates and invertebrates, he made further subdivisions. This is all part of the first step of classifying: dividing larger groups into smaller subgroups based on certain characteristics. The second step is to look at a particular creature—a dolphin, for example—and decide which subgroups it belongs to. He started at the top and classified the dolphin as an animal, not plant, because it can move. He classified it as a vertebrate because it has a backbone. And he worked his way down to more specific subgroups.

The following (10b) is an example of the first sense of *classify*, while the next selection (10c) is an example of the second sense of the word.

> 10b. A big study of more than 8,000 women, comparing results among those given one of the new drugs—letrozole—after surgery, and those given tamoxifen, reports particularly impressive results among women with a high chance of breast cancer returning....
>
> In an accompanying editorial, Sandra Swain, of the National Cancer Institute, in Bethesda, Maryland, said experts were now trying to **classify** breast cancers into multiple categories. "It is essential to define each subgroup precisely and delineate distinct characteristics and targets that will lead us to tailored therapies that are better than the ones we have now."
>
> James Meikle, Fresh Hopes for Life-saving Breast Cancer Drug, *The Guardian* (London), 12/29/05

Question: What large group are experts trying to classify? What is their purpose in dividing the large group into subgroups? What do they hope to accomplish?

> 10c. It was, however, with the Inquisition, beginning in the thirteenth century, that the intolerance of the Middle Ages reached its most perfect organization.... It was sufficient to **classify** a suspected heretic as an Albigensian, or Waldensian, or a member of some other heretical

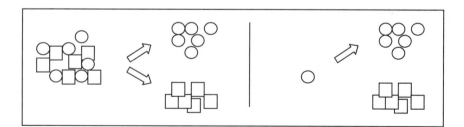

Figure 2.4
The word *classifying* has two meanings. It can mean dividing a group into subgroups, like the illustration on the left. Or it can mean putting an individual into the appropriate group, like the illustration on the right.

Figure 2.5
Many towns want people to classify their garbage as metal, glass, and paper; some suggest more categories. *Source: © prism_68/Shutterstock Images LLC*

sect. There was no use in his trying to explain or justify; it was enough that he diverged.

James Harvey Robinson, *The Mind in the Making*, Harper, 1921, p. 130

Comment

Robinson is using the word *classify* in the second sense because he says an individual with unusual opinions might be lumped together with a group of known heretics, like the Albigensians, or the Waldensians. A person classified in that way was doomed.

10d. Fanon's respect for traditional cultural patterns stopped short of their interfering with modern medical techniques. He **classified** the medicine men, witch doctors, and marabouts operating in the Algerian countryside as agents of Western colonialism helping to keep the territory enslaved in ignorance and weakness.

Peter Geismar, *Fanon:The Revolutionary as Prophet*, Grove Press, 1969, p. 87

(A *marabout* is a saintly hermit in North Africa. The word comes from the Arabic word for stork, which is a sacred bird in Islam.)

Comment

Geismar is using *classify* in the second sense, but his example shows that one *group* can be classified as belonging to a larger group. Franz Fanon put the group of witch doctors in rural Algeria into the larger class of people working for Western domination of less developed countries.

11. criterion.

11b. Ken-L Ration has been giving the Dog Hero award since 1954. Every year many dogs are nominated for the honor, all having rescued people from a variety of perils including traffic accidents, drowning, illness, animal attacks, and burglary, as well as fires and snowstorms. Somehow, these animals recognize dangers to humans and figure out ways to save or protect them. Unfortunately, these sorts of occurrences do not meet the **criteria** of science. They can't be repeated, and so we do not know what mental capabilities allow dogs to behave in these ways.

Dorothy Hinshaw Patent, *How Smart Are Animals?* Harcourt, Brace, Jovanovich, 1990, pp. 93–94

Question: A criterion is a characteristic that a person uses as a test for classifying something. What characteristic must events have to be classified as science, according to Patent?

11c. The issue of authenticity in pop music is hotly debated by music scholars. Anything symbolising music as a craft, a culture or an aesthetic is respected as authentic, while anything that symbolises music as a disposable, marketable product is deemed inauthentic.

Playing an instrument is a mark of authenticity, as is writing songs that reflect personal experience and performing live. Slogging it out at the lower end of the industry is also authentic, as is a love of music for its own sake rather than as a path to fame.

On these **criteria,** there are plenty of talented female singers who fit the "authentic" bill: PJ Harvey, Tori Amos, Ani DiFranco, Fiona Apple, to name a few. But it's subjective. The same sort of yardstick can easily be applied to Britney Spears: a singer from before she started school; a veteran of the Mickey Mouse Club before she hit her teens; a hard worker and entertaining stage performer.

Mel Campbell and Graeme Hammond, Is She for Real? *Sunday Telegraph Magazine* (Sydney, Australia), May 18, 2003

11d. Basrur insisted there's no comparison between Toronto and Asian centres hit by the disease [SARS].

"In my opinion, SARS is primarily a disease of health-care workers, largely in hospital settings," Basrur said. "It has occurred in some community settings, but not to any great extent, and to categorize us as close to Beijing or other parts of China, I think is a gross misrepresentation of the facts."

But WHO [World Health Organization] defended its decision, saying the spread of SARS overseas by people from Toronto gave it no choice.

"The **criteria** are there," WHO's Dr. David Heymann said, referring to the world body's decision to treat Toronto the same way as SARS hot spots in Asia, including China and Hong Kong.

"On a lesser magnitude, but still a high magnitude, Canada has met the same **criteria** that those other places are meeting," Heymann said.

"It has nothing to do with whether Canada and Beijing can be compared. They can't be compared. They're each different situations."

Nicolaas van Rijn, Britain Warns Its Citizens Not to Travel to Toronto, *Toronto Star*, April 24, 2003

Comment

People can get into disagreements over criteria in two ways. Consider the example of authentic musicians. One kind of disagreement is: Does a person (Britney Spears, for example) meet the criteria for being an authentic musician (loving music for its own sake, etc.)? Some might say yes and some no. The second kind of disagreement over criteria is: Are these the right criteria for being an authentic musician (loving music, playing an instrument, etc.)? Maybe writing songs is the only criterion we should use. People can disagree about what the criteria should be, as well as about whether an individual actually meets the criteria.

In Example 11d, Mr. Basur and Dr. Heymann disagree about whether Toronto should be classified as a SARS hot spot. Mr. Basur doesn't explain his point of view in detail, but he seems to disagree with Dr. Heymann over what the criterion for classifying cities should be. The fact that people from Toronto spread SARS overseas (the WHO's criterion) is apparently well established.

Part 3. Applying the Words

Exercise 1:   Choose the Right Word

For each sentence, choose the best word (or an appropriate form of the word) to fill in the blank.

7. to generalize
8. sample
9. stereotype
10. to classify
11. criterion

a. The _____ for being classified as a teenager is being between 13 and 19 years old, but I know some 30-year-olds who behave like teenagers.
b. Europeans who have visited the United States and met a number of Americans often _____ and say, "Most Americans are very friendly."
c. The Environmental Protection Agency said the water was safe to drink, based on _____ taken from around the city.

   d. Mike was afraid of beetles because he had a very limited understanding of insects; he relied on a _____ and thought all insects were alike.

   e. Rick wrote down all the things he ought to do next week, and then _____ them as "very important," "important," and "not important."

Exercise 2:   Apply the Words

Read each example and answer the questions that follow.

> 1. No professional diplomatists worried about falsehoods. Words were with them forms of expression which varied with individuals, but falsehood was more or less necessary to all.
>
> Henry Adams, *The Education of Henry Adams*, Modern Library, 1931, p. 133

Adams is making a generalization about a group. What group is he thinking of? Is his generalization a universal generalization or a limited generalization?

> 2. Over the past few months I've spent several hours a day, five days a week, watching talk shows. From *Rolonda* to *Geraldo* to *Jenny Jones* to *Richard Bey* to *Donahue* to *Ricki Lake* to *Gordon Elliott* to *Jerry Springer* to *Sally Jessy Raphael* to *Maury Povich* to *Montel Williams* to *Oprah*. I've watched shows on mate swapping, men who beat women, fat women who are porno stars, ... You name it, I've probably seen it; I've seen it all.
>
> Jill Nelson, Talk Is Cheap, in Robert Atwan, ed., *Our Times: Readings from Recent Periodicals*, Fifth Edition, Bedford, 1998, p. 373

Nelson has collected a sample of talk shows. If she made a generalization based on her sample, would you accept it? In other words, do you think her sample is good enough to give her an understanding of the whole class of talk shows?

> 3. When General Wojciech Jaruzelski imposed martial law in Poland on December 12th 1981, most of the male leaders of the trade union Solidarity were imprisoned. It was women who kept the organisation going. They dodged the secret police, forged papers, gave underground seminars and produced a clandestine mass-circulation newspaper, which the authorities repeatedly, but vainly, tried to suppress. Their chauvinism meant they assumed that the conspirators they were seeking must be men. During house searches, the secret police would usually neglect to investigate anything connected with women or children. Consequently, piles of nappies [diapers] became one of the most preferred hiding places.
>
> Brave Women, but Not Sisters, *The Economist*, 7/30/05

The Polish authorities were guilty of applying stereotypes to women. What generalizations did they make about women? Why were those generalizations stereotypes?

> 4. When Fanon arrived at Blida there were six medical doctors in charge of two thousand patients. Slightly more than half were

European, the rest *indigenes* (natives), in the official language of the colonial epoch. The two groups were kept separate, the settlers receiving favored treatment....

In Fanon's service the distinction between "native" and European was prohibited. On the other hand, the doctor planned a new kind of segregation based on the patient's aggressiveness.

Peter Geismar, *Fanon: The Revolutionary as Prophet*, Grove Press, 1969, pp. 64–66

Geismar describes two classifications: the original doctors' classification and Fanon's classification. What group were they classifying? What subgroups did the original doctors create, and what subgroups did Fanon set up?

5. At what point in altering ourselves, would we lose our essential humanity? Are there any traits that make us essentially human? When might we become monsters or marvels, or are we already there? I vividly remember reading a book by a woman named Martha Beck. She had given birth to a Down's syndrome child and she wrote in a few chilling sentences that because of one tiny chromosome, her child, Adam, is "as dissimilar from me as a mule is from a donkey. He is, in ways both obvious and subtle, a different beast." Is it really that simple, that small? One tiny chromosome severs us from the human species?

Lauren Slater, "Dr. Daedalus" in Matt Ridley, ed., *The Best American Science Writing 2002*, HarperCollins Publishers, 2002, p. 16

Slater is thinking about the criterion, or criteria, for belonging in the class of humans. What criterion does Martha Beck use to decide that her son is not part of the human species ["a different beast"]?

Exercise 3:   Types of Generalizations

There are two types of generalizations, universal and limited. Universal generalizations are statements about an entire group of things. Limited generalizations are about only part of a group. You can find both universal generalizations and limited generalizations in the following examples. Read each example and answer the questions that follow.

1. As a result of the excessive cold which produces killing frosts, none of the lands of the high sierra can be used to grow fruits and vegetables.

Bernabe Cobo, quoted in Filipe Fernandez-Armesto, *Civilizations: Culture, Ambition, and the Transformation of Nature*, Free Press, 2001, p. 229

(The word *sierra* means a rugged range of mountains. It is Spanish for "saw.") Cobo makes a generalization about the lands in the mountains. Is it universal or limited?

2. For Confucius, every person is potentially a sage, defined as one who acts with extreme benevolence.

Leslie Stevenson and David L. Haberman, *Ten Theories of Human Nature*, Third Edition, Oxford University Press, 1998, p. 28

Is Confucius' generalization universal or limited?

> 3. The special information which lawyers derive from their studies ensures them a separate station in society, and they constitute a sort of privileged body in the scale of intelligence.... A portion of the tastes and of the habits of the aristocracy may consequently be discovered in the characters of men in the profession of the law.... [But] A privileged body can never satisfy the ambition of all its members....
>
> I do not, then, assert that all the members of the legal profession are at all times the friends of order and the opponents of innovation, but merely that most of them usually are so.
>
> Alexis de Tocqueville, *Democracy in America*, trans. by Henry Reeve, Bantam, 2000 [originally published 1835], pp. 316, 317

In the sentence that begins "I do not, then, assert...," does Tocqueville make a universal generalization or a limited generalization? (To be absolutely precise, Tocqueville makes two generalizations about two groups in this sentence. Can you see the two groups he is talking about?)

Exercise 4:   Types of Classifications

Remember that the word *classify* has two meanings: first, to divide a group into subgroups, and second, to place an individual into an appropriate group. For each of the following passages, try to decide whether the writer is using the first kind or the second kind of classifying.

> 1. Songbirds are divided into two major branches: the Corvida, with more than 1,000 species, including crows and ravens, and the Passerida, with nearly 3,500 species, including cardinals, robins, and finches. The Corvida are most diverse in Australia, so biologists assumed that they had evolved down under. The Passerida are more diverse in the Northern Hemisphere, so they were assumed to have evolved there.
>
> Erik Stokstad, Songbirds Have Southern Roots, *Discover*, January, 2005, p. 68

> 2. I have always believed that there are two kinds of literary fiction writers. The first are the story tellers. They are the yarn spinners, the narrators, the parable writers. A story teller is someone like Flannery O'Connor or Yann Martel, a writer who can engage and teach and give a deep sense of the world of his characters. The metaphor for this kind of writing is the windowpane through which the world of the novel is clearly visible.
>
> The other kind of writer is the wordsmith. These are the careful crafters of sentences, the meditative cabbalists of words. These are the writers who must be read slowly because every sentence is rich and beautiful in its own right. These are writers like Michael Ondaatje, Faulkner and Morrison. The metaphor for their writing is

the stained-glass window. One does not need to look beyond the pane to see its beauty.

Ragan Sutterfield, Review: Gilead Provides a Balm for World-weary Reader, *Arkansas Democrat-Gazette* (Little Rock), 2/20/05

(The Cabala was a secret interpretation of the Hebrew scriptures, transmitted among rabbis in the Middle Ages. *Cabalistic* means hidden, symbolic, hard to interpret; a cabalist is one who writes the complicated message.)

3. Why did Cortes conquer Baja California? Was it his ambition? ... [H]ow do we identify Cortes as an ambitious man? We must first have a theory about what constitutes ambition and how it will manifest itself under a large number of circumstances. Second, we must be able to distinguish types of ambition from each other, for the rubric undoubtedly covers many different kinds of personal characteristics....

Morton A. Kaplan, *On Historical and Political Knowing: An Inquiry into Some Problems of Universal Law and Human Freedom*, University of Chicago Press, 1971, p. 63

(Nowadays the word *rubric* usually means a name for a class of things, and that's how Kaplan uses it here: Ambition is the name of a class of traits. But if you look up the word in a good dictionary you'll see that it has several other meanings as well.)

Exercise 5: Apply the Ideas in Writing (Generalize)

Write a paragraph or two in which you make a generalization, and you explain how you arrived at your generalization. (What kind of sample did you use? Was it skewed or representative?) For example, can you see anything that most of the students in your school have in common? Anything that fashion magazines have in common? Professional athletes? Newspaper stories? Reality shows on TV? Horror movies or TV shows? (How do they try to frighten people? Do most of them use similar methods? How many have you seen?)

Exercise 6: Apply the Ideas in Writing (Classify)

Write a paragraph or two in which you classify things, in the sense of dividing a group into subgroups. For example, can you divide up the songs people listen to on the radio into types? (How do the people who give Grammy awards each year classify popular music?) What criterion do you use to divide up the whole group? Can you classify food into types? Cars? Pets? Clothes? Explain your classification clearly, and give examples.

It may be fun to classify people, but usually the people who are classified don't like it. Why not?

Improving Your Writing 2: Grammar

A sentence is different from a fragment. A *sentence* is a group of words that expresses a complete thought. A *fragment* does not express a complete thought;

it does not have both a subject and a verb. For example, "went to the store" is a fragment. Who went to the store? (The subject is missing.) "Marilyn went to the store" is a sentence. "Jodi's big interview last week" is a fragment. What about the interview? (The verb is missing) "Jodi's big interview last week went well" is a sentence.

A sentence can be about one thing or more than one thing. "Sheila is outside." "The boys are outside." "Sheila," is singular; "the boys" is plural. "Sheila" and "the boys" are the subjects of the sentences. "Is" and "are" are the verbs of the sentences. And notice that when the subject is singular, the verb is also singular—"is." When the subject is plural, the verb is plural—"are." "The mother *goes* to work." "The parents *go* home." "The bus *takes* the children to school." "The buses *take* the children to school." Matching the subject and the verb is called "subject–verb agreement." When subject and verb do not agree, the sentence sounds strange. "The third baseman run to home plate." "The players runs to home plate." The way to check to see if the subject and verb agree is to read the sentence out loud and decide if it sounds strange or sounds natural.

Paying attention to little things like subject–verb agreement probably will not improve your thinking. So why worry about it? You might have wonderful ideas, even if you write fragments and your verbs are wrong. The problem is communication. You can have the best ideas in the world, but if you can't communicate them to others, those excellent ideas won't help you very much. When you talk to others or write essays, your sentences and subjects and verbs are the first things people hear and see. If your sentences are sloppy and full of mistakes, other people will decide that your ideas are sloppy and full of mistakes, too, even if they aren't. First impressions are important.

Reasoning

So far you have learned about several relationships: between objects (comparing), among many things (generalization), and between an object and the group it belongs to (classification). Now you can learn about another very important relationship: a relationship between statements.

First, what is a statement? *Statement* is one of the words in this chapter, so you can study the meaning in more detail later. For now, let's say a statement is a sentence that can be true or false. "Roses are red" is a statement; "Roses are green" is a statement. But "Give him some roses," "Are roses green?," and "bought a dozen roses" are not statements.

The idea is that some statements are related in such a way that if you believe one or two of them, you have to believe a third one. Of course, no one will force you. But you "have to" if you want to be rational and reasonable. Here's an example of three statements that are related: "All men are mortal." "Socrates is a man." "Therefore, Socrates is mortal." If the first two statements are true, then the third has to be true. There's no way it could be false, so long as the first two are true.

Is that right? Suppose I said I believed Socrates is *not* mortal, because when he dies his soul will go to heaven. So I do not believe statement number three. But if I say that, then I am rejecting the first statement, "All men are mortal." The idea here is that, *if* you believe the first two statements are true, *then* you have to believe the third statement. That is not saying that you must believe the first two statements. The essential thing is the relationship.

Seeing relationships among statements like these is what we call "reasoning."

Here's another example. Suppose I believe that everyone who tries hard will be successful in life. You might not believe that, but suppose I do. And now I meet Frank in criminal court. Frank is a failure in every way: financially, socially, and psychologically, a real loser. But Frank tells me that he has always tried hard throughout his whole life. Will I believe him? All I have to go on are the two previous statements that I believe: (a) "Everyone who tries hard will be successful," and (b) "Frank is a failure." Now I have to decide whether to believe (c) "Frank has tried hard" or to believe "Frank has not tried hard" instead. If I'm convinced that everyone who tries hard will be successful, and I can see clearly that Frank is *not* successful, then I have to believe "Frank has not tried hard," even though he says he has. (I have to if I want to think clearly.)

Now maybe I'm being unfair. Maybe Frank was born with a handicap, or an abusive family, or something else, and he really has tried hard. That happens. Perhaps I should be more sympathetic and accept his claim. But now I have a logical problem. If I'm going to believe Frank, I have to give up one of my other beliefs. I'm assuming he's obviously a failure; there's no doubt about that. If I believe him when he says he has tried hard, then I have to give up my belief that "Everyone who tries hard will be successful." Frank has tried hard, but he is not successful. I might decide that "*Most* people who try hard become successful." But that's a different belief, and the main point still holds. These beliefs are related in such a way that you can't just pick and choose which you will believe. If you believe two of them, you have to believe a third one.

Relationships among statements are a little more abstract than relationships among physical objects or events, and they may be harder to see. But you get better with practice. A good place to begin is to learn labels for the relations and the parts. That makes them much easier to recognize and analyze.

Figure 3.1
Reasoning means seeing relationships among statements. Suppose E stands for the statement "Senator Kennedy is now in Los Angeles" and C stands for the statement "Senator Kennedy is now in the United States." You can see that if E is true, then C must also be true.

Part 1. Definitions

12. statement. a sentence that can be true or false. "When the spokesperson said the product is safe, she made her statement in a loud and firm voice."

In order to think clearly about statements, you need to know what a sentence is. A sentence is a set of words expressing a complete thought. It is different from a fragment, or phrase, which is a set of words that does not express a complete thought: "drank a bottle of beer," "the cold weather in Moscow," "which was built last year."

Statements are types of sentences, but not all sentences are statements. "Close the door" is a sentence but not a statement. It expresses a complete thought; it's not a fragment. But it can't be true or false. "Where is Kathy?" is a sentence but not a statement. In other words, statements can be classified as types of sentences. "Sentence" is the broad category. Statements are a subset of sentences. (Commands and questions are other types of sentences.)

Example

> 12a. According to a study conducted by researchers at the University of Maryland, during and immediately following the Iraq War more than half of Americans believed that Saddam was a major supporter of al-Qaeda. Roughly a third believed that Iraq had deployable or deployed WMD [weapons of mass destruction, e.g., chemical, biological, or nuclear weapons] and that most of the world supported the U.S.-led invasion of Iraq. The first and the third **statements** are known to be false; the second is widely accepted to be. So how did so many people get so much wrong?
>
> Attitudes/Knowledge Networks, Misperceptions, the Media and the Iraq War, Program on International Policy, quoted in *The Atlantic Monthly*, Jan-Feb, 2004, p. 46

13. argument. the reasons for believing something or doing something; statements that, if true, make some other statement more likely to be true. "Bob's main argument for going to Florida instead of Bermuda was that Florida was cheaper." "Carol's argument for saying dinosaurs were warm-blooded is that their bones are very similar to birds' bones, and birds are warm-blooded." The purpose of arguing and arguments is to persuade others to believe something or do something.

Some people also define *argument* to mean the reasons *and* the statement they want people to believe.

to argue (verb). to give reasons for doing something or believing something. "The Senator argued for an increase in the minimum wage."

In many contexts, *to argue* means to disagree with someone or engage in a dispute. "Vic and Dave argued over who was responsible for the accident." But the word also has the special meaning indicated here, i.e., giving reasons. This special sense is a very important concept and tool to use in understanding how people think.

Example

> 13a. That same year [1972], the eminent economist Milton Friedman published an essay in Newsweek in which he called for legalizing

heroin. His **argument** was on two grounds: as a matter of ethics, the government has no right to tell people not to use heroin (or to drink or to commit suicide); as a matter of economics, the prohibition of drug use imposes costs on society that far exceed the benefits. Others, such as the psychoanalyst Thomas Szasz, made the same **argument**.

John D. Ramage and John C. Bean, eds., *Writing Arguments: A Rhetoric with Readings*, Third Edition, Allyn and Bacon, 1995, pp. 579–580

14. conclusion. what someone decides to believe after seeing or hearing something, or after accepting other statements. "Historians must examine all the relevant documents before they draw their conclusions."

Conclusion also means "the end," as in "At the conclusion of the play the curtain closed." In connection with thinking, the word means the logical end—the result—of an investigation, or the final product of a thinking process.

to conclude. "When she saw Jacob and Marcie holding hands, she concluded that they had talked and made up."

Example

14a. Let us take [Konrad] Lorenz's last book, *On Aggression*.... What it has to say is that you only have to look at mammals in general in order to see that most of them require some built in aggressive behavior in order to maintain themselves. Therefore the **conclusion** is that human beings, who are obviously mammals, display aggressive behavior and therefore it is very important in their lives.

Jacob Bronowski, *The Origins of Knowledge and Imagination*, Yale University Press, 1978, p. 8

15. evidence. the facts or information that make it reasonable to hold another belief, i.e., that lead to a conclusion. "My statement that he's making a bad investment is no idle guess or groundless speculation; I have solid evidence to support my claim."

Example

15a. During or just after the Fourth Ice Age, Neanderthal Man was burying his dead, and remains from burials added to the **evidence** that would survive to the present time. Because of burial remains it is now possible to trace Neanderthal Man in many parts of Europe and the Middle East.

Carlton J. Hayes, James H. Hanscom, *Ancient Civilizations*, Macmillan, 1968, p. 24

16. to infer. to decide to believe something on the basis of something else; to decide that if one statement is true, then another statement is true as well. "When Holmes saw the footprints, he inferred that two men had left the building."

inference (noun). a decision to believe one statement because you believe another statement; a mental leap from one statement to another. Inferences can be correct or incorrect.

Example

16a. [S]uffice it here to say that a comparison of the Jewish law to the Code of Hammurabi discloses many similarities—so close, indeed, that one may well **infer** that substantial borrowings were made by the Jews from their Babylonian neighbors, perhaps during the Babylonian captivity.

Rene A. Wormser, *The Law*, Simon and Schuster, 1949, p. 30

17. reason. a belief or statement or fact that justifies an action, including the act of deciding to believe something. "The fact that Becky has won every match she's played is a pretty good reason to believe she will win this match."

The word **reason** can also mean the mental ability or faculty we have of making inferences and seeing logical connections. See Definition 18.

Example

17a. George Eighmey, executive director of Compassion in Dying of Oregon, which works with the terminally ill, said that the main **reason** people sought lethal prescriptions was not the fear of pain, but the fear of losing their autonomy.

Nicholas D. Kristof, Choosing Death, *New York Times*, 7/14/04

18. reasoning. thinking about the relations among statements; the mental process of making inferences. "Doing well on the Law School Admissions Test requires careful reasoning."

reason. The mental ability or faculty that enables us to make inferences, understand logical relations, and solve problems. "Some say the main difference between animals and humans is that humans possess reason and animals do not."

Example

18a. More recently, when Slavs found themselves ruled by tyrants and saw no hope of escape, some gloomily concluded that there must be something in the character of Slavs which dooms them to being enslaved. This is false **reasoning**, pretending that what has happened had to happen. No free person can believe that: it is a **reasoning** imposed on slaves to make them despair.

Theodore Zeldin. *An Intimate History of Humanity*. Harper Perennial, 1994, p. 8

Test Yourself

Match each word with its definition.

12. statement
13. argument
14. conclusion
15. evidence

16. to infer
17. reason
18. reasoning

  a. to decide that some statement is true, because you already know that another statement is true

  b. what you decide to believe after thinking about the relevant facts and the situation

  c. the process of comparing statements to see how they are related and which ones make others more likely to be true

  d. a fact or statement that persuades you to believe something or do something

  e. a statement or set of statements intended to convince people that some other statement is true

  f. a sentence that can be true or false

  g. the facts or statements that make some other belief more likely to be true

Part 2. Understanding the Meaning

12. statement.

> 12b. That is the *can-can*. The idea of it is to dance as wildly, as noisily, as furiously as you can; expose yourself as much as possible if you are a woman; and kick as high as you can, no matter which sex you belong to. There is no word of exaggeration in this. Any of the staid, respectable, aged people who were there that night can testify to the truth of that **statement**.
>
> Mark Twain, *The Innocents Abroad, Roughing It,* The Library of America, 1984, p. 108

Comment

The word *claim* means almost exactly the same as the word *statement*. Words that have the same meaning are called synonyms. If you say someone made a claim, you are emphasizing the fact that the speaker believes it, but it may not be true. You are reminding people that the statement may be false. The word *statement* doesn't carry that reminder.

> 12c. The anti-bacterial category continues to grow broader and more intriguing with the recent introduction of a whole genre of bacteria-busting home appliance. Namely: the toothbrush sanitizer....
>
> We turned to six medical/health professionals for some answers.
>
> We asked them to respond to some of the startling **statements** about bacteria and toothbrushes that are being made by the makers of toothbrush sanitizers that hit the market recently....
>
> But the bottom line from our pool of experts is this: The toothbrush is not the bio-hazard that these manufacturers would like Americans to believe.

Only the dental hygienist sang the praises of sanitizing. The others we consulted said there is no scientific evidence to support the need for it—and perhaps, more important, that some of the information being presented by the makers of these appliances is just plain misleading.

Karen Klages, Man vs Toothbrush: Should We Be Afraid? (The Chicago Tribune), *AM New York*, 3/2/05

Comment

Examples 12b and 12c are about the truth or falsity of statements. You can also think about how statements are related to each other as far as their truth is concerned. That is a very important skill to practice. Remember that thinking is recognizing relationships. You can think about the relations between two similar things, or between a sample and a whole group. And you can also think about the relations between two statements. For example, Statement 1: "A majority of the 20 people we randomly selected said they liked the teacher in our class." Statement 2: "Therefore, a majority of the class of 100 probably likes the teacher." If Statement 1 is true, then Statement 2 is probably true as well. When you tell others what you have discovered in your thinking, you make statements and you put them together in arguments. Analyzing arguments means focusing on statements and thinking about how they are related.

12d. A federal prosecutor yesterday wrapped up the government's case against Lynne F. Stewart, a lawyer accused of aiding terrorists, by charging that she had released a bellicose **statement** to the news media on behalf of an imprisoned client....

The case centers on a **statement** Ms. Stewart gave to a reporter after visiting Mr. Abdel Rahman in jail in May 2000, in which the sheik said he was withdrawing his support for a cease-fire his followers in Egypt had observed since 1997. Ms. Stewart had agreed in writing to prison rules that barred her from helping the sheik communicate with the press.

Julia Preston, Saying Sheik's Lawyer Hoped to Aid Militants, U.S. Rests Case, *New York Times*, 1/4/05

Question: Who made the statement at the center of this legal case, Stewart or Abdel Rahman?

13. argument.

13b. The most powerful **argument** against using torture as a punishment or to secure confessions is that such practices disregard the rights of the individual. Well, if the individual is all that important—and he is—it is correspondingly important to protect the rights of individuals threatened by terrorists. If life is so valuable that it must never be taken, the lives of the innocents must be saved even at the price of hurting the one who endangers them.

Michael Levin, The Case for Torture, in Linda H. Peterson et al., eds., *The Norton Reader: Shorter Ninth Edition*, W. W. Norton and Company, 1996, p. 428

13c. Part of the essay *On Liberty* is spent in **arguing** that a man's beliefs and his expressed opinions practically always should be guaranteed from interference by the state, and that no pressure group such as a religious sect or trade union should be supported by the government if they clamoured for a man to be silenced because he was expressing opinions which the pressure group thought were evil. This **argument** rests on Mill's belief that the only way for truth to out is for ideas to be thrown into the market place to be discussed and fought over; for unless men are able to pursue truth society will stagnate and progress will be halted.

Noel Annan, "John Stuart Mill," in Maurice Cranston, ed., *Western Political Philosophers*, Capricorn Books, 1964, p. 111

Comment

Arguments (in the logical sense of the word, not the barroom brawl sense of the word) have two parts: the conclusion, or main point, and the evidence, or reasons to believe the main point. When you see the word *argument*, sometimes the writer will mean the conclusion, and sometimes he or she will mean the evidence. In Example 13c, when Annan says, "This **argument** rests on Mill's belief that...," he means that the conclusion rests on the belief. In Example 13b, when Levin says, "The most powerful **argument** against using torture...," he means the most powerful reasons. The way to avoid confusion is to remember that arguments always have two parts, and sometimes writers emphasize one part, sometimes the other, and sometimes they mean both parts.

14. conclusion.

14b. That the duke would emerge victorious Machiavelli had under-stood from the very first day....Machiavelli had come to this **con-clusion** through a subtle chain of reasoning that flew in the face of common sense: the duke would win in the end, he thought, because he "was alone" and faced many enemies. His strength lay precisely in his apparent weakness. Alone, he could act quickly and decisively; his enemies, divided by hostility and mistrust, would never be able to agree on an effective course of action.

Maurizio Viroli, *Niccolo's Smile: A Biography of Machiavelli*, Farrar, Straus and Giroux, 2000, p. 60

Question: What reasons led Machiavelli to his conclusion?

14c. Intensely ambitious, Lavoisier thought he was in a position to put forward a comprehensive chemical theory of acidity. Generalising from a few examples such as nitric acid and sulphuric acid, he con-

cluded that all acids contained a principle similar to the purest part of the air, which he called *oxigine*. ...

Roy Porter, ed., *Man Masters Nature: Twenty Five Centuries of Science*, George Braziller, 1988, pp. 106–107

Comment

The words *conclusion* and *evidence* always go together. That is, a conclusion is always based on some evidence, and evidence always points to some conclusion. But not every belief or statement is a conclusion. People can hold a belief without any evidence for it. Then it is not a conclusion. And they can believe something without seeing what conclusion it leads to. Then their belief is not evidence. But if you say that a statement is a conclusion, then it must rest on some evidence. If you say a belief is evidence, it leads to some conclusion. The words are also connected with arguments. When people point out evidence, they are arguing for a conclusion. In example 14c, Lavoisier pointed out that nitric acid and sulphuric acid both contain the purest part of air. He was arguing for the conclusion that *all* acids contain the purest part of air.

15. evidence.

15b. "The human race has witnessed," writes Condoleezza Rice, "in little more than a generation, the swiftest advance of freedom in the 2,500-year story of democracy." American scholars, of both left and right, have gathered **evidence** to support this bold claim. At the turn of the nineteenth to the twentieth century, some ten to twenty countries in the world could make some plausible claim to having their governments changed by popular vote, although none of them met today's requirements for being full liberal democracies. ... In the spring of 1974, with the "revolution of the carnations" in Portugal, there began an extraordinary rolling wave of democratization around the world. Greece followed, and Spain, and much of Latin America, and the Philippines, and then, after the velvet revolutions of 1989, most of the post-communist world.

Timothy Garton Ash, *Free World: America, Europe, and the Surprising Future of the West*, Random House, 2004, pp. 128–129

15c. Mr Evans has produced a rich and detailed description of just what the Third Reich did in every compartment of the state and every corner of society. ... Indeed, he concludes his vast survey by reminding the reader that Hitler was always "in the driving seat, determining the general direction in which things moved". This interpretation seems irrefutable in the face of the **evidence**. Hitler is there at the heart of major affairs of state, which he viewed as the work of a messianic leader.

Nazi Germany: They Stooped to Conquer, *The Economist*, October 29, 2005

(*Messianic* means "like a messiah," a savior who will lead followers to glory.)

Comment

Evidence can be strong or weak. Strong evidence makes the inference based on it easy. You can be confident that what you infer is correct. For example, consider this evidence: Several witnesses saw Jones at the scene of the bank robbery (and identified him in a line-up), his fingerprints are found on the weapon recovered at the scene, he has been convicted of robbery before, and his debts give him a motive to commit the crime. This is strong evidence that Jones is guilty of robbing the bank and it's easy to make that inference. But evidence can be weak. Suppose the only evidence is that, after the bank was robbed, one of Jones' acquaintances reported to the police that Jones told him earlier that he intended to rob the bank. That is evidence that Jones is guilty, but it's weak

Figure 3.2
Jurors must decide whether the evidence in a trial leads to the conclusion "Guilty" or "Not Guilty." *Source: Ingram Publishing/Fotosearch*

evidence. The acquaintance could be lying; and even if he isn't, intending to do something doesn't always lead to doing it. You would hesitate to infer that Jones is guilty if that is the only evidence you have.

In the preceding example about Hitler, the writer says that the historian has provided very strong evidence, so strong that the conclusion is irrefutable, i.e., cannot be overturned.

16. to infer.

16b. What can we **infer** from an isolated spot of furry mold [on a tomato]? We can be all but certain that a week or two before there had fallen on the smooth skin of the tomato a spore, a seed as it were, of this particular organism, a fungus. Finding a nutrient situation, just what it needed, it proceeded to grow and mature.

Philip and Phylis Morrison, *The Ring of Truth: An Inquiry into How We Know What We Know*, Random House, 1987, p. 51

Comment

The Morrisons say they make an inference from a spot of mold, not a statement. But we can treat "a spot of mold" as shorthand for the statement "There is a spot of mold on the tomato."

16c. For though other species of whales find their food above water, and may be seen by man in the act of feeding, the spermaceti whale obtains his whole food in unknown zones below the surface; and only by **inference** is it that anyone can tell of what, precisely, that food consists. At times, when closely pursued, he will disgorge what are supposed to be the detached arms of the squid; some of them thus exhibited exceeding twenty and thirty feet in length. They fancy that the monster to which these arms belonged ordinarily clings by them to the bed of the ocean; and that the sperm whale, unlike other species, is supplied with teeth in order to attack and tear it.

Herman Melville, *Moby Dick*, Bantam, 1981 [originally published 1851], pp. 261–262

Question: To infer is to begin with a statement we believe is true, and then to decide that a new statement is true because of its relation to the first statement. According to Melville, what do we know about whales, and what do we infer?

16d. [Dante encounters Cavalcante in hell.]

" 'Lives he not still? [asked Cavalcante about his son] Does not the sweet light strike his eyes?'

When he perceived that I made some delay in answering, supine he fell again, and shewed himself no more...."

As he asks his urgent questions, he is excited, almost beseeching, thus differentiating himself sharply from Farinata's imposing greatness and self discipline; and when he **infers** (wrongly) from Dante's words that his son is no longer alive, he collapses.

Erich Auerbach, *Mimesis*, Anchor, 1957, p. 154

(*Supine* means lying down.)

Comment

This example from Dante's *Divine Comedy* shows that inferences can be correct or mistaken.

17. reason.

17b. Deliberative democracy requires that citizens and their representatives give **reasons** to each other to justify their decisions.

Off the Shelf, *Harvard Magazine*, November-December, 2004

17c. In 1998, MIT social scientist Frank Sulloway and I conducted an empirical study to answer this question [how does one's environment affect one's beliefs], along with the more general one of why people believe in God.... The diversity of answers we received was staggering. Two categories predominated, however: those who primarily

Figure 3.3
When you see the expression on the girl's face and the toilet paper in the bathroom behind her, what would you infer? *Source: Design Pics*

believe in God because they "see" a pattern of God's presence in the world (that is, for intellectual or "empirical" **reasons**), and those who believe in God because such belief brings comfort (that is, for emotional **reasons**). What was most interesting about these two answers is that they neatly cleaved between why people believe in God *themselves* (for intellectual **reasons**) and why they think *other people* believe in God (for emotional **reasons**).

Michael Shermer, *How We Believe: Science, Skepticism, and the Search for God*, Second Edition, Henry Holt and Co., 2003, pp. 75–77.

17d. Although most news audience studies suggest that people want journalists to stick to the facts, a case can be made for the opposite position: that the news media include more opinions. I offer at least two **reasons**. First, opinions are desirable when journalists who have done a lot of legwork develop informed opinions, and these ought to be shared with the news audience....

The second **reason** for the inclusion of opinions is that journalists often insert opinions into their stories already, even if they usually do so unintentionally. Conversely, sometimes opinions appear because journalists hold them so firmly that they confuse them with the facts. Indeed, permitting explicit opinions may help journalists see how often they now add implicit ones.

Herbert J. Gans, *Democracy and the News*, Oxford University Press, 2003, p. 101

Comment

In Example 17c Shermer is talking about reasons to believe something. In Example 17d Gans is talking about reasons to do something.

The word *reason* has another meaning besides the idea of a statement or fact that logically supports a belief or action. It can also mean a cause of something that happens. A person can say, "The reason the house burned was that the owner was smoking in bed and fell asleep." Here the speaker is simply stating the *cause* of the fire. The two meanings are connected by the fact that both give explanations. If you know my reasons for opposing the death penalty, then you have an explanation of my belief. And if you know the reason the fire started, you have an explanation of the fire. But I would say my reason for opposing the death penalty is also a reason for you to oppose it as well.

18. reasoning.

18b. When I was a senior in high school in 1971 I became a born-again Christian. I took my commitment seriously enough to enroll at Pepperdine University, a highly regarded Christian institution affiliated with the Church of Christ.... One student in our dorm, desperately seeking a rationale for what he knew he could not control, actually prayed for God to provide him with an acceptable sexual

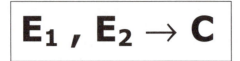

$$E_1 , E_2 \rightarrow C$$

Figure 3.4
Sometimes evidence is called a reason. And you can have more than one reason
to believe something.

outlet—read partner—because, he **reasoned**, he could witness for the
Lord better if he were not so distracted by such basic urges.

Michael Shermer, *The Science of Good and Evil*, Henry Holt and Company, 2004,
pp. 161–162

18c. "Mafia Cops" Louis Eppolito and Stephen Caracappa were denied
bail yesterday after the same federal judge who tossed out their racketeer-
ing conviction said they were "dangerous criminals" whose shame might
prompt them to flee rather than face a pending drug charge....

　　"Defendants have a high incentive to flee given that they have been
publicly shamed," [Judge] Weinstein **reasoned**.

Anthony M. DeStefano, "Mob Cops" bail request squashed, *AMNew York*, 7/26/06

Figure 3.5
Reasoning means taking a careful step from one statement to another. *Source:* ©
Jeff Gynane/Shutterstock Images LLC

18d. When animals were killed for food and their innards cut or torn out, it could be verified that their body cavities were packed tightly with viscera [internal organs] much like those of the men who were gutting them. Knowledge of human anatomy gradually expanded in this way, by **reasoning** from butchered to butcher.

Sherwin B. Nuland, *The Mysteries Within: A Surgeon Reflects on Medical Myths*, Simon and Schuster, 2000, p. 46

Question: What did the people who killed the animals know to be true, and what did they infer from it?

18e. We like to continue to believe what we have been accustomed to accept as true, and the resentment aroused when doubt is cast upon any of our assumptions leads us to seek every manner of excuse for clinging to them. The result is that most of our so-called **reasoning** consists in finding arguments for going on believing as we already do.

James Harvey Robinson, *The Mind in the Making*, Harper and Brothers, 1921, p. 37

Part 3. Applying the Words

12. statement
13. argument
14. conclusion
15. evidence
16. to infer
17. reason
18. reasoning

Exercise 1:   Choose the Right Word

For each sentence, choose the best word (or an appropriate form of the word) to fill in the blank.

1. Success in anything from real estate to police work to poker depends on _____, since people in all fields have to look at the available information and draw logical conclusions from it.
2. When Galileo saw mountains on the moon, he made an _____; he decided that the moon is made of the same material the earth is made of.
3. After examining all aspects of the global warming controversy, from several points of view, the committee reached a unanimous _____.
4. The psychologist believed that teachers' expectations strongly influence students' performance, so he began looking for _____ to support his hypothesis.
5. The prosecutor's _____ was complicated; it depended on experts' testimony as well as appeals to common sense.

6. Ms. Nelson had intended to vote for Smith, but his _____ about gun control made her change her mind.
7. Robyn's friends gave her several _____ to believe her husband was having an affair, but she wouldn't take them seriously.

Exercise 2:   Apply the Words

Read each example and answer the questions that follow.

> 1. Orb web-building spiders don't learn how to create their beautiful, perfect orbs. They are born with the knowledge. If spiderlings [baby spiders] are put into narrow glass tubes where they can't build webs for several months, they are able to make perfect ones when they are let out.
>
> Dorothy Hinshaw Patent, *How Smart Are Animals?* Harcourt, Brace, Jovanovich, 1990, p. 43

Scientists reach a conclusion about spiders. What is the conclusion, and what evidence leads them to it?

> 2. I have hoped that Mr. Boutwell [the mayor of Birmingham] will be reasonable enough to see the futility of massive resistance to desegregation. But he will not see this without pressure from devotees of civil rights. My friends, I must say to you that we have not made a single gain in civil rights without determined legal and nonviolent pressure.
>
> Martin Luther King, Jr., Letter from Birmingham Jail, in Linda H. Peterson et al., eds, *The Norton Reader: An Anthology of Expository Prose*, Shorter Ninth Edition, W. W. Norton and Company, 1996, p. 565

King presents an argument. He reasons from past experience to the present situation with Mr. Boutwell. What conclusion does he reach, and what evidence persuades him it is true?

> 3. Pope Benedict will also continue the ecumenical outreach of John Paul II, hoping to clear up magisterial differences between Orthodox Christians and Protestantism. Progress has been made in both directions and Protestant leadership is beginning to understand that something is amiss in a theological system that has spawned since the Reformation more than 400 different denominations in the U.S. alone and more than 20,000 worldwide, all claiming to be the true Church of Christ.
>
> BS, Letters: New Pope Has Made an Exciting Beginning, *Riverdale Press*, 6/16/05

What facts, or evidence, does BS describe, and what conclusion does he draw from them?

> 4. "There aren't many things in medicine you can say 'zero' about," Garner said. "But there is a zero chance you will get the bird flu in the United States right now."
>
> For one thing, no American birds have tested positive for the virus, despite a frantic testing regime. For another, this strain has been

extremely slow to jump to humans—and even slower to jump from person to person.

Since 1997, a grand total of 120 people—all in Asia—have been infected, with 63 deaths. Terrible for them of course. But in the annals of deadly diseases, this bird flu barely warrants a footnote.

"And here's an irony for all those people hoarding Tamiflu," Garner said. "If the disease does eventually mutate and infect humans in America, it'll be such a different organism that the Tamiflu won't do any good."

Ellis Henican, One for the Birds, *AMNew York*, 11/17/05

Which of the following are reasons to believe that Americans have no chance of catching bird flu (and which are not reasons)?

(a) Sixty-three people have died from bird flu.
(b) Many people are hoarding Tamiflu [a drug to fight bird flu].
(c) No birds in America have tested positive for bird flu.
(d) This strain of bird flu has been slow to jump from birds to humans.

Exercise 3:   Analyzing Arguments

Three Types of Arguments   In Chapters 1 and 2 you studied words about comparing, generalizing, and classifying. Each of those is a type of thinking, i.e., seeing relationships among things. People often use those types of thinking to construct arguments. Consider comparing. People can use a comparison to argue for a conclusion. For example, suppose you think football is fun to watch. I might say, "You know, football is a lot like soccer. If you like football, you'll probably like soccer." The idea is that if soccer is similar to football in some ways (two teams compete on a large, grassy field, both involve running, scoring goals, etc.), then it's probably similar to football in another way—it's fun to watch, and you'll like it. I am arguing for the conclusion that you will enjoy watching soccer, based on the comparison of soccer and football.

Here's another example: "I took Prof. Carson's course on American politics and it was hard, so her course on the Supreme Court will probably be hard, too." This person is saying that the two courses are similar in that they are taught by the same professor, and they are both about American government. The person took one course and knows that it was hard. He or she hasn't taken the other one yet, but on the basis of the similarity, the person decides the second one will probably be hard as well.

These arguments are called *analogical arguments* because they depend on the analogy between two things.

Analogical Arguments   Here are two examples of analogical arguments. In the first, Socrates is speaking. The situation is that he has been convicted of a capital crime in Athens, and is in jail waiting to be executed. His friends want him to escape, but Socrates says he shouldn't. He imagines the laws of Athens talking to him.

a. What two things does he (i.e., the laws) compare?
b. In what way are they obviously similar (according to the speaker?)
c. In what other way are they similar, that his friends may not see? In other words, what is he trying to get his friends to believe, based on the analogy?

> 1. Look at it this way. If, as we were planning to run away from here, or whatever one should call it, the laws and the state came and confronted us and asked: "Tell me, Socrates, what are you intending to do? Do you not by this action you are attempting intend to destroy us, the laws, and indeed the whole city, as far as you are concerned? ...Did we not, first, bring you to birth, and was it not through us that your father married your mother and begat you? ...[A]nd after you were born and nurtured and educated, could you, in the first place, deny that you are our off-spring and servant, both you and your forefathers? If that is so, do you think that we are on an equal footing as regards the right, and that what-ever we do to you it is right for you to do to us? You were not on an equal footing with your father as regards the right,... Is your wisdom such as not to realize that your country is to be honored more than your mother, your father and all your ancestors, that it is more to be revered and more sacred, and that it counts for more among the gods and sensible men, that you must worship it, yield to it and placate its anger more than your father's? You must either persuade it or obey its orders, and endure in silence whatever it instructs you to endure, whether blows or bonds, and if it leads you into war to be wounded or killed, you must obey."
>
> Plato, "Crito," trans. G. M. A. Grube, reprinted in Steven M. Cahn, ed., *Classics of Western Philosophy*, Fifth Edition, Hackett, 1999.

> 2. In the following example, what two things does Darwin compare? What is he trying to get people to believe?
>
> In 1871, Charles Darwin argued that the similarities between apes and humans pointed to Africa as the cradle of modern humans, *Homo sapiens....* [H]e argued in his book *The Descent of Man* that all the races of humans were just varieties of a single species, with Africa—the home of the world's great apes—as the most plausible birthplace of modern humans.
>
> Robert Matthews, *25 Big Ideas*, Oneworld, 2005, pp. 49–50

Arguments for Generalizations When people describe a sample from a group, and then generalize about that group, they are arguing. They are trying to get others to believe the generalization by giving them a reason to believe it. The reason is the sample. You can also say the sample is their evidence, and the generalization is their conclusion.

Read the following examples of arguments for generalizations and answer the questions about them.

> 3. At local retailers and service establishments, immigrants from Korea labor behind the counter six and seven days a week, providing your groceries and greeting cards and cleaning your clothes. You buy your magazines, candy and cigarettes from people born in Yemen or Egypt or Jordan. Recently-arrived Indians and Pakistanis staff the gas station where you fill-up your car. Israelis bake cakes and bread and slice pastrami and corned beef at the local bakery and deli. The carpenter or painter you hire to work on your house is likely to confer with you in a Greek or Irish accent, or to speak Spanish, in the dialects of the Dominican Republic, Puerto Rico, Mexico or Central America. If the supers and handymen who keep your apartment building in good repair don't speak Spanish, chances are they're Albanians, saving to buy apartment buildings nearby.
>
> You can't live in the Northwest Bronx without learning anew each day how hard immigrants work, and how important their labor and spirit is to the comfort and prosperity of all.
>
> Editorial: Slamming the Golden Door, *The Riverdale Press*, 11/1/07

In this example the writer is arguing for a conclusion, which is a generalization about a group. The evidence for the conclusion is a sample.

a. What is the conclusion?
b. Would you say the sample is large or small? Would you say it is skewed or representative?

> 4. For all previous millennia, our technologies have been aimed outward, to control our environment. Starting with fire and clothes, we looked for ways to ward off the elements. With the development of agriculture we controlled our food supply. In cities we sought safety. Telephones and airplanes collapsed distance. Antibiotics kept death-dealing microbes at bay.
>
> Now, however, we have started a wholesale process of aiming our technologies inward. Now our technologies have started to merge with our minds, our memories, our metabolisms, our personalities, our progeny and perhaps our souls.
>
> Joel Garreau, *Radical Evolution*, Doubleday, 2005, p. 6

a. This writer generalizes about a group. What is the group, and what generalization does he make?
b. What is the evidence for the conclusion? Would you say the sample is large or small?

Arguments for a Classification Remember that one meaning of *to classify* is to put an individual into a group. For example, you might say your friend

George is a liberal, he belongs in the class of liberals. But people can disagree about classifications. So you might need to present an argument for your conclusion that George is a liberal. You must explain your criterion for being a liberal (e.g., "the test for being a liberal is always voting for candidates in the Democratic Party"), and explain why George meets the test.

Read the following example of an argument for classification and answer the questions about it.

> 5. Now Ms. Gerlach is 30, and although she may continue to be an environmentalist, a federal judge said Friday that she was also a terrorist.
>
> "It was your intention to scare, frighten and intimidate people and government through the very dangerous act of arson," Judge Ann L. Aiken of Federal District Court told Ms. Gerlach at her sentencing here....
>
> Defense lawyers had argued that the environmental cases were not terrorism because they did not take aim at people's lives.
>
> "It was only intended to damage property," said Craig E. Weinerman, an assistant federal defender who represented Ms. Gerlach, of Portland. Last week Judge Aiken rejected those arguments.
>
> William Yardley, Radical Environmentalist Gets 9-Year Term for Actions Called "Terrorist," *New York Times*, 5/26/07

The judge and the defense attorney disagree about how the suspect, Ms. Gerlach, should be classified.

a. What criterion of "terrorist" is the judge using? What criterion is the defense lawyer using?
b. What do you think? Do you agree with the judge or the defense attorney?

Exercise 4:   Apply the Ideas in Writing

Watch a commercial on TV, or look at an advertisement in a magazine. First decide what is being sold or promoted. What do the sponsors want you to buy or do? Then pick out the reasons the commercial gives you to buy the product. There may be one reason or more than one. Now, write a paragraph explaining the argument in the commercial or the advertisement. The conclusion will be something like "You should buy Acme Shampoo," or "You should deposit your money in our bank," or something like that. Why should you do that? What reasons does the commercial give you? It's important that you state the reasons in your own words instead of simply copying sentences from the advertisement. You want to explain the reasons so that someone reading your paragraph can understand them.

Improving Your Writing 3: Developing Paragraphs

Remember that a good paragraph has a topic sentence, which states the main idea of the paragraph. Most of the paragraph is made up of sentences that *develop* the main idea. That means the sentences show how and why the topic sentence is true. For example, a topic sentence might be "The birthday party was fun because the parents planned a lot of different activities for the kids." Then you could develop the main idea by giving *examples* of the activities, and explaining why they were enjoyable (i.e., why they caused the kids to have fun.) Here's another topic sentence: "The Lions lost the baseball game because their pitching staff let them down." To support or develop the main idea, you may use facts, news items, reasons, examples, statistics, stories, personal experiences, or other information. If the topic sentence is about cause and effect, you might explain how you know that one event caused another event.

CHAPTER 4 ❧

Facts and Opinions

19. fact

20. opinion

21. to confirm

22. source

23. critical

24. premise

You believe that the earth is round, not flat. Why? How did you get that belief? At one time, many people believed the earth was flat. Why do you have a different belief? Well, everyone else believes the earth is round and maybe that's good enough. Maybe in school your teachers told you the earth is round, and drawings in your books showed the earth as round. Those might be good reasons to believe it. Or maybe you remember the photographs of the earth taken from the moon, and they show in a beautiful way that the earth is round. That's probably a better reason. But all your beliefs come from somewhere. They are based on something.

We all have countless beliefs—about the earth, plants and animals, other people, ourselves, other countries, companies and products, our work, and so on and so on—and they all had to come from some source. We might think that all our beliefs come from personal experience. For example, I know that honey tastes sweet because I've tasted it. But we have many more beliefs about things we haven't actually seen or heard than things we have. I believe George Washington was the first President of the United States. But of course I wasn't there, so that belief is not based on any direct experience with George Washington. Usually we believe what someone tells us, if we think that person is in a position to know. Historians say George Washington was the first President and they've looked into it, so we believe them.

The words in this chapter are about the relation between a belief and the source of the belief. Some of your beliefs come from good sources. If

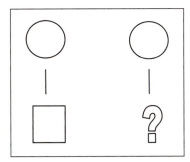

Figure 4.1
In this diagram, the circle on the left represents a factual belief. It is based on a solid
foundation, represented by the square. The circle on the right represents an opinion.
We don't know what it's based on, and it may not be based on anything.

you look up "George Washington" in a good encyclopedia, you will learn a
number of things about him. But some sources aren't so good. A newspaper
column on astrology might say that people born in September tend to be
more stubborn than other people. That source is not as good as a respectable
encyclopedia or a textbook on psychology. In many cases we believe things,
and we don't know where the belief came from, even though it had to come
from somewhere.

Normally we are interested in what a belief is about and not where it
came from. "Was Jefferson the second President? I'm not sure." But sources
are very important, especially for critical thinking. Two of the most important words you can use are *fact* and *opinion*. They describe two different
kinds of beliefs, and the beliefs are different because they come from different kinds of sources. You can avoid a lot of confusion if you understand
their precise meanings and keep those meanings in mind when you think
about things.

Part 1. Definitions

19. fact. an actual condition in the world; a state of affairs; a situation. "The
fact is that Murdock is no longer in New Orleans. He was seen yesterday in
Memphis."

A single object is not a fact. John is not a fact. But if John is 30 years old, then
that is a fact. New York is not a fact. But if New York is south of Boston, then
that situation is a fact.

factual (adjective). true, corresponding with reality, correct.

"You should separate the factual statements from the lies in this witness'
testimony." "A reporter gives a factual account of an event, whereas a novelist
might write a fictional account." **factual belief.** a belief that has been proven
true; a belief that can be shown to be accurate. "It took some time to separate

the children's factual beliefs about the 'haunted house' from their fears and imaginings."

Example

19a. The *Enterprise* [a newspaper] had earned its notable success, he was told, by printing only the truth. Rumors were never accepted. Every news story had to be based on **facts**. Personal opinions were quoted only when individual names could be used. Firsthand investigation of all events was required.

Jeanette Eaton, *America's Own Mark Twain*, William Morrow and Co., 1958, p. 136

20. opinion. a belief that has not been proven, and may or may not be true. "The doctor said it was probably a lack of iron in my diet that makes me feel so tired all the time, but she wasn't sure; that was only her opinion."

Example

20a. But I had become aware, even so early as during my college life, that no **opinion**, however absurd and incredible, can be imagined, which has not been maintained by some one of the philosophers; and afterward in the course of my travels I remarked that all those whose **opinions** are decidedly repugnant to ours are not on that account barbarians and savages, but on the contrary that many of these nations make an equally good, if not a better, use of Reason than we do.

Rene Descartes, Discourse on Method, in Charles Hirschfeld, ed., *Classics of Western Thought: The Modern World*, Harcourt, Brace and World, 1964, p. 15

(*Repugnant* means distasteful, offensive, disagreeable.)

Comment

One reason that the words *fact* and *opinion* can be confusing is that they are about different kinds of things. A fact is some condition out in the world, such as the distance from New York to Boston, or an action someone performed. ("He dropped the ball.") An opinion is a belief in someone's mind. It may be correct or incorrect. But facts are facts. They can't be incorrect. In order to put facts and opinions on the same level, we can talk about "factual beliefs" in contrast with opinions. Factual beliefs have been proven. We know they are true. Opinions have not been proven. They may be true but we can't be sure. We will examine this difference in more detail later in the chapter.

21. to confirm. to discover that a statement is true, to find something that shows that a statement is accurate. "When detectives arrived at the crime scene, they confirmed the witnesses' statement that the victim's wallet was still in his back pocket."

confirmation (noun). the act or condition of confirming a statement. "The scientist was hoping for confirmation of his theory."

Example

21a. But lighting the spark of conscience needs brave individuals—like Thomas Clarkson, the moving spirit behind the founding of the Society for Effecting the Abolition of Slavery in 1787....Clarkson fixed the strategy of the campaign. His first task was to gather evidence about the slave trade, not easy when things were so hidden from public view....One who came forward was John Newton, a former slave captain turned Anglican priest. His descriptions of the trade were very influential. Just as important was Clarkson's gathering of the physical evidence of the slave trade to **confirm** the oral and written accounts he collected. In Liverpool he picked up "collars", thumbscrews and a device for force-feeding slaves, which he would display at the hundreds of public lectures that he gave all over Britain, and France, too.

Slavery: Breaking the Chains, *The Economist*, Feb. 24, 2007

22. source. someone or something that provides information. A source can be a person, a newspaper, or a book. Or it can be other things that give us information. Historians look at birth certificates, business records, diaries, and other things to learn about life in a period of the past. "The best thing about Tim's research paper on globalization was the wide variety of sources he used."

Example

22a. The spiritual climate of the Old Kingdom [in ancient Egypt] can only be guessed at. The abundance of surviving textual **sources** from the Middle Kingdom, on the other hand, allows us to reconstruct that particular era in greater detail than any subsequent pharaonic age; in fact, very few epochs of the ancient world have left such extensive documentation.

Jan Assmann, *The Mind of Egypt: History and Meaning in the Time of the Pharaohs*, Henry Holt and Co., 2002, p. 121

(A pharaonic age in Egyptian history is a period in which Egypt was ruled by pharaohs.)

23. critical. an attitude involving a close examination of something, a search for relationships (such as cause and effect), being on guard against deception or mistakes, a reluctance to believe something, judging the strengths and weaknesses of something. "Sam watched the movie just for fun, but since Julie is a film student, she took a critical approach."

Example

23a. There was a crying need, [Richard J.] Fox decided, for an organization that would permit fringe scientists to interact with mainstream scientists and provide a forum for discussing their results. If Temple University would sponsor such a center it could make certain that high academic standards were maintained.... Temple's president, Peter Liacouras, agreed. The center's mission, he declared, was "to examine **critically** frontier research projects that hold promise of future breakthroughs."

Martin Gardner, *Did Adam and Eve Have Navels?* W. W. Norton, 2000, pp. 221–222

24. premise. one of the statements of evidence that leads to a conclusion; a fact or belief that supports another belief; a statement that someone takes for granted. "Prof. Kline first explained the premises of his argument, and then moved on to his conclusion."

Example

24a. In medicine the Greeks admitted that it was difficult to find a fundamental principle behind the working of so complex an organism as the human body, but they nevertheless began from the **premise** that the body (like the ideal city) tended towards *eunomie*—in this context, good health—and so illness suggested some aberration in the normal working of things.

Charles Freeman, *The Closing of the Western Mind: The Rise of Faith and the Fall of Reason*, Alfred A. Knopf, 2003, p. 18

Comment

The words *evidence*, *reason*, and *premise* are all very close in meaning. In many contexts they are interchangeable. But there are slight differences. For example, you can have a reason for going to the store but not evidence for going to the store. A scientist can find evidence for her hypothesis but not a premise for her hypothesis. A premise is always a statement, but a piece of evidence might be a photograph or a fossil. So premises, reasons, and evidence all have similar functions—they lead logically to further beliefs and actions—but the meanings of the words are slightly different.

Test Yourself

Match each word with its definition.

19. fact
20. opinion
21. to confirm
22. source
23. critical
24. premise

  a. to show that some statement is true
  b. a belief someone has

d. a condition or situation in the world
e. an attitude of judging something as good or bad, based on good reasons
f. the person, place, or thing from which one gets information
g. a fact or statement that one takes for granted, and that leads one to believe some other statement

Part 2. Understanding the Meaning

19. fact.

19b. There is a paradox at the heart of our lives. Most people want more income and strive for it. Yet as Western societies have got richer, their people have become no happier.

This is no old wives' tale. It is a **fact** proven by many pieces of scientific research. As I'll show, we have good ways to measure how happy people are, and all the evidence says that on average people are no happier today than people were fifty years ago. Yet at the same time average incomes have more than doubled. This paradox is equally true for the United States and Britain and Japan.

Richard Layard, *Happiness: Lessons from a New Science*, Penguin, 2005, p. 3

Comment

How do you distinguish between facts and opinions? Layard indicates one way. You ask if the statement has been proven by scientific research. Has the statement been solidly confirmed? Does the reported condition really exist, and can we explain how we know it exists? Or do reasonable people have serious doubts about it?

19c. Mr. Dobbs has stepped squarely into the debate over whether cable news anchors are breaching the bright line that has traditionally separated commentary from news. . . .

Ted Koppel, the former host of ABC's "Nightline," says that anchors and reporters who blend commentary and news should not describe themselves as journalists. "Journalism is an effort, as best you can, to establish the **fact** as dispassionately as you can," said Mr. Koppel, an occasional op-ed columnist for The New York Times. "The moment you start inserting your own passions, in whatever direction, it ceases to be journalism."

Rachel L. Swarns, Dobbs's Outspokenness Draws Fans and Fire, *New York Times*, 2/15/06

19d. For non-Muslims, one special advantage in reading the Qur'an is that it provides an authentic point of reference from which to examine the biased stereotypes of Islam to which Westerners are habitually

Figure 4.2
Good newspapers make a clear distinction between fact and opinion.

exposed. Primary information is essential to distinguish between **opinion** and **fact** in a reasonable manner.

Thomas Cleary, "The Qur'an," John Miller and Aaron Kenedi, eds., *Inside Islam*, Marlowe and Company, 2002, p. 37

Comment

Examples 19c and 19d illustrate two more ways to distinguish facts from opinions (besides having scientific proof, as in Example 19b). Koppel says that journalists try to determine the facts without letting their emotions or wishes influence their beliefs about a situation. If you know that a person's feelings have shaped his (or her) beliefs and statements, then you know he is reporting his opinions, not the facts. You know this because his statements are partly the result of his feelings, not based solely on proof that anyone can see. Of course, a person can report the facts *and* feel strongly about them. He simply shouldn't let his feelings determine his beliefs about what the facts actually are.

Cleary, in Example 19d, says that you can distinguish between facts and opinions about Islam by going to a good source, such as the Qur'an. The Qur'an tells us what good Muslims should believe and do.

> 19e. Last week, according to news service reports, the Flemish-language newspaper *De Standaard* described Defense Minister André Flahaut as "unfit or incompetent." Flahaut was accused of approving publishing as **fact** an assertion in a ministry magazine that the world's worst genocide involved the death of 15 million native North Americans from 1492 and suggesting, according to *De Standaard*, that the killing "continues to this day."
>
> The newspaper said the United States was effectively blamed by the Defense Ministry for the genocide. Its spokesman, Gerard Vareng, denied any anti-American message.
>
> John Vinocur, Politicus: Fischer's Shifting Vision of Europe's Grand Future, *International Herald Tribune*, 4/12/04

Comment

Vinocur's example shows that people can disagree on the facts. The Defense Minister of Belgium can say it is a fact that the United States government committed genocide against Native Americans. The Flemish-language newspaper can deny that it is a fact; it is only the Defense Minister's opinion. The disagreement is about confirmation: can the Defense Minister confirm his statement, or can't he? Can he prove it?

> 19f. Much research and documentation has gone into each entry in this book, and some fun, interesting, and sometimes humorous stories about various discoveries emerged. Some of the stories are historical **fact**. Others are legends or lore—stories that cannot be proved and probably cannot be disproved.
>
> Charlotte F. Jones, *Mistakes that Worked*, Doubleday, 1991, p. ix

20. opinion.

> 20b. The first **opinion** that is formed of a ruler's intelligence is based on the quality of the men he has around him. When they are competent and loyal he can always be considered wise, because he has been able to recognize their competence and to keep them loyal. But when

they are otherwise, the prince is always open to adverse criticism; because his first mistake has been in the choice of his ministers.

Niccolo Machiavelli, *The Prince*, trans. George Bull, Penguin, 1999 [originally 1514], p. 74

20c. Two publications review restaurants nationwide according to established standards—Zagat and Mobil—but few people pay serious attention. "Zagat is nothing more than a reliable phone book," scoffs Jim White, voice of WRR's "Making Reservations" and critic for eat-sanddrinks.com. "It's a bunch of **opinions** organized into an ambiguous rating system." Zagat relies on an uncertain group of diners to rate their favorites, almost like an American Idol vote.

Dave Faries, Starring Roles: Why Don't We Have a Nationwide Restaurant Rating System? *Dallas Observer*, 6/10/04

20d. Politics often calls upon more **opinion** and generalization than factual claims that can be disproved. So it went for the first 25 minutes of last night's debate between Senator Hillary Rodham Clinton and her Republican challenger, John Spencer.

In fact, on the question hanging over the race, and the first to arise in the debate—will Mrs. Clinton, a Democrat, run for president in 2008?—there is no provable answer, though it would be hard to find a politically minded American without an **opinion**.

Richard Perez-Pena, Veering From Opinions To Facts, and Slipping, *New York Times*, 10/21/06

Comment

Remember that facts are actual conditions in the world. Opinions are beliefs in people's minds. When people have true, accurate beliefs about the world, and the belief has been proven, we can say they have factual beliefs. So factual beliefs are different from opinions because opinions have not been proven. They might still be true; but the person who holds them hasn't proven that they are true.

Some beliefs are easy to prove, and some are hard to prove. In Example 20b, the great political analyst Niccolo Machiavelli says people form opinions about a leader's intelligence. But it's hard to prove a statement about someone's intelligence. Even if a leader's advisor turned against him, that would not prove that the leader made a bad choice of advisors and was stupid. Maybe no one could have known that the advisor would betray the leader. So people have opinions about the prince's intelligence, not factual beliefs, because they can't prove that their belief is true.

In Example 20c the writer is talking about people's opinions about their favorite restaurants. Some people might say, "The Blue Lagoon restaurant is better than the Uptown restaurant." But how could a person prove that one restaurant is better than another? You can think of extreme cases—spoiled food, dishonest cashiers—but in normal cases, what would prove that one restaurant is better? The problem is that some people like one kind of food, other people like other kinds of food. So beliefs about which restaurant is better are opinions, not factual beliefs, because you can't prove that they are true.

Finally, Example 20d is about a question: Will Senator Clinton run for president in 2008? When the article was written, in 2006, there was "no provable answer" to the question. It was a question about the future. Even if Senator Clinton had said "I will run," that wouldn't prove that she actually would run in 2008. It only proves that she intended to run. Anything could have happened. So beliefs about what will happen in the future are always opinions, because we cannot prove what will actually happen. Of course, some opinions about the future are much better—more believable—than others. But no one can prove a statement about the future.

Question: Do you believe Michael Phelps won eight gold medals at the Beijing Olympics in 2008? If you believe that, is it a factual belief or an opinion?

> 20e. The depositions [in court] of Schlichtman's twelve medical and three geological experts would ultimately consume fifty-three days and fill ten thousand transcript pages. Those whose **opinions** were based on quantifiable, objective measurements—the blink reflex tests and the cardiology exams, for example—fared best.
>
> Jonathan Harr, *A Civil Action*, Vintage Books, 1995, p. 254

Comment

Harr's example of court testimony by experts shows that some opinions are more reliable and more convincing than others. The medical experts were testifying about why some people were sick. Even if they couldn't prove their point, the jury believed them because their opinion about what caused the illness was based on some objective facts.

21. to confirm.

> 21b. The Ron Artest trade to Sacramento is off—for now.
>
> The [Indiana] Pacers had reportedly agreed to ship the volatile forward to the Sacramento Kings for Peja Stojakovic, but Indiana coach Rick Carlisle said last night that no deal was imminent....
>
> Artest **confirmed** to the [Indianapolis] Star that the deal had collapsed, but left open the possibility that something could still happen.
>
> Artest Isn't Moving (Yet), *AM New York*, 1/25/06

> 21c. The French minister of health insisted that doping had been going on since racing began. Two years later in a courtroom in Lille, the French sports icon Richard Virenque, five-time winner of the King of the Mountains jersey in the Tour de France, seemed to **confirm** as much when the president of the court asked him if he took

doping products. "We don't say doping," replied Virenque. "We say we're 'preparing for the race.'"

Gregory Stock, *Redesigning Humans: Our Inevitable Genetic Future*. Houghton Mifflin, 2002, p. 8

Comment

Sometimes statements can be confirmed directly by individuals, as in Examples 21b and 21c. Artest knows about a trade involving him, and the experienced racer Richard Virenque is in a position to know about doping among cyclists.

21d. When Arlene L. Weiss and her colleagues found that urban house dust tends to contain more lead the closer it is to a frequently opened window, they reasoned that most of the heavy metal arrives from outside. Their new survey now **confirms** that street grit is the probable source of lead in urban homes and that flaking paint from overpasses and bridges is a major contributor.

The researchers sampled soil and street sweepings from 255 sites throughout New York City's five boroughs. The highest lead contamination occurred directly beneath elevated train trestles, where concentrations of the metal routinely reached many thousands of parts per million (ppm). The federal limit for lead in U.S. soil is 400 ppm.

Samples of outdoor dust were much less tainted just two to three blocks away from bridges and trestles....

Janet Raloff, Leaden streets, *Science News*, 3/25/06

Comment

In Example 21d, Weiss confirms a statement about lead in street dust and on overpasses. But the way she did it is not like Artest's or Virenque's way: She isn't talking about her own career or her observations of people taking drugs. Instead, she performed a careful study to investigate the statement. She collected dust from different places and measured the amount of lead in it. That confirmed the statement.

21e. What followed, too, was the general theory of relativity, which Einstein formulated in March of 1916. The theory was **confirmed** during a solar eclipse three years later by Arthur Eddington, an English astronomer who observed that starlight actually swerved as it passed the sun, to the exact degree predicted by Einstein, proving that light has mass and that there are curvatures in space-time caused by gravity....

Michael Paterniti, *Driving Mr. Albert: A Trip Across America with Einstein's Brain*, The Dial Press, 2000, p. 6

Question: Do you think Eddington's confirmation of Einstein's theory was probably more like Artest's or like Weiss's confirmation?

Figure 4.3
This is the "Bocca della Verita," or "The Mouth of Truth," in Rome. Thousands of years ago, some people believed that if a man or woman put his or her hand into the mouth and then told a lie, the mouth would bite off the hand. How do journalists or detectives today confirm a person's statement? *Source: © Cornel Achirei /Shutterstock Images LLC*

21f. Rather than publishing another news outlet's scoop, journalists have tended to require one of their reporters to call a source to **confirm** it first. In part, this was a way of avoiding having to credit the other news organization. Yet it had another more important effect. Stories that couldn't be independently **confirmed** would not be repeated.

Bill Kovach and Tom Rosenstiel, *The Elements of Journalism*, Three Rivers Press, 2001, p. 85

(A reporter has a *scoop* when he or she has an important story and is the first to report it.)

Comment

Example 21f illustrates an important rule. To confirm a belief, you should get as many independent sources as possible. For example, suppose Tom says Rosie won the lottery. Did she really? You ask Clarence and he says she did. How does Clarence know? He heard it from Tom. Therefore Clarence is not a second, independent source. He is only repeating Tom's information. But if Maria says Rosie won, and Maria hasn't spoken to Tom, then Maria is an independent source.

22. source.

22b. Many university students in my experience would gladly pass over a section on 'source criticism', the analytical study of historical sources to determine the worth of what any of them say. However, this is an essential part of the study of history, and the study of Alexander poses a major source problem.

E. E. Rice, *Alexander the Great*, Sutton Publishing, 1997, p. 2

22c. Most of Aubrey's gossip about Shakespeare needs to be taken with a grain of salt, but this particular item has more authority than most, for he noted its source as the actor William Beeston. Beeston was the son of Shakespeare's former colleague in the Lord Chamberlain's company, Christopher Beeston. This, therefore, is a piece of biographical information that can be traced directly back to someone who actually knew Shakespeare.

Stephen Greenblatt, *Will in the World: How Shakespeare Became Shakespeare*, W. W. Norton and Company, 2004, pp. 88–89

Comment

The main question about sources is "Can you trust them? Is the information they give us true?" Greenblatt, in Example 22c, is asking that question about Aubrey. Aubrey makes a certain statement about Shakespeare. Can we trust Aubrey? Is his statement accurate? Well, Aubrey says he got the information from William Beeston. Beeston probably got it from his father, Christopher Beeston. And Christopher Beeston actually knew Shakespeare. Therefore, Aubrey's statement may be true; Greenblatt says it has more authority than statements from other sources.

22d. The use of the phrase *has learned* to mean "found out" has been growing. "CBS has learned" does three things: (1) removes the need for **sourcing** (a journalism vogue word for identifying the person responsible for a story), (2) gives the impression of being the first to know and tell the viewer and (3) plugs the network. The report is given as a certainty—much more solid than "reliable **sources** say"—

but conceals, or covers up, the fact that nobody is willing to stand behind the message except the medium.

William Safire, in Joyce S. Steward, ed., *Contemporary College Reader*, Scott Foresman and Co., 1978, p. 303

22e. The chief **source** of information about the ideas concerning love which were current in northern France in the second half of the twelfth century is Andrew the Chaplain's *De amore* [*On Love*].

Sidney Painter, *French Chivalry*, Cornell University Press, 1957 [originally 1940], p. 117

Comment

Painter's source is not a person but a book. He wants to know about the ideas that many people had in the twelfth century, and a book—which many people could read—is probably a better source than an individual for information about that.

22f. The Pennsylvania Select Committee on Academic Freedom in Higher Education was wrapping up its questioning of David Horowitz on the second of two days of hearings at Temple University....

At the hearing, Rep. Larry Curry, Democratic co-chair of the bipartisan committee, asked Horowitz about a story he has been repeating

Figure 4.4
Journalists rely on sources to get their facts. *Source: © Sergei Bachlakov/Shutterstock Images LLC*

in speeches and interviews for over a year, that a Pennsylvania State University biology professor showed his class Michael Moore's documentary "Fahrenheit 9/11" in the days before the 2004 election. Horowitz's **source**, apparently, was a posting on one of his spinoffs, the studentsforacademicfreedom.com Web site.

Trouble is, Horowitz has never provided any evidence that the screening occurred, and no other independent **source** has been able to verify it.

"The concern I have," said Rep. Curry, "is over the lack of good evidence—the vagueness being presented in both the resolution [H.R. 177] and the statements we're hearing...."

Barbara McKenna, Beware the New Thought Police, *AFT On Campus*, March/April, 2006

Comment

Curry, the state representative, wonders if he can trust Horowitz's source of information about the biology professor. Horowitz has only one source. One is better than none, but having two independent sources of the same information is much better than only one. A general rule that many journalists follow is that you can't report something as a fact unless two sources, independent of each other, confirm it. (*Verify* means confirm.) Another problem in this case is that Horowitz's source is a website that he created, a "spinoff." The example shows that if you want to know the real truth about things, finding sources of information is only part of the job: You must also decide how trustworthy your sources are.

23. critical.

23b. Many of the key texts of my religion—Hinduism—have been respectfully subjected to **critical** analysis by Western scholars—without arousing (except in a handful of cases by fundamentalist Hindutva zealots) any objection or stirring the wrath of its practitioners. The Bible is believed by many to be God's words, yet Western scholars (Jewish and Christian) have not shied away from delving **critically** into the Old Testament and the New.

DD, Letters: Could Islam Benefit from Western Critics?, *Wall Street Journal*, 1/28/08

23c. In a review of widely held medical beliefs—by public and professionals alike—two US doctors selected seven for **critical** examination and searched for evidence to support or refute them. The results suggest the beliefs are built on sand.

Rachel Vreeman of the Indiana University School of Medicine and Aaron Carroll of the Regenstrief Institute, Indianapolis, say they could find no evidence to confirm the beliefs, or there was evidence that proved them wrong.

Writing in the Christmas issue of the British Medical Journal, they say: "Physicians would do well to understand the evidence supporting their medical decision-making. They should at least recognise when their practice is based on tradition, anecdote or art. While belief in the described myths is unlikely to cause harm, recommending medical treatment for which there is little evidence certainly can."

Jeremy Laurance, Exposed: The Seven Great Medical Myths, *The Independent* (London), 12/21/07

(To *refute* a belief is to show that it is false. Evidence that *supports* a belief makes it more likely that the belief is true. An *anecdote* is a brief story, and when people base their beliefs on stories they are relying on *anecdotal evidence*.)

Comment

When the two doctors in Example 23c began their study of medical beliefs, they had open minds. They "searched for evidence to support or refute them." They did not look only for weaknesses, nor did they look only for strengths. They looked for both. Taking a critical attitude does not mean the same as criticizing (although it might lead to criticizing). A person who is examining something critically is looking for anything that might help him or her make a judgment. For example, a film critic who watches a movie critically might decide that it is an excellent film, and then write a review explaining all the reasons it is excellent. Taking a critical attitude toward statements and beliefs means, in part, asking for the source of the belief. Knowing the source will help you decide if it is a factual belief or only an opinion.

24. premise.

24b. If we want to learn anything, we must pay attention to the information to be learned. And attention is a limited resource: There is just so much information we can process at any given time.... The point is, a great deal of our limited supply of attention is committed to the tasks of surviving from one day to the next....

Some important consequences follow logically from these simple **premises**. To achieve creativity in an existing domain, there must be surplus attention available. This is why such centers of creativity as Greece in the fifth century B.C., Florence in the fifteenth century, and Paris in the nineteenth century tended to be places where wealth allowed individuals to learn and to experiment above and beyond what was necessary for survival.

Mihaly Csikszentmihalyi, *Creativity*, HarperCollins, 1996, p. 8

Question: Csikszentmihalyi thinks it is obvious that Greece, Florence, and Paris at different times were centers of creativity. That is one of his premises. He states another premise, and draws a conclusion from his premises. What is the other premise, and what is the conclusion?

Figure 4.5
Your argument for your position is only as strong as the premises holding it up. *Source:* ©
Sue Smith/Shutterstock Images LLC

24c. Human nature, evolved over millions of years and present in
our genes, expresses itself not only in bedrooms, boardrooms and
battlefields but in creative human pursuits, including literature. This,
anyway, is the **premise** of an amusing, if over-ambitious, book by psy-
chologist/zoologist David P. Barash and his college-student daughter,
Nanelle.

The Barashes line up exemplary works of fiction from Homer to
Saul Bellow alongside the major claims of evolutionary psychology.
The prehistoric origins of human conduct and desires, so the idea
goes, should be able to tell us something about the conduct and values
of characters in fiction. The results are mixed: Some of the Barashes'
explanations are far-fetched, but others have the power to jolt us into
an altered view of familiar literary stories and characters.

Denis Dutton, Survival of the Fittest Characters, review of *Madame Bovary's Ovaries: A
Darwinian Look at Literature*, By David P. Barash and Nanelle R. Barash, *Washington Post*,
8/7/05

Comment

The word *premise* means a statement in an argument that logically supports
another statement, the conclusion. People use the word *premise* when they
want to emphasize that the statement is being taken for granted; it isn't

proven. A premise is a starting point, which leads to other beliefs. A reason leads to other beliefs, too, so its function in an argument is the same. But the word *premise* includes this association of "starting point," or "taken for granted."

Part 3. Applying the Words

19. fact
20. opinion
21. to confirm
22. source
23. critical
24. premise

Exercise 1:   Choose the Right Word

In each example, the speaker is asking for a fact, an opinion, a confirmation, a source, a critical attitude, or a premise. Try to decide what the speaker is asking for.

1. "How did you find out that Senator Jones opposes the new bill?"
The speaker is asking for _____.
2. "Bob says that during the Second World War Churchill knew beforehand that the Nazis were going to bomb Coventry, but he didn't warn the citizens. That's hard to believe. Is there any proof?"
The speaker is asking for _____.
3. "I've heard all sorts of rumors and speculations about the fight, if that's what it was. You were there; what actually happened?"
The speaker is asking for _____.
4. "I agree with you that public schools are facing a crisis. What do you think should be done?"
The speaker is asking for _____.
5. "I understand the conclusion of Prof. Harkins' argument, but how did she get there?"
The speaker is asking for _____.
6. "The Greens are your friends, but how do they measure up as parents? Step back for a minute and tell me what you think."
The speaker is asking for _____.

Exercise 2:   Apply the Words

Read each example and answer the questions that follow.

1. As chief executive of CUC International, Walter A. Forbes pre-sided over a company whose books told lies for more than a decade. When the fraud was uncovered in 1998, after CUC had merged into the Cendant Corporation, it was the largest accounting fraud in American history.

This week, after a trial that lasted seven months and deliberations that lasted another month, a federal court jury convicted CUC's No. 2 executive, E. Kirk Shelton. But it was unable to reach a verdict on Mr. Forbes.

That there was a fraud is not in question. For many years, CUC inflated its revenues and hid expenses. "The defense of Walter Forbes is that he didn't know about it," said Brendan Sullivan, his lawyer, in closing arguments.

Floyd Norris, Chief Executive Was Paid Millions, and He Never Noticed the Fraud? *New York Times*, 1/7/05

"There was fraud at CUC." Does Norris present that statement as a fact or an opinion?

2. But 69 years ago the courtyard [of John Rabe's home in Nanjing] was filled with hundreds of Chinese seeking refuge from Japanese troops who were rampaging through the city, then China's capital. The invaders subjected Nanjing to a six-week reign of terror, killing large numbers of Chinese soldiers who had thrown down their weapons and murdering and raping thousands of civilians....

Since the publication of Mr. Rabe's diary in 1997, his story has become a central theme in narratives of the Nanjing Massacre, much as the massacre story itself has become an important pillar in China's emerging new nationalism....

Yet seven decades after the event there is still serious academic dispute, even over something so fundamental as the death toll....

In Japan, denial of the killings—once restricted to the far-right fringe—has entered the mainstream as the country's politics have shifted rightward. Today, in the face of the best evidence, many Japanese textbooks minimize the event, playing down suggestions of Japanese atrocities.

Experts say the fact that there were mass killings is beyond any reasonable dispute. "It was not until we toured the city that we learned the extent of the destruction," Mr. Rabe wrote on Dec. 13, 1937, just a day after Japan took control of the city. "The bodies of the civilians that I examined had bullet holes in their backs. These people had presumably been fleeing and were shot from behind."

His account is backed up by the few remaining survivors from his courtyard.... But official records tend to be scarce or unreliable.

Howard W. French, China Hails a Good Nazi and Makes Japan Take Notice, *New York Times*, 3/15/06

Is it a fact, or an opinion, that Japanese soldiers killed large numbers of civilians in Nanjing in 1937? How do we decide?

3. Founded in 1894 by Isaac Wistar, a Civil War veteran and a colorful American whose life could fill several volumes, the Wistar Institute once boasted of possessing Walt Whitman's brain, though sometime near the beginning of this century a research assistant accidentally dropped it. According to matter-of-fact newspaper accounts from the time, Whitman's brain was then tossed out in the day's garbage.

Michael Paterniti, *Driving Mr. Albert: A Trip Across America with Einstein's Brain*, The Dial Press, 2000, p. 48

What is Paterniti's source of information about Whitman's brain?

4. Our most important source for this first mission and expansion [of Christianity] is the second volume of the Gospel of Luke, called the Acts of the Apostles. It was written possibly as early as the year 85....

Luke, like all historians, is very dependent on his materials—what he had to work with, his sources. For the first part of his story, dealing with the community in Jerusalem [in about 35 AD], he probably had very little by way of real source material, perhaps only a handful of facts, which he manages to work up into a dramatic story through the use of speeches and summaries....

Whenever we can check the account of the Acts of the Apostles against other historical sources—Christian, Greco-Roman, or Jewish—Acts is accurate. It's selective; it shapes its tale; but when it says that a particular place was there, it's there. Whenever he says particular rulers or customs took place in that area, they happened there. So the Acts of the Apostles gets the world of the 1st century correct, and so—by and large—even though it has a lot of fictional rendering, scholars do well to take it seriously as a genuine historical source for Christianity's first mission and expansion.

Luke Timothy Johnson, The Great Courses: Religion, *The Teaching Company*, Chantilly, VA, 2006, p. 31

a. In this passage Johnson talks about three different types of sources. What are they? (Hint: Who uses the source? For what purpose does someone use the source?)
b. Why does Johnson believe that we can rely on the Acts of the Apostles for information?

5. Glazer claims there is no "strong evidence" that more money has educational effects. But since 1989, courts in 26 states have considered the issue of whether low levels of educational funding are depriving students of their constitutional right to an adequate education. In almost all of these cases, whether money matters has been a central issue. The leading national experts on both sides of this question have testified, and probably more evidence has been presented and thoroughly analyzed on this issue than on any other major public policy issue in recent years. The results have been astounding: plaintiffs have

prevailed in 20 of the 26 decisions of the highest state courts, and the causal relation between adequate resources and improved educational outcomes has been firmly established.

MR, Letters: Segregation Now? *New York Times Book Review*, 10/16/05

The writer says it is a fact, not an opinion, that spending more money leads to improved educational outcomes. How does he confirm his statement?

> 6. *Content of the conscience.*—The content of our conscience is every-thing that was during the years of our childhood regularly *demanded* of us without reason by people we honored or feared. It is thus the conscience that excites that feeling of compulsion ('I must do this, not do that') which does not ask: *why* must I? In every case in which a thing is done with 'because' and 'why' man acts *without* conscience— but not yet for that reason against it.

> R. J. Hollingdale, ed. and trans., *A Nietzsche Reader*, Penguin, 1977, p. 85

According to Nietzsche, if a person acts according to her conscience, is she being critical, or not being critical?

> 7. Indeed, it seems to me that the more Christian a country is the less likely it is to regard the death penalty as immoral. . . . I attribute that to the fact that, for the believing Christian, death is no big deal. Intentionally killing an innocent person is a big deal: it is a grave sin, which causes one to lose his soul. But losing this life, in exchange for the next? . . . For the nonbeliever, on the other hand, to deprive a man of his life is to end his existence. What a horrible act!

> Antonin Scalia, "God's Justice and Ours," First Things, May 2002, pp. 17–21, quoted in Sam Harris, *The End of Faith*, W. W. Norton, 2004, pp. 156–157

Supreme Court Justice Scalia's conclusion is that if a country is Christian, it will probably approve of the death penalty. What premise leads him to that conclu-sion? Is the premise a factual statement or Scalia's opinion?

Exercise 3:   Analyzing Arguments

1. In the first example, Sue Hendrickson reached a conclusion, which she said was a factual belief. (She "knew.") What proved that her belief was true?

> One August morning nine years ago, Sue Hendrickson, a field pale-ontologist for the Black Hills Institute of Geological Research, spotted some bone fragments at the base of a 57-foot cliff. "Because the frag-ments appeared to have fallen from above, I looked up," Hendrickson says. "And there, about seven feet up the cliff face, three vertebrae were sticking out of the wall. By their shape, I knew the specimen had been a meat-eater. And by their size, I knew it could only be a *T. rex* [Tyrannosaurus rex]."

> Donovan Webster, "A Dinosaur Named Sue," *National Geographic*, June, 1999

2. John Edwards presents an argument in the following passage. The conclusion is a statement of fact. What fact does Edwards say he has proven? What evidence leads to the conclusion?

> Liz Kuniholm examined several of the hospital's nurses and thereby established [the patient] E.G.'s condition at the time of admission. From them she got the doctor's order that they administer 500 milligrams, then 1000 milligrams, and finally 1500 milligrams of Antabuse. And then they testified to the dangerous side effects E.G. began to exhibit—and how one evening he was found collapsed, unconscious, on his hospital bed. In the same manner I elicited from the hospital's pharmacists that they had followed the doctor's prescriptions, despite the fact that their pharmaceutical manuals declared any dosage in excess of 500 milligrams dangerous. Clearly the hospital personnel, in violation of hospital protocols, had dispensed and administered dosages of Antabuse that far exceeded the literature's clear guidelines. The defense attorneys couldn't really challenge these facts.
>
> John Edwards, *Four Trials*, Simon and Schuster, 2004, p. 34

Exercise 4:   Apply the Ideas in Writing

Write two paragraphs about a movie or TV series you have seen, or a song or a band you've heard. In the first paragraph state the facts about the movie (if you choose a movie), and in the second paragraph explain your opinion of it. Was it good or bad, skillfully made or full of errors, interesting or boring, creative or copying others?

The first paragraph should contain only factual statements, that is, statements that someone else could confirm by looking at the movie. For example, you might say the film was 108 minutes long. It was about a bank robbery. The main character plans to rob a bank by himself, but then decides he needs others to help him. He uses a toy gun. And so on. You could not say "the main character is obviously a loser and a moron." That is your opinion, because you cannot prove that the character is a loser. Another person might watch the movie and decide he admires the robber. The way to prove your statement is to invite others to watch or listen and see if they will all agree with you. (Ask yourself "If others watched the movie, would they all agree that it's 108 minutes long? Would they agree that it's about a bank robbery?")

If you believe the character is a loser you can say that in the second paragraph, and maybe explain why you think so. You can state other opinions as well. Did the film have a message? What can you know about the main character that isn't directly stated or shown in the movie? Does he lack confidence in himself? You can try to explain why you have the opinion you do. You can have a good reason to believe the main character is a loser, even if your reason doesn't add up to proof.

Improving Your Writing 4: Organization

A good paragraph is well *organized*. That means the sentences are arranged in some order that makes the paragraph easy to understand. For example, if you are telling the story of your day, you will probably organize the details *chronologically*, according to time. You tell people what happened first, then what happened later, and then what happened after that.

If you are describing your house, you will probably begin with one room, tell your readers what is in it, then move on to another room, describe that, and so on. You follow a *spatial order*. In contrast, someone might write "I have a TV in my room, but the kitchen has a refrigerator. The walls of the living room are light blue. My room also has a desk in it." The details in these sentences are not in any particular order; the writer seems to be writing down whatever pops into his head without arranging the descriptions. As a result, the paragraph would be confusing and hard to understand.

If you write a paragraph explaining cause and effect, you might start with the effect and work your way backwards to immediate causes and then remote causes. "A cold is caused by germs multiplying in the body. The germs enter the body through openings, such as the nose or mouth. People get germs on their hands from touching doorknobs, or shaking hands with others, and then touching their nose or mouth." Or you can start with the remote causes and tell your readers what effects they produced. "When Mr. Macintosh became ill, he had to quit his job. With no income, the family's savings soon ran out and they couldn't pay their rent. Ms. Macintosh was under a lot of pressure, trying to make ends meet and care for her husband and children. Several times she became angry and screamed at the landlord. He lost patience with them and they were evicted. That's how they ended up in the homeless shelter."

CHAPTER 5

Reliable Sources

25. reliable
26. first-hand
27. expert
28. credentials
29. consensus
30. objective
31. to fabricate

Suppose I told you that I know which horse will win the Kentucky Derby next year. You would probably ask, "How do you know?" Or suppose I said I know that terrorists are planning to blow up City Hall on Thursday. The FBI would definitely ask me how I know. I might have a good answer, or I might not.

Remember that the difference between facts and opinions is that statements of fact have been proven, whereas opinions have not. How do you prove that a belief is factual and true? You consider the source, that is, where the belief came from or what it's based on. Factual beliefs come from a source that everyone can trust and that always gives correct information, such as a good encyclopedia, or someone who has a great deal of knowledge and experience. But opinions can be based on anything, or nothing. They aren't based on reliable sources.

Thinking about facts and opinions—and keeping them apart—is another way of recognizing relationships. In this case, it is recognizing the relationship between a belief and the source of the belief.

But which sources can you trust? How do you distinguish between reliable sources and unreliable sources? That's an important question, and we have several key words to use in talking about which types of sources are reliable and which aren't.

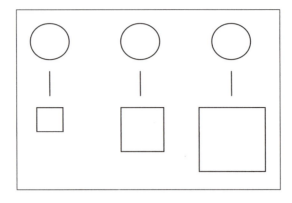

Figure 5.1
You can visualize beliefs as circles and the sources of the beliefs as squares. Some sources are more reliable than others. You can visualize reliability as size: a larger square symbolizes a more reliable source.

Part 1. Definitions

25. reliable. meets expectations, dependable; a reliable source is one that regularly provides accurate, correct information. "*The New Yorker* magazine is famous for double-checking its facts. It's highly reliable."

Example

> 25a. At one time, several years before, in 1957, Betty's sister and family had described seeing clearly an unidentified flying object in Kingston, New Hampshire, where they lived. Betty, who had confidence in her sister's **reliability** and capacity for observation, believed the story of her sighting.
>
> John G. Fuller, *The Interrupted Journey*, Dell, 1966, p. 27

26. first-hand. (adjective) based on direct experience or personal observation. "The reporter just happened to be in San Francisco when the earthquake struck, so she was able to give a first-hand report."

Example

> 26a. The defining moment of Mr. Vonnegut's life was the firebombing of Dresden, Germany, by Allied forces in 1945, an event he witnessed **firsthand** as a young prisoner of war. Thousands of civilians were killed in the raids, many of them burned to death or asphyxiated.
>
> Dinitia Smith, Kurt Vonnegut Is Dead at 84; Caught Imagination of His Age, *New York Times*, 4/12/07

27. expert. a person who is a reliable source of information, who understands some topic or has much experience in some area. "Jane Goodall is an expert on chimpanzees; she has spent years in Africa observing them in the wild."

Example

27a. Generally authority figures know what they are talking about. Physicians, judges, corporate executives, legislative leaders, and the like have typically gained their positions through superior knowledge and judgment. Thus, as a rule, their directives offer excellent counsel. Authorities, then, are frequently **experts**....In most cases it would be foolish to try to substitute our less-informed judgments for those of an **expert**.

Robert B. Cialdini, *Influence: Science and Practice*, Scott Foresman and Company, 1985, p. 192

28. credentials. whatever proves that a person is an expert or is qualified for something, usually experience, education, accomplishments, proven knowledge and ability, or evidence of those things. "The jury believed the psychiatrist because his credentials were excellent: Harvard degree, 23 years of experience, several books, numerous awards."

Example

28a. "A fellow up in New York, my former teacher Dr. Harry Zimmerman"—and an acquaintance of Einstein's—"was going to do the autopsy [on Einstein]. But then he couldn't get away. He rang me up, and we agreed that I'd do it." Harvey then trotted out his **credentials** for me: He had worked under Zimmerman, who was a neuroanatomist, at Yale and had also taught two years of neuroanatomy for Dr. Fritz Lewy at the University of Pennsylvania. He explained that Lewy had been the head of the Neurological Institute in Berlin before Hitler....

Michael Paterniti, *Driving Mr. Albert: A Trip Across America with Einstein's Brain*, The Dial Press, 2000, p. 8—

29. consensus. 1. universal agreement within a group. "After a long discussion, the committee reached a consensus on the issue." 2. the beliefs that a group shares. "The consensus was that we should split up into pairs and go in different directions."

Example

29a. It is true that 56.2 million Americans....voted for John Kerry. Kerry's vote total indicates that, without question, Bush did not win a national **consensus** on his policies.

There will still be division and debate on these matters, which is right and proper in a democracy.

John Podhoretz, What W Won, *New York Post*, 11/9/04

30. objective. 1. not influenced by personal feelings or desires; realistic; logical. "Even though his son was on the team, the coach had to think objectively about which player could do the best job." 2. outside of anyone's mind, "an objective fact." "The people in the boat were really scared, but the objective conditions were not dangerous."

Example

> 30a. The MTA provides New Yorkers with the best public transportation system in the world. By any **objective** measure—on-time performance, safety, volume of riders, customer satisfaction—we are a vastly improved system compared to the one provided New Yorkers in the past.
>
> Peter S. Kalikow, Letters, Unfounded, *AM New York*, 10/27/04

31. to fabricate. 1. to make or put together; "He fabricated a shelter from a discarded packing crate." 2. to make up a story, to report something as fact that one knows to be false; to lie. "He fabricated a ridiculous story about being kidnapped in a vain attempt to avoid prosecution." A fabrication is different from an honest mistake.

Example

> 31a. It is important to remember that this autobiography [by Charles Dickens] was written not by the child but the man, the successful author ('famous and caressed and happy' in his own words) looking back at the helpless and impoverished child. It is not, as so many commentators have assumed, a literal account but is in certain respects a **fabrication**, or, if that sounds too extreme, an imaginative reconstruction, of his childhood. After all, what autobiography is not? And as such, certain elements of fact were made subservient to the myth, or fiction, that Dickens had made out of his past.
>
> F. S. Schwarzbach, *Dickens and the City*, University of London: The Athlone Press, 1979, p. 17

Test Yourself
Match each word with its definition.

25. reliable
26. first-hand
27. expert
28. credentials
29. consensus
30. objective
31. to fabricate

a. someone who knows a great deal about some topic
b. something based on personal experience, direct knowledge
c. to make up something one knows is not true
d. dependable, something that lives up to expectations
e. agreement among almost all the members of a group
f. the proof that a person is an expert, or at least knows about something
g. based on facts rather than personal feelings or wishes

Part 2. Understanding the Meaning

25. reliable.

25b. That evening the innkeeper—a woman by the name of Domitilla—and a few stragglers who had come to drink the friars' wine lit a candle in front of the Virgin and knelt in prayer for an end to the earthquakes that were endangering the city. Earlier, the tremors had been frequent and violent, and the city lived in constant fear. Now, as everyone was kneeling in prayer, someone lifted his eyes and discovered that the face of the Madonna had suddenly turned clear and luminous. Others saw the image even open and close its eyes.... Now, you have every right to say that an innkeeper and a few townspeople (maybe even a little tipsy on monastery wine) who see a Madonna turn white and move her eyes aren't the most **reliable** witnesses.

Gian M. Rinaldi, "A Madonna's Fierce 'Armada,'" in Martin Ebon, ed., *Miracles*, New American Library, 1981, p. 68

25c. Bush included in his own State of the Union address statements about Iraq's attempt to purchase uranium from Africa that either he

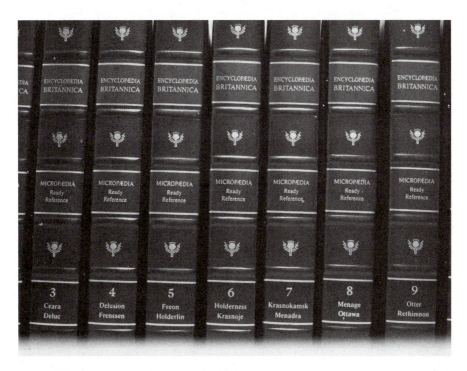

Figure 5.2
Encyclopedias try to make sure that their information is accurate.

Figure 5.3

Do you know what it's like to ride a roller coaster? Do you know what it's like if you have never ridden one but talked to many people who have? *Source: © Cary Kalscheuer/ Shutterstock Images LLC*

or his staff—or perhaps both—knew to be highly doubtful, if not false....If Bush's staff knew that the information in his speech was not **reliable**, then Bush himself should have known. And if he knew, then he is, of course, as culpable as they are.

Peter Singer, *The President of Good and Evil: The Ethics of George W. Bush*. Dutton, 2004, pp. 214–215

26. first-hand.

26b. Tom Rosenstiel, director of the project, said that reporters seemed to be increasingly shunted off to an isolated area while covering events, as they were during the recent mining disaster in West Virginia, giving them little **first-hand** access.

"The irony is that having more reporters doesn't mean more coverage," he said. "It means more reporters crowded into one corner of the scene."

Katharine Q. Seelye, Study Finds More News Media Outlets, Covering Less News, *New York Times*, 3/13/06

26c. The Titanic's stern pointed up at the night sky for a full two minutes before it finally sank, according to an account of the ship's last moments released yesterday.

"There was heard a rumbling and crashing from inside the ship, like the sound of distant thunder," wrote Second Officer Charles Lightoller, the highest ranking crew member to survive the 1912 disaster.

First-Hand Account: Titanic Story up for Auction, *Gold Coast Bulletin* (Australia), 10/31/03

Question: Lightoller was in a lifeboat some distance from the ship. Would it be possible to get a first-hand account of the last moments on the ship from someone who was actually there, i.e., someone who went down with the ship and drowned?

26d. The classical anthropologists did not write out of **first-hand** knowledge of primitive people. They were armchair students who had at their disposal the anecdotes of travelers and missionaries and the formal and schematic accounts of the early ethnologists.

Ruth Benedict, *Patterns of Culture*, Houghton Mifflin, 1934, p. 48

(An ethnologist is a person who studies different cultures in order to compare them.)

27. expert.

27b. Here at *New York* Magazine, we have no problem pointing you to a great restaurant or telling you which movie to see—but frankly, we were uncomfortable saying "Beautiful. Not beautiful," to a pile of Polaroids.

So we turned to **experts**. Which is to say, we cajoled and browbeat some of the city's most astute aestheticians (photographers, fashion designers, artists, club owners) into suggesting people they saw every day who struck them as New York's most beautiful.

Gaby Wood, The Beautiful People, *New York Magazine*, 8/15/05, p. 34

27c. In the 1930s [Clarence B.] Darrow was a stove salesman and heating engineer. The Depression was on, and time hung heavy on his hands. So he thought up a game, made the parts by hand, and began playing it with friends. It caught on locally, and he turned out sets for more friends—at first, two a day.

At a hundred sets, production went beyond Darrow's facilities. He approached toy manufacturers, but was turned down. "They told me that there were too many players in the game, that it was too complicated, that it took too long, and that it would end up in families fighting each other." (Thus, the verdict of the **experts**!). . . .

What game? "Monopoly." It is the biggest thing that ever hit the game business. And the **experts** had turned it down.

A. D. Moore, *Invention, Discovery, and Creativity*, Anchor Books, 1969, p. 40

Question: An expert is someone with extensive knowledge in some area, long experience, or proven understanding and mastery. You should always be alert to the possibility that someone who is called an "expert" isn't really an expert. Do you think there could be experts in games and toy manufacturing and sales? (A person can be an expert and still be wrong sometimes.)

27d. Any reader of this newspaper [The New York Times] knows how The Times likes to invoke the wisdom of people identified as "**experts**" or "analysts," but until I counted their presence the other day I had no idea how crowded with expertise the paper was. On Tuesday alone, such seers and sages were rolled out 33 times. . . . I'm not talking about the partisan political operatives whose apparent license to spin, sneer and smear devalues so much political reporting. I'm concerned with those **experts** rolled out to explain or contextualize complex matters (as reporters who use them would argue) or to confirm what the reporter already thinks (as far too many readers believe).

Daniel Okrent, Analysts Say **Experts** Are Hazardous to Your Newspaper, *New York Times*, 10/31/04

27e. A 61-year-old Florida man could be called an **expert** on stupidity, having written two books about it: "The Story of Stupidity" and "Understanding Stupidity." As if to further enhance his reputation as an authority on the subject, police said he tried to arrange a sexual encounter with a 15-year-old girl over the Internet only to discover, after his arrest, that he was actually communicating with an undercover male detective.

Mike Pingree, Through the Looking Glass, *The Boston Herald*, November 10, 2002

28. credentials.

28b. In the twenties and thirties the state [Kansas] was home to a quack doctor of national celebrity, Dr. John Brinkley of Milford, who claimed to cure impotence by surgically transplanting bits of goat

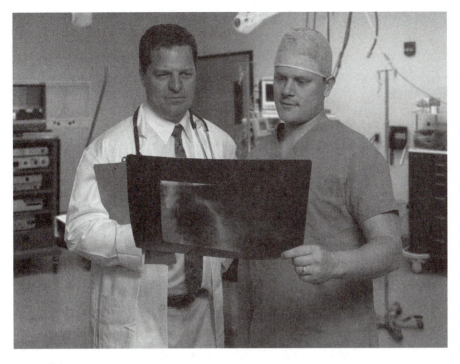

Figure 5.4
What makes a doctor an expert on X-ray photographs of patients? *Source: © James Steidl/ Shutterstock Images LLC*

testicle to humans.... Brinkley's goat operation was a fraud, though, and his medical **credentials** were questionable.... Brinkley's medical degree was from an "eclectic" institution, one of the philosophies of medicine, such as osteopathy and homeopathy, that stood apart from "regular" AMA [American Medical Association] practice, or "allopathy." At that time, Kansas was one of the few remaining states where "irregular" medical degrees were officially considered to be on an equal footing with mainstream degrees.

Thomas Frank, *What's the Matter with Kansas? How Conservatives Won the Heart of America*, Metropolitan Books, 2004, p. 196

28c. Aristide was given that rarest of political gifts—a second chance. But, reinstalled in the presidency in October 1994 by a multinational military force, he used his resurrection to perfect an autocratic style, say even those close to him who were interviewed for this story.

Today, having infuriated, humiliated, and—some allege, killed— any once-devoted followers who crossed him, Aristide has few political allies left. Even his strongest **credential**—his election to a second term in 2000—counts little as rebels gobble up territory and threaten to take the capital.

Clara Germani, Rise and Fall of a "Haitian Mandela," *Christian Science Monitor*, 2/27/04

Comment

Credentials prove that a person is qualified for something or knows about some topic. For example, an academic degree usually proves that a person is qualified in some area, such as teaching science. But as the writer says in Example 28b, not all academic degrees are equal. People questioned the doctor's credentials because the school he attended was "irregular."

Furthermore, academic degrees are only one kind of credential. To coach a volleyball team or run a business, experience is probably a better credential. Example 25c is about a rebellion in Haiti that sent the president into exile. What credentials would a person need to prove he or she is qualified to be president of a country? Not academic degrees. The writer here says that Aristide's strongest credential was being elected in 2000. But even that didn't convince the rebels. (American voters must ask themselves the same question about credentials every four years.)

> 28d. Who should run a big art museum? Executives with corporate skills that could help them manage these multimillion-dollar institutions through major expansions? Or leaders with traditional art-world **credentials**? ...
>
> So far, there are indications that the art scholars are likely to win out at some of the top institutions. ...
>
> Such skills may have helped Michael Brand clinch the directorship at the Getty Museum in Los Angeles this week. ... Mr. Brand is widely considered a respected scholar of the art of India, although the Getty isn't known for collecting in that area.
>
> Jacob Hale Russell, Art Museums Debate Skills for Top Post, *Wall Street Journal*, 8/18/05

29. consensus.

> 29b. While there is agreement that no economy can succeed under hyperinflation, there is no **consensus** about the gains from lowering inflation to lower and lower levels. ...
>
> Joseph E. Stiglitz, *Globalization and Its Discontents*, W. W. Norton, 2002, p. 220

> 29c. The River of Doubt [in the Amazon jungle] was uncharted but not unpopulated, and as the expedition made its way slowly down the river, a fierce debate raged just out of earshot. Cinta Larga tribesmen, alarmed at the intruders in their midst, considered whether to kill the strangers or let them pass through unscathed. "Given the tribe's tradition that all decisions of war be made by **consensus**, the very existence

of this debate became the thin thread on which the lives of [Theodore] Roosevelt and his men would ultimately hang," Millard writes.

Bruce Barcott, Candido and Ted's Excellent Adventure, review of Candice Millard, The River of Doubt: Theodore Roosevelt's Darkest Journey, *New York Times Book Review*, 10/16/05

29d. Also, when I say that the physics community became universally convinced of something, I am speaking loosely—this is never entirely true. If you had a lawsuit that hinged on the validity of the unified weak and electromagnetic theory, you could probably find an expert witness who is a Ph.D. physicist with a good academic position who would testify that he didn't believe in the theory. There are always some people on the fringes of science, not quite crackpots, often people with good credentials, who don't believe the **consensus**. This makes it harder for an outsider to be sure the **consensus** has occurred, but it does not change the fact of the **consensus**.

Steven Weinberg, *Facing Up: Science and Its Cultural Adversaries*, Harvard University Press, 2001, p. 90

Comment

Weinberg's statement in Example 29d reminds us that *consensus* means "all or almost all." In a relatively small group, such as a tribe of hunters in the Amazon jungle, making decisions by consensus means that every member of the tribe must agree. But in a much larger group, such as the physics community in the United States, getting every member to agree on some issue will be rarer. As Weinberg says, some physicist somewhere will disagree with the majority on just about anything. Getting a consensus in such a large group means getting almost all members to agree. When that happens, a consensus has occurred.

30. objective.

30b. What I am getting at is that there are moral principles [e.g., "Lying is wrong"] by which we can construct an ethical theory. These principles are not absolute (no exceptions), nor are they relative (anything goes). They are provisional—true for most people in most circumstances most of the time. And they are **objective**, in the sense that morality is independent of the individual. Moral sentiments evolved as part of our species; moral principles, therefore, can be seen as transcendent of the individual, making them morally **objective**.

Michael Shermer, *The Science of Good and Evil*, Henry Holt and Company, 2004, p. 168

30c. One side in the so-called science wars holds that the investigation of nature is a purely **objective** pursuit, walled off from the influences of the surrounding society and culture by built-in safeguards, such as the demand that scientific results be replicable and the requirement that scientific theories accord with nature. The gravitational force of a Marxist, in other words, is identical to the gravitational force of a fascist....

Jeffrey M. Schwartz and Sharon Begley, *The Mind and the Brain: Neuroplasticity and the Power of Mental Force*, Regan Books, 2002, p. 7

Comment

It may seem that Shermer in Example 30b and Schwartz and Begley in 30c have different ideas of objectivity. Shermer says some moral principles are objective in the sense of being independent of the individual, while Schwartz and Begley say science is objective in the sense of being independent of society and culture. But I think Schwartz and Begley agree with Shermer. Their "influences of the surrounding society" means influences on an individual scientist. The individual scientist is walled off from those influences, so science is independent of the individual's social and cultural biases. They say the law of gravity is the same for a Marxist and a fascist, even though those individuals disagree on all social and cultural questions.

30d. Incidentally, it should be clear that **objectivity** in looking at a culture is not the same as criticism of it. Some otherwise clear-thinking people confuse the two. In particular, they assume that anyone who can criticize his own society must be **objective** about it: only the conformers, those who passively accept their society's rules and stipulations, are deemed lacking in **objectivity**. Put this way, the question probably needs little further glossing, for it is apparent that criticism may lack **objectivity** too. In any event, the **objectivity** produced by participation in field work is that of unfamiliarity. The trouble about working in the culture in which one grew up is that almost everything is taken for granted.

Morton H. Fried, *The Study of Anthropology*, Thomas Y. Crowell, 1972, p. 124

30e. In "How Would Jackson Pollock Cover This Campaign?" (Oct. 10), you confuse evenhandedness with **objectivity**.

If the paper spent more of its front-page space on investigative reporting and presenting factual information about the candidates, and less time offering each of them opportunities to publicize their rhetoric, the public would be better served, and The Times would be a better newspaper.

When I write a scientific article, I present the data that I have collected. If those data support one point of view, I don't spend a lot of time describing the beliefs of people who have another point of view.

I wish The Times would model itself a little more on the scientific model, and a little less on a candidate's model (trying to say something to please everyone), in its coverage of the election.

SE, Letters to the Public Editor, Other Voices: Political Bias and the Eye of the Beholder, *New York Times*, 10/24/04

Question: Both Example 30d and Example 30e explain what objectivity is *not*. Both give examples of people who think they are being objective when they are actually substituting something else for objectivity. What mistake are the people Fried describes in Example 30d making? What mistake is *The Times* making, according to SE in Example 30e? Do the writers in these examples also tell us what objectivity *is?*

opposite. A word that has the opposite meaning from a second word is called an antonym of the second word.

subjective. the opposite of objective; based on personal, idiosyncratic feelings or preferences; existing in one person's mind. "The color of the paint is an objective fact, but Joan's feeling about the color is a subjective response."

> 30f. These days, the definition of a terrorist is quite **subjective**. For years, the Israeli Defense Forces have visited death and destruction on the occupied territories with the members of Al-Aqsa Martyrs Brigade engaging in equally violent reprisals. In Iraq, the U.S. and coalition forces have killed thousands of civilians while the equally determined insurgents try to force them out in a war of attrition. Who is the terrorist? One man's freedom fighter is another's terrorist.
>
> Dan Edanyabo, "Playing with Words," Letters, *AM New York*, 9/28/04

> 30g. Some journalists over the years have suggested substitutes for truthfulness. Probably the two most common are fairness and balance. Yet both, under scrutiny, become inadequate. Fairness is too abstract and, in the end, more **subjective** than truth. Fair to whom? How do you test fairness? Truthfulness, for all its difficulties, at least can be tested.
>
> Balance, also, is too **subjective**. Balancing a story by being fair to both sides may not be fair to the truth, if both sides do not in fact have equal weight. Is global warming a fact? The preponderance of scientists argued for years that it was, but the press coverage continued long past the time of the scientific debate to give equal weight to both sides. And in those many cases where there are more than two sides, how does one determine which sides to honor?
>
> Bill Kovach and Tom Rosenstiel, *The Elements of Journalism*, Three Rivers Press, 2001, p. 46

Question: Is the statement "Studying critical thinking is a lot of fun" objective or subjective? Is the statement "The Clinton presidency from 1992 to 2000 was a success" objective or subjective?

31. to fabricate.

> 31b. A German university has revoked the doctoral degree of the former Bell Labs scientist who claimed a series of research breakthroughs, then was fired two years ago when it was discovered that he had manipulated data and **fabricated** results.

Kenneth Chang, Researcher Loses Ph.D. over Discredited Papers, *New York Times*, 6/15/04

31c. The historians of ancient Rome considered themselves free to write imaginary speeches for their historical characters, and to include or even to invent anecdotes about them; their accounts of events were subjective, literary, and often deliberately inaccurate; far from quoting precise references, the sources which they deigned to mention were more often than not false ones, and occasionally they were pure **fabrications**.

Einhard and Notker the Stammerer, *Two Lives of Charlemagne*, translated by Lewis Thorpe, Penguin, 1969, p. 28

31d. The Village Voice suspended one of its editors [Nick Sylvester] after he admitted **fabricating** material for this week's cover story, a look at "The Secret Society of Pickup Artists."...

"I deeply regret this misinformation," Sylvester wrote....

In an August story about cheating on college campuses, Sylvester described...a Boston College junior named Simeon Criz who cheated using a specially designed deck of playing cards....

Boston College said it had no record of a student named Simeon Criz.

David B. Caruso, Voice: Editor **Fabricated** Scene, *AM New York*, 3/3/06

Question: Is fabricating material different from being subjective? Could Sylvester defend himself by saying he was expressing his personal thoughts and feelings about cheating?

Part 3. Applying the Words

25. reliable
26. first-hand
27. expert
28. credentials
29. consensus
30. objective
31. to fabricate

Exercise 1:　Choose the Right Word

For each sentence, choose the best word (or an appropriate form of the word) to fill in the blank.

1. This pathologist has performed hundreds of autopsies. When it comes to dead bodies, he's _____.
2. At first, members of the committee disagreed among themselves, but after Kline's presentation they reached _____.

3. The reporter was fired when the editor learned that only parts of his stories were true, and other parts were _____.

4. Among her _____ were a degree from U.C.L.A., published studies of skin cancer, and volunteer work in Guatemala.

5. Joey based his history paper on information he got from two web sites he found on the Internet, but I'm not sure they are _____.

6. Today's umpire is from another state, and he's never even seen either team play before, so I expect him to be completely _____.

7. Grace read a history of the Vietnam War, but Roger's grandfather was there, and Roger interviewed him, so he has _____ information.

Exercise 2:   Apply the Words

Read each example and answer the questions that follow.

> 1. Since there was always the danger of people incorrectly attributing things to the Prophet [Muhammad], scholars collected and authenticated "genuine" *hadith* [sayings by Muhammad]. Intensive research was involved as each *hadith* was rejected or accepted depending on its traceable links to the Prophet. The integrity of those who formed the links needed to be unimpeachable. Thus each *hadith* required a chain of those who had actually heard the saying and could trace it to the Prophet.
>
> Akbar S. Ahmed, "Muhammad," in John Miller, Aaron Kenedi, eds., *Inside Islam*, Marlowe and Company, 2002, p. 37.

(*Unimpeachable* means unquestionable, beyond criticism.)
Those who actually heard Muhammad's statements had first-hand information, and others passed on what those people said they heard. Both groups must be reliable. How do scholars decide they are reliable?

> 2. When St. Thomas Aquinas lay dying, in 1274, it was said that he asked for herrings, which were unknown thereabouts. Yet sure enough they soon obligingly turned up at the local fishmongers. Even in the early 14th century, when Thomas's candidacy for sainthood was under investigation, and at least two miracles were required for admission, this unlikely tale did not wash not least because it emerged that the witnesses had no way of telling whether what they had seen were herrings or not.
>
> Anthony Gottlieb, When the Lights Went Out in Europe, *New York Times*, 2/15/04

In this story, the witnesses were not reliable. Why not? In other words, besides honesty and objectivity, what else must a reliable witness have, which these witnesses did not have?

> 3. "They [American news sources] just don't have enough information about what is happening there," Samy complained. "The news is almost always recorded, never covered live. I wonder what they edit out?" he questioned. Samy continued, "they always seem to favor

non-Arabs in their reports. I don't want to hear Wolf Blitzer tell me what his impressions are of how the Arabs feel! I want to hear what the people in the street think."

Mohammed El-Nawawy, Adel Iskandar, *Al-Jazeera*, Westview, 2002, pp. 12–13

Samy wants first-hand information. Why is he not satisfied with the second-hand information he gets now?

4. The common-law system...assigns an enormous value to cross-examination. Indeed, the point of the famous "hearsay rule," perhaps the most elaborate rule in the arsenal of the law of evidence, is exactly this: if at all possible we should be able to quiz a witness directly. We do not want a witness to say that Joe said this and Mary said that; we want Joe or Mary to say it themselves, so that they can be grilled on the stand by the other side.

Lawrence M. Friedman, *American Law in the 20ᵗʰ Century*, Yale University Press, 2002, pp. 263–267

Friedman gives one reason that the criminal justice system prefers first-hand testimony over second-hand testimony. What is it? Can you think of other reasons?

5. "I'm getting 10 requests a week for Tamiflu," Dr. Steven Garner said. "These are people who want to hoard the drug in case the bird flu does come. At the same time, I have people worried they're gonna get the bird flu from the Thanksgiving turkey. Impossible. This whole thing is being wildly overhyped," he said.

He ought to know. For years, Garner ran the Kennedy Medical Center at Kennedy Airport, America's frontline defense against SARS, the Ebola virus and other nasty foreign bugs. These days, he runs the radiology operation at New York Methodist Hospital in Brooklyn.

Ellis Henican, One for the Birds, *AM New York*, 11/17/05

The writer says Dr. Garner should know about the dangers of bird flu. He is an expert on contagious diseases and epidemics. What makes him an expert?

6. Schlichtman had done what he could to prepare his experts, and most stood up fairly well.

There was, for example, the case of Dr. Vera Byers, an immunologist from California who had published some eighty-five articles on tumor immunology in respected journals such as *Lancet.*

Jonathan Harr, *A Civil Action*, Vintage Books, 1995, p. 253

What are Dr. Byers' credentials?

7. As divided as the public is on political issues, there's one thing we can all agree on when it comes to schools: parental involvement is key to student success.

Andrew Friedman, Lost Without Translation, *AM New York*, 11/19/04

Friedman says there is a consensus on what is key to student success in school. Do you think he means all of the public can agree, or almost all?

8. The will is one of the chief factors in belief, not that it creates belief, but because things are true or false according to the aspect in which we look at them. The will, which prefers one aspect to another, turns away the mind from considering the qualities of all that it does not like to see; and thus the mind, moving in accord with the will, stops to consider the aspect which it likes and so judges by what it sees.

Blaise Pascal, Thoughts, in Charles Hirschfeld, ed., *Classics of Western Thought: The Modern World*, Harcourt, Brace and World, 1964, p. 54

Pascal is describing one way in which people can fail to be objective. What does the mind do, in his opinion? What makes the way of thinking he describes subjective rather than objective?

9. On several occasions, U.S. Secretary of Defense Donald Rumsfeld described Al-Jazeera's coverage as propagandistic and inflammatory. He also accused the Arab network of manufacturing footage of dead civilians. Al-Jazeera, as it had many times before, defended its journalistic integrity and the public's right to view these images.

Mohammed El-Nawawy, Adel Iskandar, *Al-Jazeera*, Westview, 2002, p. 181

If Al-Jazeera showed film of civilians who died in an earthquake in Iraq, and identified them as civilians killed in an earthquake, would that be a fabrication? If they showed civilians killed by Al Qaeda terrorists, and identified them as such, would that be a fabrication? What do you think they must do to be guilty of fabricating footage of dead civilians?

10. Much of the material [for this book] comes from my own observations over a period of eight years, beginning in the winter of 1986, and from repeated interviews of those persons directly involved. The voluminous official record, particularly some fifty thousand pages of depositions and trial transcripts, provided another vital source.

Jonathan Harr, *A Civil Action*, Vintage Books, 1995, p. vi

Did Harr use first-hand information or did he rely only on second-hand information?

11. Above all, it [the scientific method] includes a respect for reality as something outside ourselves, that we explore but do not create. The realism of the working scientist is greatly strengthened by the experience (one that has often been my privilege to enjoy) of finding one's theoretical preconceptions overturned by experimental data.

Steven Weinberg, *Facing Up: Science and Its Cultural Adversaries*, Harvard University Press, 2001, p. 43

Does Weinberg say that the scientific method (a) depends on experts, (b) depends on consensus, (c) is objective, or (d) produces fabrications?

Exercise 3:   Analyzing Arguments

1. In the following example Tocqueville's conclusion is that Jefferson was a reliable source (what he said "is of especial weight.") What reasons lead him to that conclusion?

> We learn from President Jefferson's "Notes upon Virginia," p. 148, that among the Iroquois, when attacked by a superior force, aged men refused to fly or to survive the destruction of their country; and they braved death like the ancient Romans when their capital was sacked by the Gauls. Further on, p. 150, he tells us that there is no example of an Indian who, having fallen into the hands of his enemies, begged for his life; on the contrary, the captive sought to obtain death at the hands of his conquerors by the use of insult and provocation.... What is said by Jefferson is of especial weight, on account of the personal merit of the writer, of his peculiar position, and of the matter-of-fact age in which he lived.
>
> Alexis de Tocqueville, *Democracy in America*, translated by Henry Reeve, Bantam, 2000, [originally published in 1835], p. 26, notes i and j

2. Brian Innes says that teeth are very reliable evidence of identity. What reason or reasons does he give to support that conclusion?

> The teeth ... can provide a measure of the age of the body from which they have come as well as an important means of identification.... Once all the teeth have emerged, it is possible—as with horses and other animals—to make a rough estimate of age by noting the condition of the teeth, their degree of wear, the thickness of the dentine layer, and other indications....
>
> Deducing the age of adult teeth is therefore a very approximate method, but identification of persons by their teeth, both real teeth and dentures, has proved itself many times. This can often be based upon known features, such as crooked, missing or gappy teeth, or markings due to the occupation or habits of the owner....
>
> Nowadays, most people pay regular visits to the dentist, and detailed records are kept of fillings, extractions, bridges and dentures, plus any peculiarities or deformities. Throughout the world, there are about 200 different systems for making records, but they all provide a means of identification that is relatively easy, and almost 100 percent reliable. Dental records have proved invaluable in confirming the identity either of a single person (living or dead), or of a number of victims in a mass disaster.
>
> Brian Innes, *Bodies of Evidence*, Amber Books Ltd., 2000, pp. 79–80.

Exercise 4:   Apply the Ideas in Writing

Write two paragraphs. In the first, explain some first-hand knowledge that you have. For example, you might describe one of your teachers, or a place you have been. For your second paragraph, interview someone who also has some knowledge of the same thing. You might interview a person who is in the same teacher's class, or who has been to the same place. Report that person's information about the same topic. The information in the second paragraph will be second-hand information. The person's description might be similar to yours, or it might be different.

Try to get the other person's information without influencing what he or she says. For example, you shouldn't go to your classmate and say, "Don't you think Prof. Jones is funny? Isn't she hilarious in class?" Instead, you should say something like, "I would like you to help me with a project. How would you describe Prof. Jones?" or "What was the contestant on 'American Idol' like?" Have pen and paper ready so you can write down what your friend says.

Improving Your Writing 5: Transitions

You have learned that good paragraphs have several qualities: They are unified around one main idea, they use specific information to develop the main idea, and the examples and details are organized in some sensible way, e.g., chronologically.

Another way to improve your paragraphs is to use *transition* words. Transition words are like road signs—they tell your reader what is coming next or what direction to go. *However* is a transition word that means "the next idea contrasts with, or conflicts with, the one you just read." Example: "Smith doesn't like to exercise. However, he knows it is good for him, so he does it anyway."

You can use transition words to signal other shifts besides contrasts. *First, next,* and *finally* are useful. *So,* in the preceding example, is also a transition word. It tells your reader that you are going to state a result of something, or a decision. Similar words are *therefore, consequently,* and *thus.* Transition words help your reader see the organization you are using.

CHAPTER 6 ◆

Degrees of Belief

32. possible

33. probable

34. plausible

35. convincing

36. certain

37. skeptical

38. dogmatic

Do you want to see the latest Harry Potter movie? If you've seen it do you want to see it again? Do you want to buy some new shoes or new sunglasses? Do you want to get a college degree? Do you want to have a good job? You would probably answer these questions in different ways. You want some things very much, you want other things a little, and other things you don't care about at all. In other words, desires come in degrees: intense, moderate, small, none at all.

The same applies to beliefs. You can believe something very strongly, or moderately, or slightly. For example, I'm sure that the sun is shining outside because I can see it with my eyes. I'm pretty sure that my wife is in the kitchen because she was there a few minutes ago. But I can't hear her, and she might have gone out. So I don't hold that belief as strongly as the one about the sun. I believe a washer is probably available in the laundry room downstairs because it's late afternoon and people don't usually do their laundry at this time. But I'm not sure. I could easily be mistaken about that. I think I remember reading somewhere that the circumference of the earth is about 24,000 miles. But I wouldn't bet money on it. These examples show that beliefs, like desires, come in degrees. Believing is not like being pregnant; you can't be "a little bit pregnant." But you can have "a little bit of belief" about something. We don't say "a little bit of belief," but we do have other words to describe degrees of belief, and they can be very useful.

The strength of your belief probably depends on where your belief came from, or the basis of your belief. If I can see the sun shining with my own eyes, then I have a strong belief that the sun is shining. Direct, personal experience

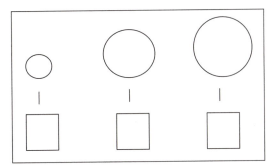

Figure 6.1
Everyone holds some beliefs (represented by circles) more strongly than other beliefs. Here the size of the circle symbolizes the degree of the belief, i.e., the degree of confidence or certainty. The size of the circle *should* depend on the size of the size of the support, i.e., the reliability of the source. But sometimes people believe things strongly regardless of the evidence.

is a solid foundation for belief. If I remember talking with a friend yesterday, I have a pretty strong belief that the conversation happened. But it could have been the day before yesterday; our memories sometimes trick us. If a documentary program on TV tells me that people lived in South America ten thousand years ago, I believe it, although I realize they could be mistaken. I don't believe it as strongly as I believe what I see with my own eyes. If a friend tells me that he heard from someone else that taking large amounts of zinc will make you immune to most diseases, I probably won't believe it at all. It conflicts with other things I believe about disease and immunity, and the source of the belief ("someone") is unknown. So your degree of belief usually depends on the relation between the belief and the basis of the belief, or why you have the belief. The better the basis, the stronger the belief.

Degree of belief is similar to fact and opinion. Remember that facts have been proven, whereas opinions have not. The words in this chapter take that two-part classification and sub-divide it further into several parts. Some beliefs are factual. You know they are true. With opinions, you aren't absolutely sure they are true, but you are more sure about some than others. The fact and opinion classification is like dividing people into "college graduates" and "non-graduates." The degree of belief classification is like recognizing that some people (seniors) are closer to graduating than others (juniors), who are closer than sophomores, who are closer than freshmen.

Part 1. Definitions

32. possible. could occur, able to happen. "It is possible to fly non-stop from Los Angeles to Hong Kong." In relation to belief, "It's possible" means that you might believe it, or you might not. You haven't decided yet.

possibility (noun). something that could happen, or that might exist; "Meeting Frank at the party is a possibility."

Example

32a. Problems have parameters—the facts behind key assumptions. We like to think of parameters as constants, but they often change dramatically. When they change, the set of **possible** solutions changes with them. Heavier-than-air flight may have been **impossible** in 1803. But by 1903, parameters had changed. Light-weight engines of sufficient power were available. Fuel efficiency had increased. There were better materials and better tools. Flight was a viable solution. Now parameters are changing faster than ever before.

Scott Thorpe, *How to Think Like Einstein*, Sourcebooks, Inc., 2000, p. 90

33. probable. more likely than not, something one can expect to happen; predictable. "The probable result of lighting a match in the garage at the present time is an explosion."

probably (adverb). a quality of an event that is likely to happen.

Comment

An adverb is a word that works with a verb—an action word—to say *how* the action occurs: quickly, brightly, completely, and so on. Many adverbs end in "ly." "Probably" indicates how something will happen.

Example

33a. In our world, causality and connectedness are everywhere. One event causes another or is associated with it in some way. If one yellow flower in a patch contains nectar, the others **probably** also will. If the sky gets dark with clouds, rain is likely to follow. If a lion crouches in the grass nearby, she is **probably** about to rush out to capture prey.

Dorothy Hinshaw Patent, *How Smart Are Animals?* Harcourt, Brace, Jovanovich, 1990, p. 163

34. plausible. believable, reasonable, seeming to be true. "Jim's explanation of the accident was plausible."

plausibility (noun). The quality of being believable, reasonable, possible.

Example

34a. Ms. Sawyer, a former science reporter for *The Washington Post*, takes a fly-on-the-wall approach as she follows, in sometimes numbing detail, the slow work of observation leading to new hypotheses, some **plausible**, some seemingly fantastic. Did meteorites from Mars, carrying primitive life forms, create life on Earth? Or as Richard

Zare, a laser chemist who worked on the rock, put it, "Is it possible that actually we're all Martians?"

William Grimes, How the Mars Rock Set the Earth Spinning, *New York Times*, 2/25/06

35. convincing. (adjective) causing belief; evidence is convincing if it leads you to adopt a belief. "The jury decided the witness's testimony was convincing so they voted unanimously to find the defendant not guilty."

People can be convinced by a person, a speech, an observation, or other experiences.

to convince (verb). to give someone evidence or facts that lead him or her to believe something.

Example

35a. Long ago, the vast majority of evangelicals became **convinced** that war is not always wrong. Drawing on the clear teachings of both Testaments, they concluded that there is such a thing as a moral right—even duty—to serve as a soldier. The biblical evidence is set forth in such passages as Romans 13. There the apostle Paul teaches that civil authority functions as "the servant of God to execute his wrath on the wrongdoer."

Kenneth S. Kantzer, in David L. Bender and Bruno Leone, eds., *War and Human Nature*, Greenhaven Press, 1983, p. 80

36. certain. (adjective) completely sure, having no doubts. "The answer is 378. I'm certain of it. I did the calculations myself and checked them twice." Being certain is a state of mind. One can be certain and still mistaken. "Jim said he was certain that he left the keys by the front door, but they were actually in the kitchen."

certainty (noun).

Example

36a. That quizzical expression on your dog's face means he didn't quite understand when you asked if he wanted to go out, so you patiently repeat it. This time he barks in response, which you take for a 'yes'. Does his behavior mean he understood the question? How could you know for **certain**? Even if you could look inside his head, you would only see his brain, not his mind. In assessing intelligence and other mental abilities, behavior is all we have to go by.

Sonja I Yoerg, *Clever as a Fox*, Bloomsbury, 2001, p. 14

37. skeptical. inclined not to believe something or someone, feeling doubtful. "Jerry told Claire he would pay her back on Thursday, but she was skeptical."

skepticism (noun). an attitude of disbelief; doubt.

Example

37a. In one of Montaigne's most notable essays on the subject of knowledge and reason (Vol II, Essay 12), he revealed himself as a philosophical relativist and **skeptic**. He spoke of the limits of reason in efforts to comprehend the universe. Neither theology, classical wisdom, nor science can provide final answers to the "big questions"; all knowledge is subject to uncertainty and doubt.

Thomas H. Greer, *A Brief History of Western Man*, Third Edition, Harcourt, Brace, Jovanovich, 1977, pp. 293–294

38. dogmatic. feeling certain about something when you have no good reason to feel certain; holding a belief in spite of evidence that it is mistaken. Some people are blindly loyal to a person when they shouldn't be; some people are blindly loyal to a belief when they shouldn't be. "We tried to talk about the other party's candidate, but the campaign worker was dogmatic and wouldn't even listen."

dogma (noun). a set of beliefs or statements that one is supposed to believe without questioning them. "Susan couldn't explain *why* she believed the soul was immortal; it was just one of the dogmas of her religion."

Example

38a. [Judith] Rich Harris has systematically demolished the **dogma** that has lain, unchallenged, beneath twentieth-century social science: the assumption that parents shape the personality and culture of their children. In Sigmund Freud's psychology, John Watson's behaviorism and Margaret Mead's anthropology, nurture-determinism by parents was never tested, only assumed. Yet the evidence, from twin studies, from the children of immigrants and from adoption studies, is now staring us in the face: people get their personalities from their genes and from their peers, not from their parents.

Matt Ridley, *Genome: The Autobiography of a Species in 23 Chapters*, HarperCollins Publishers, 1999, pp. 305–306

Test Yourself

Match each word with its definition.

32. possible
33. probable
34. plausible
35. convincing
36. certain
37. skeptical
38. dogmatic

a. causing a person to believe something
b. believable, reasonable

c. able to happen
d. holding tightly to a belief without considering the possibility that it could be wrong
e. feeling completely sure
f. likely to happen, predictable
g. being inclined not to believe something

Part 2. Understanding the Meaning

32. possible.

32b. Solar sails gain thrust from the energy of solar photons reflecting off their mirrorlike surface. The force exerted by those photons is minuscule but persistent. Because the supply of sunlight is essentially limitless, a solar sail could keep accelerating long after a conventional rocket would run out of fuel.

Huge solar sails may someday propel ships big enough to carry passengers, [Junichiro] Kawaguchi says: "Round trips between Earth's vicinity and other planets are not a dream, but realistically **possible**."

Tony McNicol, Japan Sets Sail in Space, *Discover*, January, 2005, p. 63

32c. Einstein's laws don't completely rule out the **possibility** of interstellar travel, but they do make it extremely unlikely. Any would-be starship captain faces two obstacles. First, nothing can travel faster than the speed of light. Since the closest star to Earth is about four light-years away, even a spaceship traveling at half the speed of light would need eight years for the voyage [one way]. . . . Second, Einstein's theory of special relativity dictates that time itself would flow much more slowly on a rocket moving at near light speeds than it would on Earth. . . . "The problem with interstellar travel is not really that things are so far away—it's coming back and finding that what for you was one year was 1 million years on Earth. That is pretty depressing," says physicist Joao Magueijo.

Tim Folger, At the Speed of Light: What If Einstein Was Wrong? *Discover*, April, 2003

32d. But is happiness really a single dimension of experience running from extreme misery to extreme joy? Or is it **possible** to be both happy and unhappy at the same time? The broad answer to this is no; it is not **possible** to be happy and unhappy at the same time. Positive feelings damp down negative feelings and vice versa. So we have just one dimension—running from the extreme negative to the extreme positive.

Richard Layard, *Happiness: Lessons from a New Science*, Penguin, 2005, p. 21

Figure 6.2
At the 1964 World's Fair, people thought that undersea cities were possible in the near future. *Source: Associate Press*

Comment

The term "possible" can be used in two ways, and that leads to misunderstandings. "It is possible at the present time for Queen Latifah, who weighs about 200 pounds, to run a mile in four minutes." Is that true? Some say yes, some say no. It would be easy to test the statement, but "possible" is about things that haven't been tested yet. So is it possible now?

Some say no, it's not possible. If we accept certain known facts, then it is not physically possible at the present time. We know how muscles work and the limits on them. Science tells us it is impossible for muscles to lift a certain amount of weight, or work a long time at a certain speed, or exercise without replacing oxygen and sugar. All these facts make it impossible for Queen Latifah to run a mile in four minutes. We can call this "physical possibility," or "narrow possibility."

On the other hand, some say it *is* possible at the present time. They like to use their imagination, and for them the word "possible" covers a wider range than present facts and scientific laws. Scientific facts are never absolutely certain. Very often what scientists thought was not possible turned out to be possible after all. The "facts" (as people understand them) can change. Even if the facts about muscles don't change, and no muscle can move so much weight so fast, why should we limit ourselves to the actual world? "Possible" includes what could happen if nature were different. In our world, as it is now, maybe Queen Latifah could not run a mile in four minutes, but in another world with different laws and facts, it is possible. I can imagine it, so it's possible, some people say. It's not like asking, "Can Queen Latifah be in two places at once?" or "Can the ball be red all over and green all over at the same time?" We can't even imagine those things. We can call this "logical possibility," or "wide possibility," in contrast with physical possibility. You might see the word used in either of these ways, although usually people mean physical possibility.

> 32e. Attacking Marxism, the anarchist Mikhail Bakunin pointed out that it would be **impossible** to put workers at the head of government, because then they would cease to be workers and instead would become governors.
>
> Steven Weinberg, *Facing Up: Science and Its Cultural Adversaries*, Harvard University Press, 2001, p. 253

Question: When Bakunin says it is impossible to put workers at the head of the government, does he mean impossible in the physical sense or the logical sense?

33. probable.

> 33b. [R]esearchers point out that people have a natural tendency to disregard high-consequence risks if they have a low **probability**. For example, many people are willing to live in houses built on the slopes of volcanoes, along earthquake faults, in tornado lanes and hurricane paths, and on exposed peninsulas and low-lying islands. We know that natural disasters may occur, but because the chances of a disaster striking any one particular site are low, the decision to build in a potentially dangerous area doesn't seem too risky.
>
> Ray Spangenburg, Kit Moser, *If an Asteroid Hit Earth*, Grolier, 2000, p. 48

> 33c. Major MacDonald had had no direct experience with the subject of UFO's in his Air Force career, but he had a profound respect for it.... He realized the complete **probability** of the phenomena, that the valid reports were by no means unrealistic or absurd and that extraterrestrial life was not only possible but entirely **probable**. Space programs on the earth included impact landings on Venus and a soft landing on the moon—so why couldn't the reverse process be taking place?
>
> John G. Fuller, *The Interrupted Journey*, Dell, 1966, p. 65

Question: Does the fact that human beings have sent rockets to Venus and beyond, and have visited the moon, make it probable that beings from other planets have visited Earth in their spaceships?

Comment

How do you decide whether something is probable or not? For example, if you are with your friend Derek at the ice cream shop after school, is it probable that he will order chocolate ice cream? There are two ways to decide. One way is to look at similar situations in the past. If Derek has gone with you to the ice cream shop many times, and if he has ordered chocolate every single time, then it is highly probable that he will order chocolate this time. If he's never ordered chocolate, then it's improbable. If he ordered chocolate half the time and vanilla the other times, you can say there is a 50 percent chance he will order chocolate this time. That's one way to calculate probabilities—by looking at how often something happened in the past. In Example 33a the writer is saying that biologists have seen lions crouching in the grass many times, and in most of those cases, the lion rushed out to capture prey. (That's how weather forecasters say "there is a 60 percent chance of rain tomorrow." Sixty percent of the time in the past, when conditions were similar, it rained.)

The other way to decide whether something is probable is to figure out all the possibilities, and see what percentage of them includes the event you are thinking about. For example, if you flip a coin, what is the probability of getting "heads"? It's 50 percent, of course, because there are only two possibilities: heads or tails. That is, heads make up 50 percent of all the possibilities. Suppose I say I'm holding an ace from an ordinary deck of cards. What is the probability that it is a diamond? It's 25 percent, because there are four aces (hearts, diamonds, spades, clubs), and having a diamond is 25 percent of those possibilities. Suppose you walk into the ice cream shop for the first time with Derek, and you don't know what he's ordered in the past. You have no idea what kind of ice cream he likes. But you can see that the shop serves only chocolate, vanilla, and strawberry. If that is the only information you have, you can say that the chances of Derek ordering chocolate are one in three, or 33 percent. Ordering chocolate is 33 percent of all the possibilities.

In Example 33b people are thinking that there are thousands of places that a tornado could strike, and their house is only one of them, one in thousands. So the probability that it will hit their house is small. (Or they might be calculating probability in the other way. They might be thinking that no tornado has ever struck in exactly this place before, so it's unlikely one will strike in this place in the future.)

Opposite. improbable.

> 33d. The combination lock on my bicycle has 4,096 different positions. Every one of these is equally "**improbable**" in the sense that, if you spin the wheels at random, every one of the 4,096 positions is equally unlikely to turn up.

Richard Dawkins, *The Blind Watchmaker*, W. W. Norton and Co., 1987, p. 7

Comment

The chances that any specific combination (e.g., "123") will come up are 1 in 4,096. Getting exactly that number on a random spin is improbable. It's like walking into the ice cream shop with Derek when you don't know what he likes, but they have 4,096 flavors and he could choose any of them.

33e. If Louisville's 20-point come-from-behind victory over West Virginia was **improbable**, Illinois's 90–89 overtime comeback to win its 36th game of the season was downright unbelievable.

William C. Rhoden, Unbelievably, They Made New Believers, *New York Times*, 3/27/05

33f. Not you. But yes, *you*. For Stanley Milgram proved it to be true, in Linsly-Chittenden Hall, and then later in a lab in Bridgeport, and then still later in replications all around the world. Sixty-two to sixty-five percent of us, when faced with a credible authority, will follow orders to the point of lethally harming a person.

This seems **improbable**, impossible, especially because you are—I am—a humanist at heart.

So were his subjects, many of them....

Even today, forty years after the lesson of Milgram has supposedly been learned, people still say, "Not me."

Yes you.

The power of Milgram's experiments lies, perhaps, right here, in the great gap between what we think about ourselves, and who we frankly are.

Lauren Slater, *Opening Skinner's Box: Great Psychological Experiments of the Twentieth Century*, W. W. Norton and Co., 2004, p. 40

Comment

In Examples 33e and 33f, the writers are estimating probability in a different way from Dawkins in Example 33d. Remember that you can decide what is probable or not based on what has happened in the past. If Derek chose chocolate every time, then you could say it is probable that he will choose chocolate next time, even if the shop has 4,000 flavors. Rhoden and Slater are estimating probability on the basis of what they have seen in the past (comebacks in sports, people treating others badly), not on the basis of how many possibilities there are.

33g. Creatures are not born with desires unless satisfaction for those desires exists. A baby feels hunger: well, there is such a thing as food. A duckling wants to swim: well, there is such a thing as water. Men feel sexual desire: well, there is such a thing as sex. If I find in myself a desire which no experience in this world can satisfy, the most **probable** explanation is that I was made for another world.

C. S. Lewis, quoted in Francis S. Collins, *The Language of God*, Free Press, 2006, p. 38

34. plausible.

34b. Generalization 2 said that children who are hugged are more likely to be nice, children who are beaten are more likely to be unpleasant. Turn that statement around and you get one that is equally **plausible**: nice children are more likely to be hugged, unpleasant children are more likely to be beaten. Do the hugs cause the children's niceness, or is the children's niceness the reason why they are hugged, or are both true? Do beatings make children unpleasant, or are parents more likely to lose their temper with unpleasant children, or are both true?

Judith Rich Harris, *The Nurture Assumption: Why Children Turn Out the Way They Do*, The Free Press, 1998, pp. 27–28

34c. Generally speaking, the process for determining factual issues in litigation is the same as that used by people in their ordinary affairs. When the accounts of witnesses differ, the truth is judged by estimating the witnesses' opportunities to observe, the apparent trustworthiness of their recall, and their possible bias in one direction or another. Also significant is the inherent **plausibility** of their accounts, judged by experience in everyday life.

Geoffrey C. Hazard, Jr., and Michele Taruffo, *American Civil Procedure: An Introduction*, Yale University Press, 1993, p. 79

(*Litigation* means legal proceedings, i.e., a trial or some other judicial process of resolving disputes.)

34d. Many of our interpretations of history rest on apparent **plausibility**....For instance, the Bible mentions instances of child sacrifice. Did these really occur? Some scholars believe they did not, because child sacrifice was not part of the culture and civilization of the ancient near East. But then child sacrifice is not part of the culture or civilization of contemporary India: yet it occurs in India. With respect to matters of this kind, one can usually believe what one wants to believe, for the evidence is sufficiently scanty so that competing conclusions are equally **plausible**.

Morton A. Kaplan, *On Historical and Political Knowing: An Inquiry into Some Problems of Universal Law and Human Freedom*, University of Chicago Press, 1971, pp. 64–65

Comment

Plausible means almost the same as *possible*, but not exactly the same. *Possible* usually applies to events or actions. A flood is possible, it is possible for Karen to win, selling the chair on ebay is a possibility. *Plausible*, on the other hand, usually applies to beliefs or statements or explanations, that is, it applies to the ways people think about events and actions. (The word *explanation* is similar. It can be about things that happen, but it can also be about what people *say* about things that happen: "Robin's explanation.") In the preceding examples, Harris says a statement is plausible, Hazard and Taruffo say an account—testimony—is plausible, and Kaplan says interpretations are plausible. A statement is plausible if it could very well be true.

You decide whether a statement is plausible or not by thinking about causes and effects and generalizations. If the statement does not violate any known laws of nature, and if it seems to fit in with other laws, then it's plausible. In Harris' example, she says being a nice child might cause your parents to hug you, and being unpleasant might cause them to beat you. That could happen, as far as we know, and so the statement is plausible.

35. convincing.

35b. [A European or American] has never seen an outsider, perhaps, unless the outsider has already been Europeanized. If he has traveled, he has very likely been around the world without ever staying outside of a cosmopolitan hotel. He knows little of any ways of life but his own. The uniformity of custom, of outlook, that he sees spread about him seems **convincing** enough, and conceals from him the fact that it is after all an historical accident. He accepts without more ado the equivalence of human nature and his own cultural standards.

Ruth Benedict, *Patterns of Culture*, Houghton Mifflin, 1934, pp. 5–6

35c. An effort to apply scientific methodology centered in Germany, where Leopold von Ranke launched the "objective" school of historiography. He announced that he and his students would describe the past "as it actually happened." Sentiment and national bias were to be set aside, and historical documents were to be collected and interpreted in a rigorously critical fashion. Near the end of the [nineteenth] century the scientific vogue was carried by historians from German to American universities.

Ranke wrote some laudable histories, and his stress on methodology was wholesome for the discipline. He did not **convince** all historians, however, that it is possible to reconstruct a single true picture of what "actually happened."

Thomas H. Greer, *A Brief History of Western Man*, Third Edition, Harcourt, Brace, Jovanovich, 1977, p. 455

(*Laudable* means praiseworthy, admirable.)

35d. After many months, when it had become apparent that Nancy [Cruzan] had no chance of improving, her parents asked hospital employees to terminate her ANH [artificial life support]. As in *Quinlan*, they refused, and the parents had to go to court. Evidence at trial indicated that Nancy had previously told a roommate that if sick or injured she "would not wish to continue her life" unless she "could live at least halfway normally."

Years later, the case arrived in the U.S. Supreme Court on a narrow legal issue—whether Missouri could impose an elevated standard of proof for the judicial determination of Nancy's wishes. In civil cases, the usual standard of proof is "preponderance of the evidence," meaning more likely than not. Were that the standard in *Cruzan*, Nancy's parents would have had to prove only that Nancy more likely than not would want to have her feeding tube removed and be allowed to die. Sometimes, however, in special cases, civil courts require a higher standard of proof—"clear and **convincing** evidence"—which lies somewhere between preponderance of the evidence and proof "beyond a reasonable doubt," the standard applied in criminal cases. The Missouri Supreme Court had imposed the "clear and **convincing** evidence" standard and concluded that Nancy's comment to her roommate did not meet this standard.

Jon B. Eisenberg, *Using Terri: The Religious Right's Conspiracy to Take Away Our Rights*, HarperSanFrancisco, 2005, p. 28

Question: Why do you think the testimony from Cruzan's roommate did not meet the "clear and convincing evidence" standard? Would you believe the roommate? Would you believe her strongly enough to end Cruzan's life? What would count as convincing evidence that Cruzan did not want to continue living in a permanent vegetative state?

36. certain.

36b. One of the few cases where biology has become big science is the Human Genome Project, which is the monumental effort to sequence every component of every gene of the DNA of human beings (see Chapter 23). It will give us lots of answers—and lots of questions—concerning disease. It's also going to open up new areas, including the functioning of the nervous system. Many discoveries will be made as a consequence of completing the genome. Of this much I'm **certain**.

Francisco Ayala, in Robert Lawrence Kuhn, ed., *Closer to Truth: Challenging Current Beliefs*, McGraw-Hill, 2000, p. 331

Comment

Ayala could have said, "Of this much I'm convinced." What is the difference between being convinced and being certain? Different people will use the words in slightly different ways, and for some there may be no difference. But for most people, being certain is a stronger belief. If you are certain that new discoveries will be made, then it is hard to imagine being mistaken. You can count on it. If you are convinced, then you are still confident, you fully expect new discoveries, but you realize that you could be wrong. It's just unlikely that you are.

36c. Former American hostages Chuck Scott, David Roeder, William J. Daugherty and Don A Sharer told AP that after seeing [Mahmoud]

Ahmadinejad on television, they were **certain** he was one of the hostage-takers [from 1979]. A fifth ex-hostage, Kevin Hermening, said he reached the same conclusion after looking at photos.

"I can absolutely guarantee you he was not only one of the hostage-takers, he was present at my interrogation," Roeder told AP in an interview from his home in Pinehurst, N.C., though he added, "It's sort of more mannerisms."....

Bijan Adibi, another former hostage-taker [in Iran], also viewed the photos [from 1979] and didn't believe it was Ahmadinejad. He noted the man in the picture is about the same height as everyone else in it, including the American. Adibi said Ahmadinejad is a little shorter than him—and Adibi stands at about 5 feet 2 inches.

"Look at every picture of Ahmadinejad today and he is at least a head shorter. In this picture, this man is the height of the American," Adibi said. "For many other reasons, I am **certain** that this picture is not Ahmadinejad."

Ali Akbar Dareini, Hostage-Takers: Iran's Leader Had No Role, *Associated Press*, 6/30/05

36d. Again, no person is **certain**, apart from faith, whether he is awake or asleep, seeing that during sleep we believe that we are awake as firmly as we do when we *are* awake; we believe that we see space, figure and mass; we are aware of the passage of time, we measure it; and in fact we act as if we were awake. So that half of our life being passed in sleep, we have on our own admission no idea of truth, whatever we may imagine. As all our intuitions are, then, illusions, who knows whether the other half of our life, in which we think we are awake, is not another sleep a little different from the former, from which we awake when we suppose ourselves asleep?

Blaise Pascal, Thoughts, in Charles Hirschfeld, ed., *Classics of Western Thought: The Modern World*, Harcourt, Brace and World, 1964, p. 55

Comment

Pascal, in Example 36d, says we cannot be certain whether we are dreaming or waking. I am pretty sure that I am awake right now, but maybe my feeling doesn't reach the level of certainty. For Pascal, at least, and maybe for others, being certain is rare and difficult. It means something like "absolutely sure," or "couldn't be mistaken." However, in Example 36c, the Americans say they are certain that Ahmadinejad was a hostage-taker in 1979. But Adibi is certain that the hostage-taker in the photo is not Ahmadinejad. Ahmadinejad is shorter than the man in the photo. One side is wrong, even though both sides say they are certain. How sure must you be before you are certain? Different people use the word in slightly different ways.

37. skeptical.

37b. Like many of the other scholars on the subject, Pape is deeply **skeptical** about the notion that suicide bombers are the warriors in a "clash of civilizations" between Islam and the West. Pape's survey reveals that there is nothing intrinsically "Islamic" about the suicide bomber. By his estimate, Islamist groups account for no more than 34.6 percent of the suicide terrorist attacks staged in the past 20 years. The real common denominator of suicide terrorism campaigns, he argues, is that they are all, in one form or another, responses to occupation or foreign control of a national homeland.

Christian Caryl, Why They Do It, *New York Review of Books*, 9/22/05

Figure 6.3
Does this woman appear to be skeptical, or receptive, toward the man's ideas? *Source: © Nicholas Sutcliffe/Shutterstock Images LLC*

37c. About 100 years ago, vigorous exercise was considered danger-ous, possibly even fatal. It wasn't until the 1970s that this fear was replaced with the opposite, equally pervasive view that intense exer-cise would actually prolong life. New York Times science writer Gina Kolata explores the origins of such "facts" about exercise, and how much truth they hold, in her fascinating new book, *Ultimate Fitness: The Quest for Truth About Exercise and Health....*

   Kolata is also a natural **skeptic** whose research with leading experts led her to conclude that many current popular beliefs about exercise are unproven.... Kolata warns that sound research gets lost in the claims of companies that sell fitness and nutritional products.

Nicole Gregory, The Truth About Exercise and Health, *Shape*, Aug, 2003

38. dogmatic.

38b. While Aristotle believed that an underlying unity would be found to all knowledge, he accepted that in the present state of knowledge much must remain provisional and unsure. Take, for example, a difficult question in the natural world, how to differentiate between "plants" and "animals." A **dogmatic** scientist might have drawn up some arbitrary rules and simply classified each organism as one or the other. Aristotle realized that this was to avoid the real issue. He took some examples from the marine world, the sponge, the jellyfish, sea anemones, razor shells. He noted that when a sponge was pulled from a rock to which it was attached, it reacted by clinging to the rock. So perhaps it was some kind of animal. Yet it could not live detached from a rock, as an animal would.... Aristotle's genius lay in realizing that these issues had to be worked out **undogmatically**, that observation had to continue and that sometimes the boundaries between categories would have to be redrawn as a result.... It was this openness to the provisional nature of knowledge that helps make Aristotle one of the truly great philosophers.

Charles Freeman, *The Closing of the Western Mind: The Rise of Faith and the Fall of Reason*, Alfred A. Knopf, 2003, 2021

38c. A devout Christian can practice an uncompromising skepticism toward the mythologies of other faiths and cultures, in the fashion of Charlemagne striking down the Saxon idols and defying their wrath, confident that no such heathen divinities existed. But a Christian's skepticism is necessarily partisan, sparing the believer any critical examination of his own **dogmas**.

Theodore Roszak, *The Making of a Counter Culture*, Doubleday, 1969, p. 211

Question: Being dogmatic and being skeptical are attitudes. Do you know anyone who is often dogmatic, about many things, or anyone who is often skep-tical? Why do you think they are like that?

Figure 6.4
People who hold beliefs dogmatically see others' ideas and points of view as threats, and defend themselves by shouting and throwing tantrums. *Source: © Nicholas Sutcliffe/ Shutterstock Images LLC*

Part 3. Applying the Words

32. possible
33. probable
34. plausible
35. convincing
36. certain
37. skeptical
38. dogmatic

Exercise 1:   Choose the Right Word

For each sentence, choose the best word (or an appropriate form of the word) to fill in the blank.

1. The prospector said he was sure he would strike a rich vein of gold in just a few more days, but his friends were _____.
2. The defense attorney's case was _____ because he produced a great deal of specific, factual evidence to support it.

3. Polls have been wrong in the past. The election is two weeks away, so Jones can still win. It's _____.
4. Mike said he was _____ that Jill was at the party because he had spoken to her.
5. It doesn't matter that you are advertising more. If you raise prices by five percent, I believe your sales will decrease. That's the most _____ outcome.
6. I have a hunch about this applicant for the job, and I'm sure he wouldn't be a good fit, but I don't want to be _____ about it.
7. Although people believe their horoscopes, is it really _____ that stars and planets millions of miles away will determine whether you get a job or meet an interesting person?

Exercise 2: Apply the Words

Read each example and answer the questions that follow.

> 1. It is reasonable to assume that being reared by smart parents increases a child's IQ, but it is not reasonable to assume, for example, that being reared by bossy parents makes a child bossier. Maybe being reared by bossy parents makes a child meek and passive.
>
> Judith Rich Harris, *The Nurture Assumption: Why Children Turn Out the Way They Do*, The Free Press, 1998, p. 22

Harris' main point is to say that something is possible. What is possible? She also says something is probable. What is probable?

> 2. Intuition is tricky. Gamblers' intuitions, for example, are notoriously flawed (to the profitable delight of casino operators). You are playing the roulette wheel and hit five reds in a row. Should you stay with red because you are on a "hot streak" or should you switch because black is "due"? It doesn't matter because the roulette wheel has no memory, but try telling that to the happy gambler whose pile of chips grows before his eyes.
>
> Michael Shermer, *The Science of Good and Evil*, Henry Holt and Company, 2004, p. 170

Remember that there are two ways to decide probability: based on all the possibilities (e.g., the ice cream store sells three flavors, so the chances Derek will pick one of them is 33 percent), or based on past results (e.g., 9 times out of 10 Derek has chosen chocolate, so now the chances that he will pick chocolate are 90 percent). Which method should you use with a roulette wheel? (All the slots on a roulette wheel [except one] are either red or black.) Which method is the person who follows a "hot streak" using?

> 3. People without the slightest knowledge of economics or the slightest experience running a business will boldly assert that women are paid only 75 percent—or some other percent—of what men make for doing exactly the same work.
>
> Think about it. If an employer could hire four women for the price of hiring three men, why would he ever hire men at all?

> Even if the employer was the world's biggest sexist he could still
> not survive in business if his competitors were getting one third more
> output from their employees for the same money.
>
> Thomas Sowell, The Grand Fallacy, Part 1, *Shelby Star*, 8/3/04

Some people say it is plausible that women are paid 75 percent of what men are paid for exactly the same work. It is plausible, they say, because that belief fits in with what we know about sex discrimination. But Sowell says the belief is implausible. He says the belief does not fit in with other things we know. What other things?

> 4. But while there is little, if any, scientific evidence that genetically
> modified foods are harmful, in much of Europe they are so unpopular
> that mainstream supermarket giants like Migros will not stock them....
>
>   Biotech companies like Monsanto and Syngenta insist that the crops
> should be immediately admitted to Europe, because genetically engi-
> neered foods have been consumed in much of the world for a decade
> without obvious ill effects. Their safety, said Christopher Horner, a
> Monsanto spokesman, has been "ratified by numerous credible regu-
> latory and scientific authorities."
>
> Elisabeth Rosenthal, Biotech Food Tears Rifts in Europe, *New York Times*, 6/6/06

Monsanto says genetically modified foods have been consumed for ten years with no ill effects. Therefore, on the question of the safety of such foods, should people be (a) skeptical, (b) convinced, or (c) dogmatic (according to Monsanto)?

> 5. The fool maintains an error with the assurance of a man who can
> never be mistaken: the sensible man defends a truth with the circum-
> spection of a man who may be mistaken.
>
> De Bruix, in Norman Lockridge, ed., *The Golden Treasury of the World's Wit and Wisdom*,
> Halcyon House, 1936, p. 65

Is De Bruix saying that the fool is convinced, or that he is certain?

> 6. Don't get me wrong. I am not against the ownership of firearms. I
> recognize and understand the fear that drives some people to purchase
> guns. But I don't buy the argument that allowing average citizens to carry
> concealed handguns will cut down on crime and increase public safety.
>
> Bill Kolender, in William Dudley, ed., *Opposing Viewpoints in Social Issues*, Greenhaven
> Press, 2000, p. 25

Kolender is skeptical. Exactly what statement is he skeptical about? (a) "People buy guns because they are afraid." (b) "Carrying concealed guns will cut down on crime." (c) "People ought to be free to own guns."

> 7. But far more important than the creation of the First International
> [organization of workers] was the peculiar tone which Marx injected
> into working-class affairs. This was the most quarrelsome and intol-

erant of men, and from the beginning he was unable to believe that anyone who did not follow his line of reasoning could possibly be right.

Robert L. Heilbroner, *The Worldly Philosophers*, Touchstone, 1992, p. 152

Being dogmatic means holding a belief very firmly even though you do not have enough reason to be so confident that it is true, or even if it seems contrary to the facts. Is being quarrelsome and intolerant enough to show that Marx was dogmatic, in your opinion?

8. One thing doctors know for sure is that by the time breast tumors are discovered in young women, the masses tend to be larger and often more advanced, says Lyndsay Harris, M.D., assistant professor of medicine at Harvard School of Medicine in Boston. That's partly because their tumors may grow faster, but also because there's no reliable way to catch them early. Annual mammograms or ultrasounds are not recommended until age 40, unless you have a strong family history....

Scientists have also discovered that while older women's cancers are usually driven by hormones, young women are more likely to have hormone-negative tumors, which other, often unknown factors stimulate.

Elizabeth DeVita-Raeburn, Why Do Young Women Get Cancer?, *Self*, October, 2004

The following three statements are based on this passage. Which one is known with certainty, which one states a probability, and which one is plausible?

a. If an older woman has breast cancer, it is caused by hormones.
b. Breast tumors doctors find in young women tend to be larger than tumors in older women.
c. If women had mammograms beginning at age 20, their breast tumors would be smaller when discovered.

Exercise 3: Analyzing Arguments

The following passage is about a murder investigation. It was written by a forensic scientist investigating the evidence and drawing conclusions from it. (*Forensic* means having to do with trials and crimes.) Read the passage and answer the question that follows.

[Earl Morey's body was found near a lake; he had been shot to death. The principal suspect was Richard Duntz.] Two types of shoeprints were also found next to the body. One, having a wavy design, was consistent with that of the sole pattern of Earl's sneakers; the other had a special hexagonal design. Subsequently, at the laboratory, my assistant, Ken Zercie, discovered that a Korean company was the only one that manufactured such a sneaker with this particular sole pattern. The model name was Foot Joy. During a later search of Richard's apartment, investigators didn't find any Foot Joys, but they found the next best thing: a photograph of him wearing such a pair. This proved he had more than likely been at the scene, but it did not prove that he was the killer.

Dr. Henry C. Lee, Jerry Labriola, *Dr. Henry Lee's Forensic Files*, Prometheus Books, 2006, p. 185

After considering the evidence, Dr. Lee has several beliefs about Richard Duntz, but he doesn't hold each belief with the same degree of confidence. Which of the following statements does he believe is almost certainly true, which is probably true but could be false, and which has the least probability of being true?

a. Richard had been at the scene of the murder.
b. Richard killed Earl.
c. Richard at one time wore a pair of Foot Joy sneakers.

Exercise 4: Apply the Ideas in Writing

Tavis Smiley, the TV talk show host, recently wrote a book called "What I Know for Sure." He says that on every page he tries to answer the question "What have I learned that might help others?" At one point when he was a child his father beat him and his sister so severely that both were hospitalized for days. He says:

> "I was still in a state of shock and still in great pain. I was in no position to deal with them on any terms. I was angry at my father for doing what he did and disappointed with my mother for not stopping him. I instinctively knew what all youngsters know: that regardless of the circumstances, children are entitled to justice. Children are entitled to a fair hearing. Children are supposed to be kept safe. I realize now that that was one of the great lessons of that horrific incident—regardless of anyone's age, false accusations leave deep psychological wounds that take years to heal, if indeed they ever do heal. Now I see that clearly."
>
> Tavis Smiley, *What I Know for Sure: My Story of Growing Up in America*, Doubleday, 2006, p. 70

Write a paragraph or two explaining something you know for sure. It doesn't have to be something traumatic, like Smiley's lesson. It might be something positive and pleasant. Think about going to school, or working, or playing sports, or dating, or cooking. What is something you have learned? And what experiences led you to that understanding? Are you really sure that what you believe is true?

Improving Your Writing 6: Essays

One of the most important words in the art of writing is *essay*. There are different types of essays and much to learn about them, but here we can focus on the essentials. An essay is a short, unified piece of writing that expresses your own thoughts or feelings about something. Essays are always personal to some degree. They can be very personal—you might describe your grandmother—or much less personal and more objective—you can explain why you believe the President's new energy policy will not reduce our dependence on oil. Essays can be about anything from abacuses to zoos, but they tell your audience what you have decided about abacuses, or what you think of zoos.

You write an essay to express your opinion about something. We all form opinions all the time. "What did you think of the new movie?" "Who's going to win the game on Saturday?" "Why do you think Tom did that?" Often we don't give these opinions much thought. But if you want to stop and think, and decide why you believe what you believe, the best way to do it is to write an essay. One reason writing essays is so valuable is that they are the best way for you to figure out who you really are. You dig deeper into your own thinking and beliefs. (Another reason is that they improve your ability to communicate with people.)

Essays have the same structure as paragraphs, but on a larger scale. Remember that a paragraph conveys one main idea. So does an essay. An essay is made up of several paragraphs, but they are all related and they help convey a single main point. You read about developing paragraphs by adding details and examples. The same applies to essays. Suppose you want to make the point that zoos are very valuable parts of cities. You would develop your idea by explaining how zoos benefit people. You might say that they're educational; they're fun; they teach people to respect animals; they preserve endangered species. Each of these points requires its own paragraph, so your essay will be a set of paragraphs all pointing to one conclusion.

The word *conclusion* is related to the word *argument*. If an essay presents an argument, it's called a persuasive essay. You state your conclusion clearly in the beginning, and then you use several paragraphs to explain your reasons for believing the conclusion. You are trying to persuade your audience to agree with you. All essays have a main point, and all of them try to help the audience understand and accept the main point. But some essays are more descriptive than persuasive, and some are more narrative—they tell a story—than persuasive.

CHAPTER 7 ◞◟

Cause and Effect

39. immediate cause

40. remote cause

41. contributing factor

42. coincidence

43. necessary condition

44. sufficient condition

If you are reading this book, you already know what the words *cause* and *effect* mean. But meanings are slippery. The word *cause* is a little like the word *fruit*. Everyone knows what the word *fruit* means, at least in a general way. But is a tomato a fruit? Is a cucumber? What makes a fruit different from a vegetable, or a cereal? We can all improve our understanding of words like *fruit*, or *cause*, by learning exactly what they apply to, when we should use them and when we shouldn't, and precisely what a writer is telling us when he or she uses the word. (Tomatoes and cucumbers, by the way, are both fruits—at least for biologists.)

The word *cause* is more complicated than the word *fruit* because it *relates* two things. For example, the sentence "The lightning caused the forest fire" relates the lightning and the forest fire. In fact, if you label an event a "cause," you automatically require some event or events to be the effect, and vice versa. You can't have a cause without some effect. You can think of lightning without thinking of its effects, but if you call it a "cause," you are relating it to some later events.

Most of the words in this book are complicated because they stand for relationships, not just objects that we can picture in our minds. In the first two chapters you were studying words about similarities and differences. A similarity is one kind of relationship. When we see a similarity or difference we can compare things, or if we see the same similarity among several things ("all the kids have freckles") we can group things into a class and make a generalization. Similarities and differences allow us to group things together and distinguish different groups.

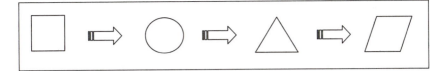

Figure 7.1
The figures represent events, earlier on the left and later on the right. The square on the left represents a remote cause of the leaning square on the far right, and the triangle represents an immediate cause of the leaning square.

Cause and effect is a different kind of relationship. For one thing, cause and effect are related in time. A cause always comes before its effect. If the attack on the World Trade Center caused the United States to invade Afghanistan, then the attack had to come first, before the invasion. But if Bill looks exactly like James, Bill doesn't exist first and then James comes along. They exist at the same time. We can think about groups of things that all exist in the present, and look for relations among them. Or we can think about changes over time, and look for patterns in those changes. Cause and effect is a relationship in time.

Another difference between these two kinds of relationships is that cause and effect is a relationship between events, not people or objects. It's true that if we aren't being careful we can say something like "Elizabeth caused the team to win" or "Elizabeth is responsible for the win today." But what we really mean is that Elizabeth's *action*—hitting a home run or scoring a goal—caused the team to win. It's also true that, since we can compare any two things, we can compare events, so similarity and difference can be a relation between events, as well as between other things. But cause and effect is always a relation between events, not between people or objects.

The main thing to keep in mind in thinking about causes and effects is that they are not simple. The relation of cause and effect is almost always more complicated than it first appears. If you get into the habit of keeping those complications in mind, and not oversimplifying matters, you will be a better thinker.

Part 1. Definitions

39. immediate cause. a cause close in time to the effect. "The immediate cause of the explosion was a spark created by faulty wiring." Sometimes the immediate cause is called the *proximate cause*.

Example

39a. While the **immediate cause** of the crash was the parachutes' failure to deploy, the reasons why that happened were far from clear.

Sensors on the spacecraft were supposed to trigger small explosives to begin the parachute deployment.

Guy Gugliotta, NASA Hopes Data Can Be Salvaged from Crashed Craft, *Washington Post*, 9/10/04

40. remote cause. a cause distant in time from the effect; an event in the distant past that helps cause some effect. "One might say that the fall of the Bastille was the cause of the French Revolution, but a remote cause was the peasants' suffering in the decades leading up to that event." Sometimes the remote cause is called the *ultimate cause*.
(Causes have both immediate and remote effects, or consequences, as well.)

Example

40a. The head of a government education panel said Sunday one of the **remote causes** for the outbreak of the 1941–1945 war in the Pacific theater was a U.S. decision to stop oil exports to Japan, stressing that Japanese were the victims of the war.

Education Panel Head Blames U.S. Oil Policy for World War II, *Japan Economic Newswire*, May 25, 2003

Comment

We all have a tendency to think of a single event as *the* cause of another single event, which is *the* effect. In Example 39a, we think the failure of the parachute caused the spacecraft to crash. But this is an oversimplification. Everything that happens is connected in many ways with other events, both before and after. Some events earlier in time caused the parachute to fail to open, and the crash of the spacecraft will have further consequences for NASA. The terms *immediate cause* and *remote cause* remind us of those connections.

How far back must one go before causes change from immediate causes to remote causes? There is no rule. It depends on the context and the purpose of the description. In talking about big events, like wars, *remote* normally means years earlier. In talking about a sudden event, like an explosion, *remote* probably means hours or days earlier.

41. contributing factor. one event or condition out of several that all together produce some effect. "The weather was a contributing factor in the plane crash. Other factors were pilot fatigue and poor maintenance of the aircraft." "One contributing factor to heart disease is too much saturated fat in the diet."

Example

41a. The [competitive] values, often promoted by overzealous parents and coaches, take a toll on the estimated 30 million children who participate in organized sports in the United States each year. Overly aggressive play fueled by a win-at-all-costs mentality are increasingly being recognized as **contributing factors** in the injuries sustained by young players.

Martin Miller, Kids Have Nothing to Gain from Pain, *AM NewYork*, 5/26/04

42. coincidence. when two events occur together, perhaps unexpectedly, but not because one causes the other. "The winning lottery numbers were the same as the first six digits of my Social Security number: what a coincidence!" "It was a lucky coincidence that I went to the PTA meeting, because I wanted to talk to Becky's parents and they were there."

Example

42a. A woman in Alabama decided to visit her sister. Her sister, unbeknownst to her, decided the same. They hit each other head-on on a rural highway. Both died. And both drove Jeeps. That counts as a rare **coincidence**, although not as rare, perhaps, as the case of Roy Cleveland Sullivan, a Virginia forest ranger who was struck by lightning seven times, or the existence of an ice dealer named I. C. Shivers.

William Grimes, The Quirky Moments When Lightning Does Strike Twice, review of Martin Plimmer and Brian King, "Beyond Coincidence," *New York Times*, 1/20/06

43. necessary condition. a condition or event which has to be present before some other condition or event can occur. "The paper in the vacuum chamber wouldn't burn because there was no oxygen, and oxygen is a necessary condition for fire." In other words, if something burns, you know that oxygen had to be present.

Example

43a. American recessions are unusual because negative consumption growth is, in most cases, a **necessary condition** for a recession. The U.S. has not experienced a quarter of negative consumption growth since a modest 0.3% drop in the seasonally adjusted annual rate (SAAR) in the fourth quarter of 1991....

John H. Makin, Recession 2008? *Wall Street Journal*, 9/8/07

44. sufficient condition. a condition or event which guarantees the occurrence of some other condition or event. "A sufficient condition for the water to freeze was that the temperature fell below 0 degrees centigrade." In other words, if the temperature fell below 0 degrees, then you know that the water froze.

Example

44a. Counselors are often surprised when confronted with camper behaviors that are difficult to manage in the cabin or in the activity area. Not recalling their own experiences as campers struggling with the many conflicts and issues of childhood and adolescence, counselors often believe that trust and kindness are **sufficient conditions** for a warm, cooperative atmosphere in the cabin setting. They sometimes feel angry and hurt when treated disrespectfully by their campers who seem unable to live and work harmoniously together.

Rabbi Ronald Garr and Minda G. Garr, Establishing Clear Limits, *The Camping Magazine*, Nov/Dec 2006

Test Yourself
Match each word with its definition.

39. immediate cause
40. remote cause
41. contributing factor
42. coincidence
43. necessary condition
44. sufficient condition

a. one event that is part of a set of events that made something happen
b. a cause that is close in time to the effect
c. an event that guarantees the occurrence of a later event
d. a relationship between to events or two conditions that is unexpected, but not a causal relationship
e. a cause that is distant in time from the effect
f. an event that has to occur before a later event can occur

Part 2. Understanding the Meaning

39. immediate cause.

39b. The Federal Government has ordered immediate setting up of an investigation committee to look into **immediate and remote causes** of the fire, which gutted the Ministry of Defence store house on Saturday.

A statement signed by the Assistant Director (Press), Adedeji Ajibade, made available to THISDAY, confirmed that an investigation committee would soon be constituted....

"Although the **immediate cause** of the fire has not been ascertained, it was observed that a bush fire at the back of the perimeter fence of the Defence building must have spilled over to the store, which is very close to the fence," Ajibade said.

Nigeria; FG to Probe Defence Ministry's Fire Incident, *Africa News, ThisDay*, January 28, 2008

Figure 7.2
The dominoes that are standing up straight will fall. What causes them to fall? *Source:* ©
Maciej Oleksy/Shutterstock Images LLC

39c. Peoples of Eurasian origin, especially those still living in Europe
and eastern Asia, plus those transplanted to North America, domi-
nate the modern world in wealth and power.... Why did wealth and
power become distributed as they now are, rather than in some other
way? ...

[One] type of explanation lists the **immediate factors** that enabled
Europeans to kill or conquer other peoples—especially European
guns, infectious diseases, steel tools, and manufactured products.
Such an explanation is on the right track, as those factors demonstra-
bly *were* directly responsible for European conquests. However, this
hypothesis is incomplete, because it still offers only a proximate (first-
stage) explanation identifying **immediate causes**. It invites a search
for ultimate causes: why were Europeans, rather than Africans or
Native Americans, the ones to end up with guns, the nastiest germs,
and steel?

Jared Diamond, *Guns, Germs, and Steel: The Fates of Human Societies*, W. W. Norton, 1999,
pp. 15, 23.

40. remote cause.

40b. An example or two may illustrate the difficulty of differentiating between cause and symptom and between proximate and **remote
causes.** We have seen how Romans or Romanized elements, those who
had the largest stake in Roman institutions, came to form a dwindling
minority in the army. The barbarization of the army and the civil
service and Rome's dependence upon barbarian allies and mercenar-
ies were undoubtedly one of the factors in the decline of Rome. But
more and more [barbarian] Germans were admitted into the army
and the civil service because Rome desperately needed men to help

defend her frontiers and administer her empire. The barbarization of the Empire is, therefore, a symptom of decay, an indication that there was a shortage of manpower in relation to the tasks which had to be performed. What caused that? Was it a declining birth rate, high mortality in wars and epidemics, or increased requirements for men? Each and all may have been **remote causes** of the barbarization of the Empire, and the process of barbarization was itself both symptom and cause of decline.

Solomon Katz, *The Decline of Rome and the Rise of Mediaeval Europe*, Cornell University Press, 1955, pp. 74–75

Question: Katz says the Roman Empire declined partly because of a shortage of manpower. What might have happened even earlier to cause that shortage?

40c. Have we been betrayed? I do not know. I have no way of coming at the facts without which considered judgment is impossible. I shall only say this: the men in charge should have known our own strength. They should have informed themselves as to the forces of the enemy. If we were the weaker, we should not have run headlong upon suicide. If we were the stronger, where did our strength go?

But our defeat has **causes more remote** than these. Here there is no need of documentation or evidence in writing: my own memory will suffice. And the memories that crowd upon me bring me to this conclusion. France died because her soul was sick....

A people is a democracy when it governs itself by means of representatives whose business is to reconcile the general interest with the liberty of the individual, in the equality of all. A people is a demagogy when its representatives neglect the general interest, and think only of their own. For long years France has been a demagogy.

"Jacques," A French Soldier Speaks (1941), in Raymond P. Stearns, ed., *Pageant of Europe*, Harcourt, Brace and World, 1961, p. 937

40d. Our curiosity is naturally prompted to inquire by what means the Christian faith obtained so remarkable a victory over the established religions of the earth. To this inquiry an obvious but unsatisfactory answer may be returned; that it was owing to the convincing evidence of the doctrine itself, and to the ruling providence of its great Author. But as truth and reason seldom find so favorable a reception in the world, and as the wisdom of Providence frequently condescends to use the passions of the human heart, and the general circumstances of mankind, as instruments to execute its purpose, we may still be permitted, though with becoming submission, to ask, not indeed what were the first, but what were the **secondary causes** of the rapid growth of the Christian church?

Edward Gibbon, *The Decline and Fall of the Roman Empire*, vol. 1, Great Books of the Western World, 1952 [originally 1776], p. 179

Question: When Gibbon speaks of "secondary causes," does he mean the remote causes or the immediate causes of the widespread acceptance of Christianity?

Comment

Often people are interested in the effects of certain events, and we can think about "immediate" effects and "remote" effects. But instead of "immediate" and "remote" most writers use the phrases "short-term" and "long-term."

short-term effect. An effect of some cause that occurs soon after the cause. "A short-term effect of taking cocaine is feeling confident and energetic."

long-term effect. An effect of some cause that occurs long after the cause has already happened. "A long-term effect of taking cocaine is becoming dependent on the drug and feeling panicky and desperate without it."

Examples

40e. Q What are the **effects** of child sexual abuse?

A The **short-term effects** on the child include behaviour problems, education and learning problems, anxiety, depression and withdrawal, while the **long-term effects** on the [child-turned-] adult include mental health problems..., sexual adjustment problems, delinquency, acts of violence, difficulty in forming relationships and problems in parenting their own children.

There is no simple, one-to-one relationship between the severity of the abuse and its impact. The consequences will depend on the severity and duration of the abuse, its associated features (for example, deprivation) and the child itself (some are more resilient than others).

Ruth Bastable, Taking Action on Suspected Child Sex Abuse, *Practitioner*, 7/21/06

40f. But what will be the lasting effect of the bombings [in London]? There is a simple rule of thumb. If it is difficult to imagine something ever returning to normal, it is likely to do so quickly. The sources of **long-term disruption** and damage are more subtle. Much of the harm will come only indirectly from the attacks, and will be caused by the responses to terror rather than the terror itself.

Any fear and anxiety whipped up by the bombings will dissipate quickly....Meanwhile, the police carry on. Their conduct over the next few months poses the greatest **long-term threat**, as well as the best hope for stopping further attacks....

The danger is that Muslims' relations with the police will sour, rather as happened with Afro-Caribbean men in the 1980s. Black anger stemmed from the seemingly prejudiced use of street searches....Between 2000–01 and 2003–04, the number of Asians stopped and searched rose by 60%, compared with an 8% rise among the population of England and Wales. Fewer of these searches led to an arrest than searches of any other ethnic group.

In the aftermath of terrorist attacks, the extravagant use of such police powers might seem tolerable, or even desirable. In the **long term**, the consequences are more likely to prove otherwise.

Learning to Live with It, *Economist*, 7/30/05

Question: The terrorist bombings in London on July 7, 2005, killed 56 people. *The Economist* magazine describes a likely short-term effect involving the police, and a long-term effect. What will be the long-term effect, in their opinion? Do they have any reason to expect these short-term and long-term effects?

Comment

The ideas of cause and effect are more complicated than many people realize, because effects extend far into the future and causes extend far into the past. Most of us are in a hurry and settle for one cause or one effect when we are analyzing an event. We don't think about more possibilities.

But the concept of cause is complicated in another way as well. An event can have several causes that occur at the same time. Of course, if you find more remote causes of an event, then you are thinking about several causes. For example, one cause of the American Civil War was the attack on Fort Sumter by South Carolina in 1861. But a more remote cause was the election of Abraham Lincoln in 1860. And there were even earlier causes. However, even if you limit yourself to one moment in time—the year 1860, let's say—you can still find many different causes of the war. Economic conditions, disagreements over slavery, changes on the western frontier, diplomatic relations with Great Britain, and many other factors contributed to the outbreak of war. This applies to any event. If you think about what causes a business to fail, you might focus on one thing: Maybe a new highway takes traffic away from the location. But other aspects of the situation had to occur as well. For example, the owners' expenses increased, or they didn't advertise in new markets, or a competitor opened a store. We might decide some events are more important causes than others, but we shouldn't ignore the others.

You can expand your idea of cause in this way as well. When someone writes about "the" cause of some event, you can remember that several different aspects of the situation contributed to the event, not just one. One term for these other causes is *contributing factors*. (Sometimes writers will use the phrase *multiple causes*.)

41. contributing factor.

41b. Popular folklore has established the stock market crash as the beginning, and even the cause, of the Great Depression. In fact, it was neither; it was, of course, the most conspicuous sign of the coming of the crisis; and it **contributed** in several ways to its severity. But the Depression had earlier beginnings and more important causes.

Frank Freidel and Alan Brinkley, *America in the Twentieth Century*, Fifth Edition, Alfred A. Knopf, 1982, p. 200

41c. To deal with Japanese beetles, here are some words of wisdom: Don't let it be. Be proactive and get rid of them....

The beetle's larvae live underground and feast upon the root systems of plants and grasses, so applying pesticides there will kill the grubs....

The Japanese beetles will not kill a tree on their own, but [Chris] Williamson said they could be a **contributing factor**. If a tree already is stressed from a disease, the beetles can kill it....

Kevin Nelson, Get Back at the Beetles, *Knight Ridder Tribune Business News*, 8/11/06

41d. Experts say it is unclear exactly why motorcycle riding in general has become so deadly, and a four-year national study is set to start this summer at Oklahoma State University to look into the causes. But health and highway-patrol officials in California, as well as riders themselves, say that the **contributing factors** are higher numbers of inexperienced riders and more traffic coupled with multitasking car drivers trying to talk on the phone, check their BlackBerries and

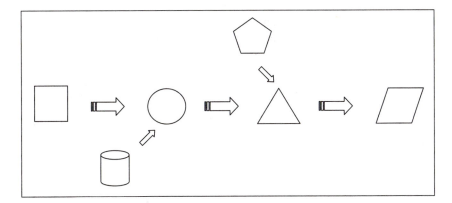

Figure 7.3
Sometimes an event has more than one cause. Several things have to happen before the event can occur. Here the circle leads to the triangle, but the pentagon at the top also influences the triangle. The circle and pentagon are contributing factors.

steer at the same time. Health officials in Los Angeles also single out S.U.V.'s, because motorcycles are less visible to drivers sitting high in their vehicles.

Mireya Navarro, California's Uneasy Riders, *New York Times*, 7/16/06

41e. The decline of the Roman Empire was neither sudden nor cataclysmic, but was a gradual process extending over several centuries....Many of the explanations have been oversimplified solutions to an immensely difficult problem. Scholars have sometimes selected one **factor**, for example, the barbarian invasions or the exhaustion of the soil, and have declared it to be the ultimate **cause** of the decline of the Roman Empire, or they have looked for one common denominator of decline to which they have reduced all other **factors**. We shall see, however, that the process of decline was due not to a single cause, but to a variety of interacting **factors**—political, economic, social, cultural, and psychological. To give priority to any one of them is virtually impossible, since each acted with and upon every other **factor**. At the outset, therefore, we should recognize the principle of multiple causation.

Solomon Katz, *The Decline of Rome and the Rise of Mediaeval Europe*, Cornell University Press, 1955, pp. 72–74

42. coincidence.

42b. Not long after the bombs went off [in London] on July 7, killing 56 people including the 4 bombers, Mr. [Magdy el-] Nashar's name surfaced. His picture appeared in newspapers and on television broadcasts around the world. Headlines talked about a young Egyptian chemist who had been arrested and was being questioned. He knew at least one of the bombers. He lived in Leeds, England, as did three of the bombers. And he left England not long before the attacks took place.

And apparently it was all a sorry **coincidence**, a case of a man who happened to befriend the wrong people at the wrong time, according to Egyptian authorities.

Michael Slackman, Egypt Releases Chemist Questioned About London Bombings, *New York Times*, 8/10/05

Comment

The word *coincidence* is a negative word, like *odorless, unqualified,* or *irrelevant.* It tells us what something is not. Specifically, it tells us that an event is not a cause or effect of some other event, even though it may appear to be. In Example 42b, several facts made some people think that Mr. Nashar was part of the cause of the bombings in London. It is unusual or surprising for one person to have all those characteristics (knowing one of the bombers, living in the same area, being a chemist, and leaving the country just before the event) without being part of the cause. But there was no relation. It was just a coincidence that Nashar happened to have those characteristics.

42c. Q. With the images on my mind of the recent transit of Venus across the sun, I was watching a TV show that depicted a solar eclipse, and I wondered: Is it just a **coincidence** that the moon is exactly the right size to block out the sun? If the size of the moon and sun, their relative distances from Earth, and other factors were different, could we inhabit a world that never experienced a full eclipse?

A.P., Dover, N.H.

A. As far as we know, there is no reason at all that things should work out so nicely, with the moon just fitting over the sun as seen from here. The sun is about 400 times larger in diameter than the moon, but it's also about 400 times farther away, so they both look about the same size to us. As far as we know, the short answer to your question is yes, it's just a **coincidence.**

Ask Dr. Knowledge, *Boston Globe,* 6/17/04

42d. Mayor William Phelan said he does not want to waste money on new dropout prevention programs if Quincy High School's problem has already been solved with new leadership.

A task force charged with finding ways to keep students in high school until graduation was formed last year after officials learned Quincy High's dropout rate had quadrupled in four years....

Following the school committee meeting, Phelan said it was no **coincidence** that the former high school principal's reign coincided with the four-year spike in the dropout rate, and that under [new principal Frank] Santoro, the outlook has changed dramatically.

"A principal was hired four years ago, and now a new principal has been hired, and it is back down," Phelan said....

But members of the task force rejected the notion of a sole origin for the dropout problem.

"There is not one reason for the spike," in dropouts, said Janet Powell, director of student support services.

Phelan emphatically disagreed. "I keep hearing that," he said. "I don't buy it. I think there is a reason. It needs to be identified. I can't believe we can't determine the reason that it happened at Quincy High School and no other school."

Jessica Van Sack, Mayor Says Dropout Problem Solved; Phelan Blames Spike on Former Principal, *The Patriot Ledger* (Quincy, MA), 5/19/05

Question: Mayor Phelan and the task force on dropout rates have a disagreement. On what do they disagree? Do you think the mayor is probably right, or the task force is probably right? (The mayor is using the word *reason* to mean cause.)

43. necessary condition.

43b. The rising violence in Los Angeles-area cities and unincorporated areas patrolled by the county Sheriff's Department is disturbing....Compton is the most acutely plagued example, with 68 killings as of Dec. 8 in a city of just under 100,000 people.... [Compton Mayor Eric] Perrodin is a deputy district attorney for L.A. County and a former police officer who was elected in 2001 on a reform platform. He inherited a nastily divided government famous for cronyism and corruption, and a school system just emerging from a fiscal meltdown and subsequent state takeover. Compton's population has shifted to majority Latino and heavily immigrant, while its voting majority remains African American. Perrodin's burdens are heavy, but making the city safer is the **necessary condition** for other improvements.

Editorial: The Saturday Page; Law and Order; Under Fire in Compton, *Los Angeles Times*, 12/17/05

Figure 7.4
Water is a necessary condition for plants to grow and remain alive. ("If a plant is green and living, then it has received water.") *Source:* © *Chris Hill/Shutterstock Images LLC*

43c. It is now conventional wisdom that the new opening to a Middle East peace is a result of Yasser Arafat's death. This is only half true, and it misses the larger point.

Arafat's death was a **necessary condition** for hope, but not a **sufficient** one. It was **necessary** because Arafat had the power to suppress and literally kill any chances of peace. But his passing would have meant nothing if it had not occurred at a time when the Palestinians finally realized that Arafat's last great gamble, the second intifada, was a disaster.

Charles Krauthammer, Why the Palestinians Came to the Table, *The Washington Post*, 2/11/05

Question: Krauthammer says the new opening to a Middle East peace and the hopefulness could not have happened without Arafat's death. But he goes farther and explains *why* that event was a necessary condition for hope. What is his explanation?

44. sufficient condition.

44b. Human beings have a tendency to maintain order and control in their lives and many will unconsciously alter innovations to fit into their existing ways of doing things. Therefore, there must be a shift in the paradigm of learning in education institutions. Learning is a continuous, cultural process and not simply a series of lectures or tutorials....

In order to respond to this challenge, educational institutions need to develop a strategic plan that mediates the shift in paradigm towards a learning culture. A strategic plan involves "the process by which the guiding members of an organization envision its future and develop the necessary procedures and operations to achieve that future."...

This paper has discussed the necessary and **sufficient conditions** for successful online learning in educational institutions. The necessary conditions include the hardware, software and financial commitment to ensure a good campus network that will support online learning. The **sufficient conditions** highlight the need for a paradigm shift in learning to build a learning culture in educational institutions, mediated by a strategic plan.

Cher Ping Lim, Online Learning in Higher Education: Necessary and **Sufficient Conditions**, *International Journal of Instructional Media*, vol. 32, issue 4, 2005

44c. Although the specific recommendations [of the commission] will not be complete for several weeks, the thinking behind them has narrowed to a central notion: the solution to poverty is employment. But in a twist on the welfare-to-work policies of former Mayor Rudolph W. Giuliani, the group has agreed that the government must use more of its resources to foster conditions that allow people to enter the work force and stay in it.

To achieve that goal, the commission has been looking at ways to increase access to child care so parents can hold on to their jobs. It has also been devising ways to use city resources to tailor training programs to an ever-changing job market, and to focus public schools on preparing students not only for college, but also for the workplace....

"I really believe that getting a good education is at the heart of any solution to poverty," Mr. Bloomberg said last month at a conference organized by the commission. "If you fix the school system, that may not solve all the problems of fixing poverty," he continued, "but it is one of those **necessary** if not **sufficient conditions** to really make progress."

Diane Cardwell, The Mayor Focuses on Poverty, and a Panel Is Ready to Help, *New York Times*, 7/17/06

Question: Mr. Bloomberg says fixing the school system is necessary but not sufficient for ending poverty. What does the commission believe *is* sufficient?

Comment

It is easier to find necessary conditions for an event than sufficient conditions. For example, if you graduated from college, a necessary condition was probably that you attended classes regularly. But that wasn't sufficient. You had to study for exams, write essays, pay fees, and do many things in order to graduate. In fact, no single thing was sufficient. It is rare that one event is sufficient to cause another. This is connected with the term *contributing factor*. In thinking about cause and effect it is important to remember that most events result from several causes, not just one. The causes may occur earlier in time (remote causes), or they may be all present at one time (contributing factors).

Comment

When people say that one event causes another, they often use "if–then statements": "If you boil the water, the germs in it will die;" "if you want better schools and government in Compton, you must first make the city safe." Looking closely at if–then statements will help you gain a deeper understanding of necessary and sufficient conditions.

For example, the statement about boiling water says that boiling water is a sufficient condition for killing the germs. If you know the water has been boiled, you know the germs are dead. Can you turn that sentence around? If you know the germs are dead, do you automatically know the water has been boiled? In other words, is killing the germs a sufficient condition for the water to boil? No. We could kill the germs in other ways, for example, by adding chlorine or some other chemical to the water. So, in general, a statement with the form "If C, then E" usually means that C is a sufficient condition for E, but E is not a sufficient condition for C.

Let's take this a step farther. A scientist says, "If you boil the water, the germs in it will die." So that's true. But suppose you know the water has *not* been boiled.

Can you then know automatically that the germs have *not* been killed? ("If not *C*, then not *E*.") No, you can't, because of what we just said about chlorine and other ways to kill germs. Maybe the germs have been killed, even though the water hasn't been boiled. Boiling is sufficient for killing the germs, but it is not necessary for killing them.

Finally, look at one last step. Suppose you know that the water still has live germs in it; the germs have *not* been killed. Can you then know anything automatically about the water, that it has been boiled or has not been boiled? In other words, can you know either of the following statements: (i) "If the germs have not been killed, then the water has been boiled;" or (ii) "If the germs have not been killed, then the water has not been boiled"? In fact, you can know the second statement. Since boiling is sufficient to kill the germs—it's a guarantee—then if they have *not* been killed, you know the water has *not* been boiled. ("If not *E*, then not *C*.") In other words, in a statement of the form "If *C*, then *E*," *E* is a necessary condition of *C*. If *C* occurs, *E* has to occur. If *E* doesn't occur, *C* can't occur.

Part 3. Applying the Words

39. immediate cause
40. remote cause
41. contributing factor
42. coincidence
43. necessary condition
44. sufficient condition

Exercise 1: Choose the Right Word

For each sentence, choose the best word (or an appropriate form of the word) to fill in the blank.

1. The area had been hot and dry for weeks, with below average rainfall, but apparently a bolt of lightning at 2:28 PM was the _____ of the forest fire.
2. Doctors now define death as the cessation of brain activity, but normally a _____ for death to occur is for the heart to stop beating.
3. To fully understand the riots, we must dig deeper into the economic and political changes of the past few years, and find the _____.
4. Halley's Comet appeared in the year Mark Twain was born, and in a strange _____, it appeared again in the year that he died.
5. Being a successful Olympic athlete requires many things, but certainly practice is one _____.
6. Possessing a particular gene on a certain chromosome is only one of many _____ that lead to musical talent.

Exercise 2: Apply the Words

Read each example and answer the questions that follow.

1. No one understands precisely how and why eating disorders develop. But experts say risk factors include an unstable environment, major life changes, feelings of inadequacy or a lack of control, depression, difficulty expressing emotions and being teased about one's weight....

"It's an absolute tightrope walk," says Dr. Ellen Rome, head of adolescent medicine at the Cleveland Clinic. "Parents have it harder than ever, especially with the rise in obesity. But a parent's negative comments can be the final straw that pushes a kid toward an eating disorder."

Shari Roan, Parents Shouldn't Take Discussing Weight Lightly, *AM New York*, 6/1/05

According to Dr. Rome, are a parent's negative comments usually an immediate cause or a remote cause of his or her child's eating disorder?

2. The roots of the capacity to implement social oppression go deep into our evolutionary history. Early human gatherer-hunters, as did all ancestral human species, lived in environments that were harsh and often limited in resources. Under such conditions, interactions between groups may have played an important role in developing aspects of human behavior, particularly aggression against other groups and social hierarchy within groups. It has been observed, in contrast to long held theories of the benign and peaceful nature of other primates, that both chimp and human societies exhibit lethal intergroup violence associated with capturing territories and resources....Clearly, we cannot understand the origins of human behavior by examining present day industrial societies. The vast majority of human evolutionary history was spent in small groups, in Africa.

Joseph L. Graves, Jr., *The Race Myth: Why We Pretend Race Exists in America*, Dutton, 2004, pp. 48, 50

Does Graves want to investigate the immediate causes of human behavior or the remote causes?

3. I know we have a fashion of saying "such and such an event was the turning-point in my life," but we shouldn't say it. We should merely grant that its place as *last* link in the chain makes it the most *conspicuous* link; in real importance it has no advantage over any of its predecessors.

Mark Twain, in Justin Kaplan, ed., *Great Short Works of Mark Twain*, Perennial Library, 1967, p. 222

Is Twain saying that immediate causes are just important in life as remote causes, or the opposite: that remote causes are just as important as immediate causes?

4. The causes of atheism are; division in religion, if they be many; for any one main division addeth zeal to both sides but many divisions

introduce atheism. Another is scandal of priests.... A third is, custom of profane scoffing in holy matters; which doth by little and little deface the reverence of religion. And lastly, learned times, specially with peace and prosperity; for troubles and adversities do more bow men's minds to religion.

Francis Bacon, *The Complete Essays*, Washington Square Press, 1963 [originally 1625], p. 45

Bacon describes several contributing factors leading to atheism in a society. Do you think he's right about those factors? Can you think of other possible causes?

5. The crime drop [in the late 1980s and early 1990s] was startling in several respects. It was ubiquitous, with every category of crime falling in every part of the country. It was persistent, with incremental decreases year after year. And it was entirely unanticipated—especially by the very experts who had been predicting the opposite....

So how did *Roe v. Wade* [the Supreme Court ruling in 1973 that made abortion legal] help trigger, a generation later, the greatest crime drop in recorded history?....

[T]he millions of women most likely to have an abortion in the wake of *Roe v. Wade*—poor, unmarried, and teenage mothers for whom illegal abortions had been too expensive or too hard to get—were often models of adversity. They were the very women whose children, if born, would have been much more likely than average to become criminals. But because of *Roe v. Wade*, these children *weren't* being born. This powerful cause would have a drastic, distant effect: years later, just as these unborn children would have entered their criminal primes, the rate of crime began to plummet.

Steven D. Levitt and Stephen J. Dubner, *Freakonomics*, William Morrow, 2005, pp. 4–6

What effect do Levitt and Dubner want to explain? What do they think caused the effect? Was it an immediate cause or a remote cause?

6. Can carrots help improve your vision?...The carrot myth dates back to World War II when the British Royal Air Force was attempting to hide the fact that it had developed a sophisticated airborne radar system to shoot down German bombers. They bragged that the great accuracy of British fighter pilots at night was a result of them being fed enormous quantities of carrots. It is true that carrots are rich in beta-carotene, which is essential for sight. The body converts beta-carotene to vitamin A, and extreme vitamin A deficiency can cause blindness. However, only a small amount of beta-carotene is necessary for good vision. If you're not deficient in vitamin A, your vision won't improve no matter how many carrots you eat.

Mark Leyner and Billy Goldberg, M.D., *Why Do Men Have Nipples?*, Three Rivers Press, 2005, pp. 47–48

What is the relation between (a) vitamin A, which one can get from eating carrots, and (b) good vision? Is (a) a necessary condition of (b) or a sufficient condition of (b)?

> 7. Knowledge had grown that if a person had smallpox and recovered, that person would never have smallpox again.... The country folk of Gloucestershire knew that anybody who suffered from a [relatively mild] disease called cowpox would never get smallpox. Cowpox, as its name implied, was a disease affecting cows and was caught by humans from cows.... [Edward] Jenner.... noted that people who had had cowpox did not contract smallpox, even though they came in contact with smallpox sufferers. He took some smallpox fluid and inserted it into the arms of these people and still they did not contract the disease.
>
> Finally—and we must pay tribute to the child's parents—Jenner inoculated a healthy eight-year-old boy, Jimmy Phipps, with cowpox virus and produced that illness in the youth. He then injected some smallpox material into the boy and into another person who had not had cowpox. Smallpox resulted, but only in the person who had not been protected by cowpox, not in lucky Jimmy Phipps.
>
> Philip Cane, *Giants of Science*, Pyramid Publications, 1961, pp. 131–133

What is the relation between (a) having cowpox and (b) being immune to smallpox? Is (a) a necessary condition for (b) or a sufficient condition for (b)?

Exercise 3:   Analyzing Arguments

1. The writer's conclusion in the following example is that access to guns is probably the cause of teenage violence. What evidence supports his conclusion?

> Although experts and sociologists have crammed TV talk shows to offer various theories about the contagion of teenage violence, it is clear that no one understands why these incidents occur. Blaming media is merely the simplest, most expedient way to explain what can't be explained....
>
> Why do so many of these school shootings occur not in media-saturated urban areas but in rural heartland communities, generally thought more conservative and traditional? Is there a connection to the rural popularity of hunting, as in Springfield?
>
> The media habits of these teenage suspect aren't yet clear. The common denominator linking them, to date, is quite clear: They can easily find guns. Why haven't journalists and politicians focused on this as the most pressing issue connecting these tragedies, a far more convincing common denominator than violence on TV?
>
> Jon Katz, Violence in the Media Does Not Cause Juvenile Crime, in Tamara L. Roleff, ed., *Crime and Criminals: Opposing Viewpoints*, Greenhaven Press, 2000, pp. 57, 59–60

2. Zimring and Hawkins' conclusion is that access to handguns is probably the cause of the higher homicide rate in the United States. What evidence supports their conclusion?

> Franklin Zimring and Gordon Hawkins of the University of California write: "The reported rates [per 100,000 people] of both violent and nonviolent crime in the United States...are quite close to those found in countries like Australia, Canada and New Zealand." The rate of criminal assault is higher in those countries than here....
>
> So it is not crime that sets us apart. We have no more pick-pockets, shoplifters, burglars, robbers or brawlers than Western Europe or the British Isles. But we have a surplus of killers—a large surplus. Our homicide rate is 20 times the rate in England and Wales, 10 times the rate in France and Germany....
>
> Zimring and Hawkins conclude that the one "causal" factor that sets us apart from the rest of the world is the huge arsenal of handguns—estimated at from 50 million to 70 million—that makes it possible to settle with finality the passionate domestic arguments and street disputes that produce most of our homicides.
>
> Richard Harwood, Gun Control Laws Reduce Crime, in Tamara L. Roleff, ed., *Crime and Criminals: Opposing Viewpoints*, Greenhaven Press, 2000, pp. 65, 67

3. In the next example Cantor reaches a conclusion about the cause of the growth in population in Europe that began around 950 CE. What does he believe caused that growth? What reasons does he give to believe that event was the cause?

> The introduction of watermills greatly facilitated the grinding of grain and contributed to an increase in the food supply.... These social and technological changes go a long way toward explaining the steady growth in the population of Europe from the middle of the tenth century. There was no alteration in the extremely primitive conditions of European medicine and no apparent improvement in the pitifully short average life expectancy, but the increased food supply must have resulted in a marked decrease in infant mortality.
>
> Norman F. Cantor, *The Civilization of the Middle Ages*, HarperPerennial, 1994, p. 229

Exercise 4: Apply the Ideas in Writing

Write a paragraph or two in which you describe some cause and effect. Here are some examples you could write about:

(a) More and more Americans are becoming overweight. What do you think the cause or causes might be?

(b) Recently, gasoline prices have risen a great deal. What do you think the effects might be?

(c) Some colleges do not give grades. If everyone in your school received either a "P" for pass or an "F" for fail, what do you think the effects of that change would be?

(d) If you have seen a nature program on TV, describe the program's explanation of the causes of some effect.

(e) If a team loses (or wins) a game, read several accounts in newspapers and summarize the causes of the loss or the win.

Improve Your Writing 7: Choosing a Topic

How do you choose a *topic* for an essay? The first thing to consider is length. Your topic shouldn't be too large or too small. For example, "my childhood" is probably too large for an essay. "My ballpoint pen" is probably too small. "Learning to write in the first grade" might be a good topic for an essay.

The next thing to consider is what interests you. You should choose a topic that you want to write about because your enthusiasm and excitement will energize your essay. Another consideration is your own knowledge and experience. Do you know anything about the topic? If not, can you learn enough so that you can explain something about the topic to others? Someone suggested that the first rule of good writing is "Have something to say."

You should also think about your audience. It's always helpful to picture in your mind the people who will read your essay. Are they your age? Older? Younger? How much do they already know about the topic? What would they like to know? If you are writing about your experiences in the first grade, you will write one way for your friends who were there, another way for a meeting of first grade teachers, and still another way for kids who are in the first grade now.

Scientific Thinking

Science impacts all of our lives in countless ways every day. The food we eat, the synthetic fabrics we wear, the cars we drive, the cell phones and computers we use, the medicine we take, and on and on, all testify to the importance of science. Our beliefs about how the world works are all shaped by science. ("What causes heart attacks? Cholesterol builds up in the arteries and cuts off oxygen to the heart muscle." "Why do earthquakes happen? One of the huge plates that cover the earth slides against another.") For several hundred years science has not only given us better food, clothes, houses, and other comforts; it has also given us a better and more accurate picture of the world we live in.

How did it do it? How did science transform our environment and our minds so completely? The short answer is "the scientific method." And the heart of the scientific method is experiment. Scientists try to understand nature not only by observing it very closely. Painters and poets do that. Scientists actually manipulate parts of the world in order to see what happens. For example, Galileo observed moving bodies of all kinds—falling objects, cannonballs fired from cannons, pendulums swinging—and he saw patterns in their motions and made generalizations. But then he took the next step. He intervened, and set up situations in which different objects moved in different ways. For example, he rolled small and large balls down ramps and measured the times it took them to get to the bottom. He made pendulums of different lengths and swung them in wide and narrow arcs. He tested his generalizations. By manipulating objects in all sorts of creative ways, and very carefully measuring the results, he was able to discover many laws of nature (for example, all objects fall at the same rate, all same-size pendulums swing at the same rate).

Before the Scientific Revolution (1600–1700), people had observed the natural world, and had made hypotheses about causes and effects. But they had not conducted experiments in the systematic, extensive way people did after the Revolution. In the Middle Ages (500–1500), Europeans formulated theories about the human body, about the elements that things are made of, about animals and plants and so on. But their theories were often based more on respected authorities, such as the Greek philosopher Aristotle, or the Bible, than on personal experience. Or they were based on very limited experience. Perhaps one year planting the crops on the second Tuesday in April led to a good harvest, so every year after that people planted their crops on the second Tuesday in April. Or a man with a fever was hot and red-faced, so they might hypothesize that draining "the excess blood" from him would help. If he happened to get better (in spite of the treatment), then people were convinced that "bleeding" was the best cure for fevers. When people disagreed about the way nature worked, they would make up ingenious arguments instead of performing a test.

Scientists, in contrast, perform tests, that is, experiments. They often want to discover some relation of cause and effect. "What causes food to spoil? Is it something in the food or in the air? If I seal up food and allow no contact with air, will it stay fresh?" "If living germs cause smallpox, what will happen if I inject dead germs into a healthy person?"

This is an oversimplification of history, and of scientific method, but I believe the basic idea is correct. To get a better understanding of the complexities of the method, you can learn more about science and scientific thinking. And I believe the best preparation for that is to learn more about some basic words.

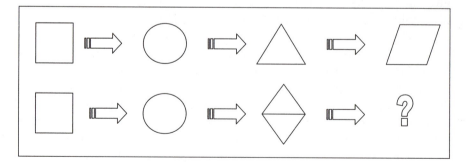

Figure 8.1
Scientific thinking often revolves around experiments. In an experiment, the scientist intervenes, and changes things to see what will happen. Here the scientist has changed the triangle on top to two triangles, to see it they will still produce a leaning square.

The words in this chapter are all connected in some way with experiments, because to think like a scientist is to think about experiments: how to design them, how to conduct them, how to judge them. Virtually all scientific knowledge is based on experiments, and when you hear about science in the news or study it in school, you usually learn about experiments. You already have some understanding of experiments, and in fact you perform them yourself. By learning more about exactly what the words in this chapter mean, you will have a vocabulary to describe and think about experiments in more detail.

Part 1. Definitions

45. hypothesis. a possible explanation of something; a statement describing what might happen to explain something else, or a statement of a possible general law. "Jenner's hypothesis was that a small amount of a disease in the body would cause the body to build up resistance to that disease."

Example

45a. On January 14 the Huygens probe will enter Titan's atmosphere [near Saturn] and parachute down for 2½ hours, snapping photos and collecting data. Scientists hope they can confirm a leading **hypothesis** that Titan's composition is similar to that of early Earth.

Maia Weinstock, Hello, Saturn, *Discover*, January, 2005, p. 48

46. experiment. a test in which an investigator changes or manipulates some feature of the world to see what will happen. An experiment differs from an observation in that an experimenter actually creates a situation or modifies objects in some way, and then observes the results. "The students performed an experiment to discover the effects of artificial light on the growth of bean plants."

Example

46a. Sharlene George works with Tetrahymena because it is an organism whose cells resemble those of humans more than do the cells of bacteria.... Hundreds, literally hundreds of **experiments** are made by first growing large laboratory cultures of cells, then adding to these cells a mutagenic compound that produces hundreds of random mutations, then screening repeatedly for the mutation that will yield up useful results. After which begins the real work: observing keenly, intently, endlessly the results of these mutation **experiments** to make both large and small sense of them. What's alike here? What's different?

Vivian Gornick, *Women in Science*, Touchstone Book, 1990, pp. 44–45

47. variables. factors in a situation that may affect other factors, e.g., amount of study time (a variable) may affect performance on a test. Every aspect of an experimental situation—including the outcome—is a variable. Scientists try to determine which variables influence other variables. "In trying to predict the weather, an important variable to keep in mind is atmospheric pressure."

Example

47a. What we are trying to do is to explain the variation in the children's IQ scores—the fact that some children score high, some score low, and some have average IQs—in terms of another **variable**, the number of books in the house. If our hypothesis is correct we will find that children who live in homes with lots of books have high IQs, children who live in homes with no books have low IQs, and children who live in homes with an average number of books have average IQs. In other words, we hope to find a positive correlation between IQ and books.

Judith Rich Harris, *The Nurture Assumption: Why Children Turn Out the Way They Do*, The Free Press, 1998, p. 18

48. controlled experiment. an experiment in which a scientist compares two groups; in one, she changes some variable, and in the other she does not; the first group is called the experimental group, and the other group is called the control group, or the control. For example, students might plant two groups of seeds. They should be alike in every way except one. They could leave one group in the natural light, but keep the second group in the dark, and see what effect the darkness has.

The point is to make sure that any outcomes are the results of the changed variable (darkness) and not results of some other cause (e.g., more water). "The students in Prof. Adams' class all did better on the second test after they made presentations in class, but we can't be sure the presentations made the difference, because the there was no control group for comparison."

Example

48a. The first high-resolution M.R.I. study of methamphetamine addicts shows "a forest fire of brain damage," said Dr. Paul Thompson, an expert on brain mapping at the University of California, Los Angeles....

The brain's center for making new memories, the hippocampus, lost 8 percent of its tissue, comparable to the brain deficits in early Alzheimer's. The methamphetamine addicts fared significantly worse on memory tests than healthy people the same age.

The study examined 22 people in their 30's who had used methamphetamine for 10 years, mostly by smoking it, and 21 **controls** matched for age. On average, the addicts used an average of four grams a week and said they had been high on 19 of the 30 days before the study began.

Sandra Blakeslee, This Is Your Brain on Meth: A "Forest Fire" of Damage, *New York Times*, 7/20/04

49. a study. a scientific survey designed to test some hypothesis; the careful observation of many examples or individuals, to determine if some generalization applies to them. "A study of American teenagers found that about a third ranked math as their least favorite subject in school."

A study is different from an experiment because in a study the investigators only observe a large number of cases; they do not intervene and change some factor to see what happens.

Example

49a. New research suggests that media portrayals of surgeons as caustic or career-driven people leading unbalanced lives might affect medical students' decisions about whether to specialize in surgery....

The **study**, published in the June 15 issue of the Journal of Surgical Research, reported that second-year medical students are influenced in their choice not to pursue surgery, in part, by images of surgeons in the media. Researchers at the University of Texas–Houston Medical School and Stanford University Medical Center conducted focus groups with 29 medical students in Houston.

Kelly Young, Med Students Need to Get Real, *AM New York*, 7/19/04

(*Caustic* literally means "able to burn or dissolve things, as acid does." A caustic person is one who has a tendency to say things that hurt others.)

50. correlation. when two events regularly occur together, so that if you find one you will probably find the other, but not necessarily because one causes the other. For example, most men shave in the morning, and they also brush their teeth. But shaving doesn't cause them to brush their teeth, and brushing their teeth doesn't cause them to shave. "Some psychologists claim that creativity is correlated with neurosis, but I don't think anyone seriously believes being creative causes neurosis or vice versa."

Correlation can be evidence of a causal relation, even though it is not proof. One must perform repeatable experiments, manipulating variables, to prove cause and effect.

Example

50a. It has long been known that mixed groups are better at problem solving than like-minded ones. But the benefits of diversity are greater than this. Research by Catalyst, an American organisation that aims to expand "opportunities for women and business", found a strong **correlation** between the number of women in top executive positions and financial performance among *Fortune* 500 companies between 1996 and 2000.

Special Report: Women in Business, The Conundrum of the Glass Ceiling, *Economist*, 7/23/05

Test Yourself

Match each word with its definition.

45. hypothesis
46. experiment
47. variables
48. controlled experiment
49. a study
50. correlation

a. the aspects of a situation that affect later events
b. a careful survey of many examples, to see what generalization one can make about them, or what correlations one can find
c. when a scientist arranges two situations or groups, exactly alike except for one factor, to see what consequences the one factor will have
d. a statement of a possible cause of something, or a possible explanation
e. a test in which the scientist changes some factor to see what will happen
f. when two events regularly occur together, but not necessarily because one causes the other

Part 2. Understanding the Meaning

45. hypothesis.

45b. Fascinated as they were by reports of China, some thinkers [of the seventeenth century] discovered that Chinese imperial genealogies went further back in time than biblical ones. Thus Isaac de la Peyrere in 1655...ventured the provocative **hypothesis** of a mankind prior to Adam. The whole of Hebrew and Christian sacred history (comprehending original sin and the mission of Jesus Christ) thus concerned only the Hebrew people but not the peoples of more ancient lands such as China. Needless to say, this **hypothesis** was considered heretical and did not enjoy great success, but it is worth recalling because it shows to what an extent China was increasingly seen as the land of an unknown wisdom.

Umberto Eco, *Serendipities: Language and Lunacy*, Columbia University Press, 1998, p. 64

Comment

Hypothesis is one of my favorite words because it expresses the *attitudes* of critical thinking so well. Just think about what's going on in the mind of a person who proposes a hypothesis. Suppose Nancy suggests that some kids aren't doing well in elementary school because they aren't getting a good breakfast before they come to school. The hypothesis may be good or bad, true or false. But what attitudes does Nancy have? First, she is curious. She is looking for answers. Second, she is imaginative. She is thinking of possibilities beyond the observable facts. Third, she is bold; she is willing to go out on a limb and say something that may sound strange. Fourth, she is open-minded and not stubborn, because she is proposing her idea as a possibility that needs to be tested, not a sure thing that others must accept because she says so. Creating hypotheses is a crucial part of effective thinking. If you become alert to this term, notice the ways writers use it, and deliberately imagine hypotheses yourself, you will be taking a big step toward improving your own thinking.

> 45c. Charles Darwin was once asked whether he thought that natural historians should go out and collect data without the prejudice of a preformed **hypothesis,** or whether they should be observing nature with a particular theory in mind. Darwin was unusually emphatic in his reply. If they did not have a **hypothesis,** he wrote to his friend the economist Henry Fawcett, they may as well "go into a gravel-pit and count the pebbles and describe the colours".
>
> Jared Diamond, I am sure, would agree. But he goes further than Darwin. In *Guns, Germs and Steel*, Diamond suggests that historians of humans, as well as of nature, should be scientific **hypothesis** testers.
>
> Laurence Hurst, Epidemics of Culture, *New Scientist*, May 24, 2003

to hypothesize (verb). to propose something as a hypothesis.

> 45d. "Some people argue that every time we recall a memory, the old memory is erased and a new memory is created," [Vadim Bolshakov] said. Others argue that the same old memory is being stored again. Some even **hypothesize** that the old memory is not destroyed, but that many copies of the same memory could exist in parallel.
>
> Carey Goldberg, A Smudge on Indelible Memories, *International Herald Tribune*, 12/31/03, p. 5

hypothetical (adjective). possible; something that could happen or could exist but hasn't actually happened.

> 45e. Here are the results of an informal poll about a third, **hypothetical,** case. Suppose a terrorist group kidnapped a newborn baby from a hospital. I asked four mothers if they would approve of torturing kidnappers if that were necessary to get their own newborns back. All said yes, the most "liberal" adding that she would like to administer it herself.
>
> Michael Levin, The Case for Torture, in Linda H. Peterson et al., eds., *The Norton Reader: Shorter Ninth Edition*, W. W. Norton and Company, 1996, p. 428

46. experiment.

46b. Faraday was wondering what would happen if he mounted a disk of copper between the poles of a horseshoe magnet. As the disk revolved an electric current was produced. This would doubtless have seemed the idlest kind of an **experiment** to the staunch business men of the time.

James Harvey Robinson, *The Mind in the Making*, Harper and Brothers, 1921, p. 55

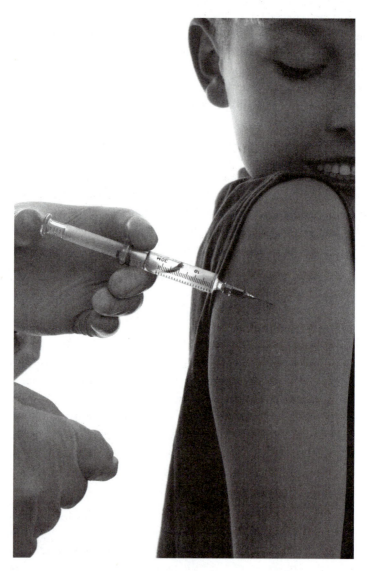

Figure 8.2

In 1796 Edward Jenner injected an 8-year-old boy with a smallpox vaccine in an experiment to test immunity. *Source: © Leah-Anne Thompson/Shutterstock Images LLC*

46c. To the extent that lie detection through the observation of body language and facial expressions is accurate (overall not very), women are better at it than men because they are more intuitively sensitive to subtle cues. In **experiments** in which subjects observe someone either truth telling or lying, although no one is consistently correct in identifying the liar, women are correct significantly more often than men.

Michael Shermer, *The Science of Good and Evil*, Henry Holt and Company, 2004, p. 176

Question: In the experiments that Shermer mentions, what part of the world is being manipulated or varied by the experimenters?

46d. Apart from the famous cases in which a strategic **experiment** might bring the solution of a particular problem, Galileo gives the impression of having **experimented** so constantly as to gain an intimacy with movement and structures—he has watched the ways of projectiles, the operation of levers and the behaviour of balls on inclined planes, until he seems to know them, so to speak, from the inside in the way that some men know their dogs.

Herbert Butterfield, *The Origins of Modern Science, 1300–1800*, Revised Edition, The Free Press, 1957, p. 105

Comment

Experiments are very common, and aren't just tests done in labs. You have conducted many experiments yourself, although probably not with the care and precision of a professional scientist. If you try on different pieces of clothing to see how they look, you are conducting an experiment. You are "manipulating some feature of the world to see what will happen." You might try a new recipe, a new route to your work, or a new way of talking with your spouse. The main reason these are not scientific experiments is that scientists define and measure the features they change very precisely, they define and measure the results very precisely, and they repeat their experiments as many times as possible. They also manipulate features in unusual circumstances, such as very low temperatures, or on an extremely small scale. But the basic process is the same in science and in your own thinking.

47. variables.

47b. One of the most important things scientists do when they conduct an experiment is to attempt to find out what the relationship is among different **variables**.

Let's consider what is meant by a relationship between **variables**. How fast can you run 100 yards? ... What if you were running on grass? What if you were running uphill? Or after a large Thanksgiving dinner? What if you wear hip boots? What if it were raining? Such things as the kind of track, the slope of the ground, the time since you last ate, the kind of clothes you are wearing, and the weather conditions are all **variables**.

Garvin McCain, Erwin M. Segal, *The Game of Science*, Fifth Edition, Brooks/Cole Publishing Company, 1988, p. 102

47c. Today, segments of Western society publicly repudiate racism. Yet many (perhaps most!) Westerners continue to accept racist explanations privately or subconsciously....

A seemingly compelling argument goes as follows. White immigrants to Australia built a literate, industrialized, politically centralized, democratic state based on metal tools and on food production, all within a century of colonizing a continent where the Aborigines had been living as tribal hunter-gatherers without metal for at least 40,000 years. Here were two successive experiments in human development, in which the environment was identical and the sole **variable** was the people occupying that environment. What further proof could be wanted to establish that the differences between Aboriginal Australian and European societies arose from differences between the peoples themselves?

Jared Diamond, *Guns, Germs, and Steel: The Fates of Human Societies*, W. W. Norton, 1999, p. 19

Question: Diamond says the Aborigines' settlement of Australia and the white Europeans' settlement of the same continent were two experiments, and the only difference between the processes was the settlers' race. But the eventual outcomes were very different. Can you think of any other differences between the two processes, besides race?

47d. Harlow graphed the mean amount of time the monkeys spent nursing versus cuddling,..."We were not surprised to discover that contact comfort was an important basic affectional or love **variable**, but we did not expect it to overshadow so completely the **variable** of nursing;...

Here Harlow was establishing that love grows from touch, not taste [or food], which is why, when the mother's milk dries up, as it inevitably does, the child continues to love her....

In Harlow's lab, at this time, there rose an air of great excitement. The researchers had stumbled into a major love **variable** and had discounted another love **variable**—feeding—as of minimal importance, and they could show all this on a graph.

Lauren Slater, *Opening Skinner's Box: Great Psychological Experiments of the Twentieth Century*, W. W. Norton and Co., 2004, pp. 139–140

Question: Harry Harlow, a psychologist, experimented with baby monkeys. He manipulated the time and manner of nursing, and also the time and manner of physical contact between a baby monkey and its mother. He wanted to see how those changes affected the bond of love between them. Can you think of any other variables, besides food and physical contact, that might affect the love between a baby monkey and its mother?

48. controlled experiment.

48b. Deutsch's and Gifford's organizations unveiled what is thought to be the city's first green roof on a downtown commercial property last week at 1425 K St. NW. A phenomenon in Europe that has been catching on across the United States, with installations in Maryland and Virginia, green roofs offer a host of environmental benefits, including reduced stormwater runoff, lower building temperatures and improved air quality—effectively reversing the impact of plant loss in some urban areas over the past 30 years.

The roof includes a 3,500-square-foot garden containing 9,730 plants, a weather station and an unplanted **control** area to compare temperature, rainfall and runoff.

Arielle Levin Becker, On K Street, a Building with a Cultivated Facade; Green Roof Called Environmental Boon, *Washington Post*, 6/28/04

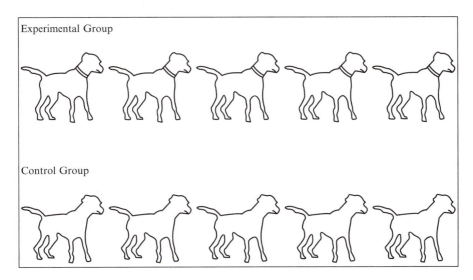

Figure 8.3
"Collars make dogs more obedient." You could perform a controlled experiment to test this hypothesis by using the two groups of dogs pictured here. The two groups are as alike as possible, except for the one variable you want to test (i.e., collars).

48c. From Chubby Hubby ice cream to Trailer Park red nail polish, marketers using ambiguous or surprising descriptions for new flavours and colours are likely to win sales by making consumers go through the effort of understanding an off-beat name, according to recent Wharton research....

Gauging the effects of such names on consumer behaviour is hard because so many other variables come in to play. So Kahn and Miller constructed **controlled experiments** of product names....

In an initial experiment testing flavour names, 100 undergraduates were asked to complete an unrelated questionnaire on a computer. After finishing the questionnaire at the computer, the students were told they could take some jellybeans. The jellybeans were in six cups each with a sign attached listing the flavour. Half the subjects saw jellybean names that were common descriptives: blueberry blue, cherry red, chocolate brown, marshmallow white, tangerine orange and watermelon green. The other half saw flavours with ambiguous names: Moody blue, Florida red, Mississippi brown, white Ireland, Passion orange and Monster green. Researchers observed that the less common names were more popular.

Shades of meaning, *Knight Ridder Tribune Business News*, 7/6/05

Question: Here, the investigators manipulated a variable to see what would happen; therefore, they conducted an experiment. What makes it a controlled experiment?

48d. In 1969, Tarjan and Kemeny, in Hungary, feeding low dosages [of DDT] to successive generations of a strain of inbred mice, reported a higher tumor incidence among the experimental animals than the **controls**, becoming statistically significant in the third and fourth generations. But there were puzzling features. For one thing, tumors were lower in the **controls** than in the breeding stock [the original group from which both experimental and control animals were taken,] indicating some factor in the experiment that was not accounted for. Further, while the strain used was supposed to be leukemia-free, leukemia in fact occurred in both the experimental and **control groups**.

James P. Hogan, *Kicking the Sacred Cow: Questioning the Unquestionable and Thinking the Impermissible*, Baen Publishing, 2004, p. 276

Comment

Occasionally you will read a passage in which a person describes a "controlled experiment," but means that the experiment is carefully managed, "under control," or regulated. That is not how the word *control* is used in the context of science, and anyone who uses it that way isn't using it in the scientific sense. The person may not know the scientific sense. Everyone is ignorant about many, many things, so that's not a scandal. Furthermore, as you have already learned, people use these key words in different ways. That's also unavoidable. Language is a living, growing system, not a set of definitions and rules set in stone forever.

The purpose of learning the standard meanings of these words is not to "sound educated." It is to give yourself the tools to think more clearly about complicated matters, such as scientific experiments. You can probably judge how strong an experiment is without knowing the word *control*. But if you know the word, judging and assessing scientific results becomes much easier, and you can advance to a higher level. Of course, using words correctly may have additional benefits. Other literate people will recognize that you know what you are talking about and will respect you for it.

49. a study.

49b. Television these days is loaded with sex, sex, sex—double the number of sex scenes aired seven years ago, says a **study** out yesterday....

There were nearly 3,800 scenes with sexual content spotted in more than 1,100 shows researches studied, up from about 1,900 such scenes in 1998, the first year of the Kaiser Family Foundation survey....

The **study** examined a sample of a week's worth of programming on ABC, CBS, NBC, Fox, WB, PBS, Lifetime, TNT, USA Network and HBO. Sexual content, as defined in the study, could be anything from discussions about sex to scenes involving everything from kissing to intercourse.

Sex Scenes on TV Are on the Rise, *AM New York*, 11/10/05

Question: Can you think of a hypothesis to explain these findings?

49c. Consistent with these experimental results are **studies** that show people are more likely to rate themselves superior in "moral goodness" than in "intelligence," and community residents overwhelmingly see themselves as caring more about the environment and other social issues than other members of the community do. In one College Entrance Examination Board survey of 829,000 high school seniors, none rated themselves below average in the category "ability to get along with others," 60 percent rated themselves in the top 10 percent, and 25 percent said they were in the top 1 percent.

Michael Shermer, *The Science of Good and Evil*, Henry Holt and Company, 2004, p. 178.

49d. In one of the most comprehensive **studies**, a 2003 report by C.D.C. [Centers for Disease Control] scientists examined the medical records of more than 125,000 children born in the United States from 1991 to 1999. It found no difference in autism rates among children exposed to various amounts of thimerosal.

Parent groups, led by SafeMinds, replied that documents obtained from the disease control centers showed that early versions of the study had found a link between thimerosal and autism.

But C.D.C. researchers said that it was not unusual for studies to evolve as more data and controls were added. The early versions of the study, they said, failed to control for factors like low birth weight, which increases the risk of developmental delays.

The Institute of Medicine said that it saw "nothing inherently troubling" with the C.D.C's adjustments and concluded that thimerosal did not cause autism. Further studies, the institute said, would not be "useful."

Gardiner Harris and Anahad O'Connor, On Autism's Cause, It's Parents vs. Research, *New York Times*, 6/25/05

Comment

Scientists conduct experiments to discover causal relations between things. But they can use studies to look for causes and effects as well. For example, the parents in SafeMinds have surveyed a large number of children, and they've noticed that very often when the children took the drug thimerosal, they became autistic. Other children who did not take thimerosal did not become autistic, these parents believe. They say that shows that the drug is probably part of the cause of autism.

C.D.C. researchers disagree with the parents. They say early versions of the study "failed to control for factors like low birth weight." They mean early versions did not specifically compare children with low birth weight to children with normal birth weight, to see if there was any difference in autism. When later versions of the study did compare those groups, they showed that the low birth weight might be part of the cause of autism, not the thimerosal.

The scientists are applying the word *control* to a study rather than an experiment, but the meaning is similar. They have 125,000 subjects to work with. They can arrange the subjects in groups that are as alike as possible, except for one variable (e.g., low birth rate) and see if the children with that variable tend to be autistic compared with the other group.

When scientists look for causes affecting people they sometimes use studies rather than experiments, because they do not want to manipulate people or variables that affect people. Universities set very strict guidelines for experiments involving human subjects.

50. correlation.

50b. Doug Sanderson, an old friend from college and a lawyer in the Washington, DC, area, recently sent me an article from *The New York Times* that claimed that "early maternal employment has negative effects on children's intellectual development." I surprised him by replying that the study cited in the article showed no such thing.... The *Times* study was "**correlational**," not "experimental," and **correlational** studies don't shed light on causes. This study merely showed a statistical relationship between the number of hours moms spent working during the first nine months of their children's lives and the scores those children received on a test at age 3. Scores were slightly better for those children whose moms stayed at home, but not necessarily *because* they stayed at home.

Robert Epstein, Editor's Pet Peeve, *Psychology Today*, December, 2002

50c. At Iowa State University in Ames, social psychologist Craig Anderson tested college students' willingness to provide help to others after playing 20 minutes of benign games like Glider Po or malignant ones like the pedestrian-plowing Carmageddon. Anderson timed how long his subjects waited before responding to a person left whimpering in the hallway after a staged attack. "The people who played a violent video game took about four times as long to come to the aid of the victim as people who played a non-violent game," says Anderson.

Skeptics like [Jonathan] Freedman say such **correlations** don't amount to causation and that other, well-established risk factors such as poverty and neglect are important to consider.

Karen Wright, Guns, Lies, and Video, *Discover*, April, 2003

Question: In Anderson's results, what is correlated with what?

50d. Why should any brain event be associated with conscious awareness....? Why can't the rest of the brain do without consciousness?

We can't yet answer this question directly but as scientists the best we can do is establish **correlations** and try to home in on the answer. We can make a list of all brain events that reach consciousness and a list of those brain events that don't. We can then compare the two lists and ask whether there is a common denominator in each list that distinguishes it from the other.

V. S. Ramachandran, *A Brief Tour of Human Consciousness: From Impostor Poodles to Purple Numbers*, Pi Press, 2004, pp. 29–30

Comment

Finding correlations is one of the first steps toward finding causes. Ramachandran describes the standard methods scientists use to look for causes. (They are called "Mill's Methods," after the philosopher John Stuart Mill.) He is wondering why some brain events cause us to be conscious of them (e.g., imagining a red rose) while others do not (e.g., the brain sends a signal to the lungs to make us breath regularly, but we aren't conscious of it). He suggests we first look at those brain events that are correlated with consciousness, and try to find something they all have in common. That might be what causes them to be conscious. For the sake of illustration, let's suppose that all those conscious events occur in the rear section of the brain.

Second, we look at those brain events that do not produce consciousness, and try to find out how they are different from the first set. Let's suppose they occur somewhere else besides the rear section. Since they lack the factor that all the events in the first set possess—occurring in the rear section—we have a reason to believe that the difference (i.e., the location) is the cause of consciousness. But no one has actually made such a study. Moreover, even this would not prove cause and effect. Two things (e.g., consciousness and occurring in the rear section of the brain) can be correlated without one causing the other. We would need more experimental evidence to prove cause and effect.

> 50e. Of the many theories addressing the problem of state origins, the simplest denies that there is any problem to solve. Aristotle considered states the natural condition of human society....
>
> A third theory, still popular with some historians and economists, sets out from the undoubted fact that, in both Mesopotamia and North China and Mexico, large-scale irrigation systems began to be constructed around the time that states started to emerge. The theory also notes that any big, complex system for irrigation or hydraulic management requires a centralized bureaucracy to construct and maintain it. The theory then turns an observed rough **correlation** in time into a postulated chain of cause and effect.
>
> Jared Diamond, *Guns, Germs, and Steel*, W. W. Norton, 1999, pp. 282–283

Comment

Diamond wants to know what caused political states to appear in history. He makes a list of ancient places that had states, and he looks for something all those places had in common. They all had large irrigation systems. That correlation suggests that irrigation systems may have been the cause of political states. In the previous example (50d), Ramachandran suggested a second step in finding the cause of something. What should Diamond do next?

to correlate (verb)

> 50f. If you do well on the Weschler vocabulary test, you'll probably also score high on Miller's analogies. In fact, a given person's scores on the different subtests that make up standard intelligence tests do **correlate** highly, though not perfectly; overall scores can be estimated using only the scores from a subtest or two.
>
> Sonja I. Yoerg, *Clever as a Fox*, Bloomsbury, 2001, pp. 19–20

Comment

Yoerg's example shows that correlation is not the same as causation. A person's skill with vocabulary is correlated with her skill with analogies; if one is high, the other will probably be high. But no one believes one skill causes the other. Instead, some psychologists believe both skills are effects of some underlying, general ability.

Part 3. Applying the Words

45. hypothesis
46. experiment
47. variables
48. controlled experiment
49. a study
50. correlation

Exercise 1:   Choose the Best Word

For each sentence, choose the best word (or an appropriate form of the word) to fill in the blank.

1. We found a _____ between annual income and low rates of heart disease, but that isn't enough to show that money itself causes people to have healthy hearts.
2. It was an excellent _____ because a large number of people participated and the investigators gathered and cataloged the data very carefully.
3. In the _____, the two groups were the same in age, in male–female ratio, in occupations, and in other ways, except one group gave up coffee for six weeks and the other didn't.
4. The most famous _____ in history, where Galileo dropped unequal weights from the Leaning Tower of Pisa, probably never happened.
5. Cliff's _____ is that the car stopped because it's out of gas, but I think something is wrong with the engine.
6. Semmelweis found that if surgeons washed their hands before operating, patients had a much better chance of surviving, but he had to consider many _____ before he made his discovery.

Exercise 2:   Apply the Words

Read each example and answer the questions that follow.

> 1. In a family of brown eyes and brown hair, I grew into the oddball with blue eyes and blond hair. A running joke among my high school friends was that I looked suspiciously like the garbageman.
>
> Michael Paterniti, *Driving Mr. Albert: A Trip Across America with Einstein's Brain*, The Dial Press, 2000, p. 45

Paterniti's friends were humorously offering a hypothesis. What was it?

> 2. Another kind of wasp paralyzes crickets and carries them to the burrow containing its larvae. Before the turn of the century, the French naturalist Jean-Henry Fabre discovered how "mindless" the apparently caring and intelligent behavior of the wasp really was. The wasp always followed a certain routine when she brought food to the burrow. She set the cricket on its back with its antennae just touching the burrow entrance. Then she carefully looked over the tunnel.

Fabre moved the cricket a fraction of an inch away while the wasp carried out her inspection. Upon finding the cricket out of position, she would put it back in place and again check over the tunnel. Even after forty repetitions, the wasp reacted like the needle on a scratched record, returning to inspect the tunnel again and again, never able to get on to the next step of carrying the food down to her offspring.

Dorothy Hinshaw Patent, *How Smart Are Animals?* Harcourt, Brace, Jovanovich, 1990, p. 30

What did Fabre discover? Did he perform an ordinary experiment, or a controlled experiment?

3. Socialization research is the scientific study of the effects of the environment—in particular, the effects of the parents' child-rearing methods or their behavior toward their children—on the children's psychological development. It is a science because it uses some of the methods of science, but it is not, by and large, an experimental science. To do an experiment it is necessary to vary one thing and observe the effects on something else. Since socialization researchers do not, as a rule, have any control over the way parents rear their children, they cannot do experiments. Instead, they take advantage of existing variations in parental behavior. They let things vary naturally and, by systematically collecting data, try to find out what things vary together. In other words, they do correlational studies.

Judith Rich Harris, *The Nurture Assumption: Why Children Turn Out the Way They Do*, The Free Press, 1998, p. 15

Socialization researchers are trying to understand children's psychological development. What variable that affects this development do they focus on? If they are studying a variable and what happens when a variable changes, why shouldn't we say their investigations are experiments?

4. When in 1980 they returned to San Diego to take up their new jobs, the Garlands found themselves stalled. They had all sorts of circumstantial evidence that vitamin D, whether generated by sunlight or diet, may prevent colon cancer, but they had no proof. The only way to establish the notion one way or another was to conduct a clinical trial, a so-called intervention experiment, in which they would give vitamin D to some people, wouldn't give it to others, and would keep track of who came down with colon cancer. That would show, once and for all, if vitamin D forestalled the disease.

Peter Radetsky, "Pulling the Handle off the Pump: Sunlight, Cancer, and the Brothers Garland," in William H. Shore, ed., *Mysteries of Life and the Universe*, Harcourt Brace and Company, 1992, p. 242

Is the "intervention experiment" that the Garlands wanted to perform a simple experiment, or a controlled experiment? What factor (or variable) did they want to manipulate?

5. More than 10 years ago, Jim Quinn, a behavioral ecologist at McMaster University in Hamilton, Ontario, determined that herring gulls nesting near steel mills around the Great Lakes displayed higher heritable mutation rates than their rural cousins. In May Quinn and one of his students, Chris Somers, were finally able to pin the blame on airborne particles just a few micrometers in diameter.

They found that offspring born from male mice exposed to industrial air pollution [in the laboratory] showed twice the mutation rate of those whose fathers breathed rural or filtered polluted air. The most likely cause, Quinn says, are small particles that can carry known mutation-causing compounds, such as polycyclic aromatic hydrocarbons, deep into the lungs.

Ken Kostel, Air Pollution Linked to Genetic Mutations, *Discover*, January, 2005, p. 72

When Quinn observed the gulls around the Great Lakes (paragraph 1), did he conduct a simple experiment, a controlled experiment, or a study? Later, when he observed mice exposed to pollution, which type of investigation did he conduct? (Did he manipulate the environment? Did he expose one group to a variable and not another group?)

6. According to one survey, only a third of people who take drugstore painkillers bother to read the package directions; 64 percent said they were unconcerned about side-effects....

The wide selection of pain relievers also makes it difficult for many consumers to know which to take for which kind of pain.

"When I ask patients why they use a certain pain reliever, they say, 'Well, one day Joe gave me this one for my headache and it really took care of it, so I always take that,'" Dr. Montauk said.

Mary Duenwald, Choosing a Pain Remedy Carefully, *New York Times*, 7/6/04

Does the first paragraph of this example describe an experiment or a study? Is the patient that Dr. Montauk describes relying on a study, or a correlation, or a superstition?

7. Unfortunately, the American public was being hoodwinked by the popularization of pseudoscientific intelligence testing carried out on both immigrants and U.S. Army recruits from 1917 to 1919....Of course, the army intelligence tests showed that both Negroes and foreigners were of less intelligence than native-born whites....These results were not surprising given that the army mental tests really only tested the degree to which one was a member of white American society. Furthermore, the army tests showed that social factors, such as education, had powerful impacts on the results.

Joseph L. Graves, Jr., *The Race Myth: Why We Pretend Race Exists in America*, Dutton, 2004, p. 168

The Army thought they observed a correlation between test scores and intelligence, but Graves says the correlation was really between test scores and something else. What? He also says that another variable influenced the test scores. What was it?

> 8. A survey by the Pew Research Center shows that conservatives are happier than liberals— in all income groups. While 34 percent of all Americans call themselves "very happy," only 28 percent of liberal Democrats (and 31 percent of moderate or conservative Democrats) do, compared with 47 percent of conservative Republicans. This finding is niftily self-reinforcing: It depresses liberals.
>
> Election results do not explain this happiness gap. Republicans have been happier than Democrats every year since the survey began in 1972. Married people and religious people are especially disposed to happiness, and both cohorts vote more conservatively than does the nation as a whole.
>
> People in the Sun Belt—almost entirely red [conservative] states— have sunnier dispositions than Northerners, which could have as much to do with sunshine as with conservatism. Unless sunshine makes people happy, which makes them conservative.
>
> Such puzzles show why social science is not for amateurs.
>
> Geroge F. Will, Smile If (and Only If) You're Conservative, *Washington Post*, 2/23/06

(A cohort is a group of people who share some common trait, e.g., being married, being religious.)

Will (a conservative columnist) says there is a closer correlation between happiness and being conservative than between happiness and being liberal. What other correlations does he describe?

> 9. Especially good experiences can have long-lasting effects on our health. If we take the 750 actors and actresses who were ever nominated for Oscars, we can assume that before the award-panel's decision the winners and losers were equally healthy on average. Yet those who got the Oscars went on to live four years longer, on average, than the losers. Such was the gain in morale from winning.
>
> Richard Layard, *Happiness: Lessons from a New Science*, Penguin, 2005, p. 24

Is Layard describing a study or an experiment? Layard says that winning an Oscar caused the winners to live an average of four years longer than the losers. Can you think of any other possible reasons that many of the winners would live longer than the losers, besides the "gain in morale"?

> 10. According to a new study by the American Association of University Women (AAUW), women already earn 20 percent less than men at the same level and in the same field one year after college graduation....

A 12 percent gap appeared even when the AAUW Educational Foundation, which did the research, controlled for hours, occupation, parenthood and other factors known to directly affect earnings.

The remainder of the gap is unexplained by any other control factors. That may mean, Hill said, that discrimination is the root cause.

Amy Joyce, Same Degree, Smaller Paycheck, *AM New York*, 5/7/07

When the Foundation says they "controlled for hours, occupation, parenthood and other factors," they mean that they compared two groups that were very similar in those respects (worked the same number of hours per week, etc.) and where the only apparent difference between the groups was that one was male and the other was female. Men still earned 12 percent more than women. What hypothesis is proposed to explain the difference in earnings?

Exercise 3: Analyzing Arguments

The following passage describes a classic controlled experiment. Try to state Redi's reasoning in the form of an argument. His experiment confirmed his hypothesis about flies, so the hypothesis is his conclusion. How would you state the evidence in the form of premises that lead to his conclusion?

In the process of spontaneous generation, living creatures are derived from inorganic, or nonliving, materials. This idea was widely accepted until the mid-1600s when it was finally challenged by experimental procedures. In 1668, the Italian Francesco Redi (1628–1694) designed a series of experiments to test the validity of spontaneous generation. Prior to Redi's experiments it was widely believed that maggots were generated from rotting meats. However, Redi was convinced that flies visiting the decaying material were contributing to the formation of the maggots. To test his hypothesis, Redi prepared a series of jars that contained various types of meat. Half of the jars were sealed while the other half remained exposed to the environment. After a period of time, only the jars that were left exposed revealed the presence of maggots. Based on these results, Redi concluded that the maggots were not developing directly from the decaying meat as was previously suggested by believers of spontaneous generation. However, the possibility still existed that the maggots were being generated from fresh air and subsequently being deposited on the meat. This would offer a possible explanation as to why the meats in the sealed jars did not generate maggots. To test the contribution of this second variable, Redi once again placed meats in two sets of jars. As with the previous experiment, he left one set exposed to the environment; however, this time the second set was sealed with gauze. The gauze allowed fresh air to reach the meat, but not the flies. Once again his results indicated the presence of maggots on the exposed meat, but not on the meat contained within the jars covered with gauze....

While Redi suggested that the maggots were formed from eggs deposited by the flies, it would not be until two decades later that the Dutch biologist Anton van Leeuwenhoek (1632–1723), using one of the new generation of powerful microscopes…, confirmed Redi's experiments.

Michael Windelspecht, *Groundbreaking Scientific Experiments, Inventions and Discoveries of the 17th Century*, Greenwood Press, 2002, p. 8

Exercise 4:   Apply the Ideas in Writing

Here is a hypothesis: "Drinking coffee thirty minutes before a math test in college improves students' performance on those tests." How would you test this hypothesis? Write a paragraph or two describing what you would do to test the hypothesis. Would you set up an experiment, or do a study? How would you do it? What specific factors must you keep in mind? What would you need to do to test the hypothesis? (You may imagine that you are a student in college taking math, or that you are a professor in a college and students are willing to cooperate, or that you are a government scientist who can set up a table in the college cafeteria. Or imagine any situation you like.)

Improving Your Writing 8: Thesis

A good essay always has a *thesis*. A thesis is the main point you want to get across in your essay. Essays are made up of several paragraphs, and the thesis holds the paragraphs together. When your reader finishes your essay, all the examples and quotes and explanations he or she remembers should be circling around one main conclusion in his or her mind, like the planets circling around the sun.

A thesis is not a topic. "Melting glaciers" could be a topic, but it's not a thesis. A thesis expresses your opinion about the topic. The statement "Melting glaciers might be the worst catastrophe in human history" is a possible thesis, because it expresses an opinion. "Competitive sports in high school" is a topic. "Competitive sports in high school are too dangerous" is a thesis. Or "Competitive sports in high school build character" is another thesis.

Your thesis should be interesting and informative. It should not be so obvious that everyone already knows that it's true. "Many high schools have sports teams" is not a good thesis because it would be easy to prove this (factual) statement; no one would disagree with it. But if you said, "Competitive sports in high school are too dangerous," you would grab people's attention. Some would disagree with you. Most readers would want to know why you hold that opinion. What makes you think that? Then you would use the main part of your essay to explain why you believe your thesis and to persuade your audience to agree with you. Finding a good thesis means discovering something on your own that other people might not have discovered.

CHAPTER 9

Explaining

51. to explain

52. theory

53. to predict

54. story

55. motive

56. superstition

The word *explanation* is very flexible and can mean several things. At the most basic level, an explanation is an answer to a question. Since we ask different kinds of questions, we have different kinds of explanations. You can explain how to do something, like how to get to Route 80. Or you can explain what someone meant, or what a word means. You can explain what happened, or what will happen next week. Probably the most basic kind of explanation is the answer to the question "why?" In other words, explaining is often giving the cause of something.

In Chapter 7 you studied words about causes and effects. The words in this chapter are about answering questions. For example, you can think about what caused a forest fire. You would think about immediate causes, remote causes, and contributing factors. After you have figured out the causes, if people ask you about it, you can tell them. And then you can think about the way you told them. Were you brief or long-winded? Did you give examples? Did you think about multiple causes? Now you are asking questions about your explanation. Consider an analogy. If you are in a biology class, the teacher might be talking about a bird's wing and how similar it is to your hand. You would be focusing on the bones of the wing and the bones of human hands. But the principal of the school might come in and listen for a while, to see how the biology teacher teaches. The principal is focusing on the way the teacher talks, the pictures he uses, the questions he asks, and the answers he gives to students' questions. The

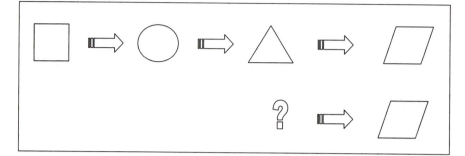

Figure 9.1
Usually when people ask for an explanation of an event, they are asking for the cause, or causes. Sometimes we can figure out the cause of an event (e.g., Smith's house burned) if we know it is very similar to another event (Jones' house burned), and we know what caused the other event.

wing and hand are not the important things to the principal. In this chapter you are like the principal. You are stepping back from comparisons and causes and thinking about how people describe those things.

That means the words in this chapter are a little different from the words in the previous chapters. The words in the previous chapters were about various relations: between things, between events, and between beliefs and sources. For example, two sisters can be similar and different; if you see dozens of cars in a parking lot you can make a generalization about them; the student's illness might cause her to miss school; you believe it is a fact that measles is contagious because your school nurse told you it is.

Seeing these relationships is thinking. Telling someone about the relationships is explaining. We have words to talk about cause and effect, but we also have words to talk about telling someone else what we've seen. That is, we can talk about explanations. We can look at different aspects of what the person says, just as we looked at different aspects of cause and effect. For example, if someone says Julie's measles caused her to miss school, we can ask more questions about measles: What does it feel like to have measles? How do you get measles? What is measles, anyway, and why did measles make her stay at home? Then we are asking for a *theory* of the cause and effect. Or we can ask for more details about what happened: When did she find out she was ill? Who decided she should stay at home? Did they call a doctor? Then we are asking for a *story* about the cause and effect. We can describe different kinds of explanations, and it's useful to learn these words.

Part 1. Definitions

51. to explain. to make understandable, in any of several ways: to show why something happened, or how something fits into a larger pattern, or how it is made of simpler elements. "Paul explained the funny shape of the cake by saying that the oven wasn't hot enough."

In the narrower sense of the word, to explain is to describe the causes of something. In the broader sense, to explain is to make something clear and comprehensible. People can explain the meaning of a word, or how to get to Chicago, or the goals of the project, without mentioning causes.

explanation (noun). a description of something that makes an event or situation more understandable. "The mayor's explanation of the recent traffic problems was that tourism has increased, and more tourists mean more traffic."

Example

51a. Past G-8 summits have drawn more than 100,000 activists. Gasink and William Pleasant, another organizer, had forecast 5,000. Most of the news media Tuesday centered on why so few turned out this time.

Explanations varied, from the busy protest schedule ahead with the upcoming Republican and Democratic national conventions, to the logistics of getting to South Georgia, to a general fear generated from the massive law enforcement build-up and past experiences at recent events, where police cracked down heavily on demonstrators.

Jim Schoettler and Teresa Stepzinski, Protests Fizzle in Brunswick and Savannah; few incidents; *The Florida Times-Union*, 6/9/04

52. theory. a set of interconnected ideas designed to explain a variety of observed phenomena; usually theories are about things we can't easily see, such as genes or atoms. That means they cannot be tested directly, as "laws" or "facts" can be. "Hank's theory about the powerful hurricanes is that the atmosphere and the oceans are getting warmer and that leads to bigger hurricanes." "Newton published his theory of universal gravitation in 1687."

Example

52a. From looking at his own farmland, he [James Hutton] could see that soil was created by the erosion of rocks and that particles of this soil were continually washed away and carried off by streams and rivers and redeposited elsewhere. He realized that if such a process were carried to its natural conclusion then Earth would eventually be worn quite smooth. Yet everywhere around him there were hills. Clearly there had to be some additional process, some form of renewal and uplift, that created new hills and mountains to keep the cycle going.... Above all, what Hutton's **theories** suggested was that Earth processes required huge amounts of time, far more than anyone had ever dreamed.

Bill Bryson, *A Short History of Nearly Everything*, Broadway Books, 2003, p. 65

53. to predict. to make an educated guess about what will happen in the future. "Based on his surveys, the pollster predicted that the Democrat would win the election."

prediction (noun).

Example

53a. For some, it is not enough to learn that thunderstorms may be passing through the area this afternoon. They crave far more specific information—say, will it rain between 5 and 7 p.m. today on the tennis court?

The National Centers for Environmental Prediction, which create the models for basic weather forecasts issued in the United States,
do not **predict** at that minute a level. But some companies equipped
with supercomputers and weather-modeling programs customized to
local conditions hope to carve a niche in the forecasting business by
providing short-term, highly focused predictions that zoom in on a
particular location.

Anne Eisenberg, And Now, the Weather Report for Your Neighborhood, *The New York Times*, July 10, 2003

54. story. a description of a series of events, usually involving one or more
main characters, but the events are not necessarily connected as cause and effect.
"Homer tells the story of Odysseus' ten-year wanderings, from the time he left
Troy to the time he arrived at home."

Example

54a. Leaders achieve effects primarily by telling **stories** and by
embodying those **stories** in their own lives....Leaders sense that a
story—unlike a mere slogan or message or even a vision—is a dramatic
vehicle that features a protagonist, a set of goals, obstacles that may
thwart the goals, and a set of strategies by which to achieve the goals.
In telling **stories**, leaders create dramatic narratives about themselves,
their families, their people, and their nations. Such narratives can be
compelling, for they draw listeners into the sweep of history, causing
them to identify with and make common cause with the leader.

Howard Gardner, *Intelligence Reframed*, Basic Books, p. 126

55. motive. the belief or desire or inner state that causes a person to act. "Ms. Carter's
motive for poisoning her husband and collecting the insurance was pure greed."

Example

55a. Since it is relevant to the subject, I shall remind princes who have
recently seized a state for themselves through support given from
within that they should carefully reflect on the **motives** of those who
helped them. If these were not based on a natural affection for the
new prince, but rather on discontent with the existing government, he
will retain their friendship only with considerable difficulty and exer-
tion, because it will be impossible for him in his turn to satisfy them.

Niccolo Machiavelli, *The Prince*, trans. George Bull, Penguin, 1999 [originally 1514], p. 69

56. superstition. a mistaken belief that one thing causes another based on very little experience or even on hearsay. "Baseball players are so superstitious: The third baseman thinks carrying his rabbit's foot will help him get a hit."

Example

56a. Northwest mythology is full of stories of the raven. He is the trickster, a shape shifter who steals light from the moon and rays from the sun. He is also known as a messenger.

A native shaman once told me a raven never approaches a person unless to impart a lesson or warning. This may be **superstition**, but wishing to believe, I took notice when one landed in front of me.

James Michael Dorsey, The Wisdom Bestowed by Four Ravens and a Wrapper, *Christian Science Monitor*, 3/31/04

(A *shaman* is a person in a pre-literate society who is believed to be able to foretell the future, or heal the sick, or communicate with the dead, or perform other mysterious feats.)

Test Yourself

Match each word with its definition.

51. to explain
52. theory
53. to predict
54. story
55. motive
56. superstition

a. a description of a series of events over time, usually involving a main character
b. to make something understandable, usually by giving the cause
c. to guess what will happen in the future
d. a person's desire or belief that causes her or him to act
e. a belief that one thing causes another when one has no good evidence that it does
f. a set of general ideas that explain more specific laws and observations

Part 2. Understanding the Meaning

51. to explain.

51b. When we try to **explain** why President John F. Kennedy acted the way he did in the Cuban missile crisis, we can offer **explanations** from a wide variety of frameworks....

Morton A. Kaplan, *On Historical and Political Knowing: An Inquiry into Some Problems of Universal Law and Human Freedom*, University of Chicago Press, 1971, p. 44

51c. Why the decline in marriage? Radcons [radical conservatives] blame sexual permissiveness. They say there's less reason to get married when sex is readily available outside marriage. Liberals "bucked against the *Leave It to Beaver* family model, pushed 'open marriages' and, in turn, redefined the family," [says Michael Savage, in *The Savage Nation*].

Wrong again. There's a much easier **explanation**. A lot of men no longer represent particularly good economic deals, and women no longer have to marry in order to have economic security. Thirty years ago, most men had stable jobs in a mass-production economy that earned them paychecks big enough to support families. And most women didn't have paid jobs, so they had to get married in order to have food on their tables and a roof over their heads.

Since then, stable mass-production jobs for men have dwindled, and their paychecks have shrunk. Meanwhile, women have streamed into the workforce....

Robert B. Reich, *Reason: Why Liberals Will Win the Battle for America*, Knopf, 2004, p. 68

51d. But what kind of **explanation** will satisfy us if we wonder how a complicated machine, or a living body, works? The answer is the one that we arrived at in the previous paragraph. If we wish to understand how a machine or a living body works, we look to its component parts and ask how they interact with each other. If there is a complex thing that we do not yet understand we can come to understand it in terms of simpler parts that we do already understand.

Richard Dawkins, *The Blind Watchmaker*, W. W. Norton and Co., 1987, p. 11

Comment

Dawkins is describing a kind of explanation that does not depend on cause and effect, at least initially. We can explain something by showing what parts it is made of. For example, someone might explain a telescope by taking it apart and showing us the lenses. Or one could explain a pencil sharpener by taking it apart and showing us the wheels that grind the wood and lead down to a sharp point. Another word for this kind of explanation is *analysis*. To analyze something is to take it apart.

52. theory.

52b. In a book written at the end of the eighteenth century, [Thomas] Malthus had maintained that there was so much poverty and misery in the world because the human population grew much faster than its food supply. The same situation, Malthus said, existed everywhere in nature....

Darwin read Malthus's book in 1836. Having seen the struggle for existence in nature for himself in South America, Darwin wrote: "It at once struck me that under these circumstances [of struggle for limited food] favorable variations would tend to be preserved, and unfavorable ones to be destroyed. The result of this would be the for-

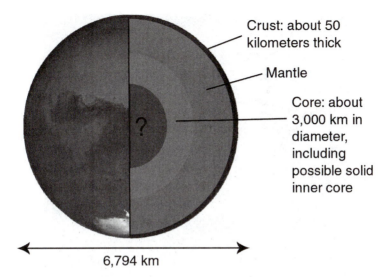

Crust: about 50 kilometers thick

Mantle

Core: about 3,000 km in diameter, including possible solid inner core

6,794 km

Figure 9.2
The drawing explains the structure of Mars. *Source: Argonne National Laboratory, managed and operated by UChicago Argonne, LLC, for the U.S. Department of Energy under contract number DE-AC02-06CH11357*

mation of a new species. Here then I had at last got a **theory** by which to work."

Harry Henderson, Lisa Yount, *The Scientific Revolution*, Lucent Books, 1996, pp. 68–69

52c. The idea that human behavior is "the product of evolution," as the *Washington Post* puts the matter, is now more than a **theory:** it is a popular conviction.

David Berlinski, On the Origins of the Mind, *Commentary*, November, 2004

52d. Norfolk- (*Walks away and turns*) All right—we're at war with the Pope! The Pope's a Prince, isn't he?
　　More- He is.
　　Norfolk- And a bad one?
　　More- Bad enough. But the **theory** is that he's the Vicar of God, the descendant of St. Peter, our only link with Christ.
　　Norfolk- (*sneering*) A tenuous link.
　　More- Oh, tenuous indeed.
　　Norfolk- (*To the others*) Does this make sense? (*No reply; they look at More*) You'll forfeit all you've got—which includes the respect of your country—for a theory?
　　More- (*Hotly*) The Apostolic Succession of the Pope is—(*Stops; interested*)…Why, it's a **theory**, yes; you can't see it, can't touch it; it's a **theory**.

Robert Bolt, *A Man for All Seasons*, Vintage, 1990, p. 91

Figure 9.3
Darwin's theory of evolution by natural selection unifies modern biology; it explains most
of the more specific facts and laws that biologists have discovered. *Source: Julia Margaret
Cameron*

Comment

A theory is a set of ideas that explains several facts and observations. Example
52c highlights another part of the meaning: Theories aren't proven, as facts are.
Good theories are probably true, but people are less sure about them than about
facts. Example 52d is a reminder that theories are usually about things we can't
see, such as the benefits to an animal of a mutation, or the connection of the Pope
with Jesus Christ. That connection is a theory that Roman Catholics believe.

53. to predict.

53b. Larry Ellison, chief executive officer of Oracle, garnered almost
36 inches of print in the *Wall Street Journal* recently with a series of
predictions about the future of the technology industry. Ellison is a
master communicator, whose reputation for talking about exciting
technologies and applications such as "vaporware" created a challenge
for his technical whizzes.

Ellison's **predictions** got attention because, like his earlier **predictions,** they were on a large scale. What makes **predictions** so powerful? Is it our desperate desire to know and therefore prepare for the future? Or to outwit others? That was certainly one of the aims of early civilizations. Or are **predictions** just fun?

Merrie Spaeth, Words Matter: The power of **prediction,** *United Press International,* April 30, 2003

(*To garner* is to get; to acquire.)

53c. Physics tells the same story as astronomy. For, independently of all astronomical considerations, the general physical principle known as the second law of thermodynamics **predicts** that there can be but one end to the universe—a "heat death" in which the total energy of the universe is uniformly distributed, and all the substance of the universe is at the same temperature. This temperature will be so low as to make life impossible.

James Jeans, The Mysterious Universe, Cambridge, 1931, in Joseph Satin, ed., *Reading Literature*, Houghton Mifflin, 1964

Comment

Jeans says the second law of thermodynamics predicts a heat death for the universe. Actually, it wasn't laws but scientists who made predictions, based on laws. Jeans is writing informally. Scientists can predict eclipses and what will happen when you combine two chemicals and so on. Do you think they can predict reliably what will happen billions of years in the future?

53d. Long Bets (www.longbets.org), a site run by the nonprofit Long Bets Foundation, uses betting as a sort of highbrow hook to encourage us to ponder the future.

Will surgical anesthesia be administered by computers in 2030? Will a world government be in control of business and environmental law by 2100? Will CDs still be popular in 2015? If you're skeptical about any of these **predictions,** or others, you can register your objections with a wager.

A funky combination of discussion forum, charity and gambling parlor, Long Bets serves as a forum for academics, entrepreneurs and self-styled intellectuals to make **predictions** about life beyond the next reality-show craze. "By 2030, commercial passengers will routinely fly in pilotless planes," reads one **prediction.** "By 2050, we will receive intelligent signals from outside our solar system," reads another.

The **predictions** should not be mere guesses, but should include an argument, a theory to back them up. The betting occurs when a **prediction** is challenged, essentially with a counter-argument. The challenger and the **predictor** agree on the stakes, with the two also choosing preferred charities for the eventual payment.

Allan Hoffman, Is "Future Site" About More Than Wagers? You Bet, *Newhouse News Service*, March 12, 2003

Comment

This example about Long Bets illustrates a good point about *prediction*. Predictions are normally based on some reason. As the writer says, people have theories to back up their predictions. If your friend is going to pick a name from a hat, and it could be any one of 100 names, you can "predict" what name it will be. But really you are just taking a wild guess. It's not a prediction in the usual sense of the word.

> 53e. In an ideal world, admission to Harvard and other elite schools would be based solely on academic merit. However, academic ability is not a **predictor** of success in the business world—charisma, energy, and motivation are often more important factors than I.Q.—and those who earn higher incomes tend to donate to the endowment of their alma mater. These universities have developed admissions policies that increase incoming dollars, a perfectly acceptable strategy in our capitalist society. Idealists may be shocked, but pragmatists know that Harvard and Yale are wise in admitting future survivors of the fittest.
>
> Robert Motta, The Mail: Making the Grade, *The New Yorker*, 11/28/05

Comment

Examples 53d and 53e both use the word *predictor*, but they mean different things. In the former example about Long Bets the word means one who predicts. In the latter example about Harvard it means a quality or factor that allows a person to predict. In this second sense, one might say, "Dark clouds are a predictor of rain."

Comment

What is the difference between a hypothesis and a prediction? The word "hypothesis" is broader. A hypothesis is any informed speculation about what is possible, in the past, present, or future. A prediction is always about the future. (So a prediction is a type of hypothesis.) You can hypothesize about the past: "I believe that the ancient Romans' use of lead pipes contributed to their health problems, and I'm looking for more evidence to prove it." However, a prediction is always about the future. "Dr. Cooper predicts that the new drug will reduce the number of heart attacks by ten percent." Dr. Cooper is thinking about what will happen in the future when patients take the new drug.

54. story.

> 54b. [The president of Planned Parenthood, Gloria Feldt, got married at 15 and had three children by age 20.] After my third child was born, I realized that someday I might have to support my kids on my own. And that's when I decided to go to college to be a teacher. I hope my **story** can help girls know that even if you make choices that set you back, you can take control of your life at any given time.
>
> Amanika Kumar (quoting Feldt), Master Planner, *Cosmogirl*, May, 2004

54c. However, historians must deal with a vanished past that has left most of its traces in written documents. The translation of these words from the documents into a **story** that seeks to be faithful to the past constitutes the historians' particular struggle with truth. It requires a rigorous attention to the details of the archival records as well as imaginative casting of narrative and interpretation.

Joyce Appleby, Lynn Hunt, and Margaret Jacob, *Telling the Truth About History*, W. W. Norton, 1994, p. 249

(*Archival* means "from archives." Archives are places where documents are stored. For example, newspapers have archives where you can find copies of the paper from years ago.)

54d. Each part of this argument is highly questionable, but Freeman tells an entertaining **story**, and on the way produces an excellent and readable account of the development of Christian doctrine. It is not easy to make an interesting or even comprehensible subject out of the angry controversies about the Trinity that preoccupied early Christians. But he manages it.

Anthony Gottlieb, When the Lights Went Out in Europe, NYT, 2/15/04

Comment

Causes and effects are events related in time, and stories describe events related in time. So what's the difference between a causal connection and a story? The difference is that causes make effects happen. The effects would not have happened without the causes. But the events in a story didn't have to happen the way they did. Twists and turns of a good plot surprise us. Telling a story is only telling *what* happened, not necessarily *why* it happened. Of course, a story can include explanations of why things happened. But then it is a description of causes, an explanation, in addition to being a story. A story, in itself, simply describes the events that happened.

For example, a newspaper story might describe how two political candidates campaigned in a state, how they gave speeches and met with groups, and it might report that finally candidate X won. The story simply reports a series of events that happened one after the other. A reporter might go farther and claim that candidate X won because she understood the voters' interest in jobs and emphasized jobs more than candidate Y. But now the reporter is explaining, not just telling the story. He would probably put his explanation on the editorial page or in a separate "analysis" piece, because he is going beyond reporting the facts. (Another reporter might give a different explanation of the results.)

54e. Contemporary medical science knows of a rare blood disease called porphyria. Porphyria may possibly be the kernel of truth buried in such a richly embroidered and widely dispersed myth as the werewolf.... The skin ulcerates, attacking cartilage and disfiguring the patient's nose, lips, eyelids, ears, and fingers. With the lips changed like this, the teeth appear to protrude more than they actually do, and the patient takes on a kind of permanent grin. The teeth are further affected by deposits of porphyrins, turning them red.... These patients also grow excessive amounts of hair, and this hirsutism makes them appear more animal-like.... As a genetic disorder, porphyria would most likely appear in localized outbreaks. This would have been especially during the Middle Ages, when people traveled less and when there was a tendency toward inbreeding. Possibly, imaginative **stories** were spun around this frightening physical phenomenon in order to make sense of it. Without an explanation, porphyria seems confusing, and the behavior would represent chaos —a state the human mind rejects. People need order, and they need to explain things.... Ancient people created myths to make sense out of confusion. The word *myth* itself means **story** in Greek, and we certainly use **stories**, even today, to explain the unknown. Sometimes only a **story**, not science, will do.

Hugh Downs, *Perspectives*, Turner Publishing, Inc., 1995, pp. 239–241

(To say the skin ulcerates is to say it forms an open wound, usually inflamed.)

Comment

Downs says we use stories to explain the unknown, such as frightening diseases we do not understand. If the word *explain* means "to describe the causes of something," then telling a story (like a story of werewolves) does not explain a disease like porphyria. But Downs is using the word *explain* in a broader sense: It can mean "bringing order to chaos," or "making sense of a confusing situation." In this broader sense, people use stories to explain things. So the word *explain* has a narrower meaning and a second, broader meaning. A good story gives us a feeling of knowing how events and people, past, present, and future, fit together. The first kind of explanation answers the question "*Why* did it happen?" It gives the causes. The second kind of explanation, based on stories, answers the question "*What* happened, or what is happening?"

   The first kind of explanation—which we might call a "causal explanation," or a "scientific explanation"—depends on finding a true causal connection. Suppose Fred dies of cancer. What explains it? You can explain it by saying he smoked a pack of cigarettes a day for years, because we know that smoking (together with other factors) does cause cancer. The value of the explanation depends directly on the truth of the causal law. In contrast, with explanations based on stories, literal truth isn't so important. In Downs' example, he says imaginative stories were woven around the frightening disease in order to make sense of it. The stories (about werewolves and full moons and so on) were reassuring—better than chaos—and they provided a sort of "explanation," although they weren't really true. Stories give us a feeling of understanding, even if they do not tell us the real causes of things.

54f. Most of us are slaves of the **stories** we unconsciously tell ourselves about our lives. Freedom begins the moment we become conscious of the plot line we are living and, with this insight, recognize that we can step into another **story** altogether. Our experiences of life quite literally are defined by our assumptions. We make up **stories** about the world and to a great degree live out their plots. What our lives are like, then, depends on the scripts we consciously or, more likely, unconsciously have adopted.

Carol S. Pearson, *The Hero Within: Six Archetypes We Live By*, HarperSanFrancisco, 1998, p. 17

54g. Human beings have always told **stories** to explain deluges such as this [tsunami in 2004]. Most cultures have deep at their core a flood myth in which the great bulk of humanity is destroyed and a few are left to repopulate and repurify the human race. In most of these **stories,** God is meting out retribution, punishing those who have strayed from his path. The flood starts a new history, which will be on a higher plane than the old.

Nowadays we find these kinds of explanations repugnant. It is repugnant to imply that the people who suffer from natural disasters somehow deserve their fate.

David Brooks, A Time to Mourn, *New York Times*, 1/1/05

55. motive.

55b. Most of us grew up with a concept of intelligence based on the traditional IQ test. The IQ test was originated by Alfred Binet (1857–1911) to measure, objectively, comprehension, reasoning, and judgment. Binet was **motivated** by a powerful enthusiasm for the emerging discipline of psychology and a desire to overcome the cultural and class prejudices of late nineteenth-century France in the assessment of children's academic potential.

Michael J. Gelb, *How to Think Like Leonardo da Vinci*, Dell, 1998, p. 3

Comment

Stories are usually about people who do certain things. If you ask why they do them, you are asking for motives. So motives are similar to causes. Even though the events in stories are not necessarily related as causes and effects, when you ask about motives, you are asking about something like the causes of people's actions.

55c. The good vs. bad attitude spans parties as well as religions. According to it, the crucifix stands for tolerance, freedom, and reconciliation and, as Social Democrat [and president of the German Parliament] Wolfgang Thierse said, is "not a symbol of oppression."…

The head scarf, on the other hand, is perceived as a symbol of intolerance, extremism, female subjugation, and, as Munich's Cardinal Friedrich Wetter put it, a "militant challenge to the values of our Basic Law."

There is a willful failure to recognize that the **motives** for covering up are as diverse as those of the people on either side of the debate. A woman may wear a head scarf for reasons of timid reserve, tradition, or old-fashioned attitudes; but she may also wear it as a form of rebellion against secular tendencies, as a demonstrative symbol of self-assertion in a foreign culture.

Astrid Holscher, The Trouble with the Head Scarf, *World Press Review*, March, 2004

Question: Are motives the same things as contributing factors? Look back at Example 41d in Chapter 7, about motorcycle accidents, and compare it with this example about head scarves. How are they similar and how are they different?

55d. Prison inmates in South Carolina could get up to six months shaved off their sentences if they donated a kidney or their bone marrow, under a proposed bill before the state Senate.

"We have a lot of people dying as they wait for organs, so I thought about the prison population," said state Sen. Ralph Anderson, the bill's main sponsor. "I believe we have to do something to **motivate** them. If they get some good time off, if they get out early, that's **motivation**." ...

Under current law, it is illegal to exchange an organ for "valuable consideration." Lawmakers are attempting to determine whether a reduced sentence constitutes a consideration.

Jenny Jarvie, Inmates Swap Organs, Time, *AM New York*, 3/12/07

56. superstition.

56b. Science, therefore, is a process. But how did it begin? It began when Man began to observe and make a note of his observations. In the Stone Age, Man lived on the flesh of the animals he could slay. Primitive men were creatures of **superstition** and probably, like the practitioners of voodoo who make wax models of their enemies and stick pins in them, they made drawings of these animals in the act of being slain in the hope that the wish would be fulfilled. So we have representations of bison in the cavern of Maux, in the south of France, which are faithful anatomical studies, with the arrow penetrating exactly where the heart would be. This, apart from any **superstition**, showed a useful "know-how" in killing animals.

Ritchie Calder, *Science in Our Lives*, New American Library, 1962, p. 35

Question: What cause-and-effect relation did primitive (i.e., pre-literate) people believe in? That is, what effect were they trying to produce, and how did they think they could produce it? Why was their belief a superstition?

56c. Many **superstitions** are so widespread and so old that they must have risen from a depth of the human mind that is indifferent to race or creed. Orthodox Jews place a charm on their doorposts; so do (or

Figure 9.4
Some "unlucky" objects, such as black cats, may make superstitious people so nervous that they have accidents. *Source: © Dwight Smith/Shutterstock Images LLC*

did) the Chinese. Some people of Middle Europe believe that when a man sneezes, his soul, for that moment, is absent from his body, and they hasten to bless him, lest the soul be seized by the Devil. How did the Melanesians come by the same idea?

Robertson Davies, "A Few Kind Words for Superstition," in Arthur M. Eastman et al., eds., *The Norton Reader*, Sixth Edition, Shorter, W. W. Norton, 1984, p. 125

Comment

A superstition is very similar to a stereotype, except superstitions are about sequences of events and stereotypes are about groups of people or things. Scientists are often trying to make generalizations about sequences of events. They are looking for laws of the form "If you do *A*, you will get *B*," or "Whenever you have *B*, it is the result of *A*." For example, a few years ago scientists discovered that whenever people have higher than normal levels of the chemical serotonin in their brains, they feel calm and secure. Lower levels make them feel anxious and depressed. Thus serotonin causes feelings of contentment. That led to the use of the drug Prozac, which blocks the absorption of serotonin, leaving more at work in the brain. In general, people who take drugs that block the absorption of serotonin feel calm and content.

A superstition is a belief in such a law based on very few observations. Perhaps one or two times a person walked under a ladder and something fell on him or her. Then people might jump to the conclusion that if anyone walks under a ladder, the chances are high that something bad will happen to that person. Walking under a ladder is "unlucky." Or a gambler in a casino wears a certain pair of socks and wins some money at the roulette wheel. If the gambler is superstitious he might think that whenever he wears the same socks he is more likely to win money. Stereotypical thinking is similar, but also different. In the case of stereotypes, people are making generalizations about groups, not sequences of events, but the mistake is the same. They look at only one or two cases and then accept a generalization about the whole group based on those limited cases.

Part 3. Applying the Words

51. to explain
52. theory
53. to predict
54. story
55. motive
56. superstition

Exercise 1:   Choose the Best Word

For each of the following examples, choose the word that best applies.

1. A statement of a probable future event. "When the spacecraft collides with the comet we should be able to see a bright flash."
2. A statement of a sequence of events in time. "Bill rose, dressed, had breakfast, and went to work."
3. A statement of the cause of some event. "The patient's death was caused by a failure of the kidneys."
4. A statement of a causal relationship based upon insufficient evidence. "Don't let the groom see the bride before the wedding; that causes bad luck in a marriage."
5. A statement of a complex set of conditions that may cause various results. "Dr. Tillman believes that when proto-humans moved from the forests to the plains, that led to upright posture, use of the hands, closer groups, and all those eventually produced human intelligence."

6. A statement of some person's reason for acting. "Jack joined the Army because he wanted to be just like his Dad and his grandfather."

Exercise 2:   Apply the Words

Read each example and answer the questions that follow.

1. Among the admirable achievements of Hannibal is included this: that although he led a huge army, made up of countless different races, on foreign campaigns, there was never any dissension, either among the troops themselves or against their leader, whether things were going well or badly. For this, his inhuman cruelty was wholly responsible.... The historians, having given little thought to this, on the one hand admire what Hannibal achieved, and on the other condemn what made his achievement possible.

Niccolo Machiavelli, trans. George Bull, *The Prince*, Penguin, 1999 [originally 1514], p. 55

What observed facts does Machiavelli want to explain? What is his explanation of them?

2. Some of the fossil creatures Cuvier identified [around 1800] were similar to living animals, but others were completely different. In time he described 150 fossil species, of which 90 appeared not to be related to any kind of animal then living. Cuvier believed that the bones he found came from animals that had lived before the flood described in the Bible. He thought God had sent many earlier floods or other catastrophes to earth. Each catastrophe killed most living things, and God created new ones when the disaster was over. "Life has often been disturbed by great and terrible events," Cuvier wrote.

Harry Henderson, Lisa Yount, *The Scientific Revolution*, Lucent Books, 1996, p. 65

Cuvier offers a theory to explain his observations. His theory consists of several statements. How would you summarize it?

3. Boeing and Airbus, the Avis and Hertz of the passenger aircraft business, say they are excited about the prospects for their newest planes, the 7E7 and the A380....

These two planes symbolize different views of the development of air travel. Boeing sees airlines serving a proliferating number of direct routes between cities, with midsize planes. Airbus sees a world of hub cities connected by high-capacity planes....

To hear Airbus and Boeing talk about each other, one would think that each had made a ruinously bad bet.

"We have no plans to make a plane larger than the 747 because we just don't think that's how people are going to fly," Mr. Mulally of Boeing said.

Mark Landler, Plane Makers at Air Show Trade Barbs on New Jets, *New York Times*, 7/20/04

What is Mr. Mulally's prediction? Would you say it is an important prediction, or not very important? What would happen if Mr. Mulally were wrong?

4. We are taught that where romance is concerned, looks are unimportant. Every novel, every screwball comedy evokes a meeting of minds. The phrase "meeting of looks" does not exist. But how many couples do you know who reflect each other's appearance?

I know a couple who met some years ago at Coffee Shop in Union Square. She was a waitress there and a model. He went for lunch and to look at her. She was Russian, he was English. Yet they shared such identically chiseled faces, it was a wonder they didn't cut themselves when they eventually kissed. Although they couldn't really speak to each other, they fell in love and he paid for her to have English lessons. Then he asked her to marry him, and they were still happily together the last I heard. Sometimes beauty is enough.

Gaby Wood, The Beautiful People, *New York Magazine*, 8/15/05, p. 91

The writer in this example tells a story. Who are the two main characters? How does it begin? How does it end? Do you think the story helps us understand something?

5. My own father, who fought on the American side in World War II, explained to me that he and his fellow soldiers never saw themselves as fighting for grand and abstract ideals like freedom and democracy when they were wallowing in the mud on the front lines. What they were fighting for at that micro-level was their own buddies, their tiny group of comrades-in-arms.

Christian Caryl, Why They Do It, *The New York Review of Books*, 9/22/05

What was the soldiers' motive in fighting in World War II, according to the writer?

6. A discussion I was party to recently comes to mind. Historians of religion were asking themselves why the passion for justice surfaces more strongly in the Hebrew scriptures than in others, and when someone came up with the answer it seemed obvious to us all. No other sacred text was assembled by a people who had suffered as much *injustice* as the Jews had, and this made them privy from the inside to the pain injustice occasions.

Huston Smith, *Why Religion Matters*, HarperSanFrancisco, 2001, p. 63

You could say that Smith describes a hypothesis, or you could say he describes an explanation. Many of the terms in this book are not specific and precise. They can apply to a wide range of situations. Nevertheless, it is probably better to say Smith describes an explanation. Why?

7. For centuries, much of science has been tied up in a philosophy called *reductionism*. The idea is that if you understand the parts, you

understand the whole. A biologist, for example, can learn a great deal about living organisms by studying their genes. To understand the DNA that makes up an individual gene, we consult the biochemist, who looks at its molecular structure.

Dan Falk, *Universe on a T-Shirt: The Quest for the Theory of Everything*, Arcade Publishing, 2004, p. 185

Falk is saying a biologist can explain many things about an organism by describing its genes. Biochemists can explain genes by looking at the molecules they are made of. They are explaining *how* things work more than *why* things happen, although the two kinds of explanations fit together. What is another example of explaining something by looking at the parts it is made of?

> 8. He told me, with great solemnity, I must go back to Covey; but that before I went, I must go with him into another part of the woods, where there was a certain *root*, which, if I would take some of it with me, carrying it *always on my right side*, would render it impossible for Mr. Covey, or any other white man, to whip me. He said he had carried it for years; and since he had done so, he had never received a blow, and never expected to while he carried it. I at first rejected the idea, that the simple carrying of a root in my pocket would have any such effect as he had said, and was not disposed to take it; but Sandy impressed the necessity with much earnestness, telling me it could do no harm, if it did no good. To please him, I at length took the root, and, according to his direction, carried it upon my right side.
>
> Frederick Douglass, Narrative of the Life of Frederick Douglass, an American Slave (1845), reprinted in Lynn Z. Bloom, ed., *The Lexington Reader*, D.C. Heath and Company, 1987, p. 158

Douglass' friend Sandy has observed a correlation between carrying the root and escaping beatings. Should Douglass, therefore, decide that Sandy's belief is not a superstition, or is he right to think it is a superstition?

Exercise 3: Analyzing Arguments

Scientists, police detectives, and others sometimes use what is called "an argument to the best explanation." They have some facts, and they know that a certain event in the past would explain the facts. For example, they know a bedroom window is broken and jewelry is missing. If a robbery was committed, that would explain the two facts. Therefore, they say, it is likely that a robbery was committed.

1. Look at the following example. What facts do people have, and what would explain those facts?

> For from their point of view, original sin is not like other facts about human life. It stands by itself. It does not have specific causes and conditions, and it cannot be handled in the way that senility, or any other human trait, can be handled. We can prevent a glutton from

over-eating by limiting his supply of food; we can keep a potential murderer from killing by locking him up. But no matter what we do, we cannot keep man from sinning, or even slow down the rate of sin.

Now why does Mr. Niebuhr believe that sin has this unique status in human life? The ultimate fact about human life, says Mr. Niebuhr, is that evil, which does not exist in nature, exists in human history. And only the doctrine of original sin, he believes, can explain this fact.

Charles Frankel, *The Case for Modern Man*, Beacon Press, 1959, pp. 94–95

2. Example 2 is about people migrating from Asia into America thousands of years ago. What important facts do scientists have about the process? The writer mentions several possible explanations of those facts. What is the best explanation?

For more than 60 years most archaeologists have believed that the first humans to reach the Americas were immigrants from Siberia who trekked across the Bering land bridge less than 12,000 years ago. Called the Clovis people, they were named after a site in New Mexico where archaeologists first found a fluted stone spearpoint that has become their signature.

But over the past few days these scientists had seen persuasive evidence that, far to the south, people had occupied Monte Verde [in Chile] at least a thousand years *before* the oldest Clovis settlement....

[Most archaeologists believed that] Ice Age glaciers across Canada had barricaded passage from Siberia into the heart of North America and beyond before 12,000 years ago. Many scientists had long been unhappy with that time constraint, especially since several sites even farther south than Monte Verde were about 11,000 years old.

"How cold people possibly have raced all the way down there from Alaska in a few hundred years?" asked David Meltzer, an archaeologist at Southern Methodist University in Dallas....

Since Monte Verde now proves people were in the Americas earlier, how and when did they arrive? Could they have skirted the glaciers, coming down along the coast by boat from Alaska? ... Sailing across the Pacific from Asia to South America in numbers large enough to colonize seems too difficult a journey for primitive seafarers.

A more likely explanation: They migrated into the lower reaches of North America even before the ice sheets developed more than 20,000 years ago.

Rick Gore, The Most Ancient Americans, *National Geographic*, Oct, 1997

Exercise 4:   Apply the Ideas in Writing

(a) Read about dinosaurs in an encyclopedia, or online, or in a book from a library. Why did they all die out and become extinct? Write a paragraph or two explaining why the dinosaurs disappeared about 60 million years ago.

(b) Read about the Black Plague in Europe around 1348. About a third of all the people in Europe died. Why? Write a paragraph or two explaining why the people died.

(c) Read about global warming. What is global warming and why is it happening? It's a controversial topic, and not everyone agrees on all the details. Write a paragraph or two using the words *hypothesis*, *theory*, and *prediction*.

Improving Your Writing 9: Research

Let's say that you have chosen a topic and stated a provisional thesis. (You can change your mind, and your thesis, as you think more about the topic or as you write.) Suppose your topic is immigration to the U.S. from Latin America, and your thesis—for now—is that we should welcome anyone who wants to come to the U.S. The next step is *research*. Research means finding information and ideas to explain what your thesis means and to persuade others to agree with you.

Where do you find information and ideas about immigration? The best place to begin is your own experience and observations. What do you know about immigration and immigrants? (Maybe some of your own relatives or ancestors immigrated to the U.S.) What led you to think that we should open the borders with Latin America and let anyone in?

After thinking about what you already know, of course you can talk to people who have more information, you can read newspapers and magazines, and go to a library to find books on your topic. But your best source is your own thinking. You can ask the same questions that journalists ask: "who, what, when, where, why, and how?" Who immigrates to the U.S. from Latin America? What is an immigrant? When have people immigrated? Where do most immigrants come into the country? Why do people immigrate? How do they immigrate? If you aren't sure of the answers to these questions, then you can go to a librarian and ask how to find out more. As you dig into your topic you will probably modify your thesis. You might change it to "We should expand our border crossings so more people can enter the country legally." Or you might change your thesis in other ways. Changing your mind based on what you learn is a big part of educating yourself.

CHAPTER 10 ❧

Valuing

57. to value

58. priority

59. goal

60. means and ends

61. principle

62. to evaluate

63. to recommend

It's hard to think clearly about values. The fact that reasonable people can disagree so strongly is evidence of that. For example, should teachers say prayers in school? Should we have a national health insurance system? Should I give part of my income to foreign aid agencies? People disagree. So if you want to improve your thinking, a good topic to work on is values because it's easy to get lost and confused in that area. And a good way to begin is to focus on the words we all use to talk (and think) about values.

You can recognize value judgments when you see them. A person might say this: "The tree in our yard is beautiful. It stands about 50 feet high." The first statement is a value judgment and the second isn't. "Susan got angry at Ted, but she shouldn't have let herself do that." The first half of this sentence simply describes the situation (Susan got angry), but the second expresses a value judgment. We can call the opposite of a value judgment a "neutral statement."

While we can recognize value judgments when we see them, it's difficult to say what makes something a value judgment. Even if we avoid the deep issues and just focus on English words, it's difficult to find something that all value words and value judgments have in common and that neutral statements don't have. "Susan got angry" is about feelings, but it's not a value judgment, so you can't define value judgments as judgments about feelings. "The tree stands about 50 feet high" is an opinion (not proven), but it's not a value judgment, so you can't define value judgments as opinions. (They may all be opinions, but there is more to it than that.)

198

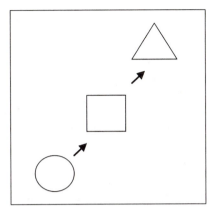

Figure 10.1
To value something is to have positive feelings about it. You can feel degrees of value. In this diagram, the figures represent things that are valued and height represents valuing. A person might value circles, but value squares more, and triangles even more than squares.

This is only a minor problem, not a major problem, because as I said, you can recognize value judgments when you see them, even if you can't define them. But I will offer a theory about them, which you may accept or reject. The theory is not essential to learning the key words and improving your thinking, but it may help. The theory fits in with the idea that the key words in effective thinking are about relationships among things. I suggest that value judgments are about relations between people and their goals, desires, or what they want to achieve or preserve. "The tree is beautiful" means that the person who makes that statement wants to enjoy the tree and preserve it. The person who says, "Susan shouldn't have gotten angry" wants people to remain calm and rational, and wants to preserve good relations among people. "You ought to keep your promises" means that the speaker wants you to keep your promises, in a particularly strong way, and will be disappointed if you don't. We use value judgments to express our wishes, including the wish that other people value the same things we do.

You can probably see problems with this theory, and we could discuss it in more detail. But we shouldn't get sidetracked into technicalities about theories. The important thing for now is to learn how people use the key words about value judgments.

Part 1. Definitions

57. to value. to want to possess something, or experience it, or promote and support it; to approve or respect something. "He values his privacy very highly."
values (noun). the things that one values. "We raised her with strong moral values: honesty, hard work, and respect for others." "This company places a value on integrity."

Example

57a. Every society features its ideal human being. The ancient Greeks **valued** the person who displayed physical agility, rational judgment, and virtuous behavior. The Romans highlighted manly courage, and followers of Islam prized the holy soldier. Under the influence of Confucius, Chinese populations traditionally **valued** the person who was skilled in poetry, music, calligraphy, archery, and drawing. Among the Keres tribe of the Pueblo Indians today, the person who cares for others is held in high regard.

Over the past few centuries, particularly in Western societies, a certain ideal has become pervasive: that of the *intelligent person*.

Howard Gardner, *Intelligence Reframed*, Basic Books, p. 1

58. priority. something that a person values more than another thing. "His priority is to get to the airport on time, so he won't be able to tour the U.N." "Her first priority is her career, and her husband understands that."
priorities. a ranking of the things a person values. "His priorities are different from mine, so he chose to go to the ball game rather than work late at the office."

Example

58a. Keeping nuclear material off international black markets needs to be the top **priority** of the next Energy Secretary, Rep. Jerry Nadler told amNewYork.

Chuck Bennett, Nadler: Put the Focus Back on Nukes, *AM New York*, 11/16/04

Comment

We use the word *priorities* to express the fact that our values have degrees. We value some things more than others. For example, I value a quick and easy commute to work. But I also value a large salary. I might decide to drive for an hour every morning to a high-paying job, rather than walk five minutes to a low-paying job closer to home. In other words, the higher salary takes priority over the easy commute.

59. goal. something one wants to accomplish or achieve in the future; aim, objective, end. "Her goal is to become a doctor."

Example

59a. But Jacob's first important service to Picasso was to keep him alive during his third stay in Paris from October 1902 to January 1903.

Picasso's **goals** were to continue his study of French art as well as to sell paintings. Although he succeeded on the first point, he failed in the latter, and this stay was a miserable one. He was flat broke, living in incredible squalor, until Jacob offered to share his room.

Arthur I. Miller, *Einstein, Picasso: Space, Time and the Beauty that Causes Havoc*, Basic Books, 2001, p. 13

60. means and ends. ends are goals, and means are the steps a person can take to reach those goals. "Charlie's goal was to make money, and he realized the best means available was to learn all he could about computers." "The operation was dangerous, but it was necessary in order to save both the mother's and the baby's lives; the ends justified the means."

The word *end* has two common meanings. Most often it means the stopping point or the conclusion: "the end of the game," "the end of the road." But it also means the place one is trying to reach, the goal: "the money was spent on worthwhile ends," "to this end he introduced himself to the vice president."

Example

60a. [Four years ago Olympic swimmer] Jenny Thompson's photograph appeared in Sports Illustrated—with only her fists covering her breasts—and generated controversy. At the time, Donna Lopiano, the executive director of the Women's Sports Foundation, told reporters, "Any exposure in a sports magazine that minimizes athletic achievement and skill and emphasizes the female athlete as a sex object is insulting and degrading."

Now, most of the athlete-models say they have enjoyed the exposure and look at it as **a means to an end**. . . . "It's a chance for me to branch out of swimming and kind of experience some other things like modeling and stuff," [said Amanda Beard].

Joe Drape, Lots of Skin but Not Much Fuss as Olympians Strike Pinup Pose, *New York Times*, 8/12/04

61. principle. a general rule, or basic fact, that provides a foundation for more specific actions or events or facts. A moral principle is a rule that guides one's actions. "The law of gravity is one of the basic principles of physics." "I'm not surprised that Roger quit his job. Loyalty to friends is a sacred principle for him."

Example

61a. "Now, what I want is, facts. Teach these boys and girls nothing but facts. Facts alone are wanted in life. Plant nothing else and root out everything else. You can only form the mind of reasoning animals upon facts: nothing else will ever be of any service to them. This is the **principle** on which I bring up my own children, and this is the **principle** on which I bring up these children."

Mr. Gradgrind, in Charles Dickens, *Hard Times*, in Gerold B. Kauvar and Gerold C. Sorensen, eds., *The Victorian Mind*, Capricorn Books, 1969, p. 66

62. to evaluate. to decide how valuable something is; to judge. "Cathy took her jewelry to the jeweler to have it evaluated." "The museum called in a world-renowned expert to evaluate the painting."

To evaluate is not the same as to value. When you evaluate something you make a decision about value, and you might decide something has very little value. For example, you might decide the lamp at the garage sale is worth ten dollars and the owner is only asking for six, so you buy it. Or you might evaluate the broken chair and decide it is completely worthless. To value something, in contrast, is to want it, admire it, prize it, and so on. After you have evaluated something you may value it, or you may not.

Example

62a. A National Intelligence Estimate on terrorism in 1997 had only briefly mentioned Bin Ladin, and no subsequent national estimate would authoritatively **evaluate** the terrorism danger until after 9/11.

Thomas H. Kean and Lee H. Hamilton et al., *The 9/11 Commission Report*, W. W. Norton, no date, p. 118

Comment

In this example, *to evaluate* means to judge the importance or the severity of the terrorism danger. No estimate did that between 1997 and 2001. Obviously, it does not mean *to value* the danger.

63. to recommend. to urge others to value something; to advise others to pursue some goal; to endorse, to praise. "Robertson's new novel is terrific. I recommend it." "You have a temperature of 101. I strongly recommend that you go to bed immediately."

Example

63a. Not long ago, a young woman and her husband came to see me at my office. Thirty-six weeks pregnant, Jennifer had been referred to me by a cardiologist because she had developed a disorder called peripartum cardiomyopathy, which can lead to congestive heart failure....

After reviewing the reports that had been faxed to my office and obtaining another ultrasound, I sat down with the young couple and discussed my **recommendations**. I expressed my concern that heart failure could develop quickly if Jennifer went into labor. In my view, the risks to her and her baby were prohibitively high. I **recommended** an elective Caesarean section.

Sandeep Jauhar, A Doctor Brings His Family to the Delivery Room, *New York Times*, 3/15/05

Test Yourself

Match each word with its definition.

57. to value
58. priority

59. goal
60. means and ends
61. principle
62. to evaluate
63. to recommend

  a. something that a person is trying to achieve, something he or she is pursuing
  b. to decide the worth of something, to decide how good or how bad it is
  c. to tell others that something is very good
  d. the steps a person takes to reach a goal, together with the goal itself
  e. to admire something, or to want to possess it, or enjoy it, or feel positive feelings about it
  f. a general rule that guides one's actions, or a general law or fact that explains things
  g. the degree of worth that something has relative to other things, its rank in one's values

Part 2. Understanding the Meaning

57. to value

> 57b. In the United States Mr. Guzman also played baseball and football. But his favorite sport was boxing, at least until he returned to South America as an adolescent and discovered that the behavior of his opponents in the ring was different from what he was used to.
>
> "There were a lot of low blows to the kidneys and testicles that went unpunished, so instead of boxing being something enjoyable, with clear rules in which you know where and how to defend yourself, it became a different sport altogether," he recalled. "I liked to play within the rules, and still do today, so I wasn't prepared for that. I **valued** fair play, and I was shocked to encounter this admiration for cheating, for using one's wits to get around the rules."
>
> Larry Rohter, Shining a Light Into the Abyss of Chile's Dictatorship, *New York Times*, 2/25/06

Comment

We use many words to talk about the things we value. If you want to begin thinking more systematically about values you can become more sensitive to these value words. They are perfectly familiar to us, but you can step back, take notice, and pay attention to the way the writer uses them. Some typical value words are *good, bad, evil, right, wrong, should, ought, beautiful, ugly, gorgeous, excellent, worthy, despicable, wonderful, offensive, admirable, atrocious, deplorable, desirable,* and many more. A brief glance at a thesaurus will give you hundreds of such words.

All these words *express* the speaker's positive or negative feelings about something. They do not *describe* a person's feelings. Jim might say, "The meal was disgusting." And later I might tell Rachel, "Jim was disgusted by the meal." Jim's statement is completely different from mine. Jim is expressing a strong feeling by using the word *disgusting,* but I am describing Jim's feelings. I am not revealing how I feel about the meal or about Jim. I'm just reporting what happened. But Jim is revealing and expressing his values.

57c. TV and the movies have replaced the family in generating **values**. The average American teenager watches 21 hours of TV per week while spending five minutes per week alone with his or her father and 20 minutes alone with his or her mother.... One can argue about the exact extent to which TV violence causes real violence and what happens when the number of TV murders per hour doubles, but no one can doubt that **values** are heavily influenced by what we see on TV.

Lester C. Thurow, *The Future of Capitalism*, Penguin, 1996, pp. 82–83

57d. Likewise, discriminating human females are central to the world of Jane Austen, whom the Barashes call "the poet laureate of female choice." Selecting a good mate is Austen's major theme. She is particularly adept at bringing out, against the vast intricacies of a social milieu, the basic **values** women seek in men, and men tend to want

Figure 10.2
For many people, what they value most is their families. *Source: © Monkey Business Images/ Shutterstock Images LLC*

in women (shortlist: good looks, health, money, status, IQ, courage, dependability and a pleasant personality—in many different weightings and orderings).

Denis Dutton, Survival of the Fittest Characters, review of Madame Bovary's Ovaries: A Darwinian Look at Literature, by David P. Barash and Nanelle R. Barash, *Washington Post*, 8/7/05

Comment

Notice that Thurow, in Example 57c, and Dutton, in Example 57d, use the word *values* in slightly different ways. Thurow means the feelings and judgments that one makes, while Dutton means the things out in the world that one judges and wants. Thurow can talk about values without mentioning *what* one values. When Dutton talks about the values that women and men seek, he is talking about the qualities in another person that they admire and want to have in their partners. It's a small difference, but it could lead to misunderstandings.

58. priority

58b. The politics of oil and gas have a more direct impact on Western policies. They heavily influence, some would say dictate, the **priority** given to some regions and countries rather than others. They generate a constant temptation to tolerate or even prop up undemocratic regimes, as Americans and Europeans have long done in the near East, and are now inclining to do in Russia, central Asia, and the Caucasus.

Timothy Garton Ash, *Free World: America, Europe, and the Surprising Future of the West*, Random House, 2004, p. 160

58c. It is tempting to dream of a highly efficient overall plan for science, in which **priorities** are rationally ordered, but the diversity of modern society means that there is insufficient common ground to act as a basis for such policymaking.

Bernard Dixon, *What Is Science For?* Harper, 1972, p. 210

58d. Robert L. Kuhn: ... In the next ten years, how will breakthroughs happen in astronomy?

Neil de Grasse Tyson: Well, I'm not sure how the other sciences move ahead, but in astronomy and astrophysics we get together as a community once per decade to **prioritize**—to advise Congress how money should be spent on such things as space science and new telescopes....

Robert Lawrence Kuhn, ed., *Closer to Truth: Challenging Current Beliefs*, McGraw-Hill, 2000, p. 326

59. goal

59b. The great question that hovers over this issue, one that we have dealt with mainly by indifference, is the question of what people are *for.* Is their greatest dignity in unemployment? Is the obsolescence of human beings now our social **goal**? One would conclude so from our attitude toward work, especially the manual work necessary to the long-term preservation of the land, and from our rush toward mechanization, automation, and computerization. In a country that puts an absolute premium on labor-saving measures, short work days, and retirement, why should there be any surprise at permanence of unemployment and welfare dependency? Those are only different names for our national ambition.

Wendell Berry, *What Are People For?* North Point Press, Farrar, Strauss and Giroux, 1990, p. 125

Comment

What is the difference between a goal and a value? They are very similar, but I think the associations they call up in one's mind are slightly different. A goal is usually a fairly specific, future condition or achievement. For example, graduating from college is a goal. Making new friends is a goal. A value is more general, and it need not be a future state. I can value my past experiences with my grandmother. I value tolerance in myself and others.

It would be a mistake to pin down these words with definite, exact definitions because that is not how they are ordinarily used. Everyone agrees on the general meaning, but different people attach slightly different ideas, different shades of meaning to them in different contexts.

Figure 10.3
Some people set distant goals. *Source: © Ljupco Smokovski/Shutterstock Images LLC*

59c. "All Chinese media have three functions: mouthpiece for the government and party, to support themselves by making money and, thirdly, to give journalists a means to influence society," he said. "The three **goals** are irreconcilable, and if you go too far in any one direction, the result is trouble."

Howard W. French, China Tries Again to Curb Independent Press in South, *New York Times*, 4/15/04

Comment

Why are the journalists' goals irreconcilable, i.e., incompatible? Well, if they simply repeat the government propaganda, they won't sell newspapers and won't make money. To make money they have to write about interesting things besides government policies. It's very common for people to have incompatible goals. I might want to learn engineering but also hang out with friends every evening instead of studying. When we discover that our goals are incompatible we have to make a decision about our priorities.

60. means and ends

60b. The procedures and penalties of the Inquisition appear cruel and inhumane to modern minds. In the view of medieval churchmen, however, the **end** (rooting out heresy) justified the **means**. Even the "Angelic Doctor" of the Church, Thomas Aquinas, held that extreme punishments were necessary to protect souls from the contamination of false beliefs. His was no doubt an honest argument. But the Inquisition was also open to the foulest abuses. To level the accusation of heresy became a convenient way of injuring or getting rid of personal enemies, and the accusers were never identified by the court.

Thomas H. Greer, *A Brief History of Western Man*, Third Edition, Harcourt, Brace, Jovanovich, 1977, p. 199

60c. It is difficult to perceive how Dr. Woo Suk Hwang can claim that using a skin cell from a patient and introducing it into a "vacant" human egg is not a process of cloning and does not constitute the creation of an embryo.

He also proposes an ethical dilemma: a choice between the destruction of his created cells and possibly saving another human from suffering. But it is never morally permissible to kill life to save life. We must help those who are suffering, but we may not use a good **end** to justify an evil **means**.

PK, Letters: Pros and Cons of Cloning, *New York Times*, 6/7/05

Comment

The phrase *means to an end* is closely related to the words *value* and *goal*. A person who uses some means, such as working, to achieve some goal, such as having money, values both things, but he or she values them in different ways. The means is like a bridge, or a road, to get to the end, which is like a destination, or home. People call the means an "instrumental value" and the end an "intrinsic value." If something is an instrumental value, then it is valuable *only* because of its consequences or what it leads to. For example, some people work only to get paid. They don't value the work for itself. But if something is an intrinsic value, then it is valuable for its own sake. Having a nice home is intrinsically valuable, in itself. (But you need to remain flexible with all these words. Something that is an intrinsic value at one time can become an instrumental value at another time. I enjoy the taste of coffee, in itself, but sometimes I drink coffee as a means to becoming more alert.)

People can disagree about means and ends. Greer, in Example 60b, describes Saint Thomas Aquinas' belief that the Catholic Church in the Middle Ages should use terrible means, including torture, to reach a very valuable end—saving souls and ensuring that they go to heaven. (Aquinas even believed that people who converted to Catholicism but then relapsed should be executed, as a means of protecting the faithful. The Koran prescribes the same punishment.) The means—torture or execution—is valuable, but *only* because it leads to a worthy goal. It is not valuable in itself. PK, in Example 60c, disagrees and says that destroying a human embryo is never valuable, even as a means of saving other people's lives.

> 60d. It is true that the police have exercised a degree of discipline in handling the demonstrators. In this sense they have conducted themselves rather "nonviolently" in public. But for what purpose? To preserve the evil system of segregation. Over the past few years I have consistently preached that nonviolence demands that the **means** we use must be as pure as the **ends** we seek. I have tried to make clear that it is wrong to use immoral **means** to attain moral **ends**. But now I must affirm that it is just as wrong, or perhaps even more so, to use moral **means** to preserve immoral **ends**.
>
> Martin Luther King, Jr., Letter from Birmingham Jail, in Linda H. Peterson et al., eds, *The Norton Reader: An Anthology of Expository Prose*, Shorter Ninth Edition, W. W. Norton and Company, 1996, pp. 575–576

Comment

King's example in Example 60d provides an interesting contrast to PK's in Example 60c. PK, like many people, says that a person shouldn't use immoral means to achieve a moral end. "The ends do not justify the means," many say. King, on the other hand, says that people should not use moral means to achieve an immoral end. The police officers behaved well, but their good behavior was a means to the end (goal) of preserving segregation, which is immoral. Therefore the means, which is normally valuable, is not valuable in this situation.

> 60e. The ritualistic element in orthodox psychoanalysis is equally obvious. The couch with the chair behind it, the four or five sessions

every week, the analyst's silence, except when he gives an "interpreta-tion"—all these features have been transformed from what once were useful **means to an end**, into a sacred ritual, without which orthodox psychoanalysis is inconceivable.

Erich Fromm, *Sigmund Freud's Mission: An Analysis of His Personality and Influence*, Peter Smith, 1978 (originally 1959), p. 107

Comment

I said earlier that sometimes an intrinsic value (an end) becomes an instrumen-tal value (a means) for a person. The example was drinking coffee. Fromm, in Example 60e, explains that a means can also become an end. Psychoanalysts use certain methods as means of helping their patients, but for some, the means become ends in themselves, or "sacred rituals." Some people may do the same with money. For most people, money is a means to buy things, but some people may begin to treat money as an end in itself. They may try to accumulate more and more, as if it were valuable for its own sake, forgetting what it is used for.

Question: Do you value getting good grades in your courses at school? If so, is getting a good grade a means or an end?

61. principle

61b. Man is but a reed, the most feeble thing in nature; but he is a thinking reed. The entire universe need not arm itself to crush him. A vapor, a drop of water suffices to kill him. But, if the universe were to crush him, man would still be more noble than that which killed him because he knows that he dies and the advantage which the universe has over him; the universe knows nothing of this.

All our dignity consists, then, in thought. By it we must elevate ourselves, and not by space and time which we cannot fill. Let us endeavor, then, to think well; this is the **principle** of morality.

Blaise Pascal, Thoughts, in Charles Hirschfeld, ed., *Classics of Western Thought: The Modern World*, Harcourt, Brace and World, 1964, p. 53

61c. No doubt we do instinctively prefer to help those who are close to us. Few could stand by and watch a child drown; many can ignore a famine in Africa. But the question is not what we usually do, but what we ought to do, and it is difficult to see any sound moral justification for the view that distance, or community membership, makes a cru-cial difference to our obligations.

Consider, for instance, racial affinities. Should whites help poor whites before helping poor blacks? Most of us would reject such a sug-gestion out of hand: people's need for food has nothing to do with their race, and if blacks need food more than whites it would be a violation of the **principle** of equal consideration to give preference to whites.

The same point applies to citizenship or nationhood...it would be wrong to decide that only those fortunate enough to be citizens of our own community will share our abundance.

Peter Singer, "Rich and Poor," in John D. Ramage and John C. Bean, eds., *Writing Arguments: A Rhetoric with Readings*, Third Edition, Allyn and Bacon, 1995, pp. 508–509

61d. In his speech, Mr Bush said again that America was committed to the "historic long-term goal" of spreading democracy....Some of the consequences are messy. It was presumably no part of Mr Bush's design to deliver power in Iraq to Islamists friendly to Iran's ayatollahs. But the decision to allow Afghans and Iraqis a free choice was surely right in **principle**.

The One Thing Bush Got Right, *The Economist*, 2/4/06

61e. It is the function of the drama, in Hebbel's opinion, to deal with the problems raised by the individual's relation to the social, moral, or religious order of which he is a part. Though the hero in this conflict always meets his doom, the future may vindicate him by bringing victory to the **principle** for which he sacrificed himself.

T. Moody Campbell, "Hebbel, Christian Friedrich," in *Collier's Encyclopedia*, Vol. 12, Macmillan, 1983

Comment

A principle is a generalization. It can be neutral, about physical processes: "Variation between parents and offspring is one of the principles of evolution." Or it can be a value judgment: "America should promote democracy around the world." Problems with moral principles arise when we ask if they are universal or limited generalizations. And if they are limited, what are the exceptions?

The three previous examples all emphasize the general nature of principles. Singer, in Example 61c, makes the point that accidents like race and nationality are irrelevant to the principle of equal treatment, which applies to all people. *The Economist* says that the policy of promoting democracy is right, even if some accidental consequences are regrettable. Campbell says a person's principles can last longer than his or her own life.

Question: Can you think of a moral principle (e.g., "Do not kill," "Try to make people happy," etc.) that you hold and that has no exceptions whatever?

62. to evaluate

62b. Harvard's Nalini Ambady and Robert Rosenthal, for example, discovered that the **evaluations** of teachers by students who saw a mere thirty-second video of the teacher were remarkably similar to those of students who had taken the entire course. Even three two-second video clips of the teacher yielded a striking .72 correlation with the course student evaluations! How can this be? We have an intuitive sense about people that allows us to make reasonably accurate snap judgments about them.

Michael Shermer, *The Science of Good and Evil*, Henry Holt and Company, 2004, p. 175

62c. Nothing better illustrates the manner in which the idea of being set free was **evaluated** in the ancient Near East than the old Egyptian word for emancipating someone from slavery. First, there was no specific word for this experience, which immediately suggests that it could hardly have been a common or desired occurrence. More important, however, was the term used to connote emancipation. It was the word *nmh*, which literally meant "to be orphaned."...Clearly, the idea of being released from obligation, far from being a desired state, was equated with one of the saddest conditions known to human beings, that of being deprived of one's parents.

Orlando Patterson, *Freedom, Vol 1: Freedom in the Making of Western Culture*, Basic Books, 1991, p. 36

Comment

To evaluate is to judge something as good or bad. Students evaluate teachers and decide some are good teachers and some aren't so good. Patterson, in Example 62c, says that ancient Egyptians evaluated liberation from slavery and decided that it was very undesirable.

Figure 10.4
Judges in a beauty pageant evaluate the contestants. *Source: Associated Press*

62d. I would like to propose, as an hypothesis for consideration, that the major barrier to mutual interpersonal communication is our very natural tendency to judge, to **evaluate**, to approve or disapprove, the statement of the other person, or the other group.

Carl Rogers, *On Becoming a Person*, in Robert K. Miller, *The Informed Argument*, Fifth Edition, Harcourt Brace College Publishers, 1998, p. 648

62e. People are very divided on the subject of canine intelligence. To some, the dog is a most intelligent animal, while others view it as being quite stupid. Such **evaluations** are subjective and depend more on personal experience with one or a few animals than on actual canine brain power.

Dorothy Hinshaw Patent, *How Smart Are Animals?* Harcourt, Brace, Jovanovich, 1990, p. 88

63. to recommend

63b. To sneak in some tummy toning at the office, try this at your desk: "For 10 minutes each hour, inch your body away from the chair back and straighten up," **recommends** Debra Strougo, a trainer at Crunch in New York City. "Imagine there's wet paint on the seat back." *That's* middle management!

Fitness Flash, *Self*, December, 2004

63c. The late Alfred Kinsey, a biologist whose later researches turned to human sexual behavior (well known through the "Kinsey Report"), claimed to have discovered that homosexuality was rather more prevalent than previously thought. On the grounds that the phenomenon exists in nature, he **recommended** that laws prohibiting the practice be modified to reflect the conclusion that it cannot be morally wrong.

Arthur N. Strahler, *Understanding Science: An Introduction to Concepts and Issues*, Prometheus Books, 1992, p. 297

Comment

To recommend is to urge others to value something. You have seen that values can be means or ends, instrumental or intrinsic. It is useful, in thinking about recommendations, to ask yourself if the person is urging people to value something as a means to some other goal, or as an end in itself. In Example 63b, the fitness expert is recommending a way of sitting as a means of exercising your mid-section. You could call it a practical recommendation. Kinsey, on the other hand (Example 63c), was recommending that people accept homosexuality as normal, not morally wrong, because it occurs in nature. Tolerating gays is an end in itself, he would say. It is a moral recommendation.

63d. They [Franz Boas, Ruth Benedict] believed that a common obstacle for Westerners in studying remote cultures was their lack of toleration, and therefore they **recommended** that cultural anthropologists avoid passing judgments on such cultures.

Susana Nuccetelli, *Latin American Thought: Philosophical Problems and Arguments*, Westview, 2002, p. 76

Question: Do you think Boas and Benedict's recommendation was practical, or moral? Did they think that avoiding passing judgment on other cultures was a means to something else, or did they think it was an end in itself?

Part 3. Applying the Words

57. to value
58. priority
59. goal
60. means and ends
61. principle
62. to evaluate
63. to recommend

Exercise 1: Choose the Best Word

For each sentence, choose the best word (or an appropriate form of the word) to fill in the blank.

1. You can tell that Janine _____ beauty and elegance in her ordinary life, because her apartment is always so neat and nicely decorated.
2. I talked with Charlie yesterday, and he _____ the restaurant on Houston Street for our dinner.
3. All the people agreed on the _____, that is, security in retirement, but they couldn't agree on the best _____ to achieve it.
4. Nick worked very hard on his project, because his _____ was to stand out among the crowd of new employees.
5. Tina threw out the whole manuscript because she said she has a _____: she will never publish anything unless it is the very best she can do.
6. The teacher said she _____ all the students' work by the same standard.
7. Carlos turned down the promotion because he said his _____ at this point is his family, not his career.

Exercise 2: Apply the Words

Read each example and answer the questions that follow.

1. Revelations that author Doug Wead secretly taped conversations with his close friend, President George W. Bush, reveals less about the President than it does about Wead and our culture.... Wead pointed out that he recorded the conversations in states where it is legal to do so without notifying the person being taped.

Wead may have behaved legally, but not ethically. What he did was dishonest, period.

Kathleen Parker, Privacy Is Dying (from the *Orlando Sentinel*), *AM New York*, 2/23/05

Is Parker making a neutral statement, or expressing a value judgment? Can Parker prove that what Wead did was dishonest? Is she expressing a feeling that she wants others to share about Wead's action?

2. But the rains brought up edible grasses, wild berries and fruits appeared, and gradually the danger of full-scale starvation receded.... What has not grown, however, is any evidence that the Ik—even in such relatively good times—have any consideration for one another. Food is still the dominant thought, food getting the dominant activity.... The adults steal from each other and angrily denounce each other, kinship affording not the slightest bond of mutual respect.... The old people tell stories of better times when, not so long ago, Kidepo Park was theirs to hunt in as they pleased.... But even the old people, now, have only one concept of good. It is nothing that can be applied to an action, or to a relationship between one human and another; it is only a condition, clearly defined as "having a full stomach." This is the basis of their life, of their law, of their morality.

Colin M. Turnbull, "A People Apart," in Richard A. Gould, ed., *Man's Many Ways*, Harper & Row, 1973, pp. 36–37

The Ik are a tribe of people in Eastern Africa. What do they value, according to Turnbull?

3. [H]usband and wife, if they have any love for their children, will so regulate their conduct as to give their children the best chance of a happy and healthy development. This may involve, at times, very considerable self-repression. And it certainly requires that both should realize the superiority of the claims of children to the claims of their own romantic emotions.

Bertrand Russell, Marriage and Morals, quoted in Christina Sommers and Fred Sommers, eds., *Vice and Virtue in Everyday Life*, Second Edition, Harcourt, Brace, Jovanovich, 1989, p. 749

Russell indicates his priorities in this passage. What takes priority over what?

4. Administration [in ancient Egypt] was thus in the first instance administration of agricultural produce. Taxation, though important, was not as important as storage. The prime official concern was to ensure against the unpredictability of the Nile floods and against fluctuations in local harvest yields, and to keep the standard of living as consistently high as possible.

Jan Assmann, *The Mind of Egypt: History and Meaning in the Time of the Pharaohs*, Henry Holt and Co, 2002, pp. 47–48

What was the ancient Egyptian administrators' ultimate goal? What took priority over what?

5. If you want to find out about someone—if you really want to understand what makes them tick—then the last thing you should do is ask them to tell you about themselves. People make up all sorts of stuff about themselves, often without even realising it. What you do is ask them to tell you about the world. Because the world as they see it is always a reflection of them, and staring right back at you in what they tell you about the world is the person they really are.

Mark Rowlands, *The Philosopher at the End of the Universe: Philosophy Explained Through Science Fiction Films*, Thomas Dunne Books, St. Martin's Press, 2003, p. viii

Rowlands is describing a means to an end. What is the end, or goal, and what means does Rowlands recommend to reach it? (What is the wrong means to use?)

6. Enough is enough. It is time to consider term limits for this state Legislature of scandals, paralysis, noncompliance with court orders, and dereliction of duty....

I don't usually approve of term limits. They restrict the free choice of the voters to elect whomever they want. Term limits have de-stabilized the [city] council, but Albany [state government] can't get any more destabilized than it is today. It is so profoundly rotten that a radical remedy is warranted.

Jack Newfield, Now's the Time for Term Limits in the Legislature, *New York Sun*, 6/25/04

What is the end and what is the means that Newfield recommends?

7. When I first went in there, I kind of envied foremen. Now, I wouldn't have a foreman's job. I wouldn't give 'em the time of the day.

When a man becomes a foreman he has to forget about even being human, as far as feelings are concerned. You see a guy there bleeding to death. So what, buddy? That line's gotta keep goin.' I can't live like that. To me, if a man gets hurt, first thing you do is get him some attention.

Studs Terkel, *Working*, Avon Books, 1972, p. 224

The speaker here states one of his principles. What is it?

8. Even the ISI—Pakistan's Inter-Services Intelligence, which once used drug money to help finance the Taliban in Afghanistan—has become a crucial U.S. partner in the spy game. "They're really a bad intelligence service, in terms of morals, but really effective," says [Michael Swetnam, CEO of the Potomac Institute for Policy Studies].

Christopher McDougall, Reasons They Haven't Hit Us Again, *New York Magazine*, 12/6/04, p. 33

How does Swetnam evaluate the Pakistani intelligence service?

> 9. Every society, of course, has the right to protect children from adult material. But increasing censorship by the central government is the wrong way to go about this. A wiser course would be to eliminate the government's role and rely more on parents. Fortunately, changes in technology and the media industry itself now make this approach more feasible than ever....
>
> Every new television set sold in America since 2000 is equipped with a "v-chip," a blocking device that Bill Clinton forced on the media industry in 1996....
>
> Technology has offered the chance to scale back censorship and America, long a champion of free speech, should seize it.
>
> An Indecent Proposal, *The Economist*, 7/23/05

The writer for *The Economist* is making a recommendation. What is it?

Exercise 3: Analyzing Arguments

1. Friedrich Nietzsche presents an argument in the following passage about the value of custom. What is the conclusion, and what premise or premises support it?

> *Custom and its sacrifices.*—The origin of custom lies in two ideas: "the community is worth more than the individual", and "an enduring advantage is to be preferred to a transient one"; from which it follows that the enduring advantage of the community is to take unconditional precedence over the advantage of the individual, especially over his momentary well-being but also over his enduring advantage and even over his survival. Even if the individual suffers from an arrangement which benefits the whole, even if he languishes under it, perishes by it—the custom must be maintained, the sacrifice offered.
>
> R. J. Hollingdale, ed. and trans., *A Nietzsche Reader*, Penguin, 1977, p. 82

2. The following passage (by the English philosopher John Stuart Mill) is about morality. When philosophers think about morality they ask, "What makes a particular action right or wrong? How do we decide that a person has done something wrong?" Mill proposes an answer, and then he goes on to defend his answer. What is the conclusion of his argument, and what premises support it?

The creed which accepts as the foundation of morals "utility" or the "greatest happiness principle" holds that actions are right in proportion as they tend to promote happiness; wrong as they tend to produce the reverse of happiness. By happiness is intended pleasure and the absence of pain; by unhappiness pain and the privation of pleasure....

The utilitarian doctrine is that happiness is desirable, and the only thing desirable, as an end, all other things being only desirable as means to that end. What ought to be required of this doctrine, what conditions is it requisite that the doctrine should fulfill—to make good its claim to be believed?

The only proof capable of being given that an object is visible is that people actually see it. The only proof that a sound is audible is that people hear it; and so of the other sources of our experience. In like manner, I apprehend, the sole evidence it is possible to produce that anything is desirable is that people do actually desire it.... No reason can be given why the general happiness is desirable, except that each person, so far as he believes it to be attainable, desires his own happiness. This, however, being a fact, we have not only all the proof which the case admits of, but all which it is possible to require, that happiness is a good, that each person's happiness is a good to that person, and the general happiness, therefore, a good to the aggregate of all persons.

John Stuart Mill, "Utilitarianism," in Steven M. Cahn, ed., *Classics of Western Philosophy*, Fifth Edition, Hackett Publishing Co., 1999, pp. 893, 907.

Exercise 4: Apply the Ideas in Writing

Write a brief essay explaining the conflicts over values in the following passage. Your essay should have at least three paragraphs: an introduction (see "Improve Your Writing 10," later in this chapter), a main body, and a conclusion. You could have more than three paragraphs. For your research, think about these questions: What values and principles do Zola-Morgan and Slater (the writer) hold? What is Zola-Morgan's goal? Do he and Slater disagree about means or ends? What recommendation do you think Slater might make?

Zola-Morgan's surgical explorations have deepened our understanding of memory. There can be no question about that. And memory is crucial to who we are, as ensouled prismatic people. And yet, to achieve this knowledge, Zola-Morgan must anesthetize his monkey patient, then wrap a cord around the neck to cut off all blood supply to the brain, wait until the cells undergo apoptosis [cell death], and then wake the monkey up to study its ability to recall. Sometime later, the monkey is "sacrificed," and its brain examined for areas of damage, blighted, dead areas, lobes white with scar and stump.

"I think human life is more valuable than animal life," says Zola-Morgan. In an interview with Deborah Blum, he says, "We have a real obligation to care for these animals well. But is my son's life worth more than a monkey's life? I don't even have to think about that answer."

I do. I do have to think about that answer. It's not at all as clear to me that human life has some intrinsically higher worth—no, not as clear to me at all.

Lauren Slater, *Opening Skinner's Box: Great Psychological Experiments of the Twentieth Century*, W. W. Norton and Co., 2004, p. 151

(*Prismatic* means like a prism, having many different sides, giving different appearances.)

Improving Your Writing 10: Organization Again

The parts of an essay must be arranged in a sensible order, just as the details in a paragraph must be. They must be *organized*. After doing your research you should have many facts, quotes, and thoughts of your own about your topic—probably more than you can use. You should list all your information, with a word or phrase for each item. As you look over your list you will think of new points to make, and you will decide that some facts or thoughts are irrelevant or unnecessary.

The next step is to arrange similar items together into groups, so that all your information is sorted into several groups. These groups will be the paragraphs of your essay. Then you can arrange your paragraphs in the best order to persuade your audience to accept your thesis.

Your first paragraph—the introduction—and your last paragraph—the conclusion—have special functions. The introduction should do three things. First, it should explain your topic. If your topic is broad, you may need a second paragraph to give your audience more background information. Second, it should state your thesis in a clear, definite way. And finally, it should make people want to read your essay. The introduction should be interesting, thought-provoking, and appealing to your audience. You can make it interesting by asking a good question, or telling a brief story, or giving a striking quotation.

Your conclusion brings your essay to a satisfying close. You can do that in different ways. You might remind your audience of why your topic is important. You might show how your thesis leads to some action or response. You might suggest related questions that remain to be answered. In general, your conclusion should connect your thesis to the wider world.

CHAPTER 11 🦋

Justifying

"I believe we ought to have capital punishment as a last resort."

"How can you? It's so barbaric and uncivilized! Life in prison is enough."

Here you can see two value judgments that are in conflict. The first person favors the death penalty, and the second opposes it. But conflicts like these are usually only the beginning of the conversation. The next step is for the two people to explain *why* they make the value judgments they do. The first person might say, "Criminals who know they face the death penalty will think twice before they murder someone." The second could reply, "No they won't. In fact, the government is just doing what it says is so horrible—killing someone." In this second step, the two people are giving reasons to support their value judgments. They are attempting to justify their points of view.

Justifying a value judgment means explaining a relationship that exists between your value judgment and some standard, that is, some more general value judgment about good and bad, right and wrong. For example, the first person here bases her support for the death penalty partly on a belief about the facts: the death penalty deters criminals and reduces the number of murders. Saving lives is her standard. The facts, together with the standard, lead her to favor the death penalty. The second person bases his opposition on a moral principle. He says capital punishment is in conflict with the principle "Killing is wrong." The principle is his standard. If you accept the principle, you can't accept capital punishment.

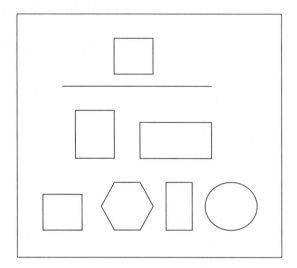

Figure 11.1
A standard is a guide for judging things. The square figure at the top represents a standard. You can judge the other figures by how closely they resemble the standard. Some of the figures at the bottom are closer to the standard than others. The figure on the lower left is the best, in the sense that it meets the standard better than the others do. You justify your judgment about the figure by showing how it meets the standard.

In a way, value judgments are like factual statements, and in another way they are like opinions. A factual statement is a statement that has been proven, i.e., confirmed. You can show that a statement is confirmed by explaining how it is related to its source, such as a reliable authority or personal observation. Value judgments are similar because you can justify a value judgment by showing how it is related to the facts, or the law, a moral principle, or something else that has been established. On the other hand, value judgments are different from facts and similar to opinions, because people don't agree on which facts or laws *do* justify value judgments. What fact or test would *prove* that capital punishment is wrong? Even if it is a deterrent, some people will still say it is wrong. Different people use different standards. We agree for the most part on what tests will confirm a factual statement. But with value judgments what counts as "proof" for one person sometimes does not mean "proof" for another, and therefore value judgments can never be confirmed the way factual statements are. This is a complicated topic, and learning a few basic terms will help you in thinking about it.

Part 1. Definitions

64. standard. the guideline or measure that a person uses to evaluate something. "Marilyn has great enthusiasm, but by the standard of scoring points, she's not a very good basketball player."

Example

64a. It is very painful to most minds to admit that the past does not furnish us with reliable, permanent **standards** of conduct and of public policy.

James Harvey Robinson, *The Mind in the Making*, Harper and Brothers, 1921, p. 130

65. to justify. to explain why some action or belief is right or appropriate or valuable. "Mickey thinks she can justify her belief by finding others who agree with her."

justification (noun). the act of justifying; or, whatever justifies a belief or action. "Thoreau's justification for refusing to pay his taxes was that the taxes were being use to support an immoral war."

Example

65a. I shall ask, then, why is it really worth while to make a serious study of mathematics? What is the proper **justification** of a mathematician's life?

G. H. Hardy, *A Mathematician's Apology*, Cambridge University Press, 1967, p. 65

66. prejudice. a value or preference that a person has that prevents the person from seeing a situation accurately; a prejudice makes a person evaluate things (praise them or condemn them) without considering all the relevant information. "Rick is an enthusiastic Red Sox fan, so he could never be an umpire; he's prejudiced." "Carolyn has had to overcome two major obstacles to get where she is: her blindness, and people's prejudice against handicapped individuals."

Example

66a. As we see him through the accounts of later writers who were for the most part his dependents Charlemagne was a man of limitless energy, great resolution, and considerable personal strength; Carloman [his brother], seen through the **prejudiced** eyes of these same writers, appears to have been peevish, given to self-pity, and the easy victim of the flatterers who surrounded him.

Einhard and Notker the Stammerer, *Two Lives of Charlemagne*, translated by Lewis Thorpe, Penguin, 1969, p. 4

67. impartial. not allowing one's values or preferences to influence one's perceptions. "The defense attorney's and prosecutor's jobs are to make the strongest cases they can, but a judge's job is to be impartial."

Example

67a. Forty years as a trial lawyer in New York have taught me that not all potential jurors are fair or **impartial**. Some potential jurors have entrenched preconceived notions that could affect deliberations.

In speaking with discharged jurors in the courthouse, I have been told such things as "Cops always lie"; "I won't take the word of a woman over any man's"; "the Lord says 'vengeance is mine'" (in a personal injury case).

SB, Letters: Is This Any Way to Pick a Jury? *New York Times*, 3/13/06

68. conflict of interest. a situation in which a person has a responsibility to do something, e.g., preside as a judge over a trial, but the person also holds some value or has some interest that interferes with doing the job fairly, e.g., the judge may be related to the individual on trial. "It is unethical for stock brokers to own shares in a company and then advise clients on whether they should buy shares in the same company, because of the clear conflict of interest."

Example

68a. The federal judge scheduled to sentence former House speaker Jim Black removed himself from the case Tuesday, marking a legal victory for Black and delaying his expected move to a federal prison.

U.S. District Judge James Dever filed an order Tuesday evening recusing himself from the case. The dramatic move comes a month after Black's lawyer asked Dever to withdraw charging that he had a **conflict of interest**. While a lawyer in private practice Dever represented the state Republican Party in a lawsuit that targeted Black and other Democratic leaders.

Mark Johnson and Gary L. Wright, Black's Case to Get New Judge, *Charlotte Observer*, 6/6/07

(In law, *to recuse oneself* means to withdraw from a position of authority, to take oneself off of a case.)

69. universal. applying everywhere. "The fear of the disease was universal." "The United States should defend universal human rights."

Example

69a. It must be added here that Newton, Hales, Cavendish, Lavoisier, Priestley, and other scientists believed that the "truths" they uncovered were **universal**, that (to use the modern way of saying it) their truths transcended race, gender, nationality, and even time itself.

Neil Postman, *Building a Bridge to the 18th Century: How the Past Can Improve Our Future*, Alfred A. Knopf, 1999, p. 63

70. relative. being related to something else; a relative term is one whose meaning depends on comparison with some standard, and whose meaning is different when people use different standards. Examples are "tall," "rich," "old," "generous," "admirable," "virtuous," "morally good." "I can't say that Ray is tall because *tall* is a relative term. Compared with Suzie, he's tall, but compared with Lawrence, he isn't."

Example

> 70a. Prior threw fastballs and curves during his side session and is not far from being able to throw a simulated game. Asked if there was any lingering pain in the elbow, Prior replied: "Pain is a **relative** term."
>
> Eventually, Prior conceded there was still some pain.

Paul Sullivan, Wood, Prior Making Strides, *Chicago Tribune*, 6/15/05

Comment

Some people say moral values are relative. That usually means moral values depend on standards set by a particular society. What is morally right in one society is not morally right in another society, according to "moral relativists." Furthermore, no moral values are universal. Each society sets its own standards, and different societies' standards are the only ones that exist. Needless to say, this is a controversial point of view.

Test Yourself

Match each word with its definition.

64. standard
65. to justify
66. prejudice
67. impartial
68. conflict of interest
69. universal
70. relative

   a. a guideline for evaluating things
   b. explaining why an action is right or a belief is true
   c. making a judgment without allowing personal preferences to influence it
   d. in all cases, all times and places
   e. something that prevents a person from seeing a situation accurately
   f. depending on something else, varying with something else
   g. having incompatible obligations or desires

Part 2. Understanding the Meaning

64. standard

> 64b. It is a commonplace of anthropology that every culture has its own set of **standards** defining beauty. But in American culture—at least from the point of view of reality television—the parameters appear to be rapidly narrowing.

Alex Kuczynski, A Lovelier You, With Off-the-Shelf Parts, *New York Times*, 5/2/04

(*Parameters* means limits or boundaries in a situation; guidelines.)

> 64c. But on the whole the history of science is fair, and this is particularly true in mathematics. No other subject has such clear-cut or unanimously accepted **standards,** and the men who are remembered are almost always the men who merit it.

G. H. Hardy, *A Mathematician's Apology*, Cambridge University Press, 1967, p. 82

Comment

The simplest kind of standard is an example of excellence. In basketball, for example, Michael Jordan is regarded by many as the best player ever. Other players can be evaluated by how close they are to Michael Jordan. So if you ask, "How good is this new rookie," you might compare him in your mind to Jordan—how does his shooting compare, how many assists does he have compared with Jordan, can he play defense like Jordan, and so on. I can justify the statement that the rookie is very good by saying he comes close to the standard of excellence, exemplified by Jordan.

Writing teachers have to evaluate students' essays, and justify their value judgments. Teachers have read many excellent writers; in fact, that's one theory of education: you expose students to examples of excellence so they can learn to recognize it when they see it (in writing, in science, in political decision-making, etc.). Teachers have been exposed to many excellent writers, and they create a

Figure 11.2
Athletes train to reach high standards. *Source: © Jim Parkin/Shutterstock Images LLC*

sort of ideal essay in their minds, based on a variety of examples of excellent writing. They do not compare a student's essay with a particular writer like E. B. White, but they might compare the student's essay with an imaginary essay created from elements of White's writing, Joan Didion's writing, Montaigne's, Maya Angelou's, and dozens of others. "Does this essay have a clear introduction like White's essays? Are the paragraphs unified like Didion's paragraphs? Do the sentences flow easily like Angelou's?"

We use other standards as well. Often we support our value judgments by relating them to a law or rule or principle. In the introduction I mentioned the example of supporting or justifying the judgment that capital punishment is wrong. Why is it wrong? Because it falls under the rule "Killing is wrong." That principle is a standard. Or a writing teacher might state a general rule for writing: "All good essays have a concluding paragraph in which the writer sums up the main ideas." People can argue over rules, too, and try to justify them by relating them to more general rules. "Good writing is coherent and unified."

But there is third way to support value judgments, besides comparing something to an example of excellence or comparing it to a rule. The third method depends on a concept you learned in the Chapter 10: means and ends. You can show that something is a means to an end that everyone wants. In other words, you can say an action is good because it leads to an outcome that is good. In the example of capital punishment, some people say it is justified because it reduces crime; it is a means to the end of reducing crime. And since everyone wants to reduce crime, capital punishment is justified. One goal of writing is to communicate effectively. If an essay achieves that end, you can say it's a good essay, and the means the writer uses are justified, even if they are unusual.

> 64d. But the fact that Cinel had not been convicted of a criminal offense did not mean he couldn't be fired. The prevailing **standard** for firing someone from an academic job, according to Ernst Benjamin, then executive director of the American Association of University Professors, is only "reasonableness." The officials who would decide Cinel's fate as a CUNY professor were to be reasonable in deciding what evidence of wrongdoing they would consider and how much weight to give it.
>
> Jon Wiener, *Historians in Trouble: Plagiarism, Fraud, and Politics in the Ivory Tower*, The New Press, 2005, p. 157

> 64e. There remains for consideration one further possible approach to the measurement of changing living **standards**. As long ago as 1816 John Rickman, the census-taker, expressed the opinion that "human comfort is to be estimated by human health and that by the length of human life." Longevity is in general a useful yardstick of changing living **standards**. . . .
>
> A. J. Taylor, Industrialization and the Standard of Living, in John C. Rule, David L. Dowd, and John L. Snell, eds., *Critical Issues in History, 1648 to the Present*, D. C. Heath and Co., 1967, p. 635

Question: If you had to rank various people's lives as "bad," "average," "good," and "best," how would you do it? What standard or standards would you use to measure the quality of people's lives? What standard did Rickman use?

64f. To write this book, I reviewed history **standards** from forty-nine states and the District of Columbia. I was pleasantly surprised to discover that history is making a comeback....As of 2002, in my judgment, there were fourteen states with strong U.S. history **standards**....The **standards** in these states clearly identify the ideas, events, and individuals that students should learn about, without prescribing interpretations. This builds a solid body of knowledge about history and provides guidance to teachers, students, assessment developers, and textbook writers....

The remaining states have **standards** that consist of concepts and skills with minimal or no historical content. The **standards** in these states are so vague that it would be hard to assess what students have learned and hard for students to know when they have achieved proficiency.

Here are some examples of standards so vague that they cannot inform teaching or assessment:

A student shall illustrate the influence of diverse ideals or beliefs on a theme or an event in the historical development of the United States. (Minnesota)

The student will understand the way people in the United States and throughout the world perceive themselves over time. (Mississippi)

Diane Ravitch, *The Language Police: How Pressure Groups Restrict What Students Should Learn*, Vintage, 2003, p. 138

65. to justify

65b. Mr. Hughes also says, "I don't care if we discover" WMDs [weapons of mass destruction in Iraq], because that was not the only reason we invaded. I do not recall any other reason given by Colin Powell in his address to the United Nations to **justify** going to war against Iraq.

NS, Letters, Why Were We in Such a Hurry to Invade Iraq? *Post-Standard* (Syracuse, NY), 3/2/04

65c. Many men actually felt a sense of religious duty to make captives of the native peoples they encountered. It was believed that only through bodily bondage to the white man could the "heathen" souls be saved....

Of course, a theory of slavery based upon saving heathen souls was bound to require new **justification** as more and more slaves became converted to Christianity. It became increasingly difficult to rationalize the enslaving of another man's body if his soul was destined for the same place as one's own. And so the belief gradually began to take hold among white men that natives were not actually human at all, that they were in fact subhuman and had not fully evolved.

Jack Conrad, *The Many Worlds of Man*, Thomas Y. Crowell Company, 1964, pp. 42–43

Comment

If you say someone justified his action, you can mean either of two things. You can mean that the action really was right. It was justified. However, you can also mean that the person gave a reason, but it wasn't a good reason. People can think they have a good reason when they don't. For example, Conrad, in Example 65c, says white conquerors justified slavery by explaining that it was necessary to save the colonized people's souls. Later they needed a new justification, he says. But Conrad himself doesn't believe it was necessary, nor does he believe the new justification was a good reason for slavery.

65d. Carol Gilligan, the psychologist and gender expert, has said that women are less predisposed to judge, and while this could be seen as moral relativism, she argues it's more a recognition of the intricacies of real-world situations. Most of the writers in "Journalistas" do have a special eye for intricacies, but they are also full of brave judgments and passion for political life in all its dimensions. Mills gets it right when she puts forward a simple **justification** for this book: "This is not just a women's collection; it reflects the great dilemmas and struggles of humanity in the last century from an often new point of view."

Jull Abramson, review of Eleanor Mills and Kira Cochrane, eds., Journalistas: 100 Years of the Best Writing and Reporting by Women Journalists, Carroll & Graf, *New York Times Book Review*, 1/8/06, p. 17

65e. More generally (and this applies to Christianity no less than to Islam), what is really pernicious is the practice of teaching children that faith itself is a virtue. Faith is an evil precisely because it requires no **justification** and brooks no argument. Teaching children that unquestioned faith is a virtue primes them—given certain other ingredients that are not hard to come by—to grow up into potentially lethal weapons for future jihads or crusades....If children were taught to question and think through their beliefs, instead of being taught the superior virtue of faith without question, it is a good bet that there would be no suicide bombers.

Richard Dawkins, *The God Delusion*, Houghton Mifflin, 2006, pp. 307–308

(*Pernicious* means harmful, usually in a secret or less obvious way.)

Question: Are some personal qualities, such as fairness, so good that they do not require any justification? Are some personal qualities the ultimate standards that justify everything else? Is faith such a quality?

66. prejudice

66b. Few readers will know that Seuss was also an able propagandist in educating grown-ups. Born 100 years ago in Massachusetts to a German-American family, he drew anti-Nazi cartoons, well selected in the book, that show his disgust at the thuggish **prejudice** of the Third Reich. That was at a time when it was still fashionable in America to see the rise of totalitarianism in Europe as a disturbance between old-world countries of no interest to the United States.

The Temple of Seuss; Theodor Seuss Geisel, *The Economist*, 4/10/04

66c. It is clear, in any case, that our convictions on important matters are not the result of knowledge or critical thought, nor, it may be added, are they often dictated by supposing self interest. Most of them are pure **prejudices** in the proper sense of the word. We do not form them ourselves. They are the whisperings of "the voice of the herd...." They are not really our own ideas, but those of others no more well-informed or inspired than ourselves, who have got them in the same careless and humiliating manner as we.

James Harvey Robinson, *The Mind in the Making,* Harper and Brothers, 1921, p. 59–60

66d. Mr Bush has bowed to Arab demands by sending a palliative letter to Palestine's prime minister, Ahmed Qurei. Despite having earlier appalled Arabs by endorsing plans by Israel's leader, Ariel Sharon, for a withdrawal from Gaza that would leave many Jewish settlements in the West Bank intact, the letter said that America "will not **prejudice**" the outcome of negotiations over the "final status" of the two states, including their borders.

Ice-cold Contempt; Iraq and the Arab World, *The Economist*, 5/15/04

(*Palliative* can mean excusing, making an action appear better, or it can mean treating the symptoms of a disease, making a person feel better.)

Comment

This example from *The Economist* (Example 66d) shows that other things besides people can be prejudiced. A procedure, a law, or a situation can be prejudiced if it is unfair to some people, or if it is based on incomplete information, or puts some people at a disadvantage. Here, President Bush was using *prejudice* as a verb, saying America will not make the situation in the Middle East unfair or unjustly designed to favor one group.

67. impartial

67b. We have sought to be independent, **impartial**, thorough, and nonpartisan. From the outset, we have been committed to share as much of our investigation as we can with the American people. To that end, we held 19 days of hearings and took public testimony from 160 witnesses.

Our aim has not been to assign individual blame. Our aim has been to provide the fullest possible account of the events surrounding 9/11 and to identify lessons learned.

Thomas H. Kean and Lee H. Hamilton et al., *The 9/11 Commission Report*, W. W. Norton, no date, pp. xv–xvi

67c. I would like to suggest that Mr. Moerdler be asked to resign his position as chairman of the land use committee of Community Board 8. It is clear that in this case he was not acting as an **impartial** judge, weighing the needs of community members versus a large institution, but urging board members to vote based on his personal concerns.

MM, Letters: Moerdler Should Resign from His Post, *Riverdale Press*, 2/23/06

67d. A senior Justice Department official, Bradley Schlozman, testified to the Senate this week that he actively recruited job applicants from conservative groups such as the Federalist Society and the Heritage Foundation.

He acknowledged trying to change the make-up of the staff of the Department civil rights office, and said he had bragged about hiring conservatives as lawyers....

It's adding up to something scandalous, and a violation of the basic trust that Americans need to have that their justice system is **impartial**.

Editorial: Politics at Justice? No Way! *Charlotte Observer*, 6/9/07

68. conflict of interest

68b. New York State Attorney General Eliot Spitzer's aggressive political fundraising raises serious **conflict of interest** questions, according to a published report yesterday.

Spitzer, who attacks corporate corruption, has raised thousand of dollars from sources close to his investigations, according to Newsweek's Charles Gasparino.

"To be clear: Spitzer has done nothing illegal; at issue is whether his own actions meet the standards he's championed," notes Gasparino.

For instance, Manhattan attorney Gary Naftalis gave Spitzer $10,000. Naftalis represents Kenneth Langone, a New York Stock Exchange committee member who was named in a civil suit by Spitzer over the $139.5 million paid to Dick Grasso, former head of the Exchange.

Chuck Bennett, **Conflicts of Interest** for Spitzer: Report, *AM New York*, 6/14/04

Figure 11.3
Why do you think the figure representing justice is blind-folded? Shouldn't she see the two parties who put their cases into her scale? *Source: © Risteski Goce/Shutterstock Images LLC*

Question: A conflict of interests is like a conflict between two of a person's goals, or a conflict between desires. What interest of Spitzer's is in conflict with what other interest of his in this example?

68c. Only now is the truth emerging about how the U.N.'s oil-for-food program became Saddam's oil-for-palaces program. And how various of the world's leading diplomats may have profited personally from it.... The U.N. isn't releasing its internal audit of the program—not to the public and not even to its own member nations. But this country's General Accounting Office has estimated that Hussein's regime siphoned off $10 billion from oil-for-food.... Saddam's regime, the report noted, also "allocated 'private oil' to individuals or political parties that sympathized in some way with the regime." Among the buyers, according to this draft report, was the U.N.'s own Benan Sevan, who was in charge of the oil-for-food program. Talk about a **conflict of interest.**

Paul Greenberg, Can We Trust the U.N.? *AM New York*, 10/27/04

68d. Both the Pentagon and a Congressionally mandated commission recently issued studies on the Chinese military that overstated the threat to the United States posed by that force. The pessimism of both studies was understandable. The Department of Defense's study—the *Annual Report on the Military Power of the People's Republic of China*—was issued by a federal bureaucracy that has an inherent **conflict of interest** in developing assessments of foreign military threats. Because the department that is creating the threat assessments is the same one that is lobbying Congress for money for weapons, personnel, fuel, and training to combat threats, its threat projections tend to be inflated.

Ivan Eland, Is Chinese Military Modernization a Threat to the United States? In John T. Rourke, ed., *Taking Sides: Clashing Views on Controversial Issues in World Politics*, Eleventh Edition, McGraw Hill/Dushkin, 2004, p. 85

69. universal

69b. Scientific research suggests that there is an automatic, **universal** standard of beauty. It has to do with the qualities of "order and symmetry" identified centuries ago by Aristotle. In one study, two American anthropologists presented a multicultural set of female faces to five groups of people in Brazil, the United States, Russia, and two isolated tribes of Indians in South America. There was a surprising amount of agreement on which faces were beautiful: those who had similar geometric proportions—large eyes in relation to a small jaw. The supermodel Paulina Porizkova got it right when she said that people finding her beautiful was really "a matter of mathematics: the number of millimeters between the eyes and chin."

Gaby Wood, The Beautiful People, *New York Magazine*, 8/15/05, p. 40

69c. Another contrast which singles out science from among the European movements of the sixteenth and seventeenth centuries is its

universality. Modern science was born in Europe, but its home is the whole world.

Alfred North Whitehead, *Science and the Modern World*, Mentor, 1948, p. 11

69d. It is highly appropriate to note at this point that the question of the **universality** of the concepts of freedom and justice, and their definitions, comprise a highly proper research topic for the anthropologist. One who pursued such an inquiry would be expected to detach himself to as great an extent as possible from currently fashionable slogans and contentions and to work comparatively.

Morton H. Fried, *The Study of Anthropology*, Thomas Y. Crowell Company, 1972, pp. 46–47

69e. The **universality** of complex language is a discovery that fills linguists with awe, and is the first reason to suspect that language is not just any cultural invention but the product of a special human instinct. Cultural inventions vary widely in their sophistication from society to society; within a society, the inventions are generally at the same level of sophistication. Some groups count by carving notches on bones and cook on fires ignited by spinning sticks in logs; others use computers and microwave ovens. Language, however, ruins this correlation. There are Stone Age societies, but there is no such thing as a Stone Age language. Earlier in this century the anthropological linguist Edward Sapir wrote, "When it comes to linguistic form, Plato walks with the Macedonian swineherd, Confucius with the head-hunting savage of Assam."

Steven Pinker, *The Language Instinct*, William Morrow and Company, 1994, pp. 26–27

Question: Languages are different. Spanish is different from German, which is different from Arabic, and so on. What do you think Pinker means when he says language is universal?

70. relative

70b. I often ask myself what advantages our "good society" possesses over that of the "savages." The more I see of their customs, the more I realize that we have no right to look down on them.... The Eskimo are sitting around me, their mouths filled with raw seal liver (the spot of blood on the back of the paper shows you how I joined in). As a thinking person, for me the most important result of this trip lies in the strengthening of my point of view that the idea of a "cultured" individual is merely **relative**.

Franz Boas, quoted in Morton H. Fried, *The Study of Anthropology*, Thomas Y. Crowell, 1972, p. 73

70c. If it were possible to teach a dog to speak, you can bet the first word from its mouth would be "food".

Dogs eat, therefore they are. Just ask our yellow lab Lottie, who is basically a life-support system for a belly, a hairy digestive system on legs.

Labradors have a reputation for intelligence, but if Lottie comes when you call her name, it's probably coincidence. Unless you happen to have something edible on your person—and "edible" is a **relative** term for Lottie.

Spurred on by some obscure inter-species peer pressure from daughter No 3's goat, Gruff, Lottie is pushing the envelope of canine alimentation. Most dogs will chase a well-thrown stick; Lottie, having

Figure 11.4
Physical beauty seems to be relative to a society. This woman might feel that American high heels, or tattoos, or breast enlargements, or mustaches, are very strange and unattractive. *Source: © Guido Vrola/Shutterstock*

studied Gruff's technique, will not only fetch it, but also patiently strip the bark and eat it.

Hal Williams, Basics of Dining with the Animals, *Daily News* (New Plymouth, New Zealand), 2/14/04

(*Alimentation* means eating.)

70d. Admittedly, there are abuses in scientific labs, fur farms, and slaughterhouses, but conditions are dramatically better for animals than they once were, and abuse, after all, is a **relative** term. Most of the people involved in the animal trade are sane and reasonable people.... They also realize that animals who live in the wild don't just die of old age; they starve, get sick, have accidents, or more cruelly, are torn apart and eaten by another animal occupying the next higher link in the food chain.

Hugh Downs, *Perspectives*, Turner Publishing, Inc., 1995, pp. 227–228

70e. Suppose you were asked to choose between living in two imaginary worlds, in which prices were the same:

In the first world you get $50 thousand a year, while other people get $25 thousand (average).

In the second world you get $100 thousand a year, while other people get $250 thousand (average).

How would you vote? This question was put to a group of Harvard students and a majority preferred the **first** type of world. They were happy to be poorer, provided their **relative** position improved. Many other studies have come to the same conclusion. People care greatly about their relative income, and they would be willing to accept a significant fall in living standards if they could move up compared with other people.

Richard Layard, *Happiness: Lessons from a New Science*, Penguin, 2005, pp. 41–42

Comment

In the first three examples here (70b, 70c, and 70d), the writers are explaining relative terms, i.e., concepts. Boas says that being cultured is relative to the society one lives in. Different people use different standards to judge "cultured." Williams says "edible" is relative for his dog. Normally the dog would not eat bark from a stick, but around a goat, bark becomes "edible." Downs says the same for "abuse." But Layard's example in 86e is different. He is describing people's social position—income—compared with others, not a term or concept. In one imaginary society, a person's income would be twice as much as in the other imaginary society, but one's relative position—compared with others—would be lower.

70f. If someone actually believes that a squabble between two children over a ball is as important as the El Salvador liberation movement, then you simply have to ask them whether they are joking. Perhaps by dint of sufficient ridicule you might persuade them to become properly hierarchical thinkers. Political radicals are quite as dedicated to the concept of privilege as their opponents: they believe, for example, that the level of food supplies in Mozambique is a weightier issue than the love life of Mickey Mouse. To claim that one kind of conflict is more important than another involves, of course, *arguing* for this priority and being open to disproval; but nobody actually believes that "power is everywhere" in the sense that any manifestation of it is as significant as any other. On this issue, as perhaps on all others, nobody is in fact a **relativist**, whatever they may rhetorically assert.

Terry Eagleton, *Ideology: An Introduction*, Verso, 1991, pp. 8–9

Part 3. Applying the Words

64. standard
65. to justify
66. prejudice
67. impartial
68. conflict of interest
69. universal
70. relative

Exercise 1: Choose the Best Word

For each sentence, choose the best word (or an appropriate form of the word) to fill in the blank.

1. Governor Schwarzenegger should have known there would be a _____ when he agreed to accept money from magazines advertising health supplements, and also had to approve or disapprove of laws regulating the health supplement industry.
2. Some people say that race, class, and gender are so important to people that they make it impossible for juries to be _____.
3. Peggy says I'm rich, and it's true that I have more money than she. But Malcolm has more than I have. I think the term *rich* is _____.
4. Joe's _____ for a good class is whether he has fun and the teacher tells jokes, but Jerry's _____ is whether he is challenged and has to work hard.
5. After being abused in the Japanese POW camp during the Second World War, O'Connor was probably _____ toward Japanese people after the war.
6. The President said if nothing is done the Social Security system will be bankrupt in a few years, and that _____ his proposal to raise Social Security taxes.

7. In every known society, past and present, most people have decorated their bodies in some way, and therefore we can conclude that a concern for how we appear to others is _____ among humans.

Exercise 2:   Apply the Words

Read each example and answer the questions that follow.

1. And, for [Argentinian philosopher Francisco] Romero, evaluative properties such as those of being a superior culture or an inferior one seem to be cashed out in terms of natural selection, for they are clearly connected to the concept of fitness for survival. Romero assumes that fitness for survival is indicative of cultural superiority, so in his view, the cultures of the native peoples of American come out as inferior. In the passage quoted above, we are told that the disadvantage or inferiority of some cultures is evident from their inability to provide anything more than myths when it comes to understanding the fundamental questions humans ask about their world.

Susana Nuccetelli, *Latin American Thought: Philosophical Problems and Arguments*, Westview, 2002, p. 85

What standard or standards does Romero use in evaluating cultures?

2. The repeated failure to reduce class size condemns us to fall short of our education goals, which shouldn't surprise anyone. Until we have smaller classes taught by qualified teachers we will not fundamentally advance teaching and learning for our children. It's common sense.

Critics say reducing class size by hiring more educators is simply a teacher union ploy to get more members and more dues. That attitude ignores research that shows that smaller classes allow teachers to give students more individual attention, reduce discipline problems, increase graduation rates and help students do better on the high-stakes tests that drive education policy from the federal level on down.

United Federation of Teachers Advertisement: Randi Weingarten, President, UFT, Common Sense on Class Size, *The Riverdale Press*, 5/18/06

Weingarten believes schools should hire more teachers to reduce the size of classes. How does she justify her belief?

3. It [the seventeenth century] is the one century which consistently and throughout the whole range of human activities, provided intellectual genius adequate for the greatness of its occasions....A mere rough catalogue of some names will be sufficient, names of men who published to the world important work within these limits of time: Francis Bacon, Harvey, Kepler, Galileo, Descartes, Pascal, Huyghens,

Boyle, Newton, Locke, Spinoza, Leibniz. I have limited the list to the sacred number of twelve, a number much too small to be properly representative. For example, there is only one Italian there, whereas Italy could have filled the list from its own ranks. Again Harvey is the only biologist, and also there are too many Englishmen. This latter defect is partly due to the fact that the lecturer is English, and that he is lecturing to an audience which, equally with him, owns this English century. If he had been Dutch, there would have been too many Dutchmen; if Italian, too many Italians; and if French, too many Frenchmen.

Alfred North Whitehead, *Science and the Modern World*, Mentor, 1948, pp. 42–43

Whitehead admits that he is prejudiced, and says other historians would be prejudiced as well. What preferences or feelings cause Whitehead to be prejudiced?

4. My own impression, from having divided my life between United States cities and New Guinea villages, is that the so-called blessings of civilization are mixed. For example, compared with hunter-gatherers, citizens of modern industrialized states enjoy better medical care, lower risk of death by homicide, and a longer life span, but receive much less social support from friendships and extended families. My motive for investigating these geographic differences in human societies is not to celebrate one type of society over another but simply to understand what happened in history.

Jared Diamond, *Guns, Germs, and Steel: The Fates of Human Societies*, W. W. Norton, 1999, p. 18

Diamond says he wants to be impartial between two sides, or two points of view. What are the two sides?

5. The brain damage Mrs. Schiavo suffered left her able to breathe on her own but not to ingest food or drink. Doctors have said she is in a persistent vegetative state, meaning her eyes are open and might widen, stare and follow objects, but her brain is incapable of emotion, memory or thought....

The family rift kept deepening, and in 1998, when Mr. Schiavo went to court for permission to remove his wife's feeding tube, the Schindlers [Mrs. Schiavo's parents] immediately challenged him. They believed, and still do, that Mrs. Schiavo is conscious and responds to them especially to her mother, whose voice, they say, elicits frequent smiles from their daughter....

For a long time, the Schindlers accused Mr. Schiavo of wanting his wife dead so he and Ms. Centonze [Mr. Schiavo's girlfriend] could spend her settlement money.

Abby Goodnough, With His Wife in Limbo, Husband Can't Move On, *New York Times*, 11/2/03

Mrs. Schiavo's parents say that Mr. Schiavo has a conflict of interest. What two interests do they see that are in conflict?

> 6. The Maya and Romans had no connection with each other. They arose at similar times but in separate social laboratories: the New World and the Old. This makes them useful for recognizing human behaviors that transcend specifics of time, place and culture—patterns that I think can help us answer two of Gauguin's questions, *What are we?* and *Where are we going?*
>
> Ronald Wright, *A Short History of Progress*, Carroll and Graf, 2004, p. 82

Wright is looking for human behaviors that are universal. How does he try to find them?

> 7. We mistakenly believe that altering our bodies will fix *everything*.... Perhaps our worst mistake is believing that being thin equals being loved, being special, being cherished. We couldn't be more wrong.
>
> Think of the women who live in Samoa. Legend has it that a woman there is not considered attractive unless she weighs more than 200 pounds.... Samoans might equate being fat with being cherished, and being thin with being miserable. (Forget about booking a one-way trip to Samoa. It's too expensive.) The truth is that beauty standards vary from culture to culture....
>
> Geneen Roth, It'll Be Better When I'm Thin, *Prevention*, October, 2004

Roth is saying that standards of beauty vary and are relative. Relative to what?

> 8. In your statement you assert that our actions, even though peaceful, must be condemned because they precipitate violence. But is this a logical assertion? Isn't this like condemning a robbed man because his possession of money precipitated the evil act of robbery? Isn't this like condemning Socrates because his unswerving commitment to truth and his philosophical inquiries precipitated the act by the misguided populace in which they made him drink hemlock? Isn't this like condemning Jesus because his unique God-consciousness and never-ceasing devotion to God's will precipitated the evil act of crucifixion?
>
> Martin Luther King, Jr., Letter from Birmingham Jail, in Linda H. Peterson et al., eds, *The Norton Reader: An Anthology of Expository Prose*, Shorter Ninth Edition, W. W. Norton and Company, 1996, p. 569

King says the ministers to whom he writes are wrong. But he also describes their justification of their view. What is it? Why is it wrong?

Exercise 3: Analyzing Arguments

In the following passage, some people justify cutting trees and plants, and others justify preserving them. In your own words explain the reasons for cutting, and then the reasons for preserving. Which justification makes more sense or is stronger, in your opinion?

> A wealthy eccentric bought a house in a neighborhood I know. The house was surrounded by a beautiful display of grass, plants, and flowers, and it was shaded by a huge old avocado tree. But the grass required cutting, the flowers needed tending, and the man wanted more sun. So he cut the whole lot down and covered the yard with asphalt. After all it was his property and he was not fond of plants....
>
> But I could not help but wonder, "What sort of person would do a thing like that?"
>
> Many Californians had a similar reaction when a recent governor defended the leveling of ancient redwood groves, reportedly saying, "If you have seen one redwood, you have seen them all."
>
> Incidents like these arouse the indignation of ardent environmentalists and leave even apolitical observers with some degree of moral discomfort. The reasons for these reactions are mostly obvious. Uprooting the natural environment robs both present and future generations of much potential use and enjoyment. Animals too depend on the environment; and even if one does not value animals for their own sakes, their potential utility for us is incalculable. Plants are needed, of course, to replenish the atmosphere quite aside from their aesthetic value.

> Thomas E. Hill, Jr., "Ideals of Human Excellence and Preserving Natural Environments," in Christina Sommers and Fred Sommers, eds., *Vice and Virtue in Everyday Life*, Second Edition, Harcourt, Brace, Jovanovich, 1989, pp. 294–295

Exercise 4: Apply the Ideas in Writing

Write an essay about a time when you were evaluated in some way. Have you ever won an award? Have you ever been praised by a coach or anyone in sports? Have you received grades in school? Planned a party that people said was successful? What happened? Who was involved? Where? How did you feel?

Do you want to write about a positive or negative experience? Have you ever tried to do something and people said you failed? Were you judged fairly or unfairly?

You can't write about all your experiences. Pick one and describe it. The focus of your essay should be the *standards* people used in evaluating you. What did "success" mean in your experience? How did others know that you achieved excellence? Or failed?

Improving Your Writing 11: A First Draft

It is easier to write an essay if you break up the process into small steps:

1. Choose a topic.
2. Form a tentative thesis.

3. Research your topic, and think about ways to support your thesis.
4. Review all your points, and group related ones into paragraphs.
5. Organize your paragraphs in an order that will help your audience understand your essay.

After going through these steps you are ready to write a *first draft*.

Your goal is to translate your fragmentary and sketchy ideas into readable sentences and paragraphs. You should have a list of key points—paragraphs—with notes about the examples and details to support each one. It is probably best to skip the introduction at first, and write it last. Begin with the next paragraph and take each one in order. For now, write out your ideas in complete sentences without paying any attention to grammar or spelling or choosing exactly the right word. You will focus on those things later. At this stage you want to produce a rough version of the whole essay. Just write out your ideas as if you were writing a letter to a good friend. Don't worry about how it sounds. Write quickly and try to get the whole essay on paper. Later you can correct your spelling or change the tone or find a better word.

CHAPTER 12

Types of Reasoning

71. to imply

72. to support

73. to suggest

74. to prove

75. to refute

76. to deduce

A chain of statements that leads to a conclusion is an argument. Arguments are extremely common. Any time you explain why you believe something, you are stating an argument. You might say, "I think there's a good chance of rain this afternoon. Those clouds in the west look dark, and the wind is picking up." The facts about clouds and the wind are your premises, and the prediction about rain is your conclusion. Any time you explain why you are doing something, you are stating an argument. "Why are you going out?" "To get milk. We don't have any."

Nine times out of ten, when you produce arguments or assess other people's arguments, everything goes smoothly. They are simple and easy to understand. But when you think about more complicated matters than looking at clouds and predicting rain, it helps to focus on the arguments involved. Politicians use arguments about the kind of society we live in, journalists use arguments about our health and food, psychologists use arguments about our relationships, and financial advisors use arguments about our investments. In school, historians, biologists, literary critics, and virtually all writers use arguments to make their points. Learning to recognize arguments can be very useful in all sorts of areas.

Arguments depend on the logical relationships between statements. The statements about clouds and wind make it more likely that the statement about rain is true. In contrast, if I said "Isn't the grass pretty here? I think it's going to rain," I would not be presenting an argument, because there is no logical relation between these two statements. But the logical relation between reasons and

$$\boxed{\textbf{E} \equiv \textbf{C} \qquad \textbf{E} = \textbf{C} \qquad \textbf{E} - \textbf{C}}$$

Figure 12.1

If evidence <u>implies</u> a conclusion, the connection is very strong. Three lines represent a strong connections.

If evidence <u>supports</u> a conclusion, the connection is not as strong. Two lines represent a weaker connection.

If evidence <u>suggests</u> a conclusion, the connection is weak. One line represents a weak connection.

the beliefs based on them can come in different forms. It can be very strong, or sort of strong, or weak. We have words to talk about those different forms of logical relationship.

You have already learned words for the essential parts of any argument: *conclusion* and *evidence* (or *reasons*, or *premise*). And you learned words about the different degrees of confidence you have in different beliefs (*probable, convincing, certain*). This chapter builds upon those previous chapters. It is about words for the different strengths of logical relationship between evidence and conclusions.

Part 1. Definitions

71. to imply. 1. to guarantee the truth of a statement; one statement implies a second statement if the truth of the first guarantees the truth of the second. "The fact that Jones is dead implies that he will not attend tomorrow's meeting." "'Miller is President' implies 'Miller is commander in chief.'"

2. to indicate the truth of a statement indirectly, by use of other statements. "When Smith said that honesty is the best policy, he implied that Green was wrong to conceal the truth." "She didn't say she would vote for Garcia, but she implied it."

Statements can imply other statements, as in Definition 1, or people can imply statements, as in Definition 2.

implication (noun). 1. the statement that is implied by some other statement; "The implication of Brown's testimony was that Black wasn't involved in the crime." 2. the act of implying. "White preferred implication over direct accusation."

Comment

We can say that one statement implies another, or that a person implies something without saying it outright. Statements can imply, and people can imply. But the two kinds of implication are a little different. When one statement implies another, that means the first guarantees that the second is true. When a person implies something, that means she hints at it without stating it directly. For example, suppose Jillian says, "I think Garcia is the better candidate in this election. Hernandez has no administrative experience." Her statements logically imply that there is an election, that Garcia is a candidate, and that Hernandez has never been a mayor, among other things. That is, if her two statements are true, these other implications must be true as well. She is also implying—hinting, indicating—that she will vote for Garcia. But her statements do not logically imply that she will vote for Garcia. Her statements could be true and yet, for some reason, she could vote for Hernandez.

Example

71a. For more than a century, researchers have used the word "subjects" to describe the college undergraduates and other brave souls who volunteer for psychology experiments.

Now the American Psychological Association wants to retire the term. It is, the group says, too impersonal, stripping people of their individuality, their humanity. "Participants" is a better word, the association's publication manual advises. It **implies** consent. Unless, of course, the subjects—er, participants—are infants or Alzheimer's patients, in which case they have not technically consented and are better referred to, the manual suggests, as "individuals."

Benedict Carey, The Subject Is…Subjects, *New York Times*, 6/15/04

72. to support. to supply a reason to believe something, to make a conclusion more likely to be true. "She supported her position with a lot of evidence and sound arguments."

support (noun). the evidence that makes a conclusion more likely to be true. "I understand Nick's interpretation, but I don't see the support for it."

Example

72a. Europe and the U.S. have been arguing over beef hormones since the late 1990s. North American ranchers inject cattle with hormones to make them grow faster. The Europeans banned the products but lacked scientific evidence to **support** those worries, and lost the WTO [World Trade Organization] ruling.

Scott Miller, EU Renews Fight Over Hormones in Beef Products, *Wall Street Journal*, 11/9/04

73. to suggest. to increase slightly the probability that something is true, but not guarantee it. One statement (or set of statements) suggests a second statement if it slightly increases the probability that the second is true, but doesn't guarantee it. "The presence of a bloodstain on the sidewalk suggests that there was a fight, but there may be a different explanation."

In many contexts the word *suggest* means to propose a plan, or urge people to do something. "I suggest we have lunch." "The Scouts offered several suggestions about how to cross the river." But in this part of the book we are looking at words about reasoning. And in the context of reasoning, the word *suggest* means to lead to a conclusion.

Comment

The word *suggest* is similar in meaning to the word *support*. The difference is that *support* is stronger. Compare the following two statements: (a) "The report *supports* the conclusion that the corporation has falsified its records." (b) "The report *suggests* that the corporation has falsified its records." Statement (a) asserts a stronger, more definite link between the report and the conclusion about the corporation than (b) does. Statement (a) says the report gives a good reason to believe the corporation is guilty, but (b) says the report only provides some sort of reason, and perhaps a weak one.

Example

> 73a. The decline in marriage is no more a public issue than is the rise in premarital sex. Of course it's good for children to know their fathers. But kids aren't necessarily better off just because their parents are married. Research **suggests** that children do better with single parents who are stable and loving than with married parents who are angry and miserable with each other.
>
> Robert B. Reich, *Reason: Why Liberals Will Win the Battle for America*, Knopf, 2004, p. 69

74. to prove. to show conclusively, without doubt, that something is true by citing evidence. "Ladies and gentlemen of the jury, the evidence presented to you will prove beyond a reasonable doubt that the defendant, James Carpenter, murdered Peter Goodman and threw his body into the Potomac River." If the lawyer proves that the defendant is guilty, then her evidence implies that he is guilty.

    proof (noun).

Example

> 74a. NASA's twin rovers, Spirit and Opportunity, reached Mars in January with one goal: **Prove** the Red Planet was once awash with water. In the weeks that followed, Opportunity succeeded. The rover detected a high concentration of sulfate minerals together with chloride and bromide salts in one rock outcrop. This was suggestive, but not conclusive, evidence of a previous presence of water. In another outcrop, the rover found jarosite, which on Earth forms only in water. Finally, it identified round rock formations, dubbed blueberries, that are rich in hematite, also an aqueous mineral. At last there could be no

doubt: The Meridiani Planum region where Opportunity landed was once part of a shallow, briny Martian sea.

Kathy A. Svitil, NASA's Rovers Find Evidence of Ancient Seas on Mars, *Discover*, January, 2005

75. refute. to show that some statement is false, to disprove. "Carter's claim that he hadn't been near the convenience store that night was refuted by the surveillance tape, which clearly showed him entering the store at 9:14 PM."

Example

75a. Mr. Lomborg, who is the director of the government-supported Environmental Assessment Institute, was actually a Greenpeace activist at one time. He said he set out to **refute** the claims of skeptics, but ended up being convinced by their arguments.

Gary Andrew Poole, $50 Billion Question: World, Where to Begin? *New York Times*, 6/5/04

76. to deduce. to decide that one thing is true, conclusively, without doubt, on the basis of something else. "By counting all the births in Sacramento between 1990 and 2000, the sociologist was able to deduce that the birth rate went down during that period."

deductive (adjective). having the character of a proof or demonstration that is logically conclusive and certain. "Scientific laws based on observations are highly probable, but mathematical proofs are deductively certain."

Example

76a. As to the late Soviet standard of living, this was, in its essentials, lower than in 1914 not only for the peasant but even for the worker, as could be **deduced** from Soviet statistical manuals. Much else more impressionistically confirms this fact. For example, Stalin's daughter, Svetlana Alliluyeva, said in passing that her grandfather, a skilled worker in Petrograd in the second decade of this century, had a four-room apartment—she says, "as much as a Soviet professor could dream of today."

Robert Conquest, *The Dragons of Expectation*, W. W. Norton, 2005, p. 154

Test Yourself
Match each word with its definition.

71. to imply
72. to support
73. to suggest
74. to prove
75. to refute
76. to deduce

a. to make something more likely to be true
b. to be related to a statement in such as way as to guarantee that the statement is true
c. to decide that one statement is definitely true on the basis of another
d. to show conclusively that something is true by citing evidence
e. to increase slightly the probability that something is true
f. to show conclusively that something is false

Part 2. Understanding the Meaning

71. to imply.

> 71b. The farm-to-city migration has obviously produced advantages to the corporate economy.... But these short-term advantages all **imply** long-term disadvantages, to both country and city. The departure of so many people has seriously weakened rural communities and economies all over the country. And that our farmland no longer has enough caretakers is **implied** by the fact that, as the farming people have departed from the land, the land itself has departed. Our soil erosion rates are now higher than they were in the time of the Dust Bowl.
>
> Wendell Berry, *What Are People For?* North Point Press, Farrar, Strauss and Giroux, 1990, pp. 123–124

Question: When one statement implies another, you can think of the first as a premise and the second as a conclusion. Berry describes two implications in Example 71b. What are the premises and what are the conclusions of each?

> 71c. Bill Moyers: What frightens them [religious fundamentalists] is something that Dostoevski once said—if God is dead, everything is permitted.
>
> Isaac Asimov: That assumes that human beings have no feeling about what is right and wrong. Is the only reason you are virtuous because virtue is your ticket to heaven? Is the only reason you don't beat your children to death because you don't want to go to hell? It's insulting to **imply** that only a system of rewards and punishments can keep you a decent human being. Isn't it conceivable a person wants to be a decent human being because that way he feels better?
>
> Bill Moyers, *A World of Ideas*, edited by Betty Sue Flowers, Doubleday, 1989, p. 272

Comment

Asimov is saying that the statement "If God is dead, everything is permitted" logically implies that people have no other standards or feelings about right and wrong besides fear of God. He probably also means that the fundamentalists are implying this, without saying it explicitly.

Figure 12.2
Robinson Crusoe was stranded on an island that he thought was deserted. But he found
evidence that changed his mind. *Source: © Trutta55/Shutterstock*
"It happened one day, about noon, going towards my boat, I was exceedingly surprised with
the print of a man's naked foot on the shore, which was very plain to be seen in the sand.
I stood like one thunder-struck, or as if I had seen an apparition. . . . and I went home again,
filled with the belief that some man or men had been on shore there; or, in short, that the
island was inhabited, and I might be surprised before I was aware. And what course to take
for my security, I knew not."
Daniel Defoe, *Robinson Crusoe*, 1719
Does the footprint <u>imply</u> that someone besides Crusoe is on the island?

71d. Regarding the middle and upper classes [of ancient Athens], it
should be remembered that, however confined, women did manage
what was the major part of their husband's property: his household.
Within the household, slaves would have been the main adult company of nearly all such women, and one can easily guess at the **implications** of this close association.

Orlando Patterson, *Freedom, Vol 1: Freedom in the Making of Western Culture*, Basic Books,
1991, p. 107

71e. Darwin carefully did not say anything about humans in *Origin
of Species*, but the book clearly **implied** that they had evolved just like
other animals.

Harry Henderson and Lisa Yount, *The Scientific Revolution*, Lucent Books, 1996, pp. 70

Question: Do the writers in Example 71e mean that the statements in *Origin of Species* guarantee that humans evolved just like other animals, or do they mean that Darwin was trying to convey the idea indirectly, but not stating it explicitly? This can be an important question in some cases. Often, people interpret a writer to be expressing an idea (e.g., "humans evolved"), and then the writer will deny that he or she meant to say that. The dispute boils down to whether the statements imply the idea in the strong, logical sense, or whether the writer is only implying something in the weaker, indirect sense. If the former, then the writer has to admit that he or she made a mistake, or has to retract what he or she wrote. If the latter, the writer can say people misinterpreted what was written.

72. to support.

72b. To Tertullian, one of the Fathers of the Latin Church, this pagan [Roman] empire, at the end of the second century, was "a world every day better known, better cultivated, and more civilized than before.... There are now as many cities as there were once solitary cottages. Reefs and shoals have lost their terrors. Wherever there is a trace of life there are houses and human habitations, well-ordered governments and civilized life." Other Greek and Roman writers, law codes, archaeological finds, coins, papyri, and thousands of inscriptions from all parts of the Empire **support** this Christian estimate.

Solomon Katz, *The Decline of Rome and the Rise of Mediaeval Europe*, Cornell University Press, 1955, pp. 7–8

(Papyri are documents written on papyrus, a sort of "paper" made from reeds.)

72c. Up to now, scientists have had close looks only at loose rocks on the Martian surface. The Opportunity [spacecraft] landed in a small crater with exposed bedrock along the inner rim. Because the bedrock formed at that spot, it will offer evidence of the site's geological history. Scientists are further intrigued because the bedrock consists of thin layers, which may be volcanic ash or sedimentary rock deposited by water or wind.

If the rock turns out to be sedimentary rock formed by the flow of water, it would **support** the theory that Mars was once much warmer and wetter than it is today.

Kenneth Chang, Martian Bedrock Intrigues Scientists as Rover Snaps Pictures, *New York Times*, 2/9/04

72d. [There is one point] on which left and right agree—that people consume news and opinion in order to become well informed about public issues. Were this true, liberals would read conservative newspapers, and conservatives liberal newspapers, just as scientists test their hypotheses by confronting them with data that may refute them.

But that is not how ordinary people (or, for that matter, scientists) approach political and social issues. The issues are too numerous, uncertain and complex, and the benefit to an individual of becoming well informed about them too slight, to invite sustained, disinterested attention. Moreover, people don't like being in a state of doubt, so they look for information that will **support** rather than undermine their existing beliefs. They're also uncomfortable seeing their beliefs challenged on issues that are bound up with their economic welfare, physical safety or religious and moral views.

Richard A. Posner, Bad News, *New York Times Book Review*, 7/31/05

73. to suggest.

73b. In New York City, the list of [gun] permit holders strongly **suggests** that licenses are issued on the basis of celebrity status, wealth, political influence, and favoritism. Such luminaries as journalist William F. Buckley, Jr., real estate mogul Donald Trump, publisher Michael Korda, comedians Bill Cosby and Joan Rivers, and radio shock-jock Howard Stern are among those who have been granted licenses. Meanwhile taxi drivers, who face a high risk of robbery and murder, are denied permits because they carry less than 2000 dollars in cash.

Daniel D. Polsby, The Prevalence of Guns Does Not Contribute to Violent Crime, in William Dudley, ed., *Opposing Viewpoints in Social Issues*, Greenhaven Press, 2000, p. 34

73c. But we've learned that even more diseases are linked to runaway inflammation; for instance, the consensus among cardiologists today is that inflammation in the lining of the arteries is a greater factor in the development of heart disease than the accumulation of cholesterol on artery walls. In fact, studies **suggest** that the fat buildup may be due to the body's attempt to patch areas where inflammation has done damage.

Andrew Weil, The Healthiest Way to Eat, *Self*, November, 2005

73d. When John Duncan and his colleagues at Cambridge University searched for one area of the brain that is activated when smart people perform a multitude of tasks... they found that the lateral part of the frontal lobe (on both the left and right sides) may be the resting place of general intelligence. While undergoing positron-emission tomography (PET) scans, Duncan's subjects selectively activated the lateral frontal cortex during several intelligence tests. Some researchers are skeptical of the importance of Duncan's study, saying it is **"suggestive"** at best, because we do not yet fully understand what the frontal lobes do.... Further support for the role of the frontal lobe in intelligence comes from the observation that people with frontal lobe damage usually score twenty to sixty fewer points on IQ tests than the normal population.

Michael S. Gazzaniga, *The Ethical Brain: The Science of Our Moral Dilemmas*, Harper Perennial, 2005, pp. 81–82

74. to prove.

74b. The massive trove of archival materials made available with the collapse of the Soviet Union **proves**—as if more **proof** were required— that, indeed, the Communist regime had posed the aggressive threat the reasonable anti-Communists always claimed.

Jean Bethke Elshtain, *Just War Against Terror: The Burden of American Power in a Violent World*, Basic Books, 2003, p. 72

74c. Movement appears to enhance memory, learning, attention, decision making and multitasking, among other mental functions. It also may slow or even reverse age related decline.

The **proof** comes in two forms. The first is research showing that people who exercise score better on mental tests than those who don't. The second is research showing that exercise prompts structural changes in the brains of mice, spurring the growth of new nerve cells and connections between cells.

To Sharpen the Brain, First Hone the Body, *AM New York*, 1/25/06

Comment

Example 74c shows that many people use the key words of critical thinking loosely, without being precise. The writer first says that movement "appears" to enhance memory. And then he or she says the "proof" comes in two kinds of research. A more careful writer would say the "support" comes in two kinds of research. The research does not prove that movement enhances memory and other mental functions, even if it does make it probable that movement has that effect.

74d. [Nizar Trabelis was sentenced to 10 years in prison for planning an attack on a Belgian military base.] Although Trabelis has admitted the crime and stands by his confession, his lawyers "said they would argue that admitting to a crime is no **proof**."

New York Sun, 2/20/04, p. 8

74e. Campbell, who was not injured, was described by police as unsteady on his feet and smelling of alcohol. After being placed in wrist restraints, police said, Campbell fell asleep in the rear of a police cruiser while officers investigated the crash scene. When he was wakened, police said, Campbell refused to perform field-sobriety tests and his speech was slurred.

Two empty beer cans and one full can of beer were found in the front seat of Campbell's car, police said. He was arrested and held overnight....

Campbell wore shorts and a T-shirt during yesterday's arraignment, at which court-appointed defense attorney Patrick O. Bomberg argued that his client did not cause the fatal crash. Bomberg said the description in the police report suggests that Guzman was the instigator.

Bomberg said Campbell's slurred words could be seen as his physical reaction to the fatal crash and not as **proof** he was drunk.

John Ellement and Brian MacQuarrie, Police Say Road Rage Led to Death of Boy, 5, *Boston Globe*, 11/19/04

75. refute.

75b. Overall, [the exhibition at the American Museum of Natural History called] "Darwin" is an education in the scientific method. Choosing to emphasize the facts, the exhibit never explicitly addresses intelligent design, but it **refutes** it nonetheless. It's a refreshing dose of rationality in a world where too often anti-intellectual hysteria and popular opinion dictate public discourse.

Emily Hulme, The Darwinists Strike Back, *AM New York*, 11/18–20/05

(Intelligent design is the theory that living organisms are too complicated to be explained by evolution, and therefore they must have been designed by a supernatural intelligence, or creator.)

75c. Herewith an update on the International Freedom Center at Ground Zero. The news is worrisome.

Richard Tofel, the center's president, chatted with Fox News' Neil Cavuto last week in an entirely unconvincing effort to **refute** charges that leftists and other intellectual lowlifes are out to hijack the Ground Zero memorial.

Editorial, Memo to Gov. Pataki: Retrieve the Memorial, *New York Post*, 6/20/05

75d. Of the arguments against capital punishment that issue from uplifters, two are commonly heard most often, to wit:

(1) That hanging a man (or frying him or gassing him) is a dreadful business, degrading to those who have to do it and revolting to those who have to witness it.

(2) That it is useless, for it does not deter others from the same crime.

The first of these arguments, it seems to me, is plainly too weak to need serious **refutation**. All it says, in brief, is that the work of the hangman is unpleasant. Granted. But suppose it is? It might be quite necessary to society for all that.

H. L. Mencken, The Penalty of Death, in Alfred Rosa and Paul Eschholz, eds., *Controversies: Contemporary Arguments for College Writers*, Macmillan Publishing co., 1991, p. 465

75e. South Africa's government lashed out yesterday at Gerard Latortue, Haiti's interim prime minister, **refuting** allegations that President Thabo Mbeki has allowed ousted Haitian president Jean-Bertrand Aristide to coordinate violence in the Caribbean country from his refuge in South Africa.

South Africa Angry Over Aristide Remark, *AM New York*, 10/19/04

Comment

This is an example of a word used in an extended sense. The original and basic meaning of *refute* is to prove mistaken. But here the writer uses *refute* to mean "to deny, to challenge." The South African government did not provide definitive proof that Latortue was mistaken, but only claimed that he was. It is tempting to say that you have refuted another person's statement instead of saying you have denied the other person's statement, because if you really have refuted it, then the other person is definitely wrong. But if you have only denied it, the other person may still be correct.

76. to deduce.

76b. Sudoku-style puzzles...were titled Number Place when they began appearing anonymously in 1979 in the periodical Dell Pencil Puzzles and Word Games. Will Shortz, the crossword puzzle editor of The New York Times, **deduced** the author's identity with sudoku-style argument: anytime the Dell publication contained one of these puzzles—and never otherwise—the list of contributors included Howard Garns, an architect from Indianapolis; Mr. Garns died in 1989.

Edward Rothstein, In Sudoku, 9 Little Numbers Create a Big Challenge, *New York Times*, 5/1/06

Question: In your opinion, did Shortz's evidence prove that Garns was the creator of the Number Place puzzles, or did it only support that conclusion?

76c. Like the Jesus-questers, I craved the solid rock of certainty, and, also like them, I set about finding it without benefit of history, sociology, theory, or philosophy. I did, however, have what I considered to be the handbook: the U.S. Constitution, which I regarded as being so rich in wisdom that all philosophical conclusions could be drawn from its pages.... As an adolescent, I thought the connection between Constitution and Bible was self-evident: these were the shop manuals to the human condition. They were all you needed to know, the original texts from which everything else could be **deduced**.

Thomas Frank, *What's the Matter with Kansas? How Conservatives Won the Heart of America*, Metropolitan Books, 2004, p. 145

76d. Tocqueville, an aristocratic French lawyer, wrote his classic text [*Democracy in America*] after a nine-month visit to the United States in 1831.... [I]t was a stroke of genius for The Atlantic Monthly to renew the Tocquevillian project by commissioning the distinguished French philosopher, journalist and gadfly Bernard-Henri Lévy to repeat Tocqueville's journey through America and chronicle his observations over the next several months in the magazine before they appear in book form early next year....

While Tocqueville **deduces** American character from abstract principles, Mr. Lévy wants to discover the abstract principles through observation of the American character. So the elegant logic that Tocqueville uses to outline democracy's effects is replaced in Mr. Lévy's first installment by the accumulation of anecdote and carefully observed description.

Edward Rothstein, Touring an America Tocqueville Could Fathom, *New York Times*, 4/11/05

76e. In a sense, Hobbes took up where Machiavelli had left off; accepting politics as a purely secular matter, he tried to make of it a **deductive** science. His general philosophy rests upon materialism and mechanism and reduces man to a mere physical organism, the product of complex motion and countermotion.... As Hobbes wrote in his classic study, *Leviathan*, "I put for a general inclination of all mankind, a perpetual desire of power after power, that ceases only in death."... He did not turn to history or primitive cultures to verify such generalizations; his method was logical rather than empirical, **deductive** rather than inductive. His dismal picture of the original (precivilized) condition of human beings derived from his postulates regarding their physical constitutions.

Thomas H. Greer, *A Brief History of Western Man*, Third Edition, Harcourt, Brace, Jovanovich, 1977, p. 349

Comment

One important thing to notice about the words in this chapter is that they fall into two groups. All of them are about the connection between evidence and conclusion (i.e., about inferences). But that connection can be very strong, or it can be weaker. The words *imply*, *prove*, *refute*, and *deduce* are about a very strong connection, while the words *support* and *suggest* are about a weaker connection. In other words, if one fact implies another, then you cannot accept the first without accepting the second. The connection is unbreakable. But if one fact suggests another, then you can believe the first and withhold judgment about the second. The second is probably true, but things may turn out differently.

We have special terms to name those two types of inferences. The very strong connection between evidence and conclusion is called *deductive*, and the weaker connection is called *inductive*. *Inductive* means probable but not proven beyond a doubt. The evidence makes the conclusion likely to be true, but it doesn't guarantee that it's true. It supports the conclusion, but doesn't prove it. But in a deductive inference, if the evidence is true, then the conclusion has to be true. (*Imply*, *prove*, *refute*, and of course *deduce*, all refer to deductive inferences. *Support* and *suggest* refer to inductive inferences.) In the following example, the writer is describing the two different kinds of inferences.

> 76f. Research and crime-detection have a lot in common, but the research worker is like that Scotland Yard detective and not like the fellow who writes the detective stories. The writer thinks out his plot (his theory) and then produces the facts to conform. He is rather like the classical theorists who dominated natural philosophy for two thousand years until Sir Francis Bacon defined the principles of modern research at the beginning of the seventeenth century. The classical theorists were **deductive**; they proceeded from the general to the particular; they erected a model theory as to how things ought to behave, and if they did not behave accordingly they were against reason, since reason (on their reasoning) could not be wrong. Modern science is **Inductive**, moving from the particular to the general, from the buckshot holes [that the detective noticed] to the theory of the crime. The experimental scientist finds the evidence, fits the clues together, and proves his answer before the jury of his critical colleagues.
>
> Ritchie Calder, *Science in Our Lives*, New American Library, 1962, pp. 31–32

Comment

The experimental scientist can "prove" his or her answer—his theory explaining what he observed—in the sense that he can present enough evidence to convince his critical colleagues. But he cannot "prove" his answer in the sense of showing that it is true beyond doubt, or guaranteed to be true. Inductive reasoning never produces proof in the strict sense, as deductive reasoning does. For example, making a generalization on the basis of a sample is inductive reasoning, and no generalization from a sample is ever guaranteed to be correct. Proposing a hypothesis about the likely cause of some event is inductive reasoning ("lack of water caused the plants to die in the past; it was probably lack of water that caused this plant to die"). But past examples, and even experiments, do not *prove* that a hypothesis is correct, in the strong sense, even if they confirm it.

Part 3. Applying the Words

71. to imply
72. to support
73. to suggest
74. to prove

75. to refute
76. to deduce

Exercise 1:   Choose the Best Word

For each sentence, choose the best word (or an appropriate form of the word) to fill in the blank.

1. Edward Jenner injected a young boy with a small dose of deadly smallpox, and the boy did not become ill, which _____ that vaccinations can work.
2. Three cases of tuberculosis have been confirmed in New Jersey, which _____ that the antibiotics that used to kill the germ are no longer effective.
3. The attorney dramatically _____ the charge that his client had murdered Mrs. Wagoner by simply bringing the woman into the room.
4. Julia must have gotten married since we saw her last. Russell's statement that she is divorced _____ that she had been married.
5. If we know that the boat can support only 500 pounds, and we know that each of the five fishermen weighs more than 100 pounds, we can _____ that the boat will sink when all five attempt to climb in.
6. Eastern Iowa has seen a net loss of jobs over the past year, since Wal-Mart opened its stores in the area, and that _____ the charge that Wal-Mart destroys jobs.

Exercise 2:   Apply the Words

Read each example and answer the questions that follow. I have provided an answer for Example 1.

> 1. Consider this list of the twelve largest companies in America on January 1, 1900: The American Cotton Oil Company, American Steel, American Sugar Refining Company, Continental Tobacco, Federal Steel, General Electric, National Lead, Pacific Mail, People's Gas, Tennessee Coal and Iron, U.S. Leather, U.S. Rubber. Ten of the twelve companies were natural resource companies. The economy at the turn of the century was a natural resource economy.
>
> But something else is interesting about that list. Bits and pieces of each of these companies exist inside other companies, but only one of those companies, GE, is alive today. Many of the twelve could not make it to the next century as separate entities. The moral of the story is clear. Capitalism is a process of creative destruction whereby dynamic small companies are continually replacing old large ones that have not been able to adjust to new conditions.
>
> Lester C. Thurow, *The Future of Capitalism*, Penguin, 1996, p. 66

Thurow uses evidence about large companies to reach the conclusion that capitalism is a process of creative destruction. He says the moral of his story is clear. Does he think the evidence suggests the conclusion or implies the conclusion?

Answer: He thinks the evidence implies the conclusion. The connection is stronger than merely suggesting the conclusion. He defines "creative destruction" as small companies replacing older, larger ones. His examples imply—prove, guarantee—that creative destruction in that sense occurs.

2. Claims of reincarnation are rare among children in the United States, where—according to a 2001 Gallup poll—only twenty-five percent of the population believes in it. This fact, perhaps more than any other, weakens the overall case for reincarnation. Stories of rebirth that crop up within cultures whose religious dogma doesn't include it are, for obvious reasons, stronger than cases that show up among cultures who accept it and, more to the point, expect it to happen. If a child in a Western culture begins to refer to a stranger with an unfamiliar name, his parents assume the name belongs to someone from his imagination. In a Hindu—or Druze, or Tlingit—culture, the parents are more likely to assume it's someone from his past life....

A child who is said to know things about a family of far-off strangers makes a stronger case for reincarnation than a child who is said to know things about a family in a town his parents know well. Weakest—and quite common—are the cases in which the child seems to be the reincarnation of one of his own family members. Stevenson's casebooks hold many of these. In the cultures that most often report it, within-family reincarnation is expected. It's what happens when you die.

Mary Roach, *Spook: Science Tackles the Afterlife*, W. W. Norton, 2005, pp. 35, 46

Roach describes several kinds of evidence for reincarnation. She might say the strongest evidence supports the belief in reincarnation, and the weakest evidence merely suggests that reincarnation occurs. What is the strongest evidence and what is the weakest evidence?

3. But if one cares to analyze the figures, such as we have, it is easy to trace the more frequent causes of homicide. The greatest numbers of killings occur during attempted burglaries and robberies. The robber knows that penalties for burglary do not average more than five years in prison. He also knows that the penalty for murder is death or imprisonment. Faced with this alternative, what does the burglar do when he is detected and threatened with arrest? He shoots to kill. He deliberately takes the chance of death to save himself from a five-year term in prison. It is therefore as obvious as anything can be that fear of death has no effect in diminishing homicides of this kind, which are more numerous than any other type.

The next largest number of homicides may be classed as "sex murders." Quarrels between husbands and wives, disappointed love, or love too much requited causes many killings. They are the result of primal emotions so deep that the fear of death has not the slightest effect in preventing them. Spontaneous feelings overflow in criminal acts, and consequences do not count.

Clarence Darrow, The Futility of the Death Penalty, in Alfred Rosa and Paul Eschholz, eds., *Controversies: Contemporary Arguments for College Writers*, Macmillan Publishing co., 1991, p. 460

"The death penalty deters people from committing homicides." Does Darrow believe his examples support that statement or refute it?

4. The peopling of the Pacific has been described as the greatest feat of maritime colonization in human history. Contrary to the conclusions of Thor Heyerdahl's Kon-Tiki expedition of 1946, the evidence of plant dispersal, archaeology, linguistics and genetics now shows quite conclusively that the pacific was not populated from the east by South Americans who drifted in on balsa-wood rafts and the prevailing wind and current, but from the west, by groups from mainland Asia who gradually spread from island to island out into the Pacific.

John Reader, *Man on Earth*, University of Texas Press, 1988, p. 11

According to Reader, does evidence from plant dispersal, archaeology, and so on (a) suggest, (b) prove, or (c) refute the conclusion that the Pacific was populated by people from the west, not the east?

5. Sir, – In his letter "Evolution is a blind concept", GW claims that by accepting the current scientific explanation for biological diversity (evolution), mankind will reject all moral codes and indulge in "injustice, cruelty, merciless brutality and murder." Sorry, but I think he'll find all those things existed long before Darwin published "On the Origin of Species" in 1859. According to this logic, ardent atheist and evolutionist professor Richard Dawkins should be a mass murderer.

He also claims: "For instance, anyone working among the poor to bring relief in Third World countries is completely wasting their time if evolution is true. They are working against the natural order of things in helping those who are unable to survive themselves." On the contrary, mutual co-operation within a species is common in nature because it confers a survival advantage.

GW asked if Hitler or Stalin would have killed millions had they believed there was a Creator. Well, one of them certainly would ("I believe today I am acting in the sense of the Almighty Creator. By warding off the Jews I am fighting for the Lord's work" —Adolph Hitler in a speech at the Reichstag, 1936).

DB, The Religious Can Be Cruel, *The Sentinel* (Stoke), July 1, 2003

GW seems to say that the belief in evolution implies the belief that helping the poor is a waste of time. DB says evolution does not imply that conclusion. Why not? How does he refute GW's claim?

> 6. "What killed the dinosaurs?" is such an alluring mystery that almost everyone seems to have an opinion. Many of the proposed theories are questionable in light of the full set of known facts.
>
> Thus, the theory that the dinosaurs were destroyed by a new breed of egg-eating mammals can immediately be challenged since it does not explain the simultaneous extinction of marine [sea-dwelling] dinosaurs.
>
> Jerry Lucas, *Great Unsolved Mysteries of Science*, Betterway Books, 1993, p. 73

Consider these two statements: (a) A new breed of egg-eating mammals killed all the dinosaurs (by eating their eggs when they weren't looking). (b) All the marine dinosaurs were killed at the same time. What is the relation between statements (a) and (b)? Does (a) support (b), does (b) support (a), or does (b) refute (a)?

> 7. Kenneth Kantzer, former editor and now advisory editor of Christianity Today, recently wrote an editorial in that journal (January 21) in which he defended Christian support for nuclear war, if that war seemed necessary to national defense: "100 million deaths may not be too great a price to pay" [for the freedom to worship as Christians], he said....
>
> Is it less important for Russian parents to be able freely to teach their children about God than it is for American parents to do so? Not if we love others as we do ourselves. Then would not an American war against Russia be justified in order to destroy a godless system and install one with religious and political freedom—even if 100 million or more lives were lost thereby? Such a "holy war" would seem to be logically justified by Kantzer's premises and reasoning.
>
> Reo M. Christenson, in David L. Bender and Bruno Leone, eds., *War and Human Nature*, Greenhaven Press, 1983, p. 88–89

According to Christenson, Kantzer believes that 100 million deaths would be acceptable in order to protect Americans' freedom to practice Christianity. Christenson says that belief leads to the further belief that a costly war against Russia to free the Russians to practice Christianity would be acceptable (assuming that we love others as we love ourselves). How strong is the connection between the first belief and the second, according to Christenson? Does the first imply the second, support it, or only suggest it? What do you think? [This piece was written before the fall of the Soviet Union, at a time when the Soviet government discouraged religious belief.]

> 8. There is also zoological evidence of drifting continents. For example: guinea pigs, chinchillas, peculiar land snails that must live in

woods, and giant lizards that lay their eggs in termite nests are found wild only in South America and Africa. All fish and fresh-water creatures in South America have close relatives in Africa.... Unless the two continents were once linked, how explain this amazing resemblance of unique creatures on opposite sides of the ocean?

Rutherford Platt, in Editors of Reader's Digest, *The Living World of Nature*, Berkley Books, 1980, p. 78

What conclusion does the zoological evidence support, according to Platt?

Exercise 3:   Analyzing Arguments

The following passage by Mortimer Adler is about equality. Are people basically equal? The American Declaration of Independence says they are. Does Adler agree or disagree with the Declaration? In your own words write the main point Adler wants to make and the reasons he gives to support it. Do the premises make the conclusion certain, or only probable? That is, is it possible for the premises to be true at the same time that the conclusion is false?

The statement in the Declaration of Independence that all men are created equal and endowed by their Creator with certain unalienable rights is not, on the face of it, self-evidently true. Nor can it be made self-evident by substituting "are by nature equal" for "created equal," and "endowed by nature with certain unalienable rights" for "endowed by their Creator with certain unalienable rights."

The truth of the statement, even when the substitutions are made, is the truth of a conclusion reached by reasoning in the light of factual evidence, evidence and reasoning that refutes the ancient doctrine that some human beings (all members of the same species) are by nature slaves....

The factual basis for the correct view is biological. All members of any biological species, human or otherwise, are alike in possessing the properties or powers that are genetically determined attributes of that species of living organism. These common properties, shared by all individuals of a certain species, are appropriately called species-specific....

[B]y being human, we are all equal—equal as persons, equal in our humanity. One individual cannot be more or less human than another, more or less of a person. The dignity we attribute to being a person rather than a thing is not subject to differences in degree. The equality of all human beings is the equality of their dignity as persons....

There is no other respect in which *all* human beings are equal. Two or more individuals may be personally equal in some other respect, such as height, intelligence, talent, or virtue, but equality in such respects is never true of all.

Mortimer J. Adler, *Six Great Ideas*, Collier Books, 1981, pp. 165–167

Exercise 4:   Apply the Ideas in Writing

The following passage is part of a description of an Aztec city in Mexico by Hernando Cortez, the Spanish explorer and soldier. Read the passage and then write two paragraphs using the words in this chapter. In the first, explain what the passage *implies*. What can you *prove* with the passage—about the city, the Aztecs, Mexico, Cortez, or anything else? In other words, if the passage is true, what else do you know for sure is true, even though it isn't stated directly in the passage?

In the second paragraph, explain what the passage *suggests*, but does not imply. If the passage is true, what else is *probably* true (but may not be true)?

> The city has many open squares in which markets are continuously held and the general business of buying and selling proceeds. One square in particular is twice as big as that of Salamanca [in Spain] and completely surrounded by arcades where there are daily more than sixty thousand folk buying and selling. Every kind of merchandise such as may be met with in every land is for sale there, whether of food and victuals or ornaments of gold and silver, or lead, brass, copper, tin, precious stones, bones, shells, snails, and feathers.... There is a street of herb-sellers where there are all manner of roots and medicinal plants that are found in the land.... There are barber shops where you may have your hair washed and cut. There are other shops where you may obtain food and drink.
>
> Hernando Cortez, Description of an Aztec City [1522], in Jackson J. Spielvogel, *Western Civilization*, Vol. 2, Second Edition, West Publishing Co., 1994, p. 487

Improving Your Writing 12: Evaluation Essays

There are several different kinds of essays. In a descriptive essay you describe something, such as a person or a place. In a narrative essay you tell a story, for example, about a camping trip. In an expository essay you explain something, such as the way music is stored on a compact disk and then played back.

Another type of essay is a *persuasive essay*, in which you take a stand on a controversial issue and defend your point of view. And there are different kinds of persuasive essays, depending on the sort of thesis you want to defend. You can have a comparison thesis ("The Republican candidate is very different from the Democratic candidate"), or a generalization thesis with examples ("Many of the students in our college have artistic talent"), or a cause-and-effect thesis ("The business failed because management could not adapt to new expectations from customers.")

One important kind of persuasive essay is an *evaluation essay*. The thesis of an evaluation essay is a value judgment. It says that something is good or bad, effective or ineffective, right or wrong. Examples: "A Volvo is a good automobile," "Smith is a terrible representative in Congress for our district," "The Blue Fin Grill is an excellent restaurant."

How would you support a thesis like this? You would need to do two things. First, you need to explain what makes anything a good automobile, or an excellent restaurant, or a good representative. In other words, you explain the *standards* people use in judging these things. For example, you might say that an excellent restaurant must serve delicious food at a reasonable price, with courteous service in a pleasant setting.

The second thing you need to do is explain why the item you are writing about—e.g., the Blue Fin Grill—does in fact meet those standards. You would describe the food, the atmosphere, and so on, to persuade your audience that it measures up to the standards.

People might disagree with you on both these points. Someone could say that an excellent restaurant must have soft music. They disagree with your standard. Another person might say the prices at the Blue Fin Grill are not reasonable. They disagree with your example. So you must think carefully about the best standards for evaluating things. People do agree to a large extent on many things. (What is a good bed, a good doctor, a good teacher?) You can help them understand their evaluations, and even help them improve their judgments.

CHAPTER 13 ❧

Mistakes in Reasoning

77. fallacy

78. propaganda

79. irrelevant

80. to rationalize

81. slippery slope

82. ad hominem

83. false dilemma

84. to beg the question

In the previous two chapters you learned words that help you think about arguments, their parts, and the different types of arguments. If you apply those words to the things you hear on TV and to your reading, you will see relationships that you might not have noticed before. You have been analyzing arguments for years, but now you can go into more detail and be more accurate because you have words to describe exactly what you hear and read.

You already know that sometimes people have good reasons for believing something, and sometimes they have bad reasons. For example, suppose your friend Judy is convinced that Smith will win the upcoming election. Why is she so sure? Because all her friends are going to vote for Smith. When you hear Judy say this, you know she could be wrong about who will win. All her friends may think alike, but they may think differently from the general population. Maybe Judy and her friends like Smith's position on scholarships in higher education, but most other voters don't. So all Judy's friends could vote for Smith and she could still lose. (Remember the words *sample* and *generalization*?)

This is an example of a bad argument. "All my friends will vote for Smith. Therefore most people will vote for Smith and she will win the election." It's a bad argument because Judy's reason for believing the conclusion is not a good

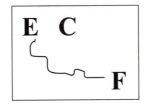

Figure 13.1
A mistake in reasoning is called a fallacy. When you commit a fallacy, your evidence leads you to a belief (F) but it is the wrong belief. There is no logical connection between the evidence and your belief. The curvy line represents an illogical connection.

enough reason. Her sample is too small, and it's biased. Judy is letting her personal interests and wishes influence her reasoning. This kind of mistake—where people make a generalization based on a sample that is too small or is skewed in some way—is very common. It's so common that it has a name. It's called a "hasty generalization." Judy is so eager to see Smith win that she believes her evidence is stronger than it really is. She thinks the statement about her friends is strong support for the statement about Smith winning, when actually it is very weak support. (Judy could say, "All my friends will vote for Smith. That suggests that she might win the election.")

A hasty generalization is one kind of mistake in reasoning, but unfortunately there are many other kinds. We all sometimes believe things for bad reasons. That is, we think that one statement makes it likely that another statement is true, when it doesn't. When you learn to recognize the mistakes we all make, you can avoid them. It's like learning the causes of automobile accidents (driving too fast, driving while intoxicated, using the cell phone while driving, etc.). Identifying the mistakes allows you to avoid them yourself, and you become a better driver. The same applies to reasoning. There are words for the most common mistakes we make in reasoning, and learning the words makes it much easier to spot the mistakes. Avoiding the mistakes will make you a much more effective thinker.

Part 1. Definitions

77. fallacy. a mistake in reasoning; an inference that is not legitimate: the evidence presented does not make the conclusion true or more likely to be true. "The students who played in the band scored higher than average on the SAT, and so Pat concluded that playing in the band will raise his SAT score. But correlation is not necessarily cause and effect. That's a fallacy."

Example

77a. The biggest **fallacy** in forecasting of any kind is to take current conditions and extrapolate forward as if those conditions won't change. President Bush could still be vulnerable politically. Same for Howard Dean in the primaries, regardless of how positive the news climate may be for both of them right now. Even with good odds, the shoo-in doesn't fit.

Jonathan Alter, The New Law of Uncertainty, *Newsweek*, 12/22/03

78. propaganda. the use of statements, stories, pictures, or other items, true or not, to influence people's beliefs and actions, to promote the propagandist's interests without regard to the audience's interests. "If the Chinese government were interested in the truth it would stop censoring the Internet and would allow people to hear something besides government propaganda."

Example

78a. All Russian history, but particularly that of modern times, was completely dominated by the party's ideological organs, which tailored the facts and interpretations to suit the current party line. Thus history was a branch of **propaganda**. Soviet historical literature had little to do with what actually happened, reflecting instead what the Establishment wanted people to believe had happened.

Richard Pipes, *Three "Whys" of the Russian Revolution*, Vintage, 1995, p. 5

79. irrelevant. in reasoning, something that does not affect the truth or falsity of the statement one is considering. "It's true that the Senator Kennedy is a Catholic, but that's irrelevant to whether he would be a good President."

Example

79a. Sir—I was outraged by your assertion that Josef Ackermann, the head of Deutsche Bank, "should not stand trial" lest "German business may suffer" (Contents, January 7th). The charges in the Mannesmann affair are serious, and the desire to avoid bad publicity is **irrelevant** to the legal proceedings.

MM, Letters: Bad business, *The Economist*, 1/21/06

80. to rationalize. to try to justify one's decision or belief, usually with bad reasons, after one has already decided to act or believe something for other reasons. "Why did I finish off the cake? Oh, I didn't want it to spoil and go to waste." "I don't care what the neighbors think; I bought the Jaguar because it gets good gas milage."

rationalization (noun). a justification of one's action or belief with reasons that one thinks may sound good to others, but that are not the real reasons for the action or belief. "Sure, I make over two hundred thousand dollars per year, much of it from capital gains. But cutting capital gains taxes is a good idea because it would stimulate the economy and help everybody."

Example

80a. In addition to developing the chivalric conceptions of prowess, loyalty, generosity, and courtesy the knights of twelfth-century France produced an ethical **rationalization** which seems to endow their endless turbulence and violence with an elevated motive.... The eleventh-century knight fought for the means of subsistence—land, plunder, ransoms....By...the latter part of the twelfth century, various circumstances had combined to encourage knights to claim a more lofty motive for their fighting.... The knight of the twelfth century passed the long evenings listening to tales of the great heroes of the past. Naturally it occurred to him that it would be pleasant to have his own deeds recounted long after his death. From this idea grew the conception that glory was the true aim of a good knight. He would, in theory at least, practice the chivalric virtues for reputation—to be known through the ages as a perfect knight.

Sidney Painter, *French Chivalry*, Cornell University Press, 1957 [originally 1940], pp. 34–36

81. slippery slope. the mistake of thinking that if we adopt a policy, e.g., legalizing marijuana, then the change will inevitably continue to an extreme degree, e.g., we will soon legalize heroin (as if one begins sliding down a slippery slope and can't stop). "We shouldn't invade Iraq. If we attack them, who's next? Egypt? France?"

Example

81a. At one point, he attacks these [biblical] standards on state-sanctioned marriage for same sex couples without expounding on the obvious effects down the road. When marriage is redefined, how can you prevent homosexual polygamy or even fathers marrying their consenting sons? Such things will happen, and these supposedly hate-filled conservatives see it coming. King's deceptive views attempt to draw an ever-changing line on the **slippery slope** of a humanistic and atheistic ideology that tries to redefine the family and morality....

SW, Letters: Attacking People's Values, *Austin American Statesman*, 4/30/05

82. ad hominem. an attempt to criticize a person's ideas or position by attacking the person herself or himself. "I can't see how anybody can agree with Bush's plan to bring democracy to Iraq. Bush is such an idiot. How could anyone agree with him?"

Example

82a. At Friday's Campus Antiwar Network-sponsored debate on the occupation of Iraq, a speaker who was advocating a continued American presence in the country was subjected to constant interruption, personal insults and unabashed disrespect from the largely antiwar, anti-occupation audience. [Students who behave like this stunt their own intellectual growth.] Not only do they deprive themselves of the chance to learn more and develop their opinions, but they also deny that opportunity to other, more civil attendees. It is truly inexcusable to take an event designed to inform and turn it into a platform for **ad hominem** attack and political dogma.

Editorial, *Washington Square News*, 2/23/04

83. false dilemma (or false dichotomy). an oversimplification of a situation, where a person says there are only two possibilities, when in fact there are other options besides the two stated. "We must invade Iraq. If we simply ignore Saddam Hussein he will destabilize the entire Middle East." Also called an "either/or fallacy."

Example

83a. Reason [magazine]: A critic once said of Thomas Pynchon that he was one of the few modern novelists for whom what the characters do for a living is more defining than what their emotional relationships are. It seems to me that you have that same focus. In *The Baroque Cycle*, the biggest romantic relationship in Daniel Waterhouse's life occurs mostly offstage, unless you count his difficult friendship with Isaac Newton.

Stephenson: There's a **false dichotomy** embedded in that. It's possible to have an emotional relationship with what you do for a living. And this is especially true when you work with other people, because naturally you form emotional relationships with those people, which get all tangled up with your relationship to the work itself.

Mike Godwin, Neal Stephenson's Past, Present, and Future, *Reason*, Feb, 2005

84. to beg the question. when you want to support some conclusion, but you use the conclusion itself as part of your support. "I asked Morgan how he knows Iraq is a threat to the U.S. and he said Saddam Hussein intends to attack us, but that just begs the question."

"A: Why do you believe astronauts never landed on the moon? B: Because Reilly says they didn't and he always tells the truth. A: How do you know he always tells the truth? B: Because the things he says are true; for example, he says that the astronauts never landed on the moon and that's true. A: Wait a minute. You're begging the question."

Example

84a. Our present use of the word "science" was coined in the nineteenth century and, strictly speaking, there was no such thing as "science" in our sense in the early modern period.... Part of our aim, in looking at the historical development of what we think of as science, should be to understand how the very concept "science" arose; we simply **beg the question** if we talk about "science" as though it always existed.

John Henry, *The Scientific Revolution and the Origins of Modern Science*, Second Edition, Palgrave, 2002, p. 4

Test Yourself
Match each word with its definition.

77. fallacy
78. propaganda
79. irrelevant
80. to rationalize
81. slippery slope
82. ad hominem
83. false dilemma
84. to beg the question

a. when something does not affect the truth or falsity of the statement one is considering
b. thinking that one step will lead to extreme, disastrous exaggerations of the same trend
c. thinking there are only two choices, when actually there are more options
d. thinking that one statement supports another statement when in fact it does not
e. bringing up reasons to try to justify a decision one has already made on other grounds
f. accepting some statement, and then using the statement itself as part of one's reason to accept that statement
g. using statements and other things to try to influence someone, without regard to whether the statements are true
h. criticizing the person rather than what the person says

Part 2. Understanding the Meaning

77. fallacy.

77b. A record-breaking new class-action lawsuit against Wal-Mart claims that this retail chain discriminates against women, for which of course vast millions of dollars are being demanded. The New York Times aptly summarized the case—"about 65 percent of the company's hourly-paid workers are women, but only 33 percent of its managers are."

The great **fallacy** of our times is that various groups would be equally represented in institutions and occupations if it were not for discrimination. This preconception has undermined, if not destroyed, the crucial centuries-old legal principle that the burden of proof is on the accuser.

Thomas Sowell, The Grand Fallacy, Part 1, *Shelby Star*, 8/3/04

Comment

Remember that a fallacy is seeing a relationship between two statements when the relationship doesn't exist. It's the mistaken belief that one statement supports the other. Here are Sowell's two statements:

(1) Various groups are not equally represented in all institutions and occupations. (For example, women make up about 50 percent of the population but only 33 percent of the managers at Wal-Mart.)

(2) Employers are discriminating against these groups. (For example, Wal-Mart is discriminating against women.)

If (1) is true, does that make it more likely that (2) is true? Sowell says no, and to say it does is a fallacy.

> 77c. For the last three decades, the scientific consensus has been that "race" is merely a social construct, since genetic variation among individuals of the same race is far greater than the variation between races. Recently, however, a **fallacy** in that reasoning—a rather subtle one—has been identified by the Cambridge University statistician A.W.F. Edwards. The concept of race may not be biologically meaningless after all; it might even have some practical use in deciding on medical treatments, at least until more complete individual genomic information becomes available.
>
> Jim Holt, Madness About a Method, *New York Times Magazine*, 12/11/05

Comment

Here are the two statements Holt is talking about:

(1) Variation among individuals of the same race is far greater than the variation between races. (For example, two white people may be more different from each other genetically—in spite of the similar color—than a white person is different from a black person.)

Figure 13.2
An argument is like a chain, and a fallacy is like a broken chain. *Source: © BruceParrott/ Shutterstock*

(2) "Race" is merely a social construct. (In other words, there is no biological basis of race. Race is just a category invented by societies, like "police officer," or "philanthropist." It's a description based on one's social role, not biology.)

If (1) is true, does that mean (2) is probably true?

Holt says scientists in the past have believed that it does. But now it seems that people of the same race have more in common than scientists thought, because medical treatments work better on people of one race than they do on people of a different race.

> 77d.   Thomas Kuhn's early book, *The Structure of Scientific Revolutions*, emphasized this process of change in our scientific standards. I think Kuhn went overboard in concluding that there was a complete incommensurability [inability to compare] between present and past standards, but it is correct that there is a qualitative change in the kind of scientific theory we want to develop that has taken place at various times in the history of science. But Kuhn then proceeded to the **fallacy**—much clearer in what he has written recently—that in science we are not in fact moving toward objective truth. I call this a **fallacy** because it seems to me a simple non sequitur. I do not see why the fact that we are discovering not only the laws of nature in detail, but what kinds of laws are worth discovering, should mean that we are not making objective progress.
>
> Steven Weinberg, *Facing Up: Science and Its Cultural Adversaries*, Harvard University Press, 2001, pp. 85–86

(*Non sequitur* is Latin for "it does not follow." It's another word for fallacy.)

Question: What two statements does Kuhn make, and why does Weinberg think the first does not support the second?

Comment

I have mentioned several words that people often use in a non-standard way. "Fallacy" is another such word. Strictly speaking, a fallacy is a mistake in reasoning, an incorrect inference. But some people use the word to mean any sort of mistake or false belief. Consider these examples:

> 77e.   Global poverty is often analyzed with more moral indignation than intellectual rigor. From the **fallacy** that economics is a zero-sum game—that someone's gain must be someone else's commensurate loss—moralists conclude that people are living badly in sub-Saharan Africa because people are living well in North America.
>
> George F. Will, The Perils of Protectionism, *Newsweek*, 3/29/04

> 77f.   Mr. Reich explodes a number of **fallacies** on the left (that manufacturing jobs can be saved) and on the right (that tax cuts and trickle-down economics reach poor people).
>
> Ted Widmer, What's Right and What's Left to Say on the Political Divide, *New York Times*, 7/7/04

In both of these examples the writers are using *fallacy* to mean a mistaken belief, not a mistaken inference. That is, if economics really *were* a zero-sum game, then the conclusion that people are living badly in one place because people are living well in another would be logically correct. The problem isn't the inference. Will says the mistake is the initial assumption that in economics some people can win only when others lose.

78. propaganda.

> 78b. The estate tax is overwhelmingly a tax on the very, very wealthy; only about one estate in 200 pays any tax at all. The campaign for estate tax repeal has largely been financed by just 18 powerful business dynasties, including the family that owns Wal-Mart.
>
> You may have heard tales of family farms and small businesses broken up to pay taxes, but those stories are pure **propaganda** without any basis in fact. In particular, advocates of estate tax repeal have never been able to provide a single real example of a family farm sold to pay estate taxes.
>
> Paul Krugman, Shameless in the Senate, *New York Times*, 6/5/06

> 78c. This is just the art of **propaganda** that it—understanding the great masses' world of ideas and feelings—finds, by a correct psychological form, the way to the attention, and further to the heart, of the great masses.... The great masses' receptive ability is only very limited, their understanding is small, but their forgetfulness is great. As a consequence of these facts, all effective **propaganda** has to limit itself only to a very few points and to use them like slogans until even the very last man is able to imagine what is intended by such a word....
>
> The people, in an overwhelming majority, are so feminine in their nature and attitude that their activities and thoughts are motivated less by sober consideration than by feeling and sentiment. This sentiment, however, is not complicated but very simple and complete. There are not many differentiations, but rather a positive or a negative; love or hate, right or wrong, truth or lie; but never half this and half that, or partially, etc.
>
> Adolf Hitler, *Mein Kampf*, Houghton Mifflin, 1939, pp. 233–234, 237

(*Mein Kampf* means "my battle," or "my struggle" in German.)

Question: What beliefs did Hitler have about ordinary people? Does anyone who uses propaganda have the same attitudes toward his or her audience?

> 78d. Competing with Montaigne as one of the earliest and most influential prose writers is the Englishman Francis Bacon, born in 1561, who used the essay form with powerful effect as **propaganda** for the importance of the scientific enterprise.
>
> Neil Postman, *Building a Bridge to the 18th Century: How the Past Can Improve Our Future*, Alfred A. Knopf, 1999, p. 59

79. irrelevant.

79b. The husband wanted to join an HMO by signing over their Medicare benefits to save money. The wife objected because it would mean she could no longer see the doctor she knew and trusted. In arguing her point of view she said, "I like Dr. B. He knows me, he's interested in me. He calls me by my first name." The husband parries the last point: "I don't like that. He's much younger than we are. He shouldn't be calling us by first name." But the form of address Dr. B. uses was **irrelevant.** The wife was trying to communicate that she felt comfortable with the doctor she knew, that she had a relationship with him. His calling her by first name was just one of a list of details she was marshalling to explain her comfort with him. Picking on this one detail did not change her view—and did not address her concern. It was just a way to win the argument.

Deborah Tannen, *The Argument Culture: Moving From Debate to Dialogue*, Random House, 1998, p. 9

79c. Robert L. Kuhn: Graham, how much of the future is dependent upon ways of thinking? Wouldn't different mechanisms of thinking lead to different futures?

Graham Molitor:...I go back and look at the crude surrogate for intellect—which is basically average brain size, the cubic-centimeter measurement. For the first [proto-humans], it was about 500 cubic centimeters, and it's about three times that today. By the year 3000, with advances in genetics, my feeling is that the size of the human brain will increase drastically, up to as much as 2000 cubic centimeters....

Edward De Bono: You can simulate a brain with only five neurons on a computer; that brain is capable of fifty billion thoughts. Five neurons, fifty billion thoughts. We've got a hundred billion neurons. So brain size, I think, is **irrelevant.** It's how we use what we've got that counts.

Robert Lawrence Kuhn, ed., *Closer to Truth: Challenging Current Beliefs*, McGraw-Hill, 2000, p. 197

80. to rationalize.

80b. Q. I am writing to express my extreme disappointment and challenge to your comment in Saturday's article. You state "...as a general rule I believe we have an obligation to obey the law." This from someone who writes a column focused on ethics, providing guidance to others on how to live more ethical lives?

Where are the ethics in picking and choosing which laws we wish to obey and which we can disobey? If a law is unjust, our system provides many remedies to changing that law, but regardless of our opinions on whether we "believe" a law is correct or not, we have a very specific ethical

Figure 13.3
If you want to persuade someone that a car is excellent, should you put a beautiful woman beside it? Source: © Andrea Leone/Shutterstock

as well as legal obligation to obey it. While we may escape legal ramifications if we choose to disregard the law, we cannot **rationalize** away that we have broken the law, and that behavior is by definition "unethical."...

A. I agree with you that we have an obligation to obey the law, but I do not believe that obligation is absolute. No law can free us from the obligation to act morally, and when our most deeply held moral principles come into conflict with the law, the moral thing to do is to obey our conscience....

Jeremy Iggers, Everyday Ethics; Plumber Sinks to Ethical Low with Enticing Offer, *Star Tribune* (Minneapolis), 10/11/03

Question: Suppose a person in the National Guard is ordered to go overseas to a war zone and refuses, on the grounds that the war is unjust. Is that reason ("The war is unjust") a rationalization? How would we decide whether it was a rationalization or not?

80c. The seal hunters are courting European politicians, hoping to defeat a seal-product ban now being debated in the European Parliament....

"We have been doing this for hundreds of years," says Jean-Claude Lapierre, president of the Sealing Association of the Magdalen Islands in eastern Canada.... The campaign calls to mind Canada's rich trapping heritage and champions the term "ultimate eco-fabric," aiming to contrast fur with less-insulating, petroleum-based, synthetic materials....

"There are all these complex sets of **rationalizations** to excuse treating animals cruelly," says Wayne Paselle, president and chief executive of the Humane Society of the U.S. "Our job is to stop it." The society is promoting a boycott of seafood from Canada until the seal hunt is abolished.

Douglas Belkin, Seal Hunters Fight Long Cruelty Label, *Wall Street Journal*, 3/23/07

81. slippery slope.

81b. Their [conservatives'] real objection is that gay marriage is a **slippery slope** to something worse. "If same-sex marriage were to prevail, society would...have to accept that marriage is an arbitrary social construct that can be...redefined by anyone laying claim to it," argues [William] Bennett. If accepted, there would be no principled grounds to "oppose the marriage of two consenting brothers...[or] deny a marriage license to three men who want to marry....

Slippery-slope arguments are always used by people who can't quite come up with a good reason for why a particular change is bad. It may not be bad in and of itself, they say, but it will inevitably *lead* to things that are bad. Radcons [radical conservatives, such as Bennett] worry a lot about **slippery slopes**. If we allow people to do what they want to do in private, all hell will break loose....

Here is a real **slippery slope** that *does* concern me. Once we allow Radcons or anyone else to decide how we should conduct our private sex lives, where would it end? If we accept the idea that one religion's view about proper sexual behavior should be the law of the land, how do we decide whose religious views should count?

Robert B. Reich, *Reason: Why Liberals Will Win the Battle for America*, Knopf, 2004, pp. 71–73

81c. The political problem with the manufacture of human embryos, however early in their development, is not just that it upsets opponents of abortion. It is that it shifts a barrier that might become porous, weakening the sacral quality of the human. And once that takes place, the **slippery slope** becomes far more slippery. Where are lines to be drawn? Will human life forms ultimately be harvested for the sake of other humans?

Edward Rothstein, The Meaning of "Human" in Embryonic Research, *New York Times*, 3/13/04

Comment

If you want to think effectively, you have to use your own judgment. You can't write down some rules, follow them closely, and expect to be a good thinker. You have to learn how to apply the rules (or words) to the various, complex situations that come up, and that requires judgment.

Figure 13.4
Starting down a slippery slope can be dangerous, but if you think you can't stop, you are committing a fallacy. *Source: © Dan Tataru/Shutterstock*

The slippery slope mistake is a case in point. Sometimes pointing to a slippery slope is a fallacy, and sometimes it isn't. Rothstein, in Example 81c, is saying that manufacturing human embryos might lead to undesirable consequences. So we must think carefully about whether we want to take that risk. He is saying there is a slippery slope here, and we may fall down it. But that isn't faulty reasoning. That is sensible caution. So what is the slippery slope mistake? It is saying that if doing something (e.g., manufacturing human embryos) *could* lead us down a slippery slope (i.e., could lead to more radical, undesirable actions), then that is *enough* to prove that we definitely shouldn't do it. But that is going too far. It isn't enough. Rothstein does not conclude that manufacturing human embryos is wrong. Nor does he say it's right. He says we should be careful.

Bennett, on the other hand (quoted in Example 81b), says that allowing two men or two women to marry might lead to terrible consequences. And that is enough to prohibit same-sex marriage, in his opinion. Once we cross that line, we will never be able to draw any more lines. But that's a fallacy. Consider a hypothetical example. Suppose a friend offers me a beer after dinner. That could lead to drinking hard liquor, and drinking during the day, and becoming addicted. It could, but it's not likely. I can avoid those things if I want to. The mere fact that we can imagine terrible consequences is not a good reason to avoid the beer. Anyone who thinks it is enough is making the slippery slope mistake.

> 81d. Though no scientists are now cloning embryos at UW–Madison, university officials told legislators Monday that it is important to leave the research avenue open in order to study genetic illnesses and pursue potential cures.
>
> Chancellor John Wiley testified before a legislative committee that is considering a proposed ban on all cloning. The ban would prohibit both therapeutic cloning, or cloning to create cells for research and medical treatments, and reproductive cloning, which is cloning to create an embryo that would result in a child....
>
> [State Rep. Steve] Kestell, as well as other cloning opponents, said allowing therapeutic cloning would create a **slippery slope** that would lead to the cloning of human beings. Jean Peduzzi, a researcher from Wayne State University Medical School who studies adult stem cells, testified in favor of the cloning ban.
>
> "Once therapeutic cloning is approved," asked Peduzzi, "who is going to object to reproductive cloning? What would some billionaire out there pay to have a replica of themselves?"
>
> But Alta Charo, the Elizabeth S. Wilson Professor of Law and Bioethics at UW–Madison, said there are already a number of protections in place to control reproductive cloning. She said the federal Food and Drug Administration has intervened to prevent such cloning.

Charo warned that outlawing all cloning would effectively bring to a standstill promising science. Instead of banning all cloning, Charo said, legislation should focus on reproductive cloning.

Ron Seely, UW Officials: Keep Cloning an Option; Bill to Ban Cloning Human Embryos Receives Testimony, *Wisconsin State Journal*, 6/21/05

Question: When Kestell uses the phrase "slippery slope," what point is he making? Is he saying we should proceed with caution? Or is he saying someone has committed a fallacy in reasoning?

Figure 13.5
Throwing a pie in another person's face is not a refutation of the person's statement. The pie is like an ad hominem. *Source: Photographers Choice/Fotosearch*

82. ad hominem.

82b. This new path moves educators away from a view of teaching as a solitary activity, owned personally by each teacher. It moves them toward a view of teaching as a professional activity open to collective observations, study, and improvement.... Petty nitpicking and **ad hominem** criticism of typical classroom lessons must give way to serious professional analysis for purposes of improving everyone's teaching.

James Hiebert, Ronald Gallimore, and James W. Stigler, Opening Classroom Doors, *American Educator*, Spring 2004

82c. Lexington [the columnist for *The Economist*] spews his venom at Michael Moore, referring to the Oscar-winning film maker as a "blowhard" and "conspiracy theorist" (Feb. 14). Lexington should avoid such unsubstantiated **ad hominem** attacks, lest his readers see him for what he is: a stupid bastard.

DW, Letters, *Economist*, 2/28/04

83. false dilemma.

83b. Jon Margolis is a big-government-loving liberal who hates and mistrusts free markets. He also hates successful entrepreneurial people who take risks, work hard and create jobs and wealth; to him, they're just "talented, ambitious and ruthless."

All of this is evident in "Market versus family values" (Perspective, March 24), in which Margolis commits the "**false dilemma** fallacy": Either we have free markets or we have family values.

But there is a third alternative. A free-market society need not be as rough as 1890s America or 1990s Russia. It can be founded on personal responsibility, tolerance and voluntary civic virtue and altruism. Cultivating these qualities is as vital as shrinking the size and power of the government.

AP, A Better Way, *Chicago Tribune*, 3/31/96

83c. For them [Shapin and Schaffer], there is nothing bad about the manufacture of facts; they want us to get used to the idea that facts in general are *made rather than found*.... Like many others who use these terms, Shapin and Schaffer want to reject a picture of the scientist as a passive receiver of information from the world. But a denial of passivity does not require this kind of talk, and it often leads to trouble. For example, at the very end of *Leviathan*, their discussion of "making" leads Shapin and Schaffer to express their overall conclusions in a way that involves a real confusion. They say: "It is ourselves and not reality that is responsible for what we know" (1985, 344). This is a classic example of a **false dichotomy**. Neither we alone nor reality alone is "responsible" for human knowledge. The rough answer is that *both* are responsible for it; knowledge involves an interaction between the two.

Peter Godfrey-Smith, *Theory and Reality: An Introduction to the Philosophy of Science*, University of Chicago Press, 2003, pp. 129–130

84. to beg the question.

84b.   There's a "God-shaped hole in many people's lives," says physicist and Anglican priest John Polkinghorne. He's right, at least about there being a hole in our lives. To call the hole "God-shaped" **begs the question**, for the affliction of our times is that we have no satisfactory image of God that rests comfortably with what scientists have learned about creation. As we approach the end of the twentieth century, many educated people in the Western world long wistfully for something akin to traditional religious faith, but they know there can be no turning back to a world of divine fiats and penny miracles. As Polkinghorne says, they can neither accept the idea of God nor quite leave it alone. .

Chet Raymo, *Skeptics and True Believers: The Exhilarating Connection Between Science and Religion*, Walker and Company, 1998, p. 1

84c.   The series [on public television] was criticized for featuring only live white males, when in fact the more pertinent criticism might have been that it addressed metaphysical and theological issues without including a metaphysician or theologian. After all, the very title "The Glorious Accident," Dr. Gould's description for the origin of human intelligence, was a metaphysical assertion.

"The Question of God" does better in its race and sex distribution, and in principle, at least, it takes on the big **question** that "The Glorious Accident" **begged**. "Whether we realize it or not," Dr. Nicholi says, "we make one of two basic assumptions. We view the universe as an accident or we assume an intelligence beyond the universe who gives the universe order, and for some of us, meaning to life."

Peter Steinfels, Existential Television, *New York Times*, 9/18/04

84d.   The expression "**begs the question**" has become so popular on the airwaves and elsewhere in the media that it begs to be dealt with in a space like this. It is almost invariably used incorrectly, which raises— rather than begs—the question, "Why?" Of course, there is no way I can know for sure, but I suspect it has something to do with failed efforts to sound intelligent. That is, people like the distinguished tone of "begs the question." It seems as if it meant the same as "raises the question," so they think, "I'll start using 'begs the question' and sound smarter."…It's a reference that arises from logic.…One begs the question when one assumes the truth of an argument or proposition to be proved, such as: "God must exist because He made the world so beautiful." Or, "Murder is illegal. So abortion should be illegal." These locutions beg the questions they purport to prove.

John Worsley Simpson, Beggars Can't Be Choosers But You Should Be, *National Post* (Canada), 4/3/04

Comment

Of all the mistakes in reasoning, begging the question is probably the most difficult one to recognize. Consider the following short dialogue.

"The invasion of Iraq was good for the people."

"Why do you think that?"

"Because any overthrow of a dictator is justified."

"Are you sure?"

"Yes, just consider the benefits that follow the overthrow. For example, just consider how much better off the people of Iraq will be after we liberate them."

Here, the first speaker's main point is (1) the invasion was good for the people of Iraq. He supports that by saying (2) overthrowing dictators is justified. And he supports that idea by saying (3) people are better off when their dictators are overthrown. Finally, he supports that idea by saying (4) Iraq is an example of a country where the people would be better off if their dictator were to be overthrown. But that is the same as (1), the main point he is trying to persuade us to accept in the first place. He can't use (1) as part of his evidence to support (1). He is going around in a circle.

Perhaps because this mistake is so difficult to detect, some people use the phrase "beg the question" in a very simplistic way. They use it to mean "raise the question," as Simpson says in Example 72d. For example, they might say the following: "The 9/11 commission concluded that the U.S. was not prepared for the attack on 9/11. But that begs the question, 'Why weren't we prepared?'"

84e. Diving to 55 feet was no sweat. I figure I could dive twice that with a little practice, reaching what scientists thought, not 50 years ago, was the body's depth limit. Today, however, that boundary has been pushed to at least 531 feet (the current no-limits world record), which **begs the question**: Just how deep can humans go? "We don't know that yet," says [Claes] Lundgren, adding ominously, "But one day someone will find out."

Logan Ward, One Dive, One Breath, *Popular Science*, July, 2003

84f. The origin of the Devil had to be explained, and when the medieval theologians proceeded with their usual scholastic logic to deal with the problem, they got into a quandary. They could not have very well admitted that the Devil, who was Not-God, came from God himself, nor could they quite agree that in the original universe, the Devil, who was Not-God, was co-eternal with God. So in desperation they agreed that the Devil must have been a fallen angel, which rather **begs the question** of the origin of evil (for there still must have been another Devil to tempt this fallen angel), and which is therefore unsatisfactory, but they had to leave it at that.

Lin Yutang, *The Importance of Living*, The John Day Co., 1937, pp. 15–16

Question: Is Yutang using the phrase "begs the question" in the original way, or in the looser way, like the writer in Example 84e?

Part 3. Applying the Words

77. fallacy
78. propaganda
79. irrelevant
80. to rationalize
81. slippery slope
82. ad hominem
83. false dilemma
84. to beg the question

Exercise 1:   Choose the Best Word

For each sentence, choose the best word (or an appropriate form of the word) to fill in the blank.

1. The state university sent information to my son trying to persuade him to enroll next year. But it was mostly glossy pictures of the champion basketball team. That's _____. How does the basketball team help him get a good education?

2. Mr. Coleman made a good point about the club president's plan. It's way over budget. But when he called him a "reckless maniac" he resorted to _____.

3. Dad says I can either work and earn some money, or I can go to school and go into debt. But I think that's a _____. I can work part-time while I go to school.

4. Karen's parents both work long hours and leave Karen with baby-sitters and her grandmother most of the time. They say they spend so much time at work so they can earn enough to buy nice things for Karen, but I think that's just a _____.

5. I don't know who reads the political bloggers' _____ on the Internet. They always look at only one side of a story, they use biased labels for things instead of neutral language, and their only goal is to make people angry. Who falls for that stuff?

6. If most Americans' incomes go up, but wealthy people's incomes go up much more than poor people's incomes, is that progress? The free market promoters say yes, and their evidence is corporations' record profits. That proves America is making progress, they say. But that argument _____.

7. Peter opposes voluntary euthanasia because he says once you allow people to choose to die, the next thing you know the government will be executing the disabled and everyone over 80. But he's committing the _____ fallacy.

8. Eva is right. Some people who smoke marijuana will use more dangerous drugs. But it's a _____ to think that what could happen will inevitably happen on a large scale, and that, therefore, we should never allow anyone to smoke marijuana.

Exercise 2:   Apply the Words

Read each example and answer the questions that follow.

> 1. The Bushies' campaign pitch follows their usual backward logic: Because we have failed to make you safe, you should re-elect us to make you safer. Because we haven't caught Osama in three years, you need us to catch Osama in the next four years. Because we didn't bother to secure explosives in Iraq, you can count on us to make sure those explosives aren't used against you.
>
> Maureen Dowd, Will Osama Help W.? *New York Times*, 1031/04

Dowd claims that the Bush campaign is committing a fallacy, that is, asserting that one statement supports another statement when actually it doesn't. What is the fallacy (according to Dowd)? (She mentions three.) That is, what is the evidence, and what is the (mistaken) conclusion?

> 2. The controversy over Sinclair Media's planned "late hit" on John Kerry has petered out. The third-tier media company showed a few minutes of the anti-Kerry film, "Stolen Honor," and a few minutes of a pro-Kerry documentary, and the whole thing disappeared without a ripple. Meanwhile, more powerful and influential media organizations have been conspiring to deliver cheap shots against Bush at the last minute in order to influence the election.
>
> On Monday, The New York Times ran a blockbuster headline— "Huge Cache of Explosives Vanished From Site in Iraq"—and an accompanying article that started strong but disintegrated like an old sweater by the end, raising a raft of questions that cannot possibly be answered with a week left in the campaign....
>
> It's hard to shake the impression that the Times was drafting talking points for the man the paper endorsed for president.... The story wasn't intended to shed light so much as to apply heat—to Bush.
>
> Jonah Goldberg, Lobbing Bombs at Bush, *AM New York*, 10/29/04

Goldberg wanted to accuse the Times of spreading propaganda. Is that a fair charge? Based on what he tells us about the story "Huge Cache of Explosives...," do you think it fits the definition of propaganda?

> 3. I have no problem with gay marriage. But liberals don't get it.
>
> If they want to live in a country where it's OK to marry the same sex, but not to smoke a cigarette, carry a gun, eat a cheeseburger or

tell an insensitive joke, then I'm not going to be supporting same-sex marriage anytime soon.

When liberals start supporting my freedoms, maybe I'll care about theirs.

HG, Gay—and in the Right, *New York Post*, 6/5/06

Someone could say, "The fact that some people oppose smoking, carrying guns, obesity, and prejudice, is irrelevant to whether or not gay marriage should be legal." Do you agree that it's irrelevant, or do you disagree?

4. Ramzan Kadyrov, the first deputy prime minister of Chechnya [and a Muslim], said that because the decade-long separatist war in the republic had taken a toll on its male population, men there should be legally allowed to have several wives, the Itar-Tass news agency reported. In an interview with Ekho Moskvy radio, Mr. Kadyrov, above, considered the most powerful man in the republic, said, "Chechnya needs that because it has a war and, statistically, the number of women is 10 percent larger than the number of men." Russian law restricts citizens to one marriage, but Islamic custom allows up to four wives.

Alexander Nurnberg, World Briefing Europe: Russia: Chechen Leader Calls for Polygamy, *New York Times*, 1/14/06

Mr. Kadyrov may be guilty of rationalizing or he may not. He favors polygamy and he gives a reason for legalizing it. How should we decide whether or not he is rationalizing in this case?

5. Observer. What is your position on child pornography?

Camille Paglia. . . . I believe that the abolition of child labor was one of the great reform movements of the last 200 years. If you have children posing for pornographic pictures and videos, that is an infringement—not of something sexual—but of what we now feel is civilized, that children should not be forced to labor.

Observer. Isn't that a dangerous opinion?

Camille Paglia. As far as any visual, imaginary representations that are sketched or painted of children in pornographic acts—again I'm considered pretty radical here, on the lunatic fringe with this one—I feel: so what? Anything that can be imagined should be depicted.

Observer. Are you sure?

Camille Paglia. I feel that that's the only way we can keep ourselves from sliding into dogmatism. To most people these kinds of things are abhorrent. They can't look at them without being disturbed. So I feel that intellectuals and artists are obliged to force themselves to depict them, to write about them.

Camille Paglia, *Vamps and Tramps: New Essays*, Vintage Books, 1994, pp. 124–125

Paglia says that outlawing imaginary representations of child pornography would lead us down a slippery slope. What harmful consequences of such a ban does she see? Do you think she is committing the slippery slope fallacy, or is she being prudently cautious?

6. To the Executive Board of the college Republicans: A few weeks ago, I published an op-ed in these pages that concerned the behavior of your club. The column was intended to illustrate a microcosm of a larger diseased anger that has systemically afflicted the Republican Party and its conservative adherents.... [Y]ou seemed to take as much time disparaging your opponents—and anyone else who disagreed with you—with personal attacks as you did discussing important political matters.

Since that column was published, members of your executive board have called me "venomously hateful," a "maggot-infested hippy," and an "SS officer."

Jan Messerschmidt, College Repubs' Ire Continues, *Washington Square News*, 11/1/04

The writer says members of the Executive Board committed the fallacy of ad hominem. Do you think he is accurate? Suppose the writer really was infested with maggots and was a hippy. Would the board still be guilty of ad hominem, or not?

7. Galbraith argued that those who disagreed with his views on "convergence" were such people as, on the one side, "right-wing members of the military and diplomatic bureaucracy in the United States" and, on the other, old-fashioned Communist dogmatists. By this ploy, he seems to have wished to say that all decent moderates and liberals everywhere must accept his line or lose their status.

Robert Conquest, *The Dragons of Expectation*, W. W. Norton, 2005, p. 153

Conquest says that Galbraith sets up a dilemma (a dichotomy). What are the two sides of the dilemma? Conquest also suggests that it is a false dilemma. Why? What makes it a false dilemma?

8. What is perception? One common fallacy is to assume there is an image inside your eyeball, the optical image, exciting photoreceptors on your retina and then that image is transmitted faithfully along a cable called the optic nerve and displayed on a screen called the visual cortex. This is obviously a logical fallacy because if you have an image displayed on a screen in the brain, then you have to have someone else in there watching that image, and that someone needs someone else in *his* head, and so ad infinitum.

V. S. Ramachandran, *A Brief Tour of Human Consciousness: From Impostor Poodles to Purple Numbers*, Pi Press, 2004, p. 24

Ramachandran describes an example of begging the question. What is the theory trying to explain? How does the theory take for granted what it is trying to explain?

Exercise 3:   Analyzing Arguments

In this example Burton Leiser says conservative opponents of abortion are begging the question. Why? How does he support his claim?

> But because the conservative claims the right to interfere in the private decisions of others and to impose restrictions upon them that can drastically alter their entire lives, surely the burden of proof is upon him: He must convince us...that abortion is in fact unjustified, that it is murder, and that human fetuses are indeed human beings. Thus far, the proofs of these propositions have amounted to nothing more than a repetition of the claim that abortion is wrong. Something more than circular, question-begging arguments is needed before the intense and widespread suffering that would follow from restrictive abortion legislation (which did exist prior to the Supreme Court's 1973 decision) can be condoned.
>
> Burton M. Leiser, *Liberty, Justice, and Morals: Contemporary Value Conflicts,* Third Edition, Macmillan, 1986, p. 118

Exercise 4:   Apply the Ideas in Writing

Imagine two fictional people with very different outlooks on life. Write a short dialogue between them. You may choose one of the starting points below, and imagine how the conversation might go from there. Try to continue the dialogue through at least two steps, like this:

1. A speaks...B replies.
2. A responds to B...B replies to that response.

You may want to imagine how the dialogue would continue through further exchanges. The purpose of the exercise is to practice looking at things from different points of view, and to practice thinking about criticisms of certain ideas. The two sides in this exercise are extreme and unrealistic, to bring out the contrast.

1. A. Liberal reformer: "The only way to reduce the gap between the rich and the poor in this country is to raise taxes and provide better government services."
   B. Conservative traditionalist:
2. A. Male chauvinist: "Electing a woman as President of the United States would be a disaster, because women are too emotional."
   B. Female feminist:
3. A. Slacker hippie: "There are many things more important than jobs and money and climbing the corporate ladder."
   B. Business school go-getter:
4. A. Religious person: "Believing in God makes people better and gives them better lives."
   B. Humanist atheist:

5. A. Parent: "You are too young to move in with your boyfriend. You don't understand what life is like or what people will say."

   B. College student:

Improving Your Writing 13: Anticipating Objections

In an essay you communicate your own particular point of view on some topic. For example, in an essay on Shakespeare's "Macbeth," you would inform your readers about the play, the setting, and the characters. But that's not the main purpose of the essay. They can read the play for themselves. The main purpose is to express *your* idea, your response to the play, your unique perspective on it. No one else has had exactly the same experiences you have, or sees things exactly the way you do, and others would like to know your opinions about things.

You develop your point of view by doing research. That means thinking for yourself, asking yourself questions and trying to answer them, as well as reading what others have said.

A very useful way to discover what you think about a topic is to state a provisional thesis, try to find facts or ideas to support it, but then try to find *mistakes* in your point of view. In other words, imagine someone who is very different from yourself. What would that person say about your thesis, or your support for it? How would that hypothetical person criticize your ideas? And can you think of any way to respond (besides bursting into tears or calling the person names)?

For example, suppose your topic is "improving the college curriculum," and your thesis is "College students should study more science." Your support is that recent developments in science like stem cell research and global warming are changing our society, and citizens should understand the changes. Can you imagine why anyone would disagree with you? Well, a hypothetical critic might say, "Students don't have time to study stem cells or other technical matters in depth, and a superficial understanding won't help anyone." If someone criticized your thesis in that way, how would you respond?

If you carry on an imaginary dialogue like this, you will greatly strengthen your essay.

CHAPTER 14 ⬥

Meaning

85. to refer
86. to mean
87. concept
88. to define
89. connotation
90. abstract

When I was in graduate school I met a woman who was a painter. We went to a few galleries and talked a few times. Once, she told me about a painting she was working on, and she said she had several ideas but wasn't sure which ones to use or how to express them exactly. As she was explaining her problem and her thinking, it suddenly dawned on me that when she said "ideas" she meant forms and colors on the canvas, not anything she could put into words. She thought of new ideas, compared different ideas, judged other people's ideas, but all this thinking was in visual images, colors, shapes, and patterns. I don't think she used words at all when she was thinking about her painting. I've heard musicians talk the same way, except they think in musical phrases, harmonies, and tones, i.e. musical ideas.

What these examples tell me is that it is possible to think without using language. But most of us, almost all the time, think in language. We talk to ourselves, maybe not in whole sentences, but in phrases and words. When I say I have an idea, I mean that I have a thought that I can express in a sentence or two (or more). If you want to understand my idea, you have to listen to my words. That's normally all you have to go on. So in most cases thinking and language are intertwined, like the strands that make up a rope, or the ingredients in a recipe. They aren't the same thing, and there are exceptions, as my friend the painter shows. But for most people, most of the time, it's difficult to separate thinking from language.

The language with which you think can influence your thinking in several ways. One of the central ideas in this book is that if you do not have the words to

$$\boxed{\ "X"\ -\ O\ }$$

Figure 14.1
We use words (represented by X) to refer to things (represented by O). The words do not resemble the things. The word *cat* does not look like a cat. But the word is still meaningful.

describe certain things, then it's much more difficult for you to see those things than it is for someone who knows the appropriate words. How much of a football game would a person miss if he didn't know what an "end run," or a "screen pass," or a "wide receiver" was? How much of a sumo wrestling match could you actually notice, compared with a native Japanese person? I know that I would miss many things until a knowledgeable fan pointed them out to me. The same applies to effective thinking.

This chapter is about the relations between language and the world. Usually what we think about is not language but people, or things, or events, or problems in the world. But our thinking depends on language. Therefore it is useful to try to separate, as far as possible, the things themselves from the words we use to think about them, and try to see how much of our understanding depends on the language we use and how much depends on the way things really are.

Part 1. Definitions

85. to refer. to pick out something, or direct attention to something; to name. Words can refer and people can refer. "The word 'President' refers to the person who has been elected as the chief executive of the United States." "*Raptor* refers to a type of bird." "Senator Brown referred to Cuba in his speech."

   reference (noun). the thing referred to, or the act of referring. "The reference of *raptor* is a kind of bird." "Senator Brown's reference was to Cuba."

Example

> 85a. In the mid-fourteenth century the civil wars in Castile [in Spain] gave rise to excesses against the Jewish community in some towns....Many unprotected Jews were forced to become Christians. From this time the *conversos* came into existence on a grand scale. Converso (or New Christian) was the term applied to one who had converted from Judaism or Islam. Their descendents were also **referred** to as conversos.
>
> Henry Kamen, *The Spanish Inquisition: A Historical Revision*, Yale University Press, 1998, p. 10

86. to mean. to convey particular ideas to people. Words can mean something and people can mean something. "The word 'quadrilateral' means having four sides." "I didn't express myself very well. What I meant was that the bride was beautiful." "When you said 'Becky's boyfriend,' what did you mean?" "I meant Frank."

meaning (noun). the ideas normally conveyed by a word, or in an extended sense, by anything. "Adele wondered what the meaning of the dream was."

Example

86a. What we really **mean** by free will, of course, is the visualization of alternatives and making a choice between them. In my view, which not everyone shares, the central problem of human consciousness depends on this ability to imagine.

Jacob Bronowski, *The Origins of Knowledge and Imagination*, Yale University Press, 1978, p. 18

87. concept. an idea; usually a general idea that holds together a group of things or refers to a type of thing. "He understands the concept of a herbivore (a plant-eating animal)." "The concept of acceleration is a basic part of physics."

Example

87a. Even physics, which seems wholly impersonal and autonomous, has been influenced by vested social interests. The **concept** of energy was developed to meet the manufacturers' need of a bookkeeping device, a way of measuring the efficiency of machines in terms of work.

Herbert J. Muller, What Science Is, in George Levine and Owen Thomas, eds. *The Scientist vs. the Humanist*, W. W. Norton and Co., 1963, p. 11

88. to define. to explain the meaning of a word. "They could avoid a lot of useless arguments if they would just define the word *opportunity*."
    definition (noun).

Example

88a. Next: how shall we **define** the whale, by his obvious externals, so as conspicuously to label him for all time to come? To be short, then, a whale is *a spouting fish with a horizontal tail*. There you have him. However contracted, that **definition** is the result of expanded meditation. A walrus spouts much like a whale, but the walrus is not a fish, because he is amphibious. But the last term of the definition is still more cogent, as coupled with the first. Almost any one must have noticed that all the fish familiar to landsmen have not a flat, but a vertical, or up-and-down tail. Whereas, among spouting fish the tail, though it may be similarly shaped, invariably assumes a horizontal position.

Herman Melville, *Moby Dick*, Bantam, 1981 [originally published in 1851], pp. 129–130

(*Cogent* means convincing, persuasive.)

89. connotation. the feelings or images that people normally associate with a word, but that are not strictly part of the meaning of the word. "The word 'fat' has a negative connotation for most people." "An undertaker performs a necessary function, but the word has a connotation of unctuousness and even insincerity."

Example

89a. For most people the term *creativity* carries strongly favorable **connotations**. Creativity is considered somehow the source of what is most valuable in the achievements of those who advance civilization by means of their skill, taste, or genius.

Stephen Barker, Scientific and Artistic Creativity According to Kant's Philosophy, in Mark Amsler, ed., *The Languages of Creativity*, University of Delaware Press, 1986, p. 142

90. abstract. meanings and concepts are abstract if they convey very general ideas, refer to types of things rather than particular objects, or to the qualities that tie a large class together. "Instead of talking about the candidates and their voting records, the professor talked about abstract ideas like 'working people' and 'dignity.'"

Example

90a. On the continent, the Swiss writer Joseph de Maistre opposed the [French] revolution not only because of its offences to Roman Catholicism, but also because it designed constitutions for an **abstract** Man. There was no such thing, complained de Maistre, as Man: there were only Frenchmen, Englishmen, Spaniards, Russians, and so forth.

George Fasel, *Modern Europe in the Making: From the French Revolution to the Common Market*, Dodd, Mead and Co., 1974, p. 60

Test Yourself
Match each word with its definition.

85. to refer
86. to mean
87. concept
88. to define
89. connotation
90. abstract

a. to use a word to pick out some object or thing
b. to explain what people have in mind when they use a word
c. a word that refers to a type of thing, or very general qualitiesd. a general idea that can apply to many specific instancese. the images and feelings associated with a word but not necessarily part of its meaning
f. to use a word to convey some idea

Part 2. Understanding the Meaning

85. to refer.

85b. When Cindy Sheehan stated "this country is not worth dying for," she was **referring** to Iraq, not the U.S. It is a shame that anyone protesting this unjust war is vilified and besmirched.

FG, Voice of the People: To Clarify, *New York Daily News*, 8/31/05

85c. I'd like to say that my use of the word 'blacks' and not 'African-American' is purely intentional. I prefer to be **referred** to as a black person, because to me the term 'African-American' denotes a connotation that I have an allegiance to Africa before America. I am an American. I was born here, my mother was born here, her mother was born here, and so on. I can trace more than five generations of my family in this country. It is my home, and it is to whom I pledge my allegiance. I am an American and very proud to be one.

Until the government can think of a term to **refer** to my race that doesn't attempt to make me feel like less of the natural-born citizen that I am, I will continue to use the term 'black.'

AL, Letter: Cosby's Comments Right on Target, *Las Vegas Review-Journal*, 6/6/04

85d. One good example of such a divergence through time is found in the pair, *master: mistress*. Once used with **reference** to one's power over servants, these words have become unusable today in their original master–servant sense as the relationship has become less prevalent in our society. But the words are still common.

Unless used with reference to animals, *master* now generally **refers** to a man who has acquired consummate ability in some field, normally nonsexual. But its feminine counterpart cannot be used this way. It is practically restricted to its sexual sense of "paramour." . . . One cannot say: "Rhonda is a mistress." One must be *someone's* mistress. A man is defined by what he does, a woman by her sexuality, that is, in terms of one particular aspect of her relationship to men.

Robin Lakoff, You Are What You Say, in Lynn Z. Bloom, ed., *The Lexington Reader*, D. C. Heath and Company, 1987, p. 87

Comment

Reference and meaning are interrelated. To refer is to pick out an object or class of things; to mean is to convey certain ideas, ideas about what is picked out. Lakoff says that the reference of the words *master* and *mistress* changed over time. The changes in reference happened at the same time as changes in meaning. The word *mistress* originally referred to a type of woman, i.e., a woman who employed servants. Now it refers to a woman who is a man's lover but not his wife. Since the word picks out a different group of people, the ideas it conveys are different as well. It is probably impossible to say one change causes the other. Reference depends on meaning, and meaning depends on reference.

86. to mean.

86b. One after another, the towns and cities that had so recently been "liberated" by the French were now being "liberated" by the [Italian] armada of Arezzo. Then, as now, the word "liberty" had a great variety of **meanings**.

Gian M. Rinaldi, "A Madonna's Fierce 'Armada'," in Martin Ebon, ed., *Miracles*, New American Library, 1981, p. 72

86c. I'm not talking about *religion* now. Obviously, particular religions and congregations can decide whether they want to confer the religious **meaning** of "marriage" on a union of two people. I'm talking about the law. Again, we need to distinguish between church and state. Under the law, married couples enjoy many benefits (such as survivor's benefits under Social Security) that are denied to unmarried couples. Why should gay couples who want these benefits be treated any differently?

Part of the problem—and confusion—[over gay marriage] is that we give *marriage* both a religious and a legal **meaning**. But they really are distinct. The difference would be clearer if we used "marriage" in the religious sphere and employed different words, such as "domestic partnership," in all laws and regulations that now refer to "marriage." In this case, government would confer the same set of benefits—Social Security survivor's benefits, alimony, a fair distribution of assets if relationships end in divorce, and so on—on any two people who sought to make a lifelong commitment to each other, even if they were never "married" in the religious sense of the term.

Robert B. Reich, *Reason: Why Liberals Will Win the Battle for America*, Knopf, 2004, pp. 69–70

Comment

It is natural to think that the meanings of words are objective facts, like state capitols, and we can confirm them by looking in a dictionary. But meaning isn't so easy to pin down. It can be controversial, as Example 86c shows. People disagree on the meaning of the word *marriage*. Some say it cannot mean a union between two people of the same sex. Others say it can. Reich says the word has two different meanings, a religious and a civil meaning. But others disagree.

86d. First, let's be clear about what we're talking about. By altruism I do not **mean** the "You scratch my back, I'll scratch yours" kind of behavior that practices benevolence to others in direct expectation of reciprocal benefits. Altruism is more interesting: the truly selfless giving of oneself to others with absolutely no secondary motives. When we see that kind of love and generosity, we are overcome with awe and reverence.

Francis S. Collins, *The Language of God*, Free Press, 2006, p. 25

Comment

The relation between language and the world is complicated. You might think that the connection is simply a matter of reference. Words are names of things, according to this view. *Peter* names an individual, *rock* names a physical object, *blue* names a color, *run* names an action. But this is a little too simple. For example, which physical object does *rock* name? Does it name every single rock? Future rocks too? And what about *unicorn*? Can that word refer to things that don't exist? Hamlet doesn't exist either; does *unicorn* refer to him too? There is no need to get tangled up in these puzzles. The only point to notice is that the relation between language and the world is more complicated that it may first appear.

That is why you are learning other words besides *refer*. In particular, referring is connected with meaning. I could ask, "What does the word *university* mean?" And you might say, "It means Harvard, Yale, Stanford, and places like those." You name places to which the word refers. In a way you would be right, but your answer isn't complete because I still might not know what the word means. I can look at some examples of universities, but what does the word mean? Am I supposed to notice the campus, the sports teams, the high costs of attending, or something else? *University* refers to Harvard and the others, but its meaning is more than the things it refers to. The preceding definition says that meaning is the ideas conveyed by the word. So to give the meaning of *university* you would not list some examples but would explain the ideas the word conveys. You might say, "*University* means a place where higher-level students come to be taught by professors in classes and laboratories." And the meaning includes other ideas as well. Because the word has this meaning, it does in fact refer to Harvard and Yale, because those places fit the definition. Meaning is the same thing as a concept, and that is another useful word to know.

87. concept.

> 87b. A great deal has been written about the renaissance **concept** of *virtu*, but Machiavelli, like his contemporaries, seems to have used it freely and loosely, nearly always in antithesis to *fortuna* [fortune, luck], sometimes with the sense of willpower, sometimes efficiency, sometimes even with the sense of virtue.
>
> George Bull, Translator's Note, in Niccolo Machiavelli, *The Prince*, Penguin, 1999 [originally 1514], p. xxxiii

> 87c. The final example I have chosen [in order] to illustrate brainwashing [namely, George Orwell's *Nineteen Eight-Four*] is fictional.... Told in the third person, it avoids the problems of unreliable narration aris-

ing when brainwashing was described either by its victims or by the US propagandists who observed them. It is as good a description of the **concept** as you will find anywhere.

Kathleen Taylor, *Brainwashing: The Science of Thought Control*, Oxford University Press, 2004, p. 20

87d. Running through the meeting was a constant tension between the ability to develop exquisitely sensitive tools to sense life as we know it—sensors to look for the spectral signature of plant chlorophyll, say—and the difficulty of looking for life as we do not know it.

"Everything we do here is hostage to our **concept** of what life is," said Dr. David Des Marais of NASA's Ames Research Center, and part of a committee charged by NASA with developing a road map of astrobiological research for the next decade. Dr. Nealson, of U.S.C., urged scientists to look for life in "non-Earthcentric ways."

Dennis Overbye, "NASA Presses Search for Extraterrestrial Life," *New York Times*, 6/4/02

Question: Could scientists discover things that were "alive," but not according to our Earthcentric concept of "life"?

87e. The **concept** of race as having a biological basis is controversial, and most geneticists are reluctant to describe it that way. But some say the genetic clustering into continent-based groups does correspond roughly to the popular **conception** of racial groups.

"There are difficulties in where you put boundaries on the globe, but we know now there are enough genetic differences between people from different parts of the world that you can classify people in groups that correspond to popular notions of race," Dr. Pritchard said.

David Reich, a population geneticist at the Harvard Medical School, said that the term "race" was scientifically inexact and that he preferred "ancestry."

Nicholas Wade, Humans Have Spread Globally, and Evolved Locally, *New York Times*, 6/26/07

88. to define.

88b. If we wish to disinfect a word or an idea from casual and false associations, we begin by trying to **define** it.... Because in the past many different things have been called romantic, some scholars have denied the possibility of giving a **definition** that will hold in all cases; or they have denied that romanticism stood for anything clear and solid.

Jacques Barzun, *Classic, Romantic and Modern*, Second Edition, University of Chicago Press, 1961, p. 3

88c. Indeed, psychologists have surveyed people's ideas about what intelligence is and have found that people generally agree on both what

defines an intelligent person and on the general concept of intelligence. In a nutshell, people think being smart means solving problems well, being good with words, and, to a smaller degree, being good with people.

Sonja I. Yoerg, *Clever as a Fox*, Bloomsbury, 2001, p. 17

88d. In 1989 I had begun reading the Austrian economist Ludwig von Mises, who **defined** *valuing* as "man's emotional reaction to the various states of his environment, both that of the external world and that of the physiological conditions of his own body."

Jeffrey M. Schwartz and Sharon Begley, *The Mind and the Brain: Neuroplasticity and the Power of Mental Force*, Regan Books, 2002, p. 87

88e. A man who was shot and killed by a Newark police officer on Sunday night had opened fire first on the officer and his partner, the police said on Monday. The police said Mr. Berger shot two people, Corey Borden, 22, ... and Keisha Young, 26. ...

"This individual showed no regard or concern for human life," Mayor Sharpe James said. "Our officers took the necessary measures, in accordance with their training and the situation, to end the violence and restore law and order at the Seth Boyden complex. They **define** the word 'courage.'"

John Holl, Man Killed By Officer Fired First, Police Say, *New York Times*, 8/9/05

Comment

We all understand what the Mayor meant. He meant the police officers *exemplify* courage, or they perfectly fit the definition of *courage*. He was using "define" in an extended sense. He was not saying that the officers explain the meaning of the word *courage*.

89. connotation.

89b. I was assigned to a committee that reviewed reading passages for the fourth grade test. ... The passage about owls was like a children's encyclopedia entry. It described how their keen eyesight and hearing enabled them to hunt at night for rodents. ... The passage was rejected [by the bias and sensitivity reviewers] because a Native American member of the bias committee said that owls are taboo for the Navajos. Consequently the entire committee agreed that the passage should be dropped. The test publisher added a notation that the owl is associated with death in some other cultures and should not be mentioned anymore, neither in texts nor in illustrations.

Here is a classic problem presented by today's bias and sensitivity review process. If any cultural group attributes negative **connotations** to anything, or considers it taboo or offensive, then that topic will not be referred to, represented, described, or illustrated on tests.

Diane Ravitch, *The Language Police: How Pressure Groups Restrict What Students Learn*, Vintage, 2003, p. 16

89c. But more to the point, who uses words like "bachelor" and "Don Juan"—or any of a number of similarly quaint synonyms (rake, rogue, roué, ladies' man)—any more? Modified by "swinging," the word bachelor used to **connote**, at least in movies and magazines, an incorrigible playboy; preceded by "confirmed," it was a euphemism for gay. Changing sexual mores—and, more to the point, changes in the way popular culture deals with sexuality—have rendered both usages obsolete.

A. O. Scott, The Two Minds of the Unmarried Man, *New York Times*, 8/7/05

(A euphemism is a nice, harmless word for something that may be offensive or harsh. *Passed away* is a euphemism for *died*. *Collateral damage* is a euphemism for civilian deaths in war.)

89d. But I shall also use the word "reality", and with two different **connotations**.

In the first place, I shall speak of "physical reality", and here again I shall be using the word in the ordinary sense. By physical reality I mean the material world, the world of day and night, earthquakes and eclipses, the world which physical science tries to describe.

I hardly suppose that, up to this point, any reader is likely to find trouble with my language, but now I am near to more difficult ground. For me, and I suppose for most mathematicians, there is another reality, which I will call "mathematical reality"; and there is no sort of agreement about the nature of mathematical reality among either mathematicians or philosophers.... I believe that mathematical reality lies outside us, that our function is to discover or *observe* it, and that the theorems which we prove, and which we describe grandiloquently as our "creations", are simply our notes of our observations.

G. H. Hardy, *A Mathematician's Apology*, Cambridge University Press, 1967, pp. 122–124

Comment

Hardy's example shows that even very good writers do not always use these words in precisely the same ways. Hardy says he gives two different connotations to the word *reality*, but it is more accurate to say he gives different meanings to the word. *Reality* can mean the world of trees and chairs we all see and touch, or it can mean the world of numbers and equations that mathematicians work with, and that we can only grasp with our minds. (You can't touch the sum of 2 and 5.) These are not just different connotations, or associations, but completely different meanings, different concepts, and different references. Connotations are images and feelings some people think of when they hear a word, but are not actually part of the meaning of the word. They are not among the ideas the word conveys to most people.

90. abstract.

90b. The performance of groups is a wonderful subject, and Surowiecki has a remarkable eye for the telling anecdote, illustrating **abstract** claims with vivid examples. His central point is convincing. Groups, and even crowds, can be wiser than most and sometimes even all of their members, at least if they aggregate information. But there is a serious problem with Surowiecki's discussion: he does not provide an adequate account of the circumstances that make crowds wise or stupid.

Cass R. Sunstein, Mobbed Up, Review of James Surowiecki, The Wisdom of Crowds, *The New Republic*, 6/28/04

90c. The term "unconsciousness," now so familiar to all readers of modern works on psychology, gives offence to some adherents of the past. There should, however, be no special mystery about it. It is not a new animistic **abstraction**, but simply a collective word to include all the physiological changes that escape our notice, all the forgotten experiences and impressions of the past which continue to influence our desires and reflections and conduct, even if we can't remember them.

James Harvey Robinson, *The Mind in the Making*, Harper and Brothers, 1921, p. 35

(*Animistic* means believing in spirits and ghosts and hobgoblins who live in trees or the wind or other places.)

90d. My problem with most fantasy and science fiction is the world-building. I haven't got the patience for the rich, laborious detail about the creatures and their machines, or for the rules about the heroes' special powers. It's all so arbitrary. Why should I bother trying to imagine scenery before I know what's happening? I want story. And story means angry, loving characters with secrets they may not even know about—not just breathless action and intricate escapes from the jaws of monsters, and not just **abstract ideas,** however clever.

Hazel Rochman, Something's Rotten in Utopia, *New York Times*, 5/16/04

Opposite

concrete. specific, particular, tangible, something you might visualize, tied to real, identifiable things. "The virus posed an immediate, concrete threat to the community, not an abstract possibility."

Examples

90e. For a colonized people the most essential value, because the most **concrete**, is first and foremost the land: the land which will bring them bread and, above all, dignity.

Frantz Fanon, *The Wretched of the Earth*, translated by Constance Farrington, Grove Press, 1968 [originally published 1961], p. 44

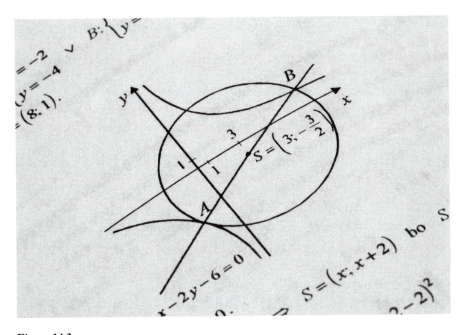

Figure 14.2
Mathematics describes broad classes of objects and events without relying on colors or sounds or smells or tastes. *Source: © Kmitu/Shutterstock*

90f. What is above all needed is to let the meaning choose the word, and not the other way about. In prose, the worst thing one can do with words is to surrender to them. When you think of a **concrete** object, you think wordlessly, and then, if you want to describe the thing you have been visualizing you probably hunt about till you find the exact words that seem to fit it.

George Orwell, Politics and the English Language, in Donald Hall and D. L. Emblen, eds., *A Writer's Reader*, Fourth Edition, Little, Brown and Company, 1985, p. 305

Part 3. Applying the Words

85. to refer
86. to mean
87. concept
88. to define
89. connotation
90. abstract

Exercise 1: Choose the Best Word

For each sentence, choose the best word (or an appropriate form of the word) to fill in the blank.

1. The words *determined* and *stubborn* have about the same meanings, but they have different _____.
2. When she instructed the jury, the judge first _____ the words *homicide* and *manslaughter*.
3. The guide _____ to Delmonico's as "the best restaurant in town."
4. Terry was trying to find another word that _____ the same as "survive."
5. Algebra is more _____ than arithmetic because it uses letters that can stand for any number.
6. Roman soldiers called Hannibal's elephants "cows with tails at both ends" because they had no _____ of an elephant.

Exercise 2:   Apply the Words

Read each example and answer the questions that follow.

> 1. It is 20 years since the term "glass ceiling" was coined by the *Wall Street Journal* to describe the apparent barriers that prevent women from reaching the top of the corporate hierarchy....

Special Report: Women in Business, The Conundrum of the Glass Ceiling, *The Economist*, 7/23/05

Does the term *glass ceiling* refer to something abstract or concrete?

> 2. In this book we shall use the term *anti-intellectualism* to describe the attempt to arrive rationally at a just appreciation of the actual roles of rationality and of nonrationality in human affairs. The term is widely used, however, to describe something quite different—the *praise* of nonrationality, the exaltation of nonrationality as the really desirable human activity, the denigration of rationality. Such an attitude of dislike for rationality and love for nonrationality we prefer to call *romanticism*, the romanticism of Goethe's "feeling is all."

Crane Brinton, *Ideas and Men: The Story of Western Thought*, Prentice-Hall, 1950, p. 504

Brinton says the same word has two different meanings. How are the two meanings different? Does the word refer to two different kinds of things?

> 3. At this point a distinction must be made between the terms *obedience* and *conformity. Conformity*, in particular, has a very broad meaning, but for the purposes of this discussion, I shall limit it to the action of a subject when he goes along with his peers, people of his own status, who have no special right to direct his behavior. *Obedience* will be restricted to the action of the subject who complies with authority. Consider a recruit who enters military service. He scrupulously carries out the orders of his superiors. At the same time, he adopts the habits, routines, and language of his peers. The former represents obedience and the latter, conformity.

Stanley Milgram, *Obedience to Authority: An Experimental View*, Perennial Classics, 2004 (originally published 1974), p. 113

Milgram distinguishes two concepts here, referring to two types of behavior. How are the concepts different?

4. In its December report, the National Assessment of Adult Literacy (NAAL), from the National Center for Education Statistics, found that prose literacy—the ability to comprehend and use information from "continuous text" such as newspaper articles—has declined significantly among college grads since 1992. Document literacy, enabling readers to understand noncontinuous text such as prescription labels and job applications, is also on the wane....

While the percentage of adults attaining higher education increased slightly between 1992 and 2003, prose literacy scores dropped among college graduates, per the NAAL survey, from 325 to 314....

Grover Whitehurst, who helped supervise the test, was quoted in the *New York Times* blaming the surge in television and Internet use for a decrease in reading for pleasure and a subsequent decline in literacy.

Campus Clips: Literacy Declines Among College Grads, *AFT on Campus*, March/April, 2006

This passage includes two definitions. What words are defined?

5. Third, don't words such as "civilization," and phrases such as "rise of civilization," convey the false impression that civilization is good, tribal hunter-gatherers are miserable, and history for the past 13,000 years has involved progress toward greater human happiness?

Jared Diamond, *Guns, Germs, and Steel: The Fates of Human Societies*, W. W. Norton, 1999, p. 18

Does Diamond believe the word *civilization* has a positive connotation or a negative connotation?

6. Defenceless villages are bombarded from the air, the inhabitants driven out into the countryside, the cattle machine-gunned, the huts set on fire with incendiary bullets: this is called *pacification*. Millions of peasants are robbed of their farms and sent trudging along the roads with no more than they can carry: this is called *transfer of population* or *rectification of frontiers*. People are imprisoned for years without trial, or shot in the back of the neck or sent to die of scurvy in Arctic lumber camps: this is called *elimination of unreliable elements*. Such phraseology is needed if one wants to name things without calling up mental pictures of them.

George Orwell, Politics and the English Language, in Donald Hall and D. L. Emblen, eds., *A Writer's Reader*, Fourth Edition, Little, Brown and Company, 1985, p. 303

Orwell gives examples of concrete words and abstract words. Why do some governments and writers use abstract words instead of the concrete ones?

7. The birth of the term 'brainwashing' reflected a need to label what were seen as terrifying new dangers. This need had become

increasingly pressing with the Soviet show trials of the 1930s, in which discredited former leaders of the Communist Party stood up and publicly denounced their entire careers, policies, and belief systems with apparently inexplicable sincerity.... [the] very fact that there was now a word for whatever mysteries had gone on in Chinese prison camps calmed the American public's fear of the unknown.

Kathleen Taylor, *Brainwashing: The Science of Thought Control*, Oxford University Press, 2004, p. 6

A new word, which is invented to refer to a new phenomenon, is called a neologism. *Brainwashing* was a neologism in the 1950s. Can you think of any other neologisms, any words for new things that didn't exist 10 or 20 years ago?

8. The glyphs [signs or symbols] are combinations of symbols enclosed in rounded squares or oblong blocks. Little circles and bars and curlicues are squeezed in each block alongside the drawing of a man in profile or a toothsome animal or a strange hybrid creature.

Don't count on the clear drawing of a bird to represent the word for bird. With flourishes and added signs, the bird glyph is made to represent a deity or some other aspect of Maya metaphysics. Variants of the glyph for the word "sky" feature an avian beak or a snake's head with menacing fangs....

In despair, I gazed on the modern international glyph on the wall at the front of the classroom. It was the ubiquitous no-smoking symbol, a red circle with a red slash through a cigarette, and wished the Maya scribes could have been so obvious.

John Noble Wilford, On Ancient Walls, a New Maya Epoch, *New York Times*, 5/16/06

(*Ubiquitous* means "occurring everywhere." *Avian* means "related to birds.")

Drawings represent things. For example, a drawing of your face represents your face. A friend who saw it would say, "That's you." Drawings can also have meaning. The no-smoking symbol means "Do not smoke." Wilford says the meaning is obvious. But the meanings of the Mayan symbols are very difficult to understand. Do you think an ancient Mayan would agree that the meaning of the symbol for "Do not smoke" is obvious?

9. Witchcraft is explained in modern literature in three ways: as a survival of paganism, as a psychological delusion, or as a social mechanism.... In origin, however, witchcraft seems adequately explained as a perfectly reasonable inference from the idea of magic. If people can harness and change nature, they can do it for ill as well as good.

Is witchcraft over? Good explanation does not always drive out bad, and science has a poor record in competition with superstition.

Would-be Western practitioners today are trying to strip the negative associations from witchcraft and revive it as a name for little more than a folksy attitude toward nature.

Felipe Fernandez-Armesto, *Ideas That Changed the World*, DK Publishing, 2003, p. 51

What is the origin of the concept of witchcraft, according to Fernandez-Armesto? Do you think modern would-be practitioners will be able to change the connotations of the word "witch" from negative to positive?

10. For intellectual circles in the past, the concept of "tradition" embraced a firm program; it appeared to be something protective on which man could rely; he could think himself safe and on the right lines if he could appeal to tradition. Today precisely the opposite feeling prevails: tradition appears to be what has been laid aside, the merely out-of-date, whereas progress is regarded as the real promise of life, so that man feels at home, not in the realm of tradition, of the past, but in the realm of progress and the future.

Joseph Cardinal Ratzinger, *Introduction to Christianity*, translated by J. R. Foster, Ignatius Press, 2004, p. 53

Do you think Ratzinger intends to say that the meaning of the word *tradition* has changed, or that the connotations of the word have changed?

Exercise 3: Analyzing Arguments

1. Malise Ruthven wonders if the word *fundamentalist* can be applied correctly outside the context where it first occurred originally *fundamentalist* referred to an American Protestant who believed the Bible was literally true, and who attempted to live in accordance with that belief. She first mentions a reason to think it can be applied to Muslims, but then gives a reason to conclude it cannot. What are the reasons?

Religious fundamentalism, as it is broadly understood, has been the principal source of conflict since the late 1980s and early 1990s.... Academics are still debating the appropriateness of using the "F-word" in contexts outside its original Protestant setting. Islamic scholars argue that since all observant Muslims believe the Koran—the divine text of Islam—to be the unmediated Word of God, all are committed to a doctrine of scriptural inerrancy, whereas for Protestants biblical inerrancy is one of the hallmarks that distinguishes fundamentalists from liberals. If all believing Muslims are "fundamentalists" in this sense of the word, then the term is meaningless, because it fails to distinguish between the hard-edged militant who seeks to "Islamize" his society and the quietist who avoids politics completely....

Malise Ruthven, *Fundamentalism: The Search for Meaning*, Oxford University Press, 2004, pp. 4, 5

302 THE VOCABULARY OF CRITICAL THINKING

2. Example 2 is a continuation of the previous passage. In your own words, what is Ruthven's argument for the conclusion that the word *fundamentalism* can be applied outside its original context? She also suggests a new criterion (different from the original one) for classifying a person as a fundamentalist. What is it?

> The applications or meanings attached to words cannot be confined to the context in which they originate: if one limits "fundamentalism" to its original meaning one might as well do the same for words like "nationalism" and "secularization" which also appeared in the post-Enlightenment West before being applied to movements or processes in non-Western societies. Applying the same restrictive logic, one should not speak of Judaism or Christianity as "religions" because that originally Latin word is found in neither Old nor New Testaments....
>
> Indeed, given the far-reaching consequences of the scientific revolution that flowed from the Enlightenment, the modern predicament against which fundamentalists everywhere are reacting has been extended to cover virtually every corner of the planet.
>
> Malise Ruthven, *Fundamentalism: The Search for Meaning*, Oxford University Press, 2004, p. 8

3. In the following passage, linguist Donna Jo Napoli is analyzing an argument about words and thinking. What is the conclusion of the argument she is analyzing? What reasons do people give to support the conclusion? (Incidentally, Napoli does not accept this argument because she says in another place that one premise – the rumor – is false.)

> Have you heard the rumor that the Inuit [Eskimos] have dozens of words for snow [words for wet snow, powdery snow, icy snow, etc.]? This rumor has been used as evidence in favor of the idea that the Inuit understand differentiations in snow types that are beyond the comprehension of, say, people from Florida, whose vocabulary lacks the equivalent words.
>
> The origin of this rumor doesn't matter to our discussion. What does matter is that people have welcomed this rumor and its ensuing conclusion—that the Inuit think differently from those who do not have as rich a vocabulary for winter events. The rumor clearly has appeal; people believe it because it seems so right to them. The Inuit live with snow most of the year, so it makes sense that they'd have lots of words for it. Furthermore, the conclusion also has appeal. If the Inuit have words we don't have, it makes sense that they have concepts (i.e., thoughts) we don't have....
>
> However, even if the rumor (that the Inuit have more words for snow) is false and its appeal is deceptive, that doesn't necessarily mean that the conclusion was false. So we must ask, if a language has a word for a given concept and another language lacks a word for that concept,

does it follow that the given concept is mentally accessible to people of the first language and inaccessible to people of the second language?

Donna Jo Napoli, *Language Matters*, Oxford University Press, 2003, pp. 41, 43

Exercise 4: Apply the Ideas in Writing

Write a four- or five-paragraph essay in which you defend one of the statements in the following list, or its denial (e.g., "The movie 'The Godfather' is a work of art," or "'The Godfather' is not a work of art.") After your introduction you should have at least one paragraph in which you explain the criteria for being _____ (a work of art, torture, etc.). And you should also have at least one paragraph in which you explain why the particular example fits those criteria. (Of course, you may decide that you need more than one paragraph for each of these two parts of your essay.)

(a) Depriving a prisoner of sleep with loud noises and bright lights for more than two days is *torture,* which is forbidden by international law.

(b) Sometimes you have to go against the majority, against national traditions, and even against the law, in order to be a true *patriot.*

(c) Mr. Smith, the boss at our company, always hugs people at our Christmas party and at birthday parties in the office. That's *sexual harassment.*

(d) Bill adopted two small children from overseas. His long-time partner, Jim, moved in and they are raising the kids. I guess they are *a family.*

(e) Coppola's film, "The Godfather," is a *work of art.*

Improving Your Writing 14: Definition Essays

In Chapter 12 you read about evaluation essays. Another kind of persuasive essay is a definition essay. It's similar to an evaluation essay, except that the thesis is a definition, or classification, not a value judgment. For example, your thesis in a definition essay could be "Seventeen-year-olds are adults," "Coppola's film, 'The Godfather,' is a work of art," or "The government of Somalia is guilty of genocide." Of course, you could argue for the denial of one of these as well ("The Somali government's actions are not genocide").

A definition essay has two parts, just as an evaluation essay does. But here, you use the first part to explain the *meaning* of the key term. What *is* genocide? Or a work of art? Or an adult? That is, you explain the criteria that anything must satisfy before it can accurately be called *genocide.* A dictionary is helpful, but it is only the first step. You need to explain and expand on the words in the dictionary definition.

The second step is closer to the second step of an evaluation essay. You need to show that your example really does meet the criteria. For example, you need to show that the government of Somalia is doing all the things that add up to genocide. It isn't just punishing law-breakers, and it isn't fighting a civil war, you could argue. Instead, their actions fit the definition of genocide.

Problems with Language

When you read a good story, or an interesting newspaper article, you are thinking about the individuals and places and events, not the words the writer is using. For example, if you are reading about the movie star governor of California, you want to learn about his policies, his political strategy, maybe his personality. You do not want to be distracted by obscure words, or long, complex sentences that are hard to understand. The best writers try to make their language perfectly transparent so you can see the topic, not the medium through which the topic is presented. Their writing is like a large, clean window that lets you see what's happening outside without any cloudy, wavy distortions.

But this may be an ideal that writers never achieve, and some may never even strive for it. Words are a writer's tools, and the tools influence the final product, no matter how well the craftsman uses them. In some kinds of writing—such as poetry—the goal is not only to describe something, but also to find words that convey the writer's particular, personal response to the topic. In other writing, such as political opinion writing, the writer intentionally uses words that influence the reader's feelings and beliefs about a topic, even if the writer knows that he or she is presenting only a part of the picture. Can that personal, limited selection ever be overcome? Can the ideal of transparency be achieved, so that the writing presents the direct,

Figure 15.1
An ambiguous word (Y) has two different meanings. A vague word (Z) refers to
something whose boundaries are not clear, something that is a matter of degree.

unbiased truth? People disagree; some say yes, some say no. But everyone agrees that
certain words can distort people's perceptions and lead to misunderstanding rather
than understanding. A careful thinker must be aware of the words that interfere
with an accurate description and convey a narrow, one-sided version of events.

There are many such words. The only way to develop your skill in detecting them
is to read widely and compare what you read with your own experience, to see how a
writer's language presents a different version of reality from the one you experience.
This chapter is not about the misleading words. There are too many of them. Instead,
it's about different *types* of misleading words. It's about the *ways* that words can mislead people. Here you can begin learning how to talk about those tricky words, as a
first step in recognizing them and avoiding the mistakes they create.

Part 1. Definitions

91. ambiguous. having two or more distinct meanings. "The word *conviction*
is ambiguous; it can mean 'a strong belief,' or 'being found guilty in a trial.'"
　ambiguity (noun).

> 91a. If an individual, says Grotius, can alienate his liberty and make
> himself the slave of a master, why could not a whole people do the
> same, and make itself subject to a King? There are in this passage
> plenty of **ambiguous** words which would need explaining; but let us
> confine ourselves to the word *alienate*. To alienate is to give or to sell.
> Now a man who becomes the slave of another does not give himself;
> he sells himself at least for his subsistence: but for what does a people
> sell itself? A king is so far from furnishing his subjects with their sub-
> sistence that he gets his own only from them....
>
> Jean-Jacques Rousseau, *The Social Contract and the Discourses*, trans. G. D. H. Cole, Revised
> Edition, Everyman's Library, 1973, p. 185

(*Subsistence* means the basic necessities of life, mainly food.)

92. vague. a word is vague if it refers to a quality that can apply in degrees, more or
less, so that the class of things picked out by the quality has indistinct boundaries.

The word "blue" is vague because there is no sharp boundary between blue and green, or blue and purple. The sky is definitely blue, but is this dress blue? Or should we say it's green? Bill Gates is rich and the unemployed, single mother is poor, but is dentist John Jones rich? The word "rich" is vague. Being rich is a matter of degree. "The principal said the program was for talented students, but that didn't help because the word *talented* is vague."

Example

> 92a. Of all the memos released by the White House last week in response to the prison abuse scandal in Iraq, none have been more incendiary than the so-called torture memo, dated Aug. 1, 2002, and written by Jay S. Bybee, the assistant attorney general in charge of the Office of Legal Counsel at the Justice Department....
>
> The memo starts by explaining that some acts may be "cruel, inhuman or degrading" but not constitute torture under Section 2340, the federal law criminalizing torture. To rise to the level of torture, it argues, the acts must be of an extreme nature, specifically intended to inflict severe pain or suffering, mental or physical. But the statute is **vague** on the meaning of "severe,"...
>
> Kate Zernike, Defining Torture: Roussian Roulette, Yes. Mind-Altering Drugs, Maybe, *New York Times*, 6/27/04

93. loaded term. a word that conveys definite feelings, positive or negative, but that also describes something; a word intended to arouse strong emotions. "Steve was biased against the chess club from the beginning, and he used all sorts of loaded terms, like 'geeks,' to describe its meeting."

Example

> 93a. [In Orwell's *Nineteen Eighty-Four*] The Party is gradually implementing Newspeak, a pared-down version of English in which "dangerous" words like "freedom" no longer exist. The idea is that without the words to express certain concepts, the concepts themselves will fade and die: "Newspeak was designed not to extend but to *diminish* the range of thought." Those words which remain are ideologically **loaded**, clear examples of Lifton's thought-terminating clichés.
>
> Kathleen Taylor, *Brainwashing: The Science of Thought Control*, Oxford University Press, 2004, p. 21

94. to characterize. to describe something in a way that emphasizes certain properties, to apply certain words to something, which other people might reject as inaccurate. "The press characterized Sam's project as a failure, but I would say it was a success." "Sue characterized him as arrogant, but really he is only confident in himself."

Example

94a. [Secretary of State Condoleezza Rice] shocked at least some of her guests by branding Iran a "totalitarian state"....A number of guests challenged her assertion, but Ms. Rice is not the type to back down. She called her **characterization** of Iran deliberate. A year ago, she said, she would have called Iran's Islamic Republic authoritarian. But after flawed parliamentary elections last spring that produced a conservative majority, she said, it moved toward totalitarian, a term that historians tend to use restrictively to define violently absolutist regimes that govern through terror.

Elaine Sciolino, The French Are Charmed and Jarred by "Chere Condi," *New York Times*, 2/10/05

95. rhetoric. statements and words, often exaggerations, that a person uses to persuade others, but that are not convincing, and are probably not sincere. "The CEO's speech to his employees was full of empty rhetoric. What else can he say when the company is on the edge of bankruptcy?"

The word "rhetoric" in this sense has a negative connotation. But the word has another meaning that is not negative. Rhetoric is also the study of the art of persuasive speaking and writing. In this sense, rhetoric is an ancient and honorable discipline.

Example

95a. As it has after other recent speeches by Mr. Gore, Mr. Bush's re-election campaign dismissed his remarks as **rhetoric** intended to aid Senator John Kerry, Mr. Bush's likely opponent.

"The anger and vitriol of this attack is so out of step with what voters need in this election. The former vice president's series of rants fits with the whole tenor of their effort to attack President Bush," [campaign spokesman Terry Holt said].

Michael Janofsky, Gore Says White House Is Eroding Democracy, *New York Times*, 6/25/04

(*Vitriol* is a strong acid; more generally, it is a powerful expression of anger and contempt.)

96. irony. the use of words deliberately to mean the opposite of what they usually mean; or an event that is the opposite of what one expected. "Jonathan Swift's essay about solving the food shortage by eating children is full of irony." "The vegetarian fitness instructor did everything to live a long, healthy life, and then he was killed at age 31 in an automobile accident. Ironic, isn't it?"

ironic (adjective)

Example

96a. **Ironically**, it was a University of California behaviorist named
Edward C. Tolman who first showed that perhaps behaviorism didn't
have all the answers.

Dorothy Hinshaw Patent, *How Smart Are Animals?* Harcourt, Brace, Jovanovich, 1990,
pp. 35–36

Test Yourself
Match each word with its definition.

91. ambiguous
92. vague
93. loaded term
94. to characterize
95. rhetoric
96. irony

  a. to apply words to something in a selective, limited way
  b. having two different meanings
  c. using words to mean the opposite of what they usually mean
  d. a quality of words that apply more or less, with hazy boundaries
  e. exaggerated language that is probably not sincere
  f. a word that is intended to make an emotional impact, beyond the factual
    meaning

Part 2. Understanding the Meaning

91. ambiguous.

91b. In the course of the 1950's the concept of mass society began
to win acceptance among the more speculative American sociologists. The publication of David Riesman's *The Lonely Crowd* at the
mid-century had both reflected and stimulated a mood of national
soul-searching....

    The term "mass society" was shot through with **ambiguities**: the ways
in which it was used were imprecise, overlapping, and frequently contradictory. Sometimes its emphasis was on undifferentiated numbers, sometimes on mechanization, sometimes on bureaucratic predominance.

H. Stuart Hughes, *The Sea Change: The Migration of Social Thought, 1930–1965*, Harper
& Row, 1975, p. 135

91c. If she [Kathia Mendez] was asked to describe herself in the United
States census, she says, she would choose the racial category selected
by nearly 15 million Hispanics in 2000: "some other race."....

Figure 15.2
Is the picture about the summer temperature, or is it about the taste of spicy food?
Source: © Peter Doomen/Shutterstock

But now census officials are hoping to eliminate the option from the 2010 questionnaire in an effort to encourage Hispanics to choose one or more of five standard racial categories: white, black, Asian, American Indian or Alaska native, or a category that includes natives of Hawaii and the Pacific Islands....

In the MARS [Modified Age/Race and Sex] file, census officials assign a race to those who select "some other race" to accommodate federal agencies who do not use the **ambiguous** racial category.

Rachel L. Swarns, Hispanics Debate Census Plan to Change Racial Grouping, *New York Times*, 10/24/04

91d. In Lacaton's case, after the torture, the police decided that he was not directly involved in F.L.N. [revolutionary, separatist] activity. But it was also clear that he was not totally dedicated to the war against Moslem separatism. It was decided to release him in the manner reserved for such **ambiguous** personalities.... Half unconscious from his treatment at the police station, Lacaton was thrown into a pigsty.

Peter Geismar, *Fanon: The Revolutionary as Prophet*, Grove Press, 1969, p. 77

Comment

The word *ambiguous* applies—in its most basic sense—to words with two or more distinct meanings. But Swarns, in Example 91c, and Geismar, in Example 91d, extend the word and apply it to other things that are similar to ambiguous words.

Swarns says the category on the census labeled "some other race" applies to two or more groups of people, and Geismar says a person who is neither strongly in favor of a political cause nor strongly against it has an ambiguous personality.

92. vague.

92b. Loving enemies is another dogma of feigned morality, and has besides no meaning. It is incumbent on man, as a moralist, that he does not revenge an injury; and it is equally as good in a political sense, for there is no end to retaliation, each retaliates on the other, and calls it justice; but to love in proportion to the injury, if it could be done, would be to offer a premium for crime. Besides the word "enemies" is too **vague** and general to be used in a moral maxim, which ought always to be clear and defined, like a proverb.

Thomas Paine, *Collected Writings*, selected by Eric Foner, The Library of America, 1995 [this selection, originally 1795], p. 823.

(*Feigned* means pretended, insincere. It rhymes with "pained.")

92c. The theories described below illustrate the diversity of scientific approaches to understanding religion.... The field suffers from vague terminology, disagreement about what exactly "religion" is, and which of its aspects are most important. Does religion consist primarily of behaviors, such as attending church or following certain moral precepts? Or does it consist of beliefs—in God or in an afterlife? Is religion best studied as a set of experiences, such as the inchoate feelings of connection to the rest of nature that can occur during prayer or meditation? Comparing studies is often an exercise in comparing apples and oranges.

John Horgan, The God Experiments, *Discover*, Dec., 2006

Comment

The word *religion* is vague. If it means attending church or following moral rules, how often must you attend church to be religious? How strict in your adherence to rules? There is no definite boundary between being religious and not being religious. But the word is also ambiguous. Horgan points out that it can mean attending services, or holding certain beliefs, or having religious experiences.

92d. In a passionate, rapid-fire speech that lasted more than an hour, Dr. Newdow described problems with the family-law system, which makes custody decisions based on the "best interests of the child."

But that is "a meaningless standard which you can't fight," Dr. Newdow said. Which is best for children, he asked, to teach them to be generous or to teach them to be stingy? To spend time on Shakespeare or on baseball?

"Which is better? We don't know," he said. And there are no valid studies that answer the question of what is best for children, he said.

Instead, judges simply impose their own biases about what they think is best, with no checks or balances.

In addition to being unconstitutionally **vague**, Dr. Newdow said, the best-interests focus puts the rights of children above the rights of parents, which is inequitable.

Leslie Eaton, Lawyer Who Fought Pledge Assails Courts on Custody, *New York Times*, 10/23/04

92e. Among the many decisions Friday by the 8 leaders was a promise to spend millions more to fight AIDS, tuberculosis, and malaria

Figure 15.3
Where on the rainbow does red stop and orange begin? The boundaries between colors in a rainbow are vague. *Source:* © *Zibedik/Shutterstock*

in Africa. The $60 billion promise remained **vague**, spread over "the coming years" without a specific time frame.

Christine Ollivier, G-8 Reaffirms Its African Aid Pledge, *Charlotte Observer*, 6/9/07

Opposite

precise. exact, definite, very specific; often involving measurement. "An architect's drawing has to give the precise dimensions of the building she designs."

Example

92f. However, to repeat an earlier point, it is a mistake to assume that someone cannot have a foreign policy philosophy until he has written a book on the subject or at least read a range of books written by others. Bush may not have spent any time consciously trying to develop a philosophy about foreign affairs. However, a lifetime of experience had left deeply formed beliefs—instincts might be more **precise**— about how the world works and, just as important, how it does not.

Ivo H. Daalder, James M. Lindsay, *America UnBound: The Bush Revolution in Foreign Policy*, Brookings Institution Press, 2003, p. 41

93. loaded term.

93b. The existence of this gray area should not be surprising, because in contemporary society the word "science" is a **loaded** and rhetorically powerful one. People will often find it a useful tactic to describe work in a borderline area as "scientific" or as "unscientific." Some will call a field scientific to suggest that it uses rigorous methods and hence delivers results we should trust.

Peter Godfrey-Smith, *Theory and Reality: An Introduction to the Philosophy of Science*, University of Chicago Press, 2003, p. 3

93c. Then there is the moral argument: torture is an abomination so profound that permitting it, even if limited to rare and dire emergencies, constitutes an indelible blight on a society and its laws. So stated, the proposition has undeniable appeal. But "torture" is a **loaded word**. No one, it is fair to say, favors a policy of complete laissez-faire. What is envisioned instead is the administration of pressure that is capable of causing extreme pain—Dershowitz gives the example of sterile needles forced under the fingernails—but is nonlethal.

Andrew C. McCarthy, Torture: Thinking About the Unthinkable, *Commentary*, July–August, 2004

93d. Burlingame, a director of the World Trade Center Memorial Foundation, specifically charged that Tofel and others are planning to host exhibits at Ground Zero devoted to such wholly off-topic issues as the alleged "genocide" of Americans Indians, the fight against slavery, the Holocaust and the Soviet Gulag.

Worthy subjects for study, each and every one—but not at Ground Zero.

Tofel, for his part, insists that the controversy is all about nothing.

But when Cavuto asked, specifically, whether the museum would feature "atrocities Americans have committed," Tofel repeatedly refused a direct answer.

"Atrocities is such a **loaded word**," he stammered, the weasel.

Tofel needed to say—unequivocally—that the museum will not impugn or disparage America in any way, shape, form or manner.

Editorial, Memo to Gov. Pataki: Retrieve the Memorial, *New York Post*, 6/20/05

Question: The New York Post calls Mr. Tofel a weasel. Can you think of any words you have studied so far that apply to this case? (For example, is the Post using a metaphor?)

94. to characterize.

94b. The Bush administration has been more forthright than any of the United Nations' 191 members states in denouncing the atrocities in Sudan—a fact that should shame European nations that pride themselves on their human rights pedigrees. The United States was the first to **characterize** the violence as genocide and the first, way back in June, to name potential perpetrators and call for punishment.

Samantha Power, Court of First Resort, *New York Times*, 2/10/5

94c. The man whose ideas once served as a barometer of change in Iranian society today expresses cynicism, disgust and concern. "Ahmadinejad's era will become like a tragedy in our history," he said of the president, Mahmoud Ahmadinejad, a **characterization** certain to further alienate—and even antagonize—Iran's leaders.

Michael Slackman, Hostage-Taker, Reformer, Pessimist: An Iranian Life, *New York Times*, 4/29/06

94d. The history of childhood, [Lloyd] deMause urges passionately, "is a nightmare from which we have only recently begun to awaken. The farther back in history one goes, the lower the level of child care, and the more likely children are to be killed, abandoned, beaten, terrorized and sexually abused."

DeMause **characterizes** all this past violence against children as mistreatment. By modern civil standards it certainly was, but judging past behavior by present standards, whatever our natural sympathies, is anachronistic: it obscures the view.

Richard Rhodes, *Why They Kill: The Discoveries of a Maverick Criminologist*, Alfred A. Knopf, 1999, p. 236

(*Anachronistic* means imagining things from one historical era—e.g., airplanes—in another—e.g., ancient Greece. More generally, it means applying standards and ways of thinking from one era to behavior or thinking from another.)

95. rhetoric.

95b. Soaring high on the hot thermal currents of his own **rhetoric**, he loses track of what words actually mean. When he drops a phrase like "the mythic cities of Tennessee," where are we exactly? Chattanooga?

William Grimes, A Modern-Day Tocqueville Finds an Uncertain America, review of Bernard-Henri Levy, American Vertigo, *New York Times*, 2/4/06

95c. America has always been a magnet for freedom-seeking people, with millions of immigrants coming to a country that promised freedom and opportunity.

Now the word "freedom" has become a newly invoked justification for the occupation of a country that did not attack us, whose people have not greeted our soldiers as liberators.

What does President Bush mean by "freedom," when he claims that "freedom is on the march" in the Middle East (front page, Oct. 21)? To call a military occupation a path to freedom is Orwellian doublespeak....

Rhetoric matters. We have already lost one word that characterized the style of American thought and life as defined at the founding of the Republic: liberal. It has become the object of vilification, as our society drifts toward intolerant radicalism and fundamentalism.

Now "freedom" is being emptied of meaning and reduced to a slogan. But one doesn't demean the concept without injuring the substance.

Fritz Stern, Freedom Has Meaning. It's Not Just a Slogan, *New York Times*, 10/24/04

95d. Unlike [Andrew D.] White, who averred that he opposed not religion but dogmatic theology, [T. H.] Huxley sought to undermine organized religion, though his **rhetoric** frequently sought to convey the impression of a disinterested defense of truth.

Colin A. Russell, The Conflict of Science and Religion, in Gary B. Ferngren, ed., *Science and Religion: A Historical Introduction*, Johns Hopkins University Press, 2002, p. 7

(To aver is to state, to maintain.)

95e. Machiavelli was a master of **rhetoric**. He had studied the classics and knew that no amount of reasoning is as powerful as an example, a story, a narrative. He found a masterful story, which would surely touch the hearts of the citizens assembled in the Great Council. He harked back to the fall of Constantinople to the Turks in 1453. The emperor,

Machiavelli wrote, summoned all the citizens to ask them for money and help against the terrible enemy drawing near. The citizenry "ridiculed him." Finally, the Turks laid siege to the city, and as soon as the citizens of Constantinople heard the cannonballs pounding against their walls and the cries of the Turkish soldiers, they ran wailing to the emperor, their pockets full of money. He spurned them with these words: "Go and die with this money, since you have not wished to live without it."

Maurizio Viroli, *Niccolo's Smile: A Biography of Machiavelli*, Farrar, Straus and Giroux, 2000, p. 70

Comment

Viroli is using *rhetoric* in its classical sense to mean the study of persuasive speaking and writing. When he says Machiavelli was a master of rhetoric, he means Machiavelli was a skillful speaker who could persuade the people of Florence by telling them exactly the right story. He does not mean Machiavelli used exaggerated language insincerely.

rhetorical question. a question that is not a real question, not a request for information, but is asked in order to make a point. "Are you going to take all day to make that sandwich?"

95f. That he himself [Muhammad], unschooled to the extent that he was unlettered (*ummi*) and could barely write his name, could have produced a book that provides the ground plan of all knowledge and at the same time is grammatically perfect and without poetic peer— this, Muhammad, and with him all Muslims, are convinced defies belief. He put the point in a **rhetorical** question: "Do you ask for a greater miracle than this, O unbelieving people, than to have your language chosen as the language of that incomparable Book, one piece of which puts all your golden poetry to shame?"

Huston Smith, "Islam," in John Miller and Aaron Kenedi, eds., *Inside Islam*, Marlowe and Company, 2002, p. 20

96. irony.

96b. Unless scientists discover a way to delay the disease [Alzheimer's], some 7.7 million people are expected to have it by 2030, the report says. By 2050, that toll could reach 16 million.

Why? **Ironically**, in fighting heart disease, cancer and other diseases, "we're keeping people alive so they can live long enough to get Alzheimer's disease," explains [Alzheimer's] association vice president Steve McConnell....

No one knows what causes Alzheimer's creeping brain degeneration. It gradually robs sufferers of their memories and ability to care for themselves, eventually killing them.

Lauren Neergaard, Alzheimer's Hits 5 M, *AM New York*, 3/21/07

96c. Is there not something deeply **ironic**, we might ask, about the international publishing success of a book entitled The Art of Happiness: A Handbook for Living, written by a Buddhist? Its author, the Dalai Lama, is by all accounts a wise and kindly man. But the fundamental revelation of the Buddha, the first of his "Four Noble Truths," is that all life is suffering. Somehow this seems to have been forgotten.

Darrin M. McMahon, *Happiness: A History*, Atlantic Monthly Press, 2006, p. 471

96d. [Adam] Smith's case for the morality of capitalism is based largely on its social consequences; it has nothing to do with the virtuous motives of entrepreneurs....Smith's confidence lies not in the character of businessmen but in the force of competition and its effect on the behavior of people in business. Smith argues that competition is the "invisible hand" that compels the businessman to devote his energies to supplying the best possible product at the lowest possible price. So greed leads to empathy. **Ironically**, the businessman is driven by his motive of self-love to seek to meet the needs and wants of others. Even more remarkable, by pursuing his own interest the businessman advances the welfare of society more effectively than when he tries to do so directly.

Dinesh D'Souza, *The Virtue of Prosperity: Finding Values in an Age of Techno-Affluence*, The Free Press, 2000, p. 117

Comment

This list of key terms should help you spot tricky words. And it reveals at least two ways in which words can cause problems in communication. They can fail to mean anything specific, so you are left wondering what the message is. And they can mean too much, so to speak; they can carry extra emotional baggage that gets in the way of clear understanding. Ambiguous and vague words fit in the first category. Imagine that you get a postcard from a friend and it says, "The beach is cool. Wish you were here." Does your friend mean the beach is fun and hip, or that the temperature is low? You can't be sure what the message is.

Other words mean too much. People use loaded terms when they not only want to describe something, but they want to make you feel what they feel about it as well. For example, one person might describe the U.S. military action in Iraq in 2003 as "an unprovoked assault on a sovereign country," while another person describes it as "a courageous liberation of an oppressed people." Both people can even agree on the verifiable facts. But they have different opinions and feelings about the facts, and they use words to convey those feelings. Another example of meaning too much is *to characterize*. Questionable characterizations are like loaded terms. They try to seduce you into seeing things in a one-sided way.

Rhetoric often commits both sins: it's vague, without any real substance, but it sounds good and generates strong responses in the audience. If a politician says he stands up for hard-working people, everyone cheers. But what does that mean, exactly? Everyone thinks of himself or herself as hard working.

Irony is like ambiguity; an ironic statement has two meanings: the superficial meaning, and the opposite meaning that the writer intends. For example, a teacher may be repetitive and speak in a monotone and put students to sleep. If I say the teacher is "a real dynamo," I'm being ironic. The superficial meaning of "dynamo" in this context is *energetic, dynamic, electrifying*, but what I mean is the opposite. Irony is only a problem when the audience doesn't understand that the writer is being ironic.

Part 3. Applying the Words

91. ambiguous
92. vague
93. loaded term
94. to characterize
95. rhetoric
96. irony

Exercise 1:   Choose the Best Word
For each sentence, choose the best word (or an appropriate form of the word) to fill in the blank.

1. The teacher said, "Write a paper about something in the news," but that's so _____ no one knew what she wanted.
2. The editorial called the corporation "a predator," but the spokesperson rejected the _____.
3. Bob was using _____ when he said he thought the history teacher should assign more reading.
4. The principal's statement of "support" for our club was _____ because we thought he would give us funds, but he only made a speech.
5. The Dean shouldn't have called George "a slacker." He should stick to the facts and avoid _____.
6. The Mayor used a lot of patriotic words like "duty" and "freedom" and "the American way," but I think it's all just _____ because he hasn't made any sacrifices himself.

Exercise 2:   Apply the Words
Read each example and answer the questions that follow.

1. Two different meanings of the word "theory" underlie the effort to frame intelligent design and Darwinian evolution as alternative scientific theories.

In popular usage, a theory is a speculation, not necessarily supported by evidence, and only in that sense is intelligent design a theory.

In science, a theory is a coherent and consistent way to account for a wide array of observations and experimental results. It also generates testable predictions. When the explanatory and predictive power of a theory becomes overwhelming, it can be regarded as fact.

Darwinian evolution has long since passed that test and is solidly established as the foundation of modern biology.

Even the most well-established scientific theory can be disproved by new contradictory evidence. It cannot be overturned, nor should it be challenged as an alternative, by a speculation based on religion.

EW, Letters: The Scopes Trial, Echoed in Dover, Pa., *New York Times*, 9/28/05

The writer says the word *theory* is ambiguous. How are the two meanings of the word different?

2. Consider a verbal description of the effect of gravity: drop a ball, and it will fall.

That is a true enough fact, but fuzzy in the way that frustrates scientists. How fast does the ball fall? Does it fall at a constant rate, or accelerate? Would a heavier ball fall faster? More words, more sentences could provide details, swelling into an unwieldy yet still incomplete paragraph.

The wonder of mathematics is that it captures precisely in a few symbols what can only be described clumsily with many words. Those symbols, strung together in meaningful order, make equations—which in turn constitute the world's most concise and reliable body of knowledge.

Kenneth Chang, What Makes an Equation Beautiful, *New York Times*, 10/24/04

One of Chang's two questions—"How fast does the ball fall?" and "Does it fall at a constant rate, or accelerate?"—shows that the verbal description is vague, and one shows that it is ambiguous. Which is which?

3. Re: the June 25 front-page story, "Off the Hook," regarding the decision by the Court of Appeals that New York's death penalty statute is unconstitutional. The headline suggests that the four men on death row will be getting away with something as a result of that decision. That is far from true. They will spend the rest of their lives behind bars, with no possibility of parole. Anyone who has spent a single day in prison knows that the prospect of living out the rest of one's life there is an extraordinary punishment. For some, it is literally a fate worse than death.

You do a disservice to your readers by suggesting that the high court's decision in any way exonerates the men on death row or gives them a windfall. The Court declared that the law used to send those men to death row is unconstitutional, not that they did not deserve the harshest punishment the law allows.

DH, Letters: Not Off the Hook, *AM New York*, 6/28/04

Why does DH believe that "off the hook" is a loaded term (or loaded phrase)?

4. Walter Dellinger, a law professor at Duke, said, "It's not legitimate to produce a legal opinion that fails even to cite the most relevant landmark Supreme Court precedent."

Douglass Cassel, a law professor at Northwestern, went further. "That's not just poor judgment," he said. "That's incompetence."

Adam Liptak, Legal Scholars Criticize Memos on Torture, *New York Times*, 6/25/04

Cassel rejects one characterization of the judge's opinion and prefers another. Do you think the two characterizations are really different? How?

5. Giving some talks in Norway, I asked a professor, one of my hosts, why he and three others were listed as Fascists in a student handout. What had they done in Nazi times? Another host told me: one had been in a concentration camp; two others had been in the underground, one of them having helped the British raiders sabotage the Nazi heavy water project; the fourth had escaped to England and joined the Norwegian democratic armed forces. They had all, however, prevented or deplored a more recent student disruption.

Robert Conquest, *The Dragons of Expectation*, W. W. Norton, 2005, p. 31

It is ironic that the student handout used the loaded term *Fascist* to characterize the professors, who had fought against the real Fascists in World War II. Does the students' use of the term fit the definition of *rhetoric*, or is it different from rhetoric?

6. I am reminded of a dispiriting moment in a cello lesson with my teacher, Mr. Herbert Withers. He was eighty-three years old, and I was eleven. I had tried to play a passage, but I couldn't make it work. I tried again, and it didn't work, and a third time, and I was no more successful. I remember making a frustrated grimace and putting down my bow. The elderly Mr. Withers leaned over me and whispered, "What? You've been practicing it for three minutes, and you *still* can't play it?"

Rosamund Stone Zander, Benjamin Zander, *The Art of Possibility: Transforming Professional and Personal Life*, Penguin, 2000, p. 5

How would you sum up the message that the cello teacher intended to convey to his student?

7. We cannot close our eyes to the fact that the great majority of the people can scarcely have any well-founded judgment concerning the correctness of certain important general ideas or doctrines. Therefore, the word "belief" can for this majority not mean "perceiving the truth of something" but can only be understood as "taking this as the basis for life." One can easily understand that this second kind of belief is much firmer, is much more fixed than the first one, that it can persist

even against immediate contradicting experience and can therefore not be shaken by added scientific knowledge.

Werner Heisenberg, "Science and Culture," in W. Warren Wagar, ed., *Science, Faith, and Man: European Thought Since 1914*, Walker and Company, 1968, pp. 29–30

Is Heisenberg saying the word *belief* is ambiguous or vague?

8. The words "existential" and "empirical" remain hazy, as much as Perl loves and uses them. The verb "existentialize" doesn't exist in my dictionary, and I groped to attach meanings to such nuanced variations of the concept as "in their wackily existentialist way" and the report that some Buckminster Fuller domes were sent out "into the world in a pure, almost existentialized form." *Almost* existential-ized—an unlucky near miss!

John Updike, Metropolitan Art, review of Jed Perl, New Art City, *New York Times Book Review*, 10/16/05

The words *existential* and *existentialist* are very difficult to define, and therefore difficult to apply to moods, gestures, or art. They are vague. Do you think vague words are useful? Or are they just excuses for lazy writing and a failure to find a more exact, descriptive word?

9. The fact is that the essential nature of Riverdale is being changed by overdevelopment. This is a statement of fact, and one can look at that fact as positive or negative.

I look at it as negative. If development continues unchecked, say bye-bye to the way of life you are all used to here. It simply will not exist anymore.

MG, Letters: The Building Boom in Riverdale, *Riverdale Press*, 8/1/04

The writer says his comment is strictly factual and neutral; the change could be positive or negative. Do you think the word "overdevelopment" can be either positive or negative? Or is it loaded?

10. It is not accurate to refer to social security as a "massive entitle-ment" program as it was stated in the Associated Press article on Greenspan's remarks about this program. Framing the issue in this way is dishonest and manipulative.

Social Security is rather an insurance program—the gem of Franklin D. Roosevelt New Deal Programs. It is based on paying it forward. People who are presently working are paying the benefits of those who have retired.

When they retire, their benefits will be paid by those who are work-ing. It is not an entitlement when we have paid into the system.

EF, Letters: Social Security Facts, *AM New York*, 2/23/05

The writer mentions two ways of characterizing the Social Security system. What are they? Which is better?

11. When the Saudi religious police objected to the use of a plus sign instead of an ampersand in a company's name because it resembled a Christian cross, a writer for the region's main newspaper, Al-Medina, suggested that perhaps the symbol should be replaced with a "tasteful Islamic crescent" in the country's math books.

William Grimes, A Glimpse of Forces Confronting Saudi Rule, *New York Times*, 8/17/05

How can we decide whether the writer for Al-Medina was being sincere or was being ironic? Do you think he or she was being sincere or ironic?

12. There are a lot of empty stores along West 231st Street.... We've been told we shouldn't blame the landlords for the higher rents they charged, that "they're looking for the chains that can pay the higher rents. It's the American way."

I always thought small business was the American way....

ND, Letters, 231st Street Is Becoming a Ghost Town, *The Riverdale Press*, 7/22/04

Rhetoric is language that is usually exaggerated, insincere, and meaningless. Which of these three characteristics of rhetoric best applies to the phrase "the American way" in ND's letter?

Exercise 3:   Analyzing Arguments

1. The following passage is about brainwashing. More specifically, it is about the idea of brainwashing. Does the idea make sense? Or is so-called "brainwashing" a mysterious process that can never be defined? The writer, Zablocki, defends the idea. He says the critics ("debunkers") have misunderstood the theory, and therefore their criticism misses its mark. (There is a word for this: the "straw man" mistake. Zablocki says the critics are attacking a "straw man," i.e., a weak substitute they have created, rather than the real theory.) The misunderstanding occurs because a key word is ambiguous. What is the key word, and what are its two meanings? What is the (weak) theory the debunkers are attacking? What is the real theory, according to the writer?

> Would-be debunkers of the brainwashing concept have argued that brainwashing theory is not just a theory of ordinary social influence intensified under structural conditions of ideological totalism [or totalitarianism], but is rather a "special" kind of influence theory that alleges that free will can be overwhelmed and individuals brought to a state of mind in which they will comply with charismatic directives involuntarily, having surrendered the capability of saying no. Of course, if a theory of brainwashing really did rely upon such an intrinsically untestable notion, it would be reasonable to reject it outright....
>
> Foundational brainwashing theory has not claimed that subjects are robbed of their free will. Neither the presence nor the absence of free will can ever be proved or disproved. The confusion stems from

the difference between the word *free* as it is used in economics as an antonym for *costly*, and as it is used in philosophy as an antonym for *deterministic*. When brainwashing theory speaks of individuals losing the ability to freely decide to disobey, the word is being used in the economic sense. Brainwashing imposes costs, and when a course of action has costs it is no longer free. The famous statement by Rousseau (1913, p. 3) that 'Man is born free, and everywhere he is in chains,' succinctly expresses the view that socialization can impose severe constraints on human behavior.

Benjamin Zablocki, Towards a Demystified and Disinterested Scientific Theory of Brainwashing, in Benjamin Zablocki and Thomas Robbins, eds., *Misunderstanding Cults: Searching for Objectivity in a Controversial Field*, University of Toronto Press, 2001, pp. 170–171

2. Malcolm Cowley presents an argument about a characterization. What is his conclusion? What reasons does he give to support it?

Yet in spite of their opportunities and their achievements the generation deserved for a long time the adjective that Gertrude Stein had applied to it ["the lost generation"]. The reasons aren't hard to find. It was lost, first of all, because it was uprooted, schooled away and almost wrenched away from its attachment to any region or tradition. It was lost because its training had prepared it for another world than existed after the war (and because the war prepared it only for travel and excitement). It was lost because it tried to live in exile. It was lost because it accepted no older guides to conduct and because it had formed a false picture of society and the writer's place in it. The generation belonged to a period of transition from values already fixed to values that had to be created.

Malcolm Cowley, *Exile's Return: A Literary Odyssey of the 1920s*, Viking, 1951, p. 9

Exercise 4:   Apply the Ideas in Writing

Find a brief story in a newspaper, magazine, or website that you can cut out or copy and give to your teacher. Read the story, and write one or two paragraphs in which you retell the story in your own words. But imagine that you are strongly biased, either against the people in the story or in favor of them. Use *loaded terms* when you retell the story. (For example, if President Bush left Washington, you could say "Bush fled Washington....") *Characterize* the people or events in a slanted way ("the pro-amnesty bill," "the anti-immigrant bill"). Use *rhetoric* to try to manipulate your audience's feelings. You may not change the facts, or make up anything that isn't in the story. However, if you choose your words carefully, you can present a completely misleading, one-sided picture of the same events that the newspaper story reported. It may be helpful to use a thesaurus. Give your teacher the original story and your biased version.

Improving Your Writing 15: Revising

If you have written a first draft, how do you revise it? You can do it the way a pilot and co-pilot prepare to fly an airplane: You can go through a checklist. The pilot and co-pilot say things like, "Fuel tank full?" "Check." "Wing flaps working?" "Check." "Global positioning system turned on?" "Check." (In case you are wondering, I am not a real pilot.) You can ask yourself the following questions—your checklist—and make changes in your draft where necessary. If you can get a "co-pilot" (a friend or classmate) to look over your revised version to make sure you have checked everything, that would be helpful, too.

1. Have you stated a definite thesis, in simple, clear language, near the beginning of the essay?
2. Have you given evidence and reasons that should make your audience agree with your thesis?
3. Should you add anything to make your ideas more appealing or convincing?
4. Should you take out anything because it's irrelevant, or repetitive, to make your essay more unified and clearer?
5. Have you written an introduction and conclusion?
6. Does each paragraph convey one, and only one, main idea?
7. Have you used transition words?
8. Is each of your sentences easy to understand? Does each one sound natural?
9. In each sentence, have you used the best words to express your ideas, or can you think of more accurate, more vivid words?

Going through a checklist takes time. But it's better to race through a rough draft quickly and leave time for your checklist than it is to try to get everything just right the first time around.

Assuming

The words in this chapter are about the relation between the things you say and the other things you don't say but take for granted. For example, you might say, "Quick, help me clean up the living room. Our friends are coming right over." Here, you are giving a reason to clean up the living room, which is that your friends are coming over. But you are taking at least one other statement for granted. You are assuming that your friends will be offended if your living room is not clean, or that they won't want to visit you again (and that you want them to visit again), or that they will think less of you if your living room is a mess.

Taking things for granted like this is a necessary part of communication. We all share a common world, and we don't need to remind each other of basic facts whenever we say something. If you shout to your friend, "Watch out for the bus!" you don't need to add, "If the bus hits you, you will die." Your friend already knows that. Sometimes movie makers put an alien from outer space or a robot among ordinary people, and then get some laughs when the alien or robot doesn't understand the basic things we all take for granted. In an episode of "Star Trek: The Next Generation," the android/robot, Data, observes the conflicts between different families at a wedding and says he is fascinated by this new facet of human behavior he's never seen before. "Please continue the petty bickering," he says. He doesn't realize that petty bickering is ridiculous and humans don't like it, even though that's what they are doing.

$$\boxed{\text{(E) – C}}$$

Figure 16.1
An assumption (E) is a belief you take for granted, which is necessary for your other
beliefs (C). For example, if I believe I will vacation in Hawaii next year, I am assuming
I will have enough money to pay for it, that I will be alive next year, that Hawaii won't be
washed away by a tsunami, and so on.

Your experience with moving buses, friends, the human body, appliances,
and everything else makes up the unspoken background of all the things you
say. Problems arise, however, because people have different experiences. This
is obvious in a movie when a prehistoric caveman gets resurrected in Encino in
1998, but it's actually true for everyone. For example, a young woman might go
to dinner with her boyfriend, and he could be disappointed that she wore her
old sweater. "If you loved me you would dress nicely," he might say. "It's because
I love you that I can be completely relaxed and don't feel like I have to put on
airs," she might say. The boyfriend has some ideas about being in love that he
never explained to her, and she has some different ideas in her background that
she never explained to him.

This relationship between what is openly stated and what is taken for granted
is like the relationship between evidence and a conclusion, except that part of the
evidence—the part taken for granted—is not stated openly. When you shout,
"Watch out for the bus," you are actually shouting a conclusion. The evidence
supporting your conclusion is, "There is a bus coming," and "You do not want to
get hit by a bus." Therefore, "Watch out!" Or you could shout out the evidence—
"There's a bus coming!"—and let the other person supply the missing evidence—
"I don't want to get hit"—and draw the conclusion—"I should move."

Taking things for granted is inevitable, and since people are different, the
resulting confusions and misunderstandings are inevitable as well. But you
can minimize them. An effective thinker can understand what a person says,
and can also figure out what the person must be taking for granted, behind the
scenes, if she says those things. Often a person doesn't even realize herself what
she is taking for granted. So it requires some imagination, putting yourself in
the other person's place, to see the relationship.

Part 1. Definitions

97. to assume. to take something for granted; to believe without evidence.
"You gave Sam advice about how to attract Gail's attention. You're assuming
Sam *wants* to attract Gail's attention."

assumption (noun). a belief that a person takes for granted, usually without stating it, often without realizing it.

Example

97a. The belief that the justice system has been undermined in modern times by plea bargaining is based on the erroneous **assumption** that it is a recent innovation. In fact, as [Charles] Silberman reports, "it has been the dominant means of settling criminal cases for the last century."

Richard Shenkman, *Legends, Lies, and Cherished Myths of American History*, HarperPerennial, 1988, p. 159

98. point of view. the particular way that a person sees a situation, which may be different from other people's way of seeing it; an interpretation. "The coach of the losing team was angry, but from the point of view of the winning coach, the referee was being fair."

Example

98a. Few personalities or events stand without comment in the historical record; contemporary accounts and documents, the so-called original sources, no less than later studies, are written by people with a distinct **point of view** and interpretation of what they see. Problems of interpretation are inseparable from the effort to achieve historical understanding.

J. Kelly Sowards, ed., *Makers of the Western Tradition: Portraits from History*, Third Edition, St. Martin's Press, 1983. p. ix

99. context. the larger situation in which something occurs; the context of a fact or a statement is the other facts or statements related to it. "If you remember that the context of Vicky's statement was a New Year's Eve party, then you can understand that she was joking."

Example

99a. KV's June 28 letter "Blame the GOP" repeats the Democrats' claim that the Reagan administration "supported and helped provide funds to Saddam Hussein."

Any allegation that doesn't at least cite the Iran hostage crisis as the **context** is absolutely dishonest. Most Americans were delighted when Saddam attacked Iran on Sept. 22, 1980. Our hostages were not released until Jan. 20, 1981....

Yes, we looked the other way when Kurds were gassed. But remember that we were traumatized by Iran at that time. We had no choice.

SR, Letters: Liberal Liars, *AM New York*, 6/29/04

100. to interpret. to see something in a certain way, to arrange facts or elements in a way that makes them comprehensible. "One can interpret the painting as a picture of a mountain." "Jill interpreted the senator's remarks to mean that he will introduce a bill to lower taxes." "According to the Freudian interpretation, Hamlet was in love with his mother."

interpretation (noun). one way of understanding something, a way of putting something into context, or seeing a pattern among parts, that makes the thing meaningful and comprehensible.

Example

100a. Citing the ancient Greek philosopher Epictetus, and the insight that it is not the events in our lives that cause us suffering but the way we **interpret** them, [Albert] Ellis sees much of our unhappiness as based on irrational assumptions, like demanding perfection from yourself and others.

Daniel Duane, The Socratic Shrink, *New York Times Magazine*, 3/21/04

101. inconsistent. in conflict; one statement is inconsistent with another if they cannot both be true at the same time. By extension we can say people's desires or actions are inconsistent. "He admitted that he cheated on the test, but then claimed that he is always honest. Those statements are inconsistent." "His love of chocolate is inconsistent with his desire to lose weight." "Her actions were inconsistent with her words."

Example

101a. See what gross **inconsistency** is tolerated. I have heard some of my townsmen say, "I should like to have them order me out to help put down an insurrection of the slaves, or to march to Mexico—see if I would go"; and yet these very men have each directly by their allegiance and so indirectly, at least by their money, furnished a substitute. The soldier is applauded who refuses to serve in an unjust war by those who do not refuse to sustain the unjust government which makes the war.

Henry David Thoreau, Civil Disobedience, in Robert A. Goldwin, ed., *On Civil Disobedience: Essays Old and New*, Rand McNally, 1969, p. 17

102. to contradict. to say the opposite; one statement contradicts another if they cannot both be true at the same time; contradictory statements are inconsistent. "Tommy's claim of innocence was contradicted by the clerk's statement that he saw Tommy put the radio in his jacket pocket and leave the store."

Sometimes people contradict themselves. "Jones said he was a firm democrat, but he contradicted himself when he added that he did not believe every adult citizen should be allowed to vote."

contradictory (adj.). the characteristic of two statements that cannot both be true, or the characteristic of one statement that contradicts another. "Simon's testimony on Monday and Tuesday was contradictory." "Bell said no one was in the house, but Walker made a contradictory claim."

(Logicians define *contradictory* more narrowly as statements that cannot both be true *and* cannot both be false either. For example, "Rachel is pregnant" and "Rachel is not pregnant" are contradictory in this sense of the word.)

Example

102a. One young man deployed as a human shield during the armed assault against the U.S. Consulate here said from his hospital bed that the most vivid moment came when the gunman who had been firing over the man's shoulder ordered him to raise his hands and scream "God is Great!"...Eight men were used as shields for one to two hours on Monday, survivors in King Fahd hospital said....

The description of what happened inside the consulate compound **contradicts** statements by officials in the State Department and the Saudi Embassy in Washington that no hostages were taken during the three-hour attack.

Neil McFarquhar, Survivors of Jidda Attack Tell of Human Shields, *International Herald Tribune*, 12/8/04

Test Yourself

Match each word with its definition.

97. to assume
98. point of view
99. context
100. to interpret
101. inconsistent
102. to contradict

a. in conflict; two statements that cannot both be true at the same time
b. to take something for granted; to believe without evidence
c. the larger situation in which something occurs; the causes and effects of something
d. the particular way that a person sees a situation, which may be different from other people's way of seeing it
e. to say the opposite; to deny by asserting the opposite of what another says
f. to see something in a certain way, to arrange facts or elements in a way that makes them comprehensible

Part 2. Understanding the Meaning

97. to assume

97b. [Some vertebrae in the spine are called "sacral vertebrae," from the word "sacred."] Actually no one is certain why they are named as they are. The easiest **assumption** is that they had some special significance in Roman religious rites, but that is just an easy **assumption**, and it is not necessarily true.

Isaac Asimov, *The Human Body: Its Structure and Operation*, New American Library, 1963, p. 44

97c. Whenever this magazine runs an article such as "Red Planet Blues" (p. 62) or "Go Somewhere!" (April 2002) we receive letters protesting that our interest in a Mars mission is misguided. A Mars mission, the argument goes, will squander tens of billions of dollars better spent on problems here on earth. This is a hopeful but unconvincing argument. It **assumes** that money not spent by Washington on one thing will be intelligently diverted to another, more important thing. It assumes proportionality in matters budgetary. Call me cynical, but that is not my understanding of the horse trading and porkbarrelling that passes for money minding on Capitol Hill.

Scott Mowbray, Mars Is Not a Money Issue, *Popular Science*, July, 03, p. 6

Question: The editor of Popular Science says critics of a Mars mission present an argument. The conclusion of the argument is that money spent on a Mars mission is wasted (squandered). On what premise or premises do the critics base their conclusion? Do you agree that it is a false assumption?

97d. [T]here is another such **assumption** that serves as perhaps the biggest single obstacle to a clear understanding of what the climate crisis is all about. Many people today still **assume**—mistakenly—that the Earth is so big that we human beings cannot possibly have any major impact on the way our planet's ecological system operates. That assertion may have been true at one time, but it's not the case anymore. We have grown so numerous and our technologies have become so powerful that we are now capable of having a significant influence on many parts of the Earth's environment.

Al Gore, *An Inconvenient Truth*, Rodale, 2006, p. 22

98. point of view

98b. In any good story there should always be two sides. But what about the truth? In the stories on Private Jessica Lynch, there is the American **point of view** of what happened and then there is the Iraqi **point of view.** In the case of Private Lynch, who was captured and then rescued during the recent Iraq War, we can't tell what is the truth. The stories do have all the makings of a dramatic movie, however.

From the American viewpoint, Private Lynch was mistreated and tortured in her stay at Saddam Hospital. Private Lynch had injuries to her right and left legs, her right arm and her spine. She had several operations. At one time, she had a temperature of 104 F. The

Figure 16.2
Former Vice President Al Gore says many people dismiss global warming because they assume that the earth is so large that humanity cannot change it. *Source:* © *Laurin Rinder/ Shutterstock*

Americans also stated that while in the custody of the Iraqis, she was starved and only survived because she was fed orange juice and crackers. But, surprisingly, Private Lynch had gained weight.

From the Iraqi **point of view,** Private Lynch was treated like a goddess. She was given supplies that the Iraqis were short of. According to the Iraqis, Private Lynch only had compound fractures to her two legs and a deep cut on her head. She was given more than enough food to stay alive. In fact, the Iraqis said they gave her more food than any other patient in the hospital even though they were low on food. An Iraqi doctor tried to return Private Lynch to the US troops, but he had to retreat when the Americans fired at his ambulance. The nurse that looked after Private Lynch said that she felt more like a mother than a nurse to her. They even gave Private Lynch a rare special bed because she was developing a bedsore.

BO, Grade 11, Are the Stories True? *Hamilton Spectator* (Ontario, Canada), 6/13/03

98c. Unfortunately, the very format of the history textbook compels distortions; it presumes that a single book can render objective and decisive judgment on hundreds or thousands of controversial issues. In fact, the only sure truths in the books are dates and names (and sometimes the textbooks get those wrong). Beyond that, there is seldom, if ever, a single interpretation of events on which all reputable historians agree. The soul of historical research is debate, but that sense of uncertainty and contingency seldom finds its way into textbooks. By its nature, the textbook must pretend that its condensation of events and its presentation of their meaning are correct. In reality, every textbook has a **point of view**, despite a façade of neutrality; the authors and editors select some interpretations and reject others, choose certain events as important and ignore others as unimportant. Even when they insert sidebars with point and counterpoint on a few issues, they give the false impression that all other issues are settled when they are not. The pretense of objectivity and authority is, at bottom, just that: a pretense.

Diane Ravitch, *The Language Police: How Pressure Groups Restrict What Students Should Learn*, Vintage, 2003, p. 134

(*Façade* literally means the front of a building, but writers often use it to mean a superficial appearance of something, which may hide a different reality.)

99. context

99b. When 20,000 to 25,000 people are being murdered every year, you've got a problem. It's not a huge problem in the **context** of death in America; more than 2.25 million of us die every year from all causes—including 30,000 to 40,000 from AIDS, 40,000 or so in automobile accidents and about 30,000 as a result of suicide.

But even in that **context**, murder is a serious problem.

Richard Harwood, The Prevalence of Guns Contributes to Violent Crime, in William Dudley, ed., *Opposing Viewpoints in Social Issues*, Greenhaven Press, 2000, p. 22

99c. Second, some argue that while terrorist acts deserve to be punished or pre-empted, we also need to look at their **context** and causes. They do not occur in a historical and moral vacuum. Their agents are human beings like the rest of us, a mixture of good and evil, and do not enjoy throwing away their lives and turning their wives into widows and children into orphans. They risk their lives in terrorist acts because they feel humiliated, trampled upon, unjustly treated, and see no other way of redressing their grievances. Rather than concentrate only on their reprehensible deeds, we must address their deeper causes.

Bhikhu Parekh, Terrorism or Intercultural Dialogue, in Ken Booth and Tim Dunne, eds., *Worlds in Collision: Terror and the Future of Global Order*, Palgrave Macmillan, 2002, p. 270

99d. Shocking footage from Jay-Z's concert film "Backstage" may come back to haunt him in his retirement. In a clip from a DVD of the 2000 documentary...Jay-Z walks down a hallway with his entourage and meets a petite woman who appears to have a camera.

Figure 16.3
This street – Park Avenue in Manhattan – looks different from different points of view. *Source A: © emin kuliyev/Shutterstock Source B: © rfx/Shutterstock*

The clip shows Jay-Z appear to get angry, then slap and shove the woman directly in the face. As he strikes her, a woman's voice yells out, "Chill! Come on, just chill!" ...

But Jay-Z's spokeswoman told us: "The person in that video is someone who he has worked with for years, and they are very close, and for it to be excerpted like that is an insult. That footage was taken completely **out of context**. They were just horsing around."

George Rush and Joanna Molloy, In DVD, Jay-Z a Hitmaker, *Daily News* (New York), 6/22/04

Question: In Example 99b, the context for understanding the number of murders in America is objective circumstances, i.e., the numbers of deaths from AIDS, accidents, and suicides. In Example 99c, the context for understanding terrorist acts is the subjective feelings of the terrorists, feelings of humiliation and so on. In Example 99d, according to Jay-Z's spokeswoman, is the necessary context for understanding Jay-Z's action objective circumstances or subjective feelings?

100. to interpret

100b. [F]acts and figures do not speak for themselves. For all their stubbornness, they are accommodating enough to allow a number of different **interpretations**—and there are always enough of them around to support almost any theory.

Herbert J. Muller, What Science Is, in George Levine and Owen Thomas, eds. *The Scientist vs. the Humanist*, W. W. Norton and Co., 1963, p. 2

100c. Between 1785 and 1840 the production of cotton goods for the home market increased ten times more rapidly than did population. An equally well-attested, if somewhat more limited, increase is to be seen in the output of soap and candles; and it is possible to infer similar increases in the production of a wide range of household articles from pots and pans to furniture and furnishings. It would be unwise to **interpret** this general expansion in output as synonymous with an equivalent increase in working-class consumption. The upper and middle class, no doubt, took a disproportionate share of the products as they did with the profits of industrialization.

A. J. Taylor, Industrialization and the Standard of Living, in John C. Rule, David L. Dowd, and John L. Snell, eds., *Critical Issues in History, 1648 to the Present*, D. C. Heath and Co., 1967, p. 635

100d. In the story of Ahab and his crew, and the one articulate antagonist, Starbuck, we discover a grimly joined inner battle, a searing and terrible symbolic representation of a profound conflict in the soul of man. There is no mistaking Melville's intent so to generalize. There is only the necessary search for applicability.

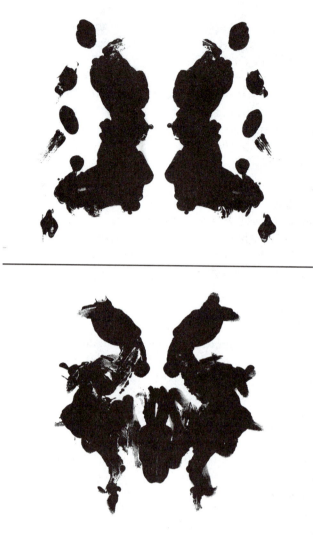

Figure 16.4
Psychologists ask a person to interpret inkblots – tell them what he or she sees – and the interpretations reveal something about the person's ways of dealing with the world. *Source:* © *Dvirus/Shutterstock*

As with *Hamlet*, where three hundred years have not sufficed for the emergence of a definitive thematic **interpretation**, we have here a host of contenders for authoritative explication. This can mean one of two things: that the text, due to confusion in concept or execution, is at fault; or that, as a sort of master metaphor, it embodies an archetypal situation capable of a considerable variation of perfectly relevant responses or "meanings."

John Parke, "Seven Moby Dicks," in Herman Melville, *Moby Dick*, edited by Charles Child Walcutt, Bantam, 1981, p. 560

(An archetype is an original example, upon which later reproductions are based. An archetypal situation is a basic type of situation, such as a couple in love, children rebelling against parents, a leader emerging from a group, and so on.)

Comment

The general meaning of "interpret" is to make comprehensible, to find the meaning of something, but there are different ways to do that. Perhaps the most basic kind of interpretation is that of an "interpreter," that is, a person who translates one language into another. Another way to interpret something is to classify it, to figure out what type of thing it is. "We should interpret the events of the Prague Spring of 1968 as a genuine revolution." "He interpreted her remark as a compliment."

On the other hand, you can interpret an event by relating it to earlier or later events. "General Brown interpreted the skirmish as the first step in a broad western offensive." If the skirmish is a part of a larger development, and has predictable consequences, then it makes sense and we know how to respond to it. "Malcolm was puzzled by the greenish color of the fluid, but Dr. Black interpreted it as the result of the rapid growth of algae." If we know the cause of something, we feel that we understand it.

We often interpret people's actions by relating them to prior intentions, or beliefs, or the goals they hope to achieve. "Now I understand why Charlie is studying like crazy: he wants to get an A in the course." "Regina spoke up in class today because she believes so strongly in women's rights."

Notice that in all these cases to interpret something is to put it into a context. It is to see a relationship between the thing interpreted and other things. Maybe the relationship is classification, or cause and effect, or being an example of a generalization. But understanding usually means making logical connections. (That's another reason that learning these key words—which are all about logical connections—is so useful.)

101. inconsistent

101b. Do American news viewers want it both ways: objective but at the same time skewed? A lengthy study from the Pew Research Center for the People and the Press finds that viewers seem to want it that way.

Pew separated viewers by the newscasts they usually watched and then asked loyal viewers of broadcast networks, CNN or Fox News how they think news organizations represent a U.S. point of view.

Nearly two-thirds, 64% of just over 1,200 respondents to the phone survey in late June and early July, said they preferred news coverage of the war on terrorism to be neutral, while 29% said they preferred pro-American coverage.

Yet about three-quarters of all polled viewers of TV news agreed with the statement that "it is good that news organizations take a pro-American point of view."

Pew Research Center Editor Carroll Doherty said, "It's easy to understand why people see these things as **inconsistent**. And it's also true that the public can often hold two seemingly conflicting opinions at the same time."

Dan Trigoboff, Do Americans Want Flag-Waving News?; Pew News Review Picks up Mixed Signals, *Broadcasting and Cable*, July 21, 2003

Question: Here are two statements: (a) I prefer news coverage of the war on terrorism to be neutral; (b) I think it is good that news organizations take a pro-American point of view. Do you think these two statements are inconsistent?

101c. Since the publication of my religious books, *Living Faith* and *Sources of Strength*, I have been asked whether my Christian beliefs ever conflicted with my secular duties as president. There were a few **inconsistencies**, but I always honored my oath to "preserve, protect, and defend the Constitution of the United States." For instance, I have never believed that Jesus Christ would approve either abortions or the death penalty, but I obeyed such Supreme Court decisions to the best of my ability, at the same time attempting to minimize what I considered to be their adverse impact.

Jimmy Carter, *Our Endangered Values: America's Moral Crisis*, Simon and Schuster, 2005, p. 57

101d. Karl Marx, who was not only on the side of the worker but wanted to see him inherit the earth, asserted that all value was created by labor. His effort to support this assertion with a theoretical justification exhibits clearly—it is perhaps the most striking example—the **inconsistency** in Dialectical Materialism between the tendency to represent everything as relative, every system of economics as an ideology projected by special class interests, and the impulse to establish principles with some more general sort of validity, upon which one's own conduct may be based.

Edmund Wilson, *To the Finland Station*, Anchor, 1953, p. 299

102. to contradict

102b. Many who have studied the lives and deaths of certain Roman emperors may perhaps believe that they provide examples **contradicting** my opinion; some emperors who led consistently worthy lives, and showed strength of character, none the less fell from power, or were even done to death by their own men who conspired against them.

Niccolo Machiavelli, trans. George Bull, *The Prince*, Penguin, 1999 [originally 1514], p. 61

102c. When the different pieces of the mind are not in harmony, a condition called cognitive dissonance results....How does this

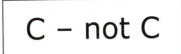

Figure 16.5
A contradiction is two beliefs that cannot both be true at the same time.

happen? Consider these statements: (1) I know cigarette smoking causes cancer; (2) I smoke. Rational people would be uncomfortable trying to live with this **contradiction**. They can solve the problem in several ways: giving up smoking; considering cancer not such a bad thing; assuming that a cure will be found by the time they get the disease; or, in the extreme, simply ignoring the evidence.

Robert Ornstein, *Multimind*, Houghton Mifflin, 1986, p. 83

Question: Statements (1) and (2) in Ornstein's example can both be true at the same time, so, by themselves, they are not contradictory. But Ornstein assumes that most people have some *other* basic desires and beliefs, e.g., "people with cancer do not live long." What other belief or desire can you add that would reveal the contradiction in a person's mind who held all of them?

102d. As reported in your Nov. 8 edition, the government has now come out with a report showing that the number of women who were incarcerated last year rose 3.6% from 2003. Since 1995, the number of women in prison rose by 48%, while the male population during that time grew by 29%.

Wasn't it just a couple of weeks ago that the government also released statistics showing how far crime has come down in this time? That the country is at an all time low in crime? There is a clear **contradiction** here, where on the one hand the government is reporting crime is down while the number of people in prison continues to soar at an alarming rate. If crime is down, how can the prison population rise at such a high rate? The Justice Department statistics for the crime rate percentage has [sic] got to be far off from the actual figures. Would the Justice Department admit that the high number of people they are incarcerating are innocent? I don't think so. Crime in this period has not dropped as far as the number of people who are being incarcerated. Therefore, crimes are still being committed.

You can't be saying crime is down to the lowest it's been in years, when the prison population is higher than it's ever been in this country. The numbers don't add up.

BH, Letters: Doesn't Add Up, *AM New York*, 11/16/04

Question: Here are two statements: "The number of crimes committed has declined over the past five years"; "The number of people convicted and imprisoned has increased over the past five years." Do you agree with the writer that these two statements are contradictory?

Comment

Inconsistencies and contradictions are lapses in thinking and mistakes you want to avoid. If you say things that are inconsistent, people will not be able to understand you and will simply not believe what you say. Suppose a wife says, "Yes, I told my friends what you wrote in your diary, and I do respect your privacy." The inconsistency is confusing. Which is it? If the person reveals secrets, then she doesn't respect the husband's privacy, and if she respects the husband's privacy, then she wouldn't reveal personal secrets. If you contradict yourself by saying inconsistent things, most people will decide that you are simply lying and they won't trust you.

People in general are honest and don't contradict themselves like this, because the inconsistency is so obvious. But we all make many assumptions that we aren't aware of, and they may not fit together logically. We all have a point of view on various matters, and that point of view includes assumptions we may not have thought about. That is inevitable. Problems come up, however, when some of the assumptions we make are inconsistent. For example, my friend Smith is a staunch Democrat who firmly believes in equal opportunity. When he reads about rundown inner city schools for minorities and new, well equipped schools for white people in the suburbs, it makes his blood boil. He is assuming that all people should have access to similar schools. Otherwise opportunities aren't equal. But when he thinks of his own beautiful children, he naturally wants the very best education for them that he can get. So he sends them to a private school. He assumes that parents should give their children the best opportunities they can, including the best schools they can afford. It's a moral duty. Both of Smith's assumptions sound reasonable. But they are inconsistent. If it's true that all children should have access to similar schools, then it can't be true that Smith's children should have access to superior schools.

Smith isn't aware of the contradiction in his assumptions. But if it comes out in conversations with others, then he will be in the same position as the partner who told secrets. He will have to find some way to reconcile the two beliefs, or give up one of them. He can't hold on to inconsistent beliefs for long, because people will not believe or trust a person who contradicts himself. Moreover, when Smith explicitly sees that his beliefs are contradictory, he won't be able to hold both of them in his mind. It would be like believing that Rachel is pregnant and not pregnant at the same time.

I've described an imaginary Democrat, but it would be just as easy to find inconsistencies in the assumptions that Republicans make. And we all make inconsistent assumptions in many areas besides politics. Our views of religion, human nature, happiness, work, personal relationships, and other areas are filled with contradictory assumptions we make. Thinking clearly about what you believe and trying to make the beliefs fit together is a lifelong challenge. And it's a lot of fun!

Part 3. Applying the Words

97. to assume
98. point of view
99. context
100. to interpret
101. inconsistent
102. to contradict

Exercise 1: Choose the Best Word

For each sentence, choose the best word (or an appropriate form of the word) to fill in the blank.

a. The story is about the parents' trials with baby-sitters, but it's told by the six-year-old daughter. She has a different _____.
b. I see that Gretchen is carrying her umbrella. She _____ it will rain today.
c. The President wants to increase spending and lower taxes at the same time, but I think those two goals are _____.
d. Remember that the professor was explaining all sides in a vigorous class discussion, and in that _____, the statement shouldn't be seen as sexist or offensive.
e. Mark knew that Diana wanted to leave the party, because after 20 years of marriage he could _____ her body language.
f. At first the suspect said he didn't own a gun, but when shown the weapon, he _____ himself and said he only owned one gun.

Exercise 2: Apply the Words

Read each example and answer the questions that follow.

> 1. We (in the sense of human beings) travel and explore the world, carrying with us some "background books." These need not accompany us physically; the point is that we travel with preconceived notions of the world, derived from our cultural tradition. In a very curious sense we travel knowing in advance what we are on the verge of discovering, because past reading has told us what we are supposed to discover. In other words, the influence of these background books is such that, irrespective of what travelers discover and see, they will interpret and explain everything in terms of these books.
>
> Umberto Eco, *Serendipities: Language and Lunacy*, Columbia University Press, 1998, p. 54

Eco says we make assumptions when we travel. Where do the assumptions come from? How do they influence us?

2. The Vietnamese villager on whose house a bomb falls may see the war in Vietnam as one producing destruction of civilians. The Vietcong soldier may see it as a struggle against imperialism. The supporter of the government in Saigon may see it as an effort to prevent Communist tyranny. The executive in Washington may see it as part of an effort to impede progress of totalitarianism and to protect American strategic interests. It is possible for all these perceptions to be correct simultaneously, depending upon the definitions of the key terms and appropriate qualifications. It is, moreover, possible for someone to write an account of the war that comprehends these different frameworks and places them in perspective....

Morton A. Kaplan, *On Historical and Political Knowing: An Inquiry into Some Problems of Universal Law and Human Freedom*, University of Chicago Press, 1971, p. 85

How many different points of view does Kaplan mention?

3. Even the FBI kept track of Harvey, clipping occasional articles about the pathologist and Einstein's brain, and adding them to the secret file on Einstein. If J. Edgar Hoover [director of the FBI] thought Albert Einstein was dangerous alive, it's quite possible he also found him dangerous in death. After all, the idea of Einstein's brain finding its way to the Soviet Union, to the Brain Institute, where Lenin's brain had already been sliced, diced, and secretly studied, would have been chilling in a Cold War environment where anything from a Martian invasion to a world-death machine seemed as immediately possible as the cloning of the world's greatest brain.

Michael Paterniti, *Driving Mr. Albert: A Trip Across America with Einstein's Brain*, The Dial Press, 2000, p. 63

J. Edgar Hoover was working in the context of the Cold War between the United States and the Soviet Union. How does that context help explain Hoover's actions, according to Paterniti?

4. In the last chapter we saw how, by looking at the policies of the IMF [International Monetary Fund] *as if* the organization was pursuing the interests of the financial markets, rather than simply fulfilling its original mission of helping countries in crises and furthering global economic stability, one could make sense of what otherwise seemed to be a set of intellectually incoherent and inconsistent policies.

Joseph E. Stiglitz, *Globalization and Its Discontents*, W. W. Norton, 2002, p. 216

How does Stiglitz interpret the IMF? What enables him to make sense of the IMF's policies?

5. I understand why Christians have defended war. The Old Testament provides numerous examples of wars seemingly sanctioned

or ordered by Yahweh. Nor is the New Testament evidence against war as crystal-clear as many of us would wish....

Where passages of Scripture may seem to be at odds with one another, the most reliable way to resolve the apparent differences is through testing them against the teachings and example of Jesus. He is the most trustworthy interpreter and exemplar of the mind and will of God.

Reo M. Christenson, in David L. Bender and Bruno Leone, eds., *War and Human Nature*, Greenhaven Press, 1983, pp. 86–87

What are the two inconsistent beliefs that seem to be taught by Scripture, according to Christenson?

6. Mp3 Joint Care Supplement helps build and maintain healthy cartilage and joints. (These products are not intended to diagnose, treat, cure, or prevent any disease.)

Advertisement for Mp3 Joint Care Supplement, CVS pharmacy, 4/24/05

Do you think the two sentences in this advertisement are consistent or inconsistent?

7. Today, with the decline of authority, one often hears people explain that they believe in this or that because it makes them better or happier. It's easy to see how one's beliefs could arise from a desire to be good or happy, but if one *knows* that this is the source of one's beliefs, how can one continue to believe? I suspect that belief is not the simple matter discussed by epistemologists, but a complicated emotion like love, and that many find it satisfactory to believe and not believe the same thing at the same time. But I think one ought at least to try to resist this temptation.

Steven Weinberg, *Facing Up: Science and Its Cultural Adversaries*, Harvard University Press, 2001, p. 45

(Epistemology is the part of philosophy that studies knowledge: what it is and how we acquire it.)

a. Does Weinberg think that Romeo can love Juliet and not love Juliet at the same time?
b. Does he think Romeo can believe Juliet is a teenager and not believe she is a teenager at the same time?
c. Does he think it can be true that Juliet is a teenager, and not true that she is a teenager, at the same time?

8. As Louis Wirth put it in his introduction to *Ideology and Utopia*, "The most important thing, therefore, that we can know about a man is what he takes for granted, and the most elemental and important facts about a society are those that are seldom debated and generally regarded as settled."

William Ryan, *Equality*, Pantheon Books, 1981, p. 39

Wirth says that societies make assumptions just as individuals do. Can you think of any assumption that American society seldom debates and regards as settled?

9. The world is a complicated place. Each group in society focuses on a part of the reality that affects it the most. Workers worry about jobs and wages, financiers about interest rates and being repaid. A high interest rate is good for a creditor—provided he or she gets paid back. But workers see high interest rates as inducing an economic slowdown; for them, this means unemployment.

Joseph E. Stiglitz, *Globalization and Its Discontents*, W. W. Norton, 2002, p. 217

Stiglitz says different groups have different points of view. *Why* do they have different points of view?

10. Roland Barthes is frequently cited as the originator of the announcement of "the death of the author." He is usually taken to mean that readers create their own meanings of a text irrespective of the author's intentions. Thus, the meanings of texts are always shifting and open to question, depending on what the reader does with the text. If this means that texts (including spoken words) may have multiple meanings, then the idea is a mere commonplace. But if it is taken to mean that there is no basis for privileging any meaning given to a text over any other meaning, then it is, of course, nonsense.

Neil Postman, *Building a Bridge to the 18th Century: How the Past Can Improve Our Future*, Alfred A. Knopf, 1999, p. 78

Postman offers two interpretations of Barthes' announcement. What are they?

11. All sensible people oppose the slaughter of innocent civilians, but an overwhelming number favor war if the evil it seeks to defeat is worth fighting against, even if war will ineluctably lead to the slaughter of innocent civilians.

Torture is not meaningfully different. Considered in a vacuum, it is a palpable moral evil. Moral evils, however, do not exist in a vacuum; they exist in collision with other evils, and sometimes we are forced to choose. Ask the average person if he opposes torture and the answer will surely be yes. But present him with a real-world scenario and the answer may well change.

Andrew C. McCarthy, Torture: Thinking About the Unthinkable, *Commentary*, July–August, 2004

Is McCarthy saying that people have inconsistent beliefs about torture?

12. In a talk at the King Juan Carlos I of Spain center, professor Eduardo Subirats detailed the two events that, to him, show the senselessness of civilization.

"Auschwitz and Hiroshima are where words break apart," Subirats said. "They are beyond linguistics, the limit to meaning—where humanity is reduced to silence."

In the talk, titled "Violence and Civilization: Critical Theory and the Progress of Warfare," Subirats proposed that the two events were not isolated, but rather resulted from a long chain of historical actions and led to the way the world functions until the present day.

Sarah Davidson, Prof: From WWII Conflict, Modern Chaos, *Washington Square News*, 11/10/04

Someone might claim that Subirats contradicts himself. Would you agree or disagree? Are his statements about Auschwitz and Hiroshima contradictory?

Exercise 3:   Analyzing Arguments

1. Read this passage about a trial reported in the Bible and answer the questions that follow.

Susanna stands accused of adultery by two elders with whom she had refused to have sex. The people of Israel hear the testimony of the elders and act as both judge and jury, sentencing Susanna to death. Susanna cries out to God at the injustice, and He rouses the spirit of Daniel to stand in her defense. Daniel then demands an opportunity to examine each of the elders separately. The elders are brought before the people and isolated from each other. Daniel then asks each elder one question: Under what type of tree did the alleged adultery take place? Each describes a different type of tree, and on hearing this the people of Israel praise God, acquit Susanna, and sentence the elders to death for bearing false witness.

Alan M. Dershowitz, *America on Trial: Inside the Legal Battles That Transformed Our Nation*, Warner Books, 2004, p. 3

The people of Israel conclude that the two elders have lied about Susanna. What evidence persuades them to believe that? The evidence would not persuade them unless they were also making an additional assumption. What assumption (or assumptions) must they be making?

2. The following passage presents two arguments about interpreting the U.S. Constitution, one from Robert H. Bork and one from the author, Harry H. Wellington. They reach different conclusions. What are the two conclusions, and what are the reasons supporting them?

2. Some politicians, judges, and legal scholars who see themselves engaged in so-called interpretive review believe that when the text of the Constitution is not clear, the question of authority and the question of control are both answered by reading the text in the light of original intent. To get away from misleading usage let's call them originalists....

As a judge on the U.S. Court of Appeals for the District of Columbia Circuit, the influential originalist Robert H. Bork put his position this

344 THE VOCABULARY OF CRITICAL THINKING

way: "[I]f we are to have judicial review, and if the Constitution is to be law, so that the judge does not freely impose his or her own values, then the only way to do that is to root that law in the intentions of the founders. There is no other source of legitimacy...."

Whatever I may believe about the utility of searching for intention in my effort to understand single-author texts (what did Shakespeare intend when he wrote *Hamlet*), I start with great skepticism where the text I am interpreting has been written by a committee. For I am impressed that a constitution is the product of negotiation (as indeed most written law is), that negotiation of complex issues usually leaves major problems unresolved, and that language on which people of divergent views can agree must often be open-textured—to say the least. Let's understand one thing: purposeful ambiguity is to legislative drafting what the fastball is to major league baseball. I doubt that it is even coherent to talk about the intention of a class consisting of the framers at Philadelphia and the ratifiers at the state conventions. How do you obtain the sum of their disagreements?

Harry H. Wellington, *Interpreting the Constitution*, Yale University Press, 1990, pp. 49, 54–55

Exercise 4:   Apply the Ideas in Writing
Read the following passage by T. H. Huxley (1825–1895). Then write one or two paragraphs explaining the assumptions that Huxley is making. Explain the connection you see between what he says and the assumptions that you think he is making. In other words, explain why you think those are the assumptions he is making.

> Education is the instruction of the intellect in the laws of Nature, under which name I include not merely things and their forces, but men and their ways; and the fashioning of the affections and of the will into an earnest and loving desire to move in harmony with those laws.
>
> T. H. Huxley, "A Liberal Education," in Mortimer J. Adler and Charles Van Doren, eds., *Great Treasury of Western Thought*, R. R. Bowker Company, 1977, p. 526

Improving Your Writing 16: Rhetoric

Remember that the word *rhetoric* is ambiguous. In can mean using language insincerely, to manipulate people. Or it can mean the study of how to speak and write persuasively.

One of the first people to study rhetoric in the second sense was the Greek philosopher Aristotle. He said a good speech or essay persuades people in three interdependent ways, which he called logos, ethos, and pathos.

Logos means logical reasons and evidence. That is the main tool a writer uses in persuasive essays, but it isn't the only one. *Ethos* means character, trustworthiness, or credibility. A good writer has to be believable. If you state that something is a fact, but your audience knows it is only your opinion, not a fact, they will have doubts about everything you say. If you are unfair to the people who disagree with you, or misrepresent their view, your audience will reject your essay. If they suspect that you are trying to trick them, or that you think they are stupid, they won't accept your thesis no matter what reasons you give them. You must avoid these mistakes if you want to have ethos.

Pathos means emotion. A good writer communicates feelings as well as ideas. You can communicate your feelings about a topic in several ways. You can use words that create sharp pictures in people's minds as they read. "The fire spread" is flat and dull. "The fire leaped to other trees" conveys drama and excitement. You can tell a story about a specific individual or event that conveys your feelings. You can make comparisons that arouse feelings (e.g., "like a hornet," "like a babbling brook," "like a Porsche, idling").

But pathos is related to ethos. Feelings support reasons, but they can't take their place. If you try to substitute feelings for reasons, your audience won't trust you. If you create strong feelings to distract people, or confuse the issue, rather than showing all sides more clearly, your audience will feel used. They will dismiss your writing as "just rhetoric."

Creative Thinking

All the previous chapters of this book have been about relationships of various kinds. This chapter is no different. Creative thinking is seeing *new* relationships among things, seeing surprising, useful relationships that other people haven't noticed. A famous example is Johannes Gutenberg. Around 1450 he put two ideas together: he saw people pressing grapes with a screw press (i.e., a square board that was screwed down against the grapes harder and harder with a large screw, like a vise). And he saw people carving designs in wood (e.g., a design of a flower), putting ink on them, and pressing them against paper to make a print (like an artificial fingerprint). Many people were familiar with both of these processes. But Gutenberg took the step no one had taken before—he put the two ideas together in his mind. He carved letters, arranged them in words, put ink on them, and pressed them onto paper over and over to print books. The printing press was born, and knowledge became available to everyone. Looking back, we might say the combination of ink printing and wine press was obvious. But it wasn't; no one had thought of it before Gutenberg.

Creative thinking occurs everywhere, not just in technology and inventing things. Of course, many artists are creative. An example is Jackson Pollack. Pollack revolutionized painting in the twentieth century when he created "action painting." Other painters had already created abstract paintings, i.e., paintings that do not represent anything, but are just interesting shapes and colors on canvas. Pollack produced a new kind of painting by putting the canvas on the floor and dripping and slinging different colors of paint onto it. The result was complex designs of loopy, wavy lines and random spots of different colors. You can almost see Pollack's arms move and the paint fly as you follow the lines and blotches around the canvas. He combined the *act* of applying paint with the appearance of the artwork. When you look at a Pollack you are not looking at a landscape, and you are not even looking at shapes and colors. You are looking at the process of making a painting. That's an interesting new kind of art.

Great artists and scientists are often called "geniuses," and many of them are extraordinary. But you don't have to be a genius to think creatively. Some people believe creativity is some sort of mystical power that can't be explained. But you should be more analytical by now. What exactly do we mean by the word *creativity*? And what kind of explanation are we looking for? You will study the word *creativity* in the next section of in this chapter, so I won't go into more detail here. But when it comes to explanations, we might look for two types. One type would be a scientific explanation of creative personalities. Psychologists study highly creative individuals to try to find out what experiences or training or circumstances led to their success. And they try to find underlying similarities that many creative people have in common. That kind of explanation is beyond the scope of this chapter.

The other kind of explanation is more practical. We can look at techniques or methods that creative people use to come up with their new ideas. Inventors, writers, marketers and others describe what they do to solve tough problems and create interesting things. They actually agree on some basic techniques. I mentioned one of them earlier: bring together two or more things that haven't been combined before. Obviously, doing that will not always lead to a creative idea. So there is more to creative thinking than following simple rules. But learning what creative people do is perhaps the first step toward developing your own creativity. And learning words to describe what creative people do will help.

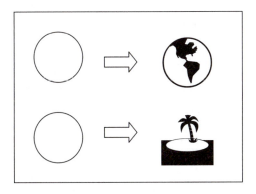

Figure 17.1
Creative thinkers modify their ideas in surprising ways to make them more useful or better solutions.

Part 1. Definitions

103. creative. quality of something that is original, new, and also valuable, excellent, or useful. You could pick letters out of a hat and form "new words." But that's not creative. "Lloyd's whole approach to keeping order in the classroom is fresh and creative." "Picasso initiated cubism, he brought African motifs into European painting, and he challenged the whole idea of representation; he is perhaps the most creative artist of the twentieth century."

creativity (noun). the ability or tendency to be creative.

Example

103a. Film-maker Shekhar Kapur reminisced about how when he started making *Elizabeth* [the film], he realised he didn't know much about English history and bluntly admitted the fact to Kate Blanchett and his crew.

"**Creativity**," he said, "is, in a sense, a denial of knowledge, an exploration of the unknown, a 'you-are-not-in-control' feeling." The only way to be **creative** is to come into harmony with the chaotic unknown.

Swati Piramal, Davos Diary: It's All About Creativity, *The Economic Times of India*, January 25, 2004

104. to associate. to see a connection, or make a relationship, between two things. Being creative often means finding new, productive relationships between things. "Newton associated the falling apple with the moon orbiting the earth, and that led him to the theory of universal gravitation." "I always associate that song with our first date."

association (noun). the relationship between two things, or the act of associating two things.

Example

104a. Absurd and unusual **associations** often lead to creative breakthroughs. Remember that even the greatest genius of all time [Leonardo da Vinci] was concerned that his "new and speculative idea...may seem trivial and almost laughable." But he did not let that stop him, and neither should you.

Michael J. Gelb, *How to Think Like Leonardo da Vinci*, Dell, 1998, p. 190

105. brainstorming. a group process in which members produce as many ideas as possible about some topic, using each others' suggestions as triggers for more ideas, and deliberately refraining from any criticisms or judgments. "In our brainstorming session we came up with 37 ways to improve a bicycle." "We need to brainstorm with Chuck and Marisa to think of more activities for the junior prom."

Example

105a. We brought together one of D.C.'s top caterers, a nightclub impresario, a Republican fundraiser, a wedding planner, the local art world's queen of hip, and a faux-finish artist known for his legendary Easter bonnet party.

Then we turned them loose for a **brainstorming** session. Their charge: to come up with a concept for the most amazing holiday party ever, the likes of which this staid, buttoned-down town has never seen.

Annie Gowan, Holiday on Ice, *Washington Post*, 11/27/03

106. stimulus. something that causes one to think, to act, or to feel something. "When Bob is working on a problem, he uses his walks in the woods as a stimulus to his imagination." "Sometimes a random list of words can stimulate new ideas and creative possibilities."

to stimulate (verb). to cause one to act, to energize, to create motion in the mind.

Example

106a. Sometimes our habits become so integral to our thinking that we fail to identify them as habits, and instead consider them "the way things are done." Thus, we need an occasional jolt to shake us out of our mental patterns. I call this jolt "a whack on the side of the head," and it can **stimulate** us to ask the questions that lead us to new answers.

Roger von Oech, *Expect the Unexpected (or You Won't Find It)*, The Free Press, 2001, p. 56

107. fantasy. the part of the imagination that produces strange, whimsical, or bizarre images and scenes, at the outer limits of possibility; or the products of such thinking. "Stories about traveling to the planets are sort of realistic, but stories about dragons and elves are pure fantasy." "At playtime some of the kids in the kindergarten talk to themselves, and they seem to be lost in a fantasy world."

Example

107a. The most notable trend in the NBC prime-time lineup for the 2007–08 season, which the network introduced yesterday, is a focus on **fantasy** and science fiction. Three of five new dramas fit that description, telling tales of time travel ("Journeyman"), a robot-human hybrid ("Bionic Woman"), and a computer geek who unwittingly downloads spy secrets into his brain ("Chuck").

Stuart Elliott, NBC, Tired of Last Place, Turns to Sci-Fi and Fantasy, *New York Times*, 5/15/07

108. to modify. to change or alter slightly; sometimes to change a part of some whole. Creating something, such as a poem, or a useful invention, is usually a process that takes time, involving more than one insight. "The tailor said he could modify the suit to make it fit." "I started with an image of a man sitting in a tree, and by adding and modifying parts, I came up with this story."

modification (noun) a change in something, usually intended to make it better.

Example

108a. Candido Jacuzzi noticed that the pumps used for his son's hydro-therapy treatments [in the hospital] were similar to the smaller pumps his company sold for industrial uses. With a few **modifications**, Jacuzzi constructed a pump that could provide hydrotherapy in the comfort of one's home. Soon he realized that the soothing jets could do more than just provide therapy, and the spa industry was born.

Scott Thorpe, *How to Think Like Einstein*, Sourcebooks, Inc., 2000, p. 64

Test Yourself

Match the words with the definitions.

103. creative
104. association
105. brainstorming
106. stimulus
107. fantasy
108. to modify

  a. something that causes one to think
  b. a process in which a group produces as many ideas as possible
  c. to change something, or a part of something
  d. to see a relationship between two things
  e. a way of thinking that produces strange, amazing images and ideas
  f. quality of something that is new and excellent

Part 2. Understanding the Meaning

103. creative

103b. Are **creative** individuals born that way? Does environment make a difference? Jane Piirto offers answers in her new book, "Understanding **Creativity**." She says, "We are all creative; those who are more creative than others have learned to take risks, to value complexity, to see the world with naiveté". And they have great motivation to work.

Dr. Piirto has identified seven I's—Inspiration, Imagery, Imagination, Intuition, Insight, Incubation, and Improvisation—all important to the creative process. Her vignettes of well-known people in creative

Figure 17.2
Thomas Edison received over 1300 U.S. and foreign patents for inventions such as the electric light, the phonograph, and a way to combine motion pictures with sound. *Source: Credit: © LH/Shutterstock*

fields—art, music, dance, theater, writing, science, math, business, and technology—provide real life examples.

Mitchell P. Davis, editor, *The Yearbook of Experts, Authorities and Spokespersons*, Broadcast Interview Source, Inc., February 4, 2004

103c. **Creative** genius is the ability to effect unusual combinations of elements nobody else would think of putting together, and to do so in a way that makes the combination click. That goes for genius in any form: artistic, literary or musical; inventive or scientific; military, political or economic.

The born genius does this instinctively, in a flash—often an emotional one.

But there are deliberate geniuses, who achieve as striking results in cold blood. They reach out, literally or figuratively, for totally unrelated elements, consider how they may be combined, effect the combination, adjust it until it works—and behold! They have a something altogether new....

Try this on a puzzling situation, adapting it to fit, and you have what the outsider would consider a flash of inspiration. Actually, it is brilliant, but by deliberate contrivance, not inspiration.

Robert R. Updegraff, quoted in David H. Killeffer, *How Did You Think of That: An Introduction to the Scientific Method*, Anchor Books, 1969, p. 133

Comment

Most writers agree that creativity is both learned and inborn. Anyone can learn to be more creative. But some people have more natural talent than others.

103d. The first and most evident way that alcohol may enhance **creativity** in some people is to "blank out the censor, or the part of you that says 'That's no good,'" says Dr. Goodwin.... Alcohol may [also] make other people and events seem more intriguing to the drinker, says Dr. Goodwin.

But with all this said, alcohol is still no magic elixir. On the contrary—it's more a Pandora's box. "Alcohol in some instances can stimulate **creativity**, but overall it will kill it," says Arnold M. Ludwig, M.D., professor of psychiatry at the University of Kentucky Medical Center.

Ellen Michaud and Russell Wild et al., *Boost Your Brain Power*, Rodale Press, 1991, pp. 200–201

104. association

104b. Dean Keith Simonton has recently proposed a theory of creative thinking that assumes that the basis for production of original ideas is the chance combination of "remotely-**associated**" mental elements.... [N]ew ideas are generated by randomly combining mental elements; Simonton calls this "chance permutation."

The second component of Simonton's theory is that the creative genius is able to generate combinations of elements that are more original than those produced by ordinary thinkers. This occurs because the genius possesses a "looser" set of **associative** connections, and is less tied to habitual **associations**, than the ordinary person, and thus more likely to think original thoughts.

Robert W. Weisberg, *Creativity: Beyond the Myth of Genius*, W. H. Freeman and Co., 1993, p. 56

104c. The words or the language, as they are written or spoken, do not seem to play any role in my mechanism of thought. The psychical entities which seem to serve as elements in thought are certain signs and more or less clear images which can be "voluntarily" reproduced and combined.... But taken from a psychological viewpoint, this combinatory play seems to be the essential feature in productive thought.... Conventional words or other signs have to be sought for laboriously only in a secondary stage, when the mentioned **associative** play is sufficiently established and can be reproduced at will.

Albert Einstein, quoted in Gerald Holton, *Thematic Origins of Scientific Thought: Kepler to Einstein*, Revised Edition, Harvard University Press, 1988, pp. 386–387

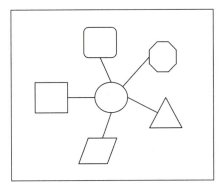

Figure 17.3
Association is bringing together things in new combinations. *Source:* © *Kelly Young/Shutterstock*

Comment

Play is a word that comes up frequently when artists and scientists and other creative people talk about what they do. Another is *childlike*.

> 104d. Carlyle habitually thought with his imagination, jumping from one **association** to another. His genius lies, not in conducting his readers along a carefully-graduated series of argumentative steps towards an irresistible conclusion, but in putting two or more seemingly very different objects or situations unexpectedly next to each other, in sudden and blinding juxtaposition, and forcing the reader, even unwillingly, to recognise likenesses where he had seen none before.
>
> A. L. Le Quesne, *Carlyle*, Oxford University Press, 1982, p. 25

(*To juxtapose* is to put two things side by side.)

105. brainstorming

> 105b. Osborn begins his analysis with the assumption that all people possess creative capacity. He divides the thinking mind into two now-familiar components: *judicial mind*, which analyzes, compares, and chooses, and *creative mind*, which visualizes, foresees, and generates ideas. Although we all have both capacities, especially when we are young, the creative capacity can dwindle over the years as one becomes increasingly judgmental. Most importantly *premature* judgment can interfere with creativity when it causes one to reject as useless those ideas that might solve the problem if given the chance. The importance of deferral of judgment has been accepted by many of those who seek to facilitate creativity.
>
> The **brainstorming** technique is designed to offset the inhibiting effect of premature judgment and to make it possible for problem

solvers to produce many wild ideas in order to maximize the chance
of producing a potentially useful idea.

Robert W. Weisberg, *Creativity: Beyond the Myth of Genius*, W. H. Freeman and Co., 1993,
p. 62

Comment

The idea of right brain–left brain, creative brain–logical brain, has become a cliché, i.e., an expression or idea that is overused, superficial, simplistic. It may be
true, in some way. Many experts believe it. But creative people always question
widely accepted assumptions. (Osborn was talking about methods, or processes,
not parts of the brain.)

> 105c. Humor, or any good mood, seems to increase creativity.
> According to Howard Lieberman, M.D., a New Jersey neurosur-
> geon, good moods are associated with an increase in the frequency
> and rapidity of electrical connections in the brain. New connections
> can often present new ideas and new ways to look at a problem.
>
> "In a **brainstorming** meeting, everyone needs to be happy and
> energetic," says [Jim] Shields. "Humor often is a catalyst for this. As a
> matter of fact, the most productive sessions are those that have a toler-
> ance for wacky and even off-color jokes."

Mark Golin et al., *Secrets of Executive Success*, Rodale Press, 1991, pp. 41–42

Figure 17.4
In a brainstorming session you let others' ideas stimulate your thinking, and say everything
that pops into your head, the crazier the better. *Source: Shutterstock/Kelly Young*

105d. This year, Manning Selvage and Lee [a public relations firm] received 200 applications for its summer internship program—the usual number, Mr. Tsokanos said—and from that group 20 were chosen to do something not quite so usual. They spent a full day at the company's headquarters on Broadway in Midtown Manhattan, trying simultaneously to shine and to be team players during exercises aimed at simulating a working day.

First up was a **brainstorming** session on how to market a hypothetical new tampon. "We chose that because it does make some people uncomfortable," Mr. Tsokanos said, "and we have to weed that out. We work on everything—above the belt and below the belt—here. Tampons are serious business."

The students threw out ideas: Hand out samples at the mall! at health clubs! on college campuses! Send guest speakers to talk to middle school health classes! Drop them from blimps at sporting events!

Then they broke into groups and created media plans: Start a Web site! Serve pizza at product-introduction events! Serve beer! Or wine! Or diet soda! Or chocolate!

Lisa Belkin, Part "Survivor," Part "Apprentice," All Reality, *New York Times*, 6/4/06

105e. A pack of Riverdale residents is hoping their neighbors will throw them a bone and donate funds to renovate the popular Seton Park dog run....

Speaking over a cacophony of barks on Sunday, [Dog Run] association members **brainstormed** ideas on how to raise the needed funds. Suggestions of bake sales, bike and iPod raffles and canvassing local businesses were all given.

Marie Villani-York, Dog Owners Unleash New Plan for Seton Park, *Riverdale Press*, 5/24/07

106. stimulus

106b. [E. L.] Doctorow's novel *Loon Lake* started when he was driving in the Adirondacks and noticed the title words on a road sign. What starts a piece, Doctorow said, "can be a phrase, an image, a sense of rhythm, the most intangible thing. Something just moves you, evokes feelings you don't even understand...."

Launching pad images and powerful but nebulous sensations like these are the alchemic grains of salt that Henry James called "germs." Unable to resist a pun, James defined germs both as an infection that sends the hapless author into a literary fever and as a seed-cell ready to germinate into a full-blown literary life-form....

James reported that a chance comment at a dinner party about a mother and son fighting over an inheritance was the seed that **stimulated** him to *The Spoils of Poynton*. That idle phrase, James said, made him instantly aware of "the *whole* of the virus" (emphasis added) that would spread to be his story.

John Briggs, *Fire in the Crucible*, St. Martins Press, 1988, pp. 281–282

(*Alchemic* means related to alchemy, the set of ideas and practices in the Middle Ages in Europe organized around the attempt to transform lead into gold, and to understand the elements in general. A crucible is a durable pot used for melting and mixing metals.)

106c. The use of random **stimulation** is fundamentally different from vertical thinking. With vertical thinking one deals only with what is relevant. In fact one spends most of one's time selecting out what is relevant and what is not. With random **stimulation** one uses any information whatsoever. No matter how unrelated it may be no information is rejected as useless. The more irrelevant the information the more useful it may be....

Physical exposure to random **stimulation**. This may involve wandering around an area which contains a multitude of different objects, for instance a general store like Woolworths or a toy shop. It may also mean going along to an exhibition which has nothing to do with the subject you are interested in.

Edward de Bono, *Lateral Thinking*, Harper Perennial, 1970, pp. 193–194

106d. I begin drawing tiny squares and rectangles to represent buildings, with gaps marking the streets. Heavy lines denote the walls of a castle; more heavy lines show the city walls. And I put gates in the walls....

For there was one gate that, in the process of drawing, I had accidently drawn with no gap between the two towers that guarded it....

Except that I believe, when it comes to storytelling—and making up maps of imaginary lands *is* a kind of storytelling—that mistakes are often the beginning of the best ideas. After all, a mistake wasn't *planned*. It isn't likely to be a cliché. All you have to do is think of a reason why the mistake isn't a mistake at all, and you might have something fresh and wonderful, something to **stimulate** a story you never thought of quite that way before.

Orson Scott Card, *How to Write Science Fiction and Fantasy*, Writer's Digest Books, 1990, p. 29

Comment

One characteristic of many creative people is that they are not afraid to make mistakes. So-called "mistakes" and "failures" are often opportunities.

106e. But by its very nature, creative thinking requires a break from habit that is, really, a kind of wooden thoughtlessness. Travel is one way, and apparently a common way, that creative people make the familiar strange again. Trying to get around in a strange culture, to feed yourself, to make sense of the news, to buy toothpaste... all are familiar gestures made highly peculiar again, as they were when you were a child.... The way [Peter] Sellars often gets "a way in" to a theater piece is to look around him for models, similar events, metaphors, analogies, and then add to that from his own observation.... These images come from a fertile life of **stimulation**—much of it foreign-derived.

Denise Shekerjian, *Uncommon Genius: How Great Ideas Are Born*, Penguin, 1990, pp. 123, 125

107. fantasy

107b. Good stories and poems work their magic by blending structure and logic with imagination and creativity, inviting listeners to suspend reality, opening a place in their minds for new realities, possibilities and strategies. There should be elements of vision and integrity, human values such as courage, vitality for life, compassion, curiosity and inventiveness subtly embedded in the structure and flow, played out through the characters and plot. The imagination of the listeners should be roused by **fantasy**, odd juxtapositions, inventions, **fantastic** creatures—for example, talking animals, amazing places. Emotions can be touched through incidents and phrasing that highlight humour, empathy, sadness, relief, fright and other shared human experiences. The story should also appeal to our senses through vibrant descriptions that paint a picture and convey movements and sounds. When a story or poem with these factors is told well, it helps us to remember the messages associated with it and the context in which it was told.

Neil Middleton, Storytelling and Learning: Power, Purpose and Popularity, *Training Journal*, February, 2004

107c. Yet maturity has not brought an end to Ms. Chouinard's **fantasy** and fertile imagination. In "24 Preludes by Chopin" and "Le Cri du Monde," two New York [dance] premieres at the Joyce Theater, Ms. Chouinard takes her creativity onto an impressive and higher formal level.

The Compagnie Marie Chouinard, which opened on Tuesday night for a run through tomorrow, is inhabited by its usual sensual creatures with primal urges. Faunlike in flat angular silhouettes and sporting either Mohawk hair crests or piled-up hair, the dancers hark back to the mythic beasts and orgiastic rites that Ms. Chouinard has brought to New York for nearly 25 years....

Provocatively and methodically, Ms. Chouinard works against the traditional music-appreciation associations of each Prelude (Opus 28). No sylphides or raindrop images here: just highly articulate bodies that have something of the animal and vegetable about them in their feline slink, birdlike flutter and blooming shapes.

Anna Kisselgoff, Creatures in Torment Seek Their True Nature, *New York Times*, 12/12/03

Comment

Using association can be a way to create new relationships. But Kisselgoff says this choreographer works against traditional associations in creating her dances. If associations have become habitual and expected, then one must break out of the expectations to create something new.

> 107d. There's no evidence, however, that technology is killing off **fantasy**. In a survey of children's invisible friends, psychologist Marjorie Taylor, of the University of Oregon, found that only 3 percent were named after superheroes like Batman or Superman. "Children are coming up with their own characters who are quite unique and idiosyncratic," she says. Some entertainment may even help nourish imagination. Anderson found that kids who watched "Mister Rogers' Neighborhood" scored higher on the Uses for an Object Test as teenagers, perhaps because Mr. Rogers often took common objects and came up with novel uses for them. Newer technology may turn out to promote **fantasy**, says Anderson.
>
> Claudia Kalb, Playing Ye Olde Way, *Newsweek*, 9/8/03

108. to modify

> 108b. When some unknown genius became sufficiently irritated by the way his cheese or butter or hard-boiled egg stuck to the knife blade instead of coming away in neat slices, he created an edge without a blade. He realized that only the edge did the cutting and the rest of the knife blade served no useful function, but only stuck to his soft cheese to tear it. Then he went the next step and cut his cheese, or his butter, or his hard-boiled egg into neat slices by using a fine wire stretched taut, the edge of a bladeless knife....
>
> Finally, you must cap the whole enterprise by trying your solution to be sure it is the solution you want. Here you learn whether your bladeless knife will really cut cheese into neat slices, or whether something else is needed, some **modification** of the taut-wire solution, to make it work. At this stage, too, it may be necessary to go back to the very beginning and start over again.
>
> David H. Killeffer, *How Did You Think of That: An Introduction to the Scientific Method*, Anchor Books, 1969, pp. 3, 6

> 108c. As you know, not one of the lower animals can read, and not one ever will. Perhaps some of them do what we call thinking, in an extremely limited way. But their lives and activities, rich and varied as they sometimes are, are nevertheless governed and limited by instincts and largely automatic responses. We humans have a brain with which we think. We have a capacity for reliving the past. We are able to anticipate the future. If an animal meets a difficulty, it may merely turn aside, and always thereafter do the same. To us, a difficulty is a

challenge. How can we surmount it? How can we change it? How might we even **modify** it and turn it into an advantage?

A. D. Moore, *Invention, Discovery, and Creativity*, Anchor Books, 1969, p. 1

108d. The Movies, published by Activision for Windows desktop computers, was produced by Lionhead Studios, a British software house....

"It literally came to me at 5 o'clock in the morning on January the 19th, 2002," Molyneux said. What the world needed, Molyneux decided, was a game that let people play at making movies. He hopped out of bed and began planning....

It's the latest in the grand tradition of "God games" like The Sims, in which the player creates and manages his own private world. In this case, it's a movie studio. Beginning in the 1920s, with a vacant lot in Hollywood, you build sets, hire actors, and crank out goofy comedies and overwrought melodramas.

But the most creative players can go even further, by creating animated movies from scratch. Players can choose from hundreds of sets, backdrops, and costumes. They can write their own scripts, and use recorded music to create an exciting soundtrack. They can even use a program called Starmaker to create actors. This sophisticated tool lets you **modify** virtually every physical feature of your star. You can tinker until he looks just like Steve McQueen or Adrien Brody, or your kid brother.

Hiawatha Bray, So You Want to Be in Pictures? *Boston Globe*, 12/17/05

Part 3. Applying the Words

103. creative
104. association
105. brainstorming
106. stimulus
107. fantasy
108. to modify

Exercise 1:   Choose the Best Word

For each sentence, choose the best word (or an appropriate form of the word) to fill in the blank.

a. The members of our group bring different qualities together and seem to stimulate each other; we have great _____ sessions.
b. Some people are practical, result-oriented, and realistic; they are uncomfortable with _____.
c. In one of the most famous discoveries in history, Archimedes made an _____ between stepping into a tub of water and immersing an object in water to measure its volume.

d. The best ideas are almost never the first ideas, but the third and fourth ideas that you get when you _____ the first idea.
e. The faculty didn't like Prof. Thompson's suggestion at first because it was strange to them, but eventually they realized that it was very _____.
f. When my friend Linda is stuck on a problem in her business she uses Marx Brothers movies as a _____ to her thinking.

Exercise 2:   Apply the Words

Read each example and answer the questions that follow.

1. First, the creative person is always operating in a domain or discipline or craft. One is not creative or noncreative in general.... Second, the creative individual does something that is initially novel, but the contribution does not end with novelty—it is all too easy to do something merely different. Rather, what defines the creative act or actor is the ultimate acceptance of that novelty [by people working in the discipline or domain]; and again, the acid test of creativity is its documented effect on the relevant domain or domains.

Howard Gardner, *Intelligence Reframed*, Basic Books, 1999, p. 117

Gardner emphasizes that being creative is not the same as doing something different or new. In your own words, how would you explain what else is involved in being creative?

2. Dicky said to me, "[Robert] Frost's wildness, his vitality, struck anyone who took his courses. His low, rumbling voice lingered over each word, with frequent pauses followed by repetitions of phrases and notions. He didn't really teach a subject so much as teach himself, his way of thinking and being in the world. His mind, his conversation, ranged widely over everything from literature to politics to sports, but he had a way of making connections, of stitching together disparate things." Frost was, in other words, an artist in the classroom, creating new wholes from matter not previously thought related.

Jay Parini, *The Art of Teaching*, Oxford, 2005, p. 87

If Frost shifted from literature to politics to sports in a class, his students might think he had attention deficit disorder and was unable to concentrate. How was his method different from ADD, according to the writer?

3. However, in my experience one thing is constant: Good stories don't come from trying to write a story the moment I think of the first idea. All but a handful of my stories have come from combining two completely unrelated ideas that have been following their own tracks through my imagination.

Orson Scott Card, *How to Write Science Fiction and Fantasy*, Writer's Digest Books, 1990, p. 33

How should we understand the one constant thing in Card's experience of writing? Is it associating things? Or modifying things?

4. Isaris Baez is 11 and waiting for heart surgery....So she was happily surprised last Wednesday when she learned that there was to be a screening of "TMNT," the latest Teenage Mutant Ninja Turtles movie, followed by a poetry jam....

"What is a poem?" he [Robert Galinsky] asked. "Rhyming!" said 11-year-old Quadri. "Literature!" said 10-year-old Terrel. "Imagination!" Isaris said.

Mr. Galinsky wrote the words on a sheet of blank paper. Then he asked the children what some of the movie's themes were.

"Brotherhood," they replied. "Working together." "It was funny," Terrell offered.

"Do you find there's a lot of funny stuff in your life?" Mr. Galinsky asked.

Terrell shook his head. "There's no comedy in my life."

Mr. Galinsky added words to the list, and soon the makings of a poem began to emerge: "Brotherhood is working together / I want adventure forever / There is no comedy in my life / There is action / There is music / There is drama."

Abby Ellin, Words That Help When Life Is All Drama, No Comedy, *New York Times*, 5/15/07

Mr. Galinsky was helping children in a hospital create a poem. Which aspect of creative thinking does this episode best illustrate?

5. My first successful creations, Barbie and Ken, came from observing my own daughter playing with paper dolls. She always chose grown-up dolls, and I realized she was using the doll to project her own dreams of her future. I was convinced that if I could turn this play pattern with paper dolls into a three-dimensional doll, I could fill a very real need in the lives of little girls.

Ethlie Ann Vare and Greg Ptacek, *Patently Female*, John Wiley and Sons, 2002, p. vii

Many people had watched their children play with dolls. Why do you think this inventor's child served as a stimulus to her creativity? (Suggestion: This famous quote from the great French scientist Louis Pasteur may be relevant: "Chance favors the prepared mind.")

6. An extremely interesting piece of research by Getzels and Jackson, of the University of Chicago, compares the highly intelligent with the highly creative adolescent. They tested 449 adolescents in a Midwestern private secondary school, both for I.Q. and creativity....

When required to write a story about a stimulus picture, there was a striking difference between the two groups. The I.Q. group tended to be conventional, stodgy. The creatives made significantly greater use of stimulus-free themes, unexpected endings, incongruities, and playfulness; they had imagination, and they turned it loose.

A. D. Moore, *Invention, Discovery, and Creativity*, Anchor Books, 1969, pp. 23–24

Schools give students feedback—grades—on their performance. Do you think it is possible to grade fantasy? Can teachers recognize one student's writing, or scientific thinking, or mathematical problem-solving, as more fantastic, fanciful, using more fantasy, than another student's work?

7. As artist Jasper Johns said when asked to describe what was involved in the creative process: "It's simple, you just take something and then you do something to it, and then you do something else to it. Keep doing this and pretty soon you've got something."

Roger von Oech, *Expect the Unexpected (or You Won't Find It)*, The Free Press, 2001, p. 112

The Russian poetess Marina Tsvetaeva wrote:
"I obey something which sounds constantly within me but not uniformly, sometimes indicating, sometimes commanding. When it indicates, I argue; when it commands, I obey....

More to the left–more to the right, higher–lower, faster–slower, extend–break off: these are the exact indications of my ear, or of something *to* my ear. All my writing is only listening."

Sven Birkerts, *Readings*, Graywolf Press, 1999, p. 170

These two artists—Johns and Tsvetaeva—both emphasize the process of modifying what they produce to make it better. Do their comments suggest any differences in their ways of working?

8. "The best way to get a good idea is to get a lot of ideas."

Linus Pauling, in Roger von Oech, *Expect the Unexpected (or You Won't Find It)*, The Free Press, 2001, p. 108

All the words in this chapter except for the word *creative* are about techniques for producing new ideas. In your opinion, which technique would probably produce the most new ideas?

Exercise 3: Analyzing Arguments

In the following passage Todd Siler presents an argument about creativity. In your own words, how would you state Siler's main point? What evidence does he provide to support it?

[A]longside our most celebrated geniuses, there are legions of everyday geniuses. They're not people who are mental giants. Nor are they intellectual heroes. Their theories and inventions don't change cultures or civilizations. But they have all experienced flights of exceptional thinking, often in some highly practical way. Such is the genius behind the invention of paper, Velcro, staples, nails, steel, glass, cement, currency, and other remarkable "simple" but useful things....

We have all experienced flights of genius. We all think things we never thought before, and we think *in ways* we never thought before, especially when we are children. We discovered how to walk and how to speak. These personal achievements have aspects of genius to them because they required us to connect information that at first seemed unrelated. We understood that a bed, chair, table, and shower are all different in appearance and function, and yet we all managed, as toddlers, to house these symbols in our mind's sense of things that belong in a home.

Todd Siler, *Think Like a Genius*, Bantam Books, 1996, pp. 5–6

Exercise 4: Apply the Ideas in Writing

1. Go back to your paragraphs for Chapter 6 where you explained something you had learned, something you know for sure. Write a fairy tale that would be interesting to a five-year-old, and that teaches the lesson you learned. The moral of the story is the lesson you learned. The more imaginative and creative your fairy tale, the better. What would hold the attention of a five-year-old? But remember that *creative* doesn't simply mean new or strange. It also means useful and effective. You should create parts of your story that reinforce the message.
2. Write a paragraph or two explaining ways to improve a coffee cup (or tea cup). Or a park bench. Or a paragraph or two explaining ways to save electricity. Or water.

Improving Your Writing 17. Why Write?

I can mention three reasons to write, and you can probably think of more. First, picking a topic and writing something about it makes you more aware of your world. It forces you to be more observant, more attentive to your topic, because you are trying to capture your experience in words and communicate it. Think about having lunch. Now think about writing an essay about having lunch. You can see how much more engaged and alert you would have to be. Think of your friend. Now think of writing an essay about your friend. Writing makes you more alive.

Writing essays is also the best way to discover who you really are. It helps you figure out what you believe and how you feel about things—your past, movies, men and women, euthanasia, human nature, goals in life, and everything else you think about. You really don't have a clear grasp of your values and beliefs until you try to explain them to someone. When you try to organize your ideas in a clear essay you see how hard it is to pin down your basic attitudes and assumptions, and how complicated they are. But those beliefs and values are you. Your identity doesn't depend on your car or your clothes or the music that's popular this year. Your real core self is deeper. It's made up of your basic values and beliefs about people and the world. They determine your direction in life and how you respond to things. Writing is the best way to explore that inner self.

Finally, your insights and opinions are valuable. Not just to you, but to other people. They're valuable because they're unique. There is no other person in the world who can see things or think about things exactly the way you do, because no other person has lived your life or has your inborn talents. If I have to go for a job interview, I would like to hear how yours went, and what you thought about your interview. Your opinions would help me. That applies to everything else, too. I'm not sure what I believe about capital punishment. Hearing your ideas will help me decide what I think. It will help me get to know myself better (besides getting to know you). Discovering your own beliefs and values is not easy, and expressing them clearly is a challenge as well. But if you do, even in part, you will do something generous and helpful. You will benefit others with your understanding.

For Further Study

In this book I have treated thinking as recognizing relationships. We do that continuously, in various ways. Thinking is central to being alive, at least in the way that humans are alive. It is a large part of what makes us human. Therefore we can look at it from different perspectives, just as we can look at human beings from different perspectives. Biologists look at humans in one way, psychologists in another, sociologists in another, economists, teachers, political candidates, office managers, telemarketers, and so on all look at people in different ways. The same goes for thinking. Different people have different interests, and so emphasize different aspects of thinking. Most books about thinking select one aspect and explain that.

1. Informal logic. Correct reasoning. Fallacies.

Many books explain thinking as the process of reasoning correctly. They teach people to analyze arguments, recognize fallacies, and construct their own arguments to persuade others.

Alec Fisher, *Critical Thinking: An Introduction*, Cambridge, 2001. Brief survey of arguments and how to analyze them, limited to the essential concepts. Very clear, no jargon or technicalities; sound, commonsense approach.

M. Neil Browne and Stuart Keeley, *Asking the Right Questions*, Eighth Edition, Prentice Hall, 2006. Chapters devoted to such questions as, "What are the issue and the conclusion," "What are the reasons," "What are the value conflicts and assumptions," "Are there rival causes," etc.

Jamie Whyte, *Crimes Against Logic*, McGraw Hill, 2005. An entertaining, very readable survey of logical mistakes people make, with amusing examples.

2. Rhetoric. The art of persuasive speaking and writing. Successful communication.

Books on rhetoric explain correct reasoning, but include more. They analyze the whole situation of persuasive writing and speaking, including the audience, the feelings one's speech creates in them, the order in which one presents arguments, and so on.

Edward P. J. Corbett and Rosa A. Eberly, *The Elements of Reasoning*, Second Edition, Allyn and Bacon, 2000. Simple discussion of the five basic questions of rhetoric: conjecture (what happened?), definition (what is it?), cause and effect (what are the causes and consequences?), value (is it good or bad?), and proposal (what should we do?), with ways to present answers.

Jay Heinrichs, *Thank You for Arguing*, Three Rivers Press, 2007. Heinrichs presents the principles of classical rhetoric in a contemporary, entertaining form. He describes and catalogs many different techniques and tricks that persuasive speakers use.

Anthony Pratkanis and Elliot Aronson, *Age of Propaganda: The Everyday Use and Abuse of Persuasion*, Owl Books, 2001. Detailed study of advertising, political campaigning, TV news and newspapers, among other contemporary phenomena, with numerous examples, by two social psychologists.

3. Psychology. Cognition. Reasoning. Decision Making.

Psychologists have always studied thinking. They study it empirically, by observing people and experimenting with them. They describe how people actually make inferences, how they perceive, classify, and remember things, the mistakes they typically make, how thinking grows during childhood, and so on.

Gary R. Kirby and Jeffery R. Goodpaster, *Thinking*, Third Edition, Prentice Hall, 2002. Many practical suggestions for improving thinking of all kinds—scientific, creative, logical, evaluative, etc.—based on psychologists' understanding of how people do those things.

Diane F. Halpern, *Thought and Knowledge: An Introduction to Critical Thinking*, Third Edition, Lawrence Erlbaum Associates, 1995. Halpern's book is similar to Kirby and Goodpaster's, with a little more emphasis on current research in psychology. She discusses judgments of probability, sampling techniques, and memory, among other things.

4. Problem solving. Scientific method.

Some writers believe that good thinking is productive thinking, in the sense of solving problems, figuring out things, or finding solutions to puzzles. They propose rules to follow if one wants to find solutions. Some think the scientific method is the best procedure; others define problem solving more broadly.

Stephen S. Carey, *A Beginner's Guide to Scientific Method*, Third Edition, Wadsworth Publishing, 2003. Clearly written chapters on some of the factors involved in scientists' observations, explanations, tests of explanations, and attempts to establish causes, among other things, with extensive exercises.

Theodore Schick, Jr., and Lewis Vaughn, *How to Think About Weird Things*, Fourth Edition, McGraw Hill, 2007. Schick and Vaughn discuss belief and knowledge, emotions, logic, and science, in relation to "miracle cures," parapsychology, UFOs, and other New Age interests.

5. Heuristics. Rules. Methods

Heuristics means guidelines or rules. These writers also view thinking as productive in some way, but they see it as even broader than scientific method or problem solving. For example, making choices, interacting with others, and creating a meal all require thought. We can improve our thinking in any task if we apply certain techniques, these writers say.

Edward de Bono, *Six Thinking Hats*, Second Edition, Penguin Books, 2000. De Bono says a main obstacle to effective thinking is trying to do several things at once. People should "separate emotion from logic, creativity from information, and so on." We can imagine putting on a white hat to think about facts and figures, a red hat to think about how we feel, a black hat to think about errors and shortcomings, etc.

Morgan D. Jones, *The Thinker's Toolkit: 14 Powerful Techniques for Problem Solving*, Revised edition, Three Rivers Press, 1998. Jones explains useful techniques such as restating the problem in a different way, trying to find flaws in your solution, assigning numerical values to all the different options, and controlling personal biases.

6. Types of thinking. Different skills and aptitudes.

Some books describe different types of thinking. For example, you can analyze something into smaller parts, or you can take a collection of pieces and put them together (synthesis) to make a larger whole. Those are two types. Other writers propose other types. Some say there are three basic types, some say seven, some more.

Robert Sternberg, *Successful Intelligence: How Practical and Creative Intelligence Determine Success in Life*, Plume, 1997. Sternberg first describes "analytical intelligence," which is solving problems, and he describes the best steps for that (like the books listed in section 4 of this chapter). But success requires two other "intelligences" as well. He emphasizes attitudes that aid creativity. The third requirement for success is practical intelligence, which is the ability to communicate and share ideas with others.

Howard Gardner, *Frames of Mind*, Basic Books, 1983. Gardner's initial presentation of his theory of the seven intelligences: verbal, mathematical, spatial, musical, bodily-kinesthetic (movement), interpersonal (understanding others), intrapersonal (understanding oneself).

Robert Ornstein, *Multimind: A New Way of Looking at Human Behavior*, Anchor, 1989. Ornstein believes we do not have one mind, but many minds. We are a collection of many different abilities and talents: comparing, searching, calculating, deciding, and so on. To improve our thinking we must first change our concept of "thinking."

7. Attitudes. Emotions. Being critical.

Everyone agrees that knowing all about how we think is not enough to make a person an effective thinker. The person has to apply what she or he knows. That means the person must have certain attitudes, or motives, or feelings about herself and what she thinks about. Some books describe those.

Vincent Ruggiero, *Beyond Feelings: A Guide to Critical Thinking*, Eighth Edition, McGraw-Hill, 2007. An elementary discussion of truth, belief, and evidence, followed by explanations of several kinds of mistakes people make, followed by suggestions for avoiding the mistakes. A good presentation of the basics of effective thinking.

Daniel Goleman, *Emotional Intelligence: Why It Can Matter More Than IQ*, Bantam, 1997. Goleman explains what psychologists are learning about how we can know our own desires and feelings, and how we can understand others' desires and feelings. Knowing the first is essential for having goals and being motivated, and knowing the second helps in all cooperative endeavors.

Michael Shermer, *Why People Believe Weird Things*, W. H. Freeman, 1997. Skeptical, debunking survey of the paranormal, near-death experiences, alien abductions, creationism, and Holocaust deniers, among other topics. People believe unfounded things "because they want to. It feels good. It is comforting."

Thomas Kida, *Don't Believe Everything You Think: The 6 Basic Mistakes We Make in Thinking*, Prometheus, 2006. We prefer stories to statistics, we seek confirmation, we fail to recognize chance and coincidence, we misperceive, we oversimplify, and we have faulty memories. Readable, with many interesting examples.

8. Language. Words.

Most thinking occurs in words. For most people, thinking means talking to oneself. And the words one uses has a very large influence on the way one thinks. The way one talks publicly, with others, and the talking one hears influence the way one talks to oneself. Some books emphasize the close connection between language and thinking.

S. I. Hayakawa, *Language in Thought and Action*, Fifth Edition, Harcourt, 1991. A famous book about how various aspects of language can influence thinking, e.g., "snarl-words" and "purr-words," "the ladder of abstraction," "the two-valued orientation" (false dilemmas), and so on.

Steven Darian, *Understanding the Language of Science*, University of Texas Press, 2003. Very detailed, sophisticated analysis of the nature of the terms and concepts used in definition, classification, determining causes, and figurative language in science, among other things. For the advanced student.

9. Being creative. Creativity.

It's not easy to define creativity, but everyone agrees that it's important. Many books try to explain what it is, and especially how anyone can be more creative. Some focus on the personal traits of creative people, others suggest techniques all of us can follow to be creative.

Anthony Weston, *Creativity for Critical Thinkers*, Oxford, 2007. Brief (80 pp.) survey of practical techniques; lively discussion of interesting examples. Weston emphasizes restating problems, or reframing situations, to open up new possibilities.

Roger von Oech, *A Whack on the Side of the Head*, Third Edition, Warner Books, 1998. Amusing survey of many emotional needs that prevent us from being more creative: the need to follow rules, to be logical, to be practical, to conform to expectations, to avoid failure, to be serious, to be clear and precise, and others. James L. Adams' classic, *Conceptual Blockbusting* (Addison-Wesley, 1986), is similar.

Edward de Bono, *Lateral Thinking: Creativity Step by Step*, Harper Perennial, 1970. De Bono contrasts lateral thinking with vertical thinking, which is logical, sequential, judgmental, and aimed at a single answer. Lateral thinking is the opposite. It is the search for new ideas rather than correct ideas. Many practical exercises.

10. Dialogue. Reflective thinking.

For complex, philosophical problems, some say the best thinking occurs in a group, with questions and answers and questions about the answers. Some books give advice on how to carry on a discussion. This high-level thinking incorporates and builds on most of the other approaches.

Mortimer J. Adler, *The Paideia Program*, MacMillan Publishing Company, 1984. Adler and his colleagues advocate restructuring education to emphasize active thinking about problems in dialogue with others. In all disciplines—including the sciences and foreign languages—they propose "group tutoring in the art of pointed criticism."

Matthew Lipman, *Thinking in Education*, Second Edition, Cambridge University Press, 2003. The way to improve students' thinking is to create "a community of inquiry," where "students listen to one another with respect, build on one another's ideas, challenge one another to supply reasons…, assist each other in drawing inferences from what has been said, and seek to identify one another's assumptions."

Roger C. Schank, *Tell Me A Story: Narrative and Intelligence*, Northwestern University Press, 1995. Schank argues that people naturally organize information into stories; it is perhaps the most basic way of understanding the world. Learning more about how we create stories and respond to them will illuminate many aspects of our basic thinking.

11. Levels of development.

Some investigators follow the great Swiss psychologist, Jean Piaget, in believing that everyone goes through similar stages as their thinking improves. For example, beginners usually think that every question has a definite answer, and they see issues in simple black and white. More mature thinkers recognize that some questions have several possible answers, and some are better than others.

Patricia M. King and Karen Strohm Kitchener, *Developing Reflective Judgment: Understanding and Promoting Intellectual Growth and Critical Thinking in Adolescents and Adults*, Jossey-Bass Publishers, 1994. King and Kitchener distinguish seven levels of development, from the tendency to trust authority and accept simple, absolute answers, through the tendency to believe everything is completely subjective and personal, to the advanced view that by working together people can get closer to the truth, even if we can never achieve an absolute truth.

Index